ANATOMY FOR ARTISTS

ANATOMY
FOR ARTISTS
by Reginald Marsh

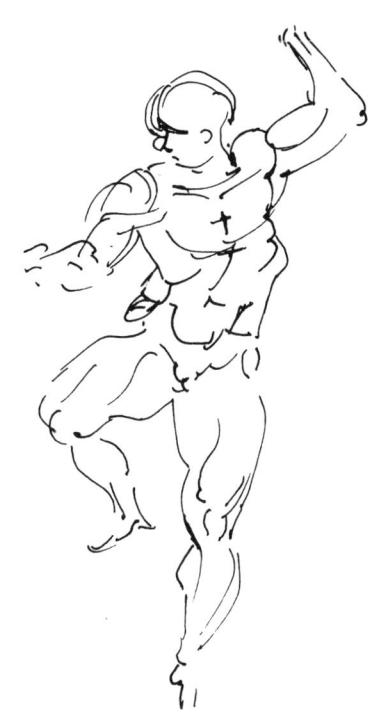

DOVER PUBLICATIONS, INC.
NEW YORK

Published in Canada by General Publishing Company, Ltd., 30 Lesmill Road, Don Mills, Toronto, Ontario.
Published in the United Kingdom by Constable and Company, Ltd.

This Dover edition, first published in 1970, is an unabridged republication of the work originally published by American Artists Group, New York, in 1945. The illustrations in this edition have been newly reproduced directly from the original drawings, and almost all of them are now shown at original size.

International Standard Book Number: 0-486-22613-1
Library of Congress Catalog Card Number: 75-129078

Manufactured in the United States of America
Dover Publications, Inc.
180 Varick Street
New York, N.Y. 10014

Preface

This anatomy book for artists is conceived on the visual principle. The drawings are arranged in such a manner that with an easy turning of the leaves the reader may find the desired or approximate view. Medical and technical nomenclature, unknown to the majority of artists, is omitted, but simple tables of proportions used throughout the ages have been included. These drawings consist of free adaptations, combinations, abbreviations and copies of works of the old masters, chiefly from the Italian and Flemish schools before the advent of academicism.

Strangely enough, in spite of the advance in medical anatomical knowledge since the Renaissance, the art of drawing and the use of anatomy has declined. It is conceded that the highest development in the art of figure drawing was bound together with the knowledge of anatomy. The artists of the Renaissance—Leonardo da Vinci, Mantegna, Durer, Michaelangelo, Raphael, Tintoretto, Titian, Rubens and Rembrandt—hardly challenged, have never been surpassed.

I have drawn also from later authorities whose contributions, though artistically uninspired, offer anatomical explanation.

R. M.

Sections

Front

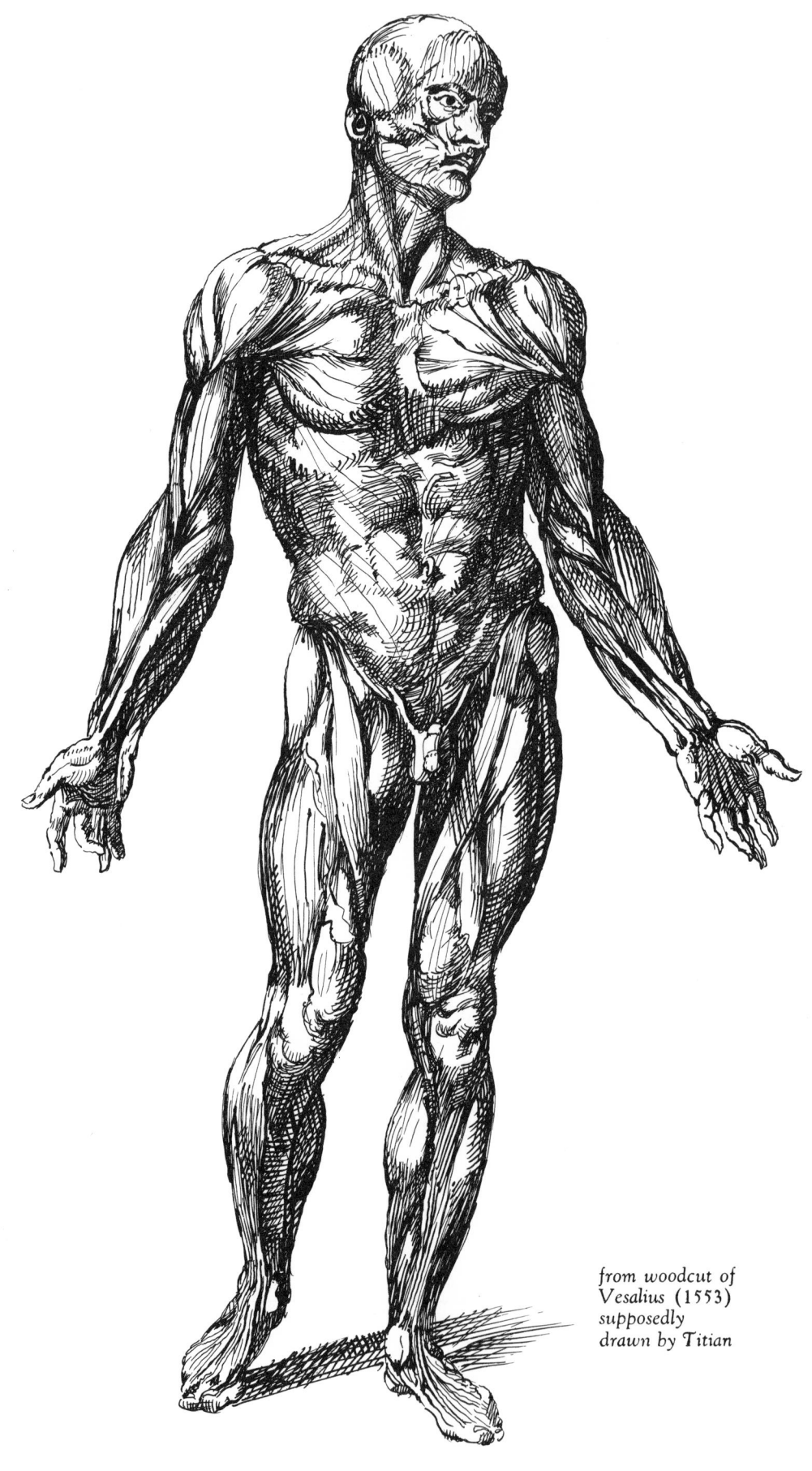

from woodcut of
Vesalius (1553)
supposedly
drawn by Titian

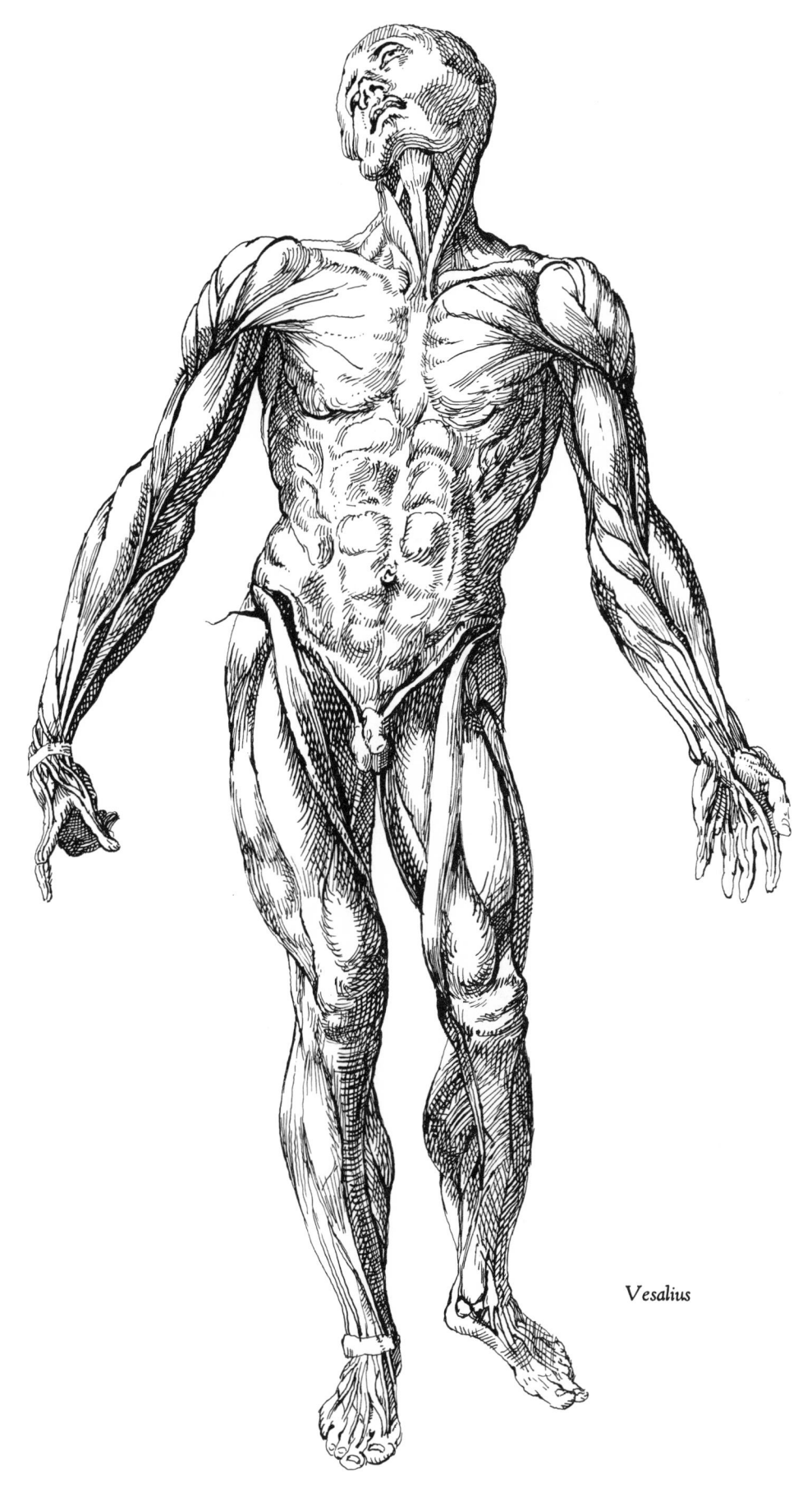

Vesalius

3

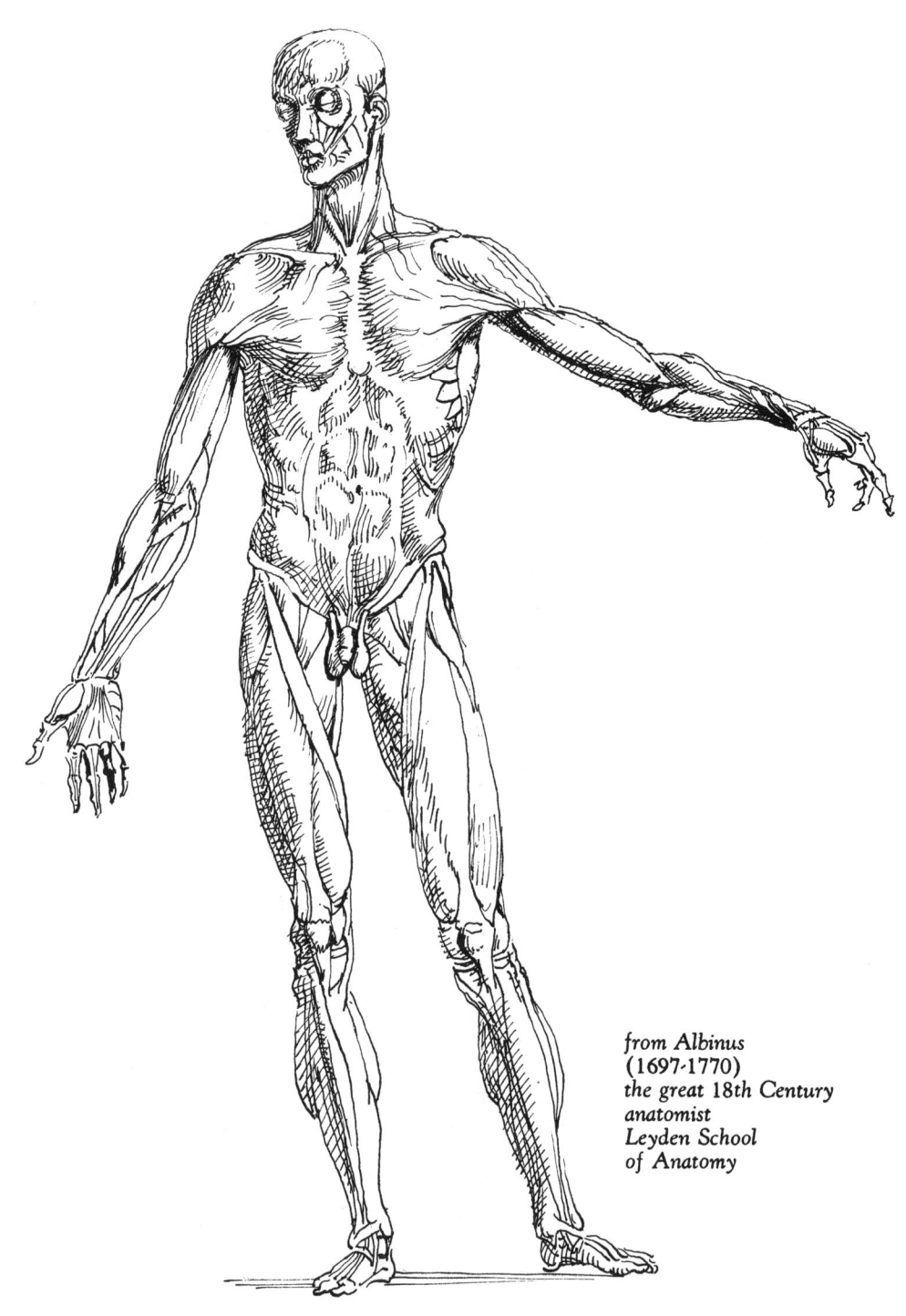

*from Albinus
(1697-1770)
the great 18th Century
anatomist
Leyden School
of Anatomy*

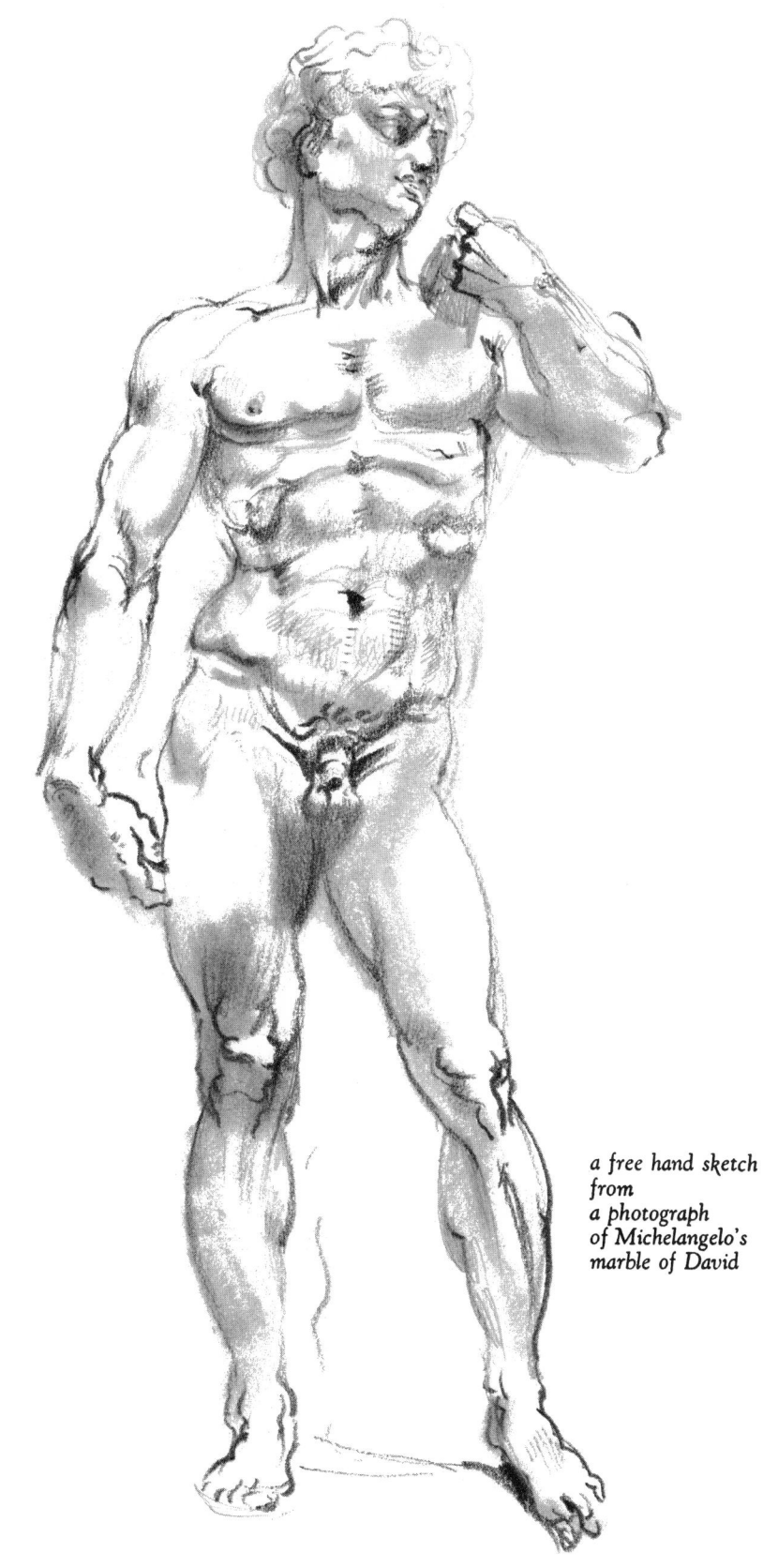

*a free hand sketch
from
a photograph
of Michelangelo's
marble of David*

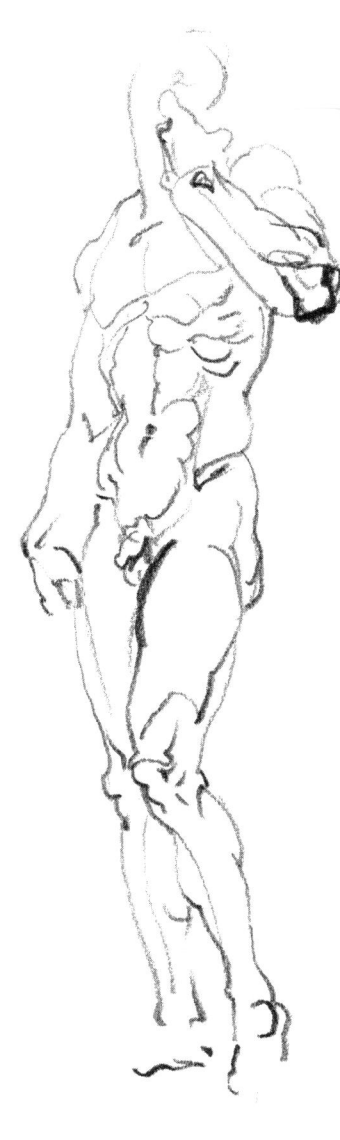

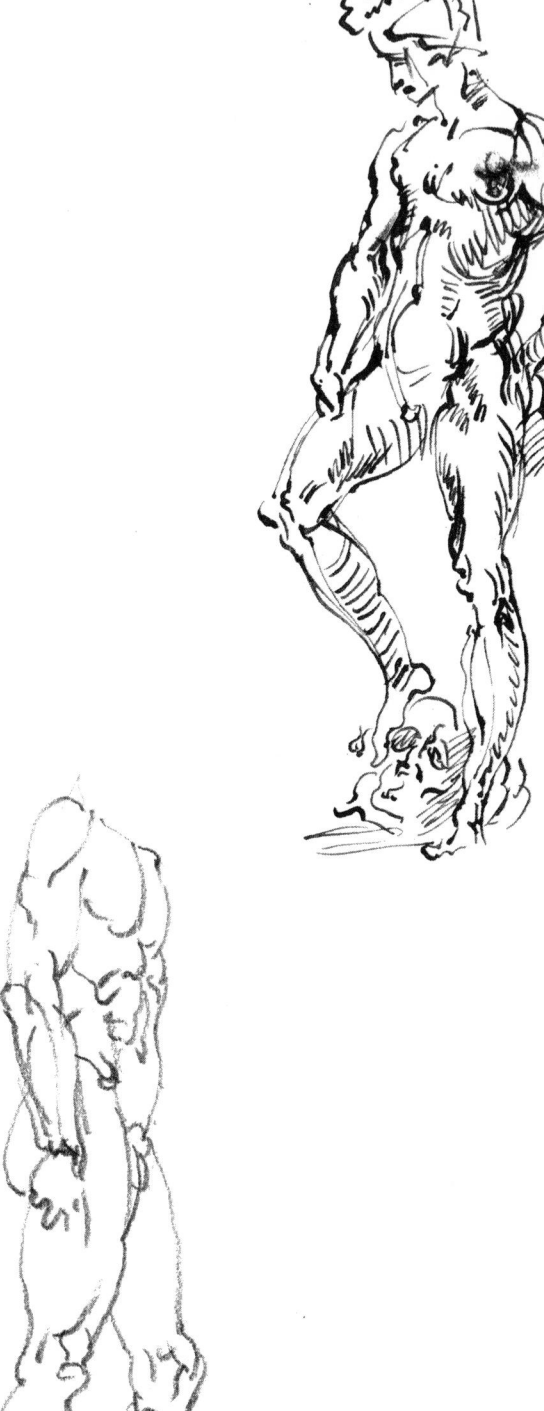

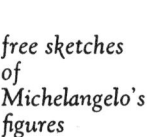

*free sketches
of
Michelangelo's
figures*

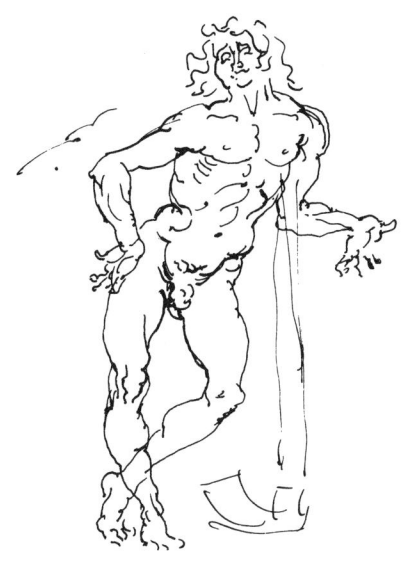

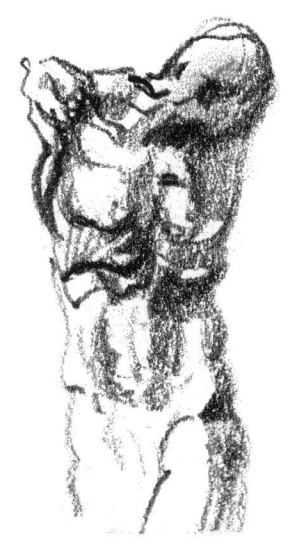

Pollaiuvolo   Michelangelo

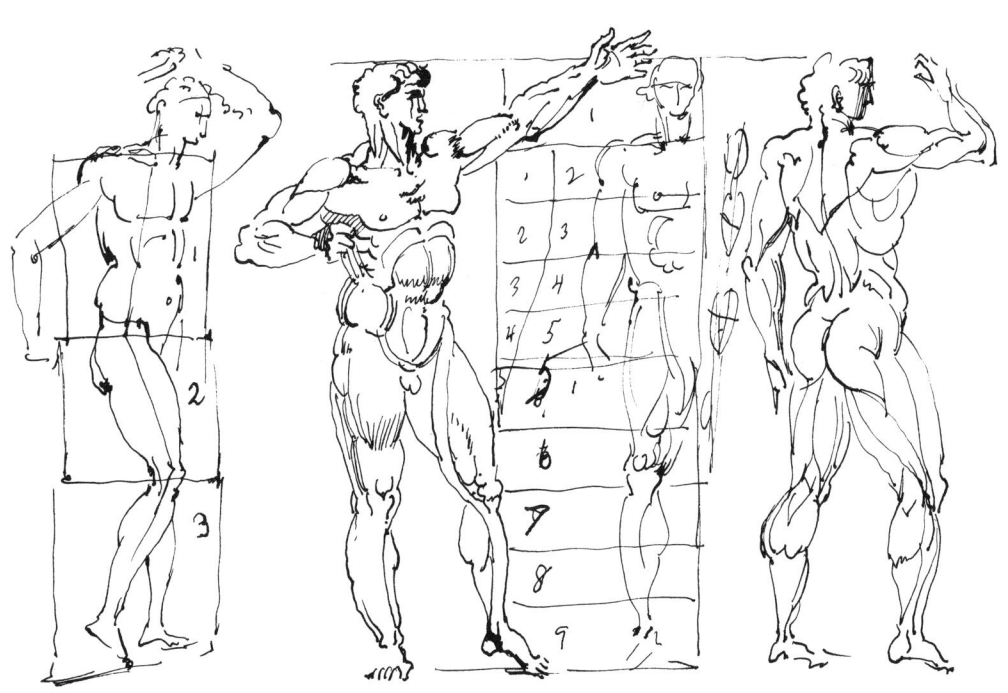

free sketch of unpublished Italian
drawings from Cooper Union Museum, N. Y.

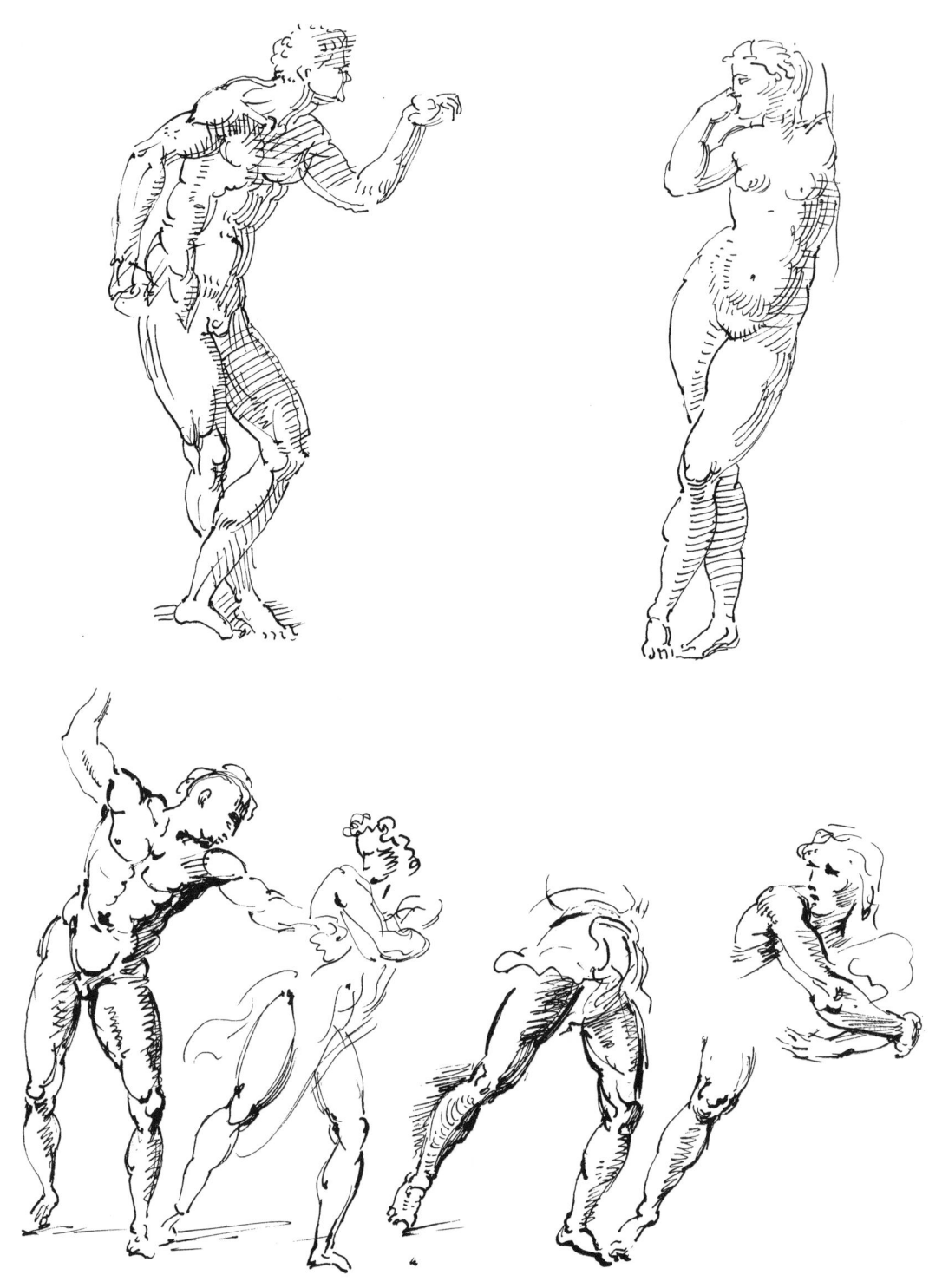

from Raphael and his engraver—Marcantonio—(Note selection of key position to convey idea of movement)

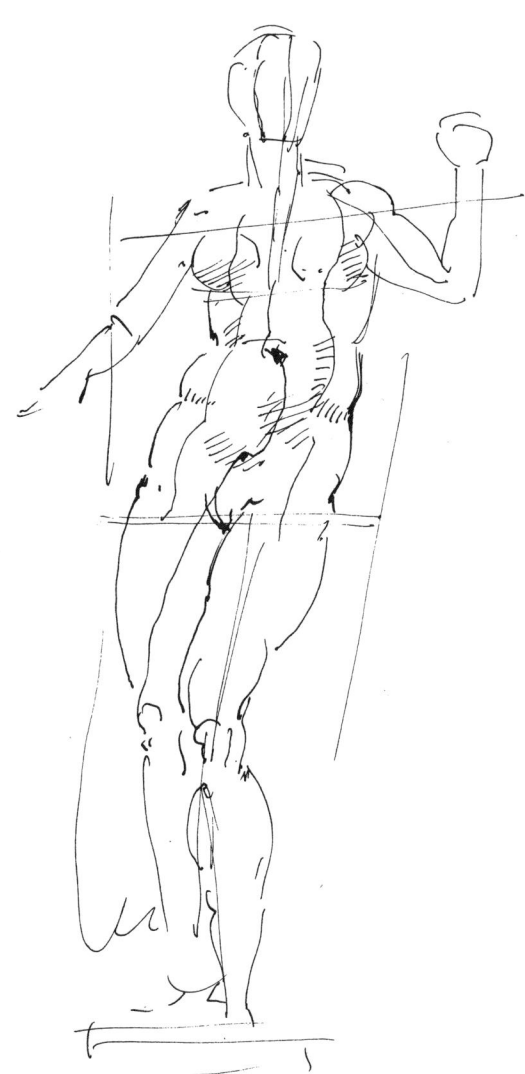

*proportion sketch
from Michelangelo*

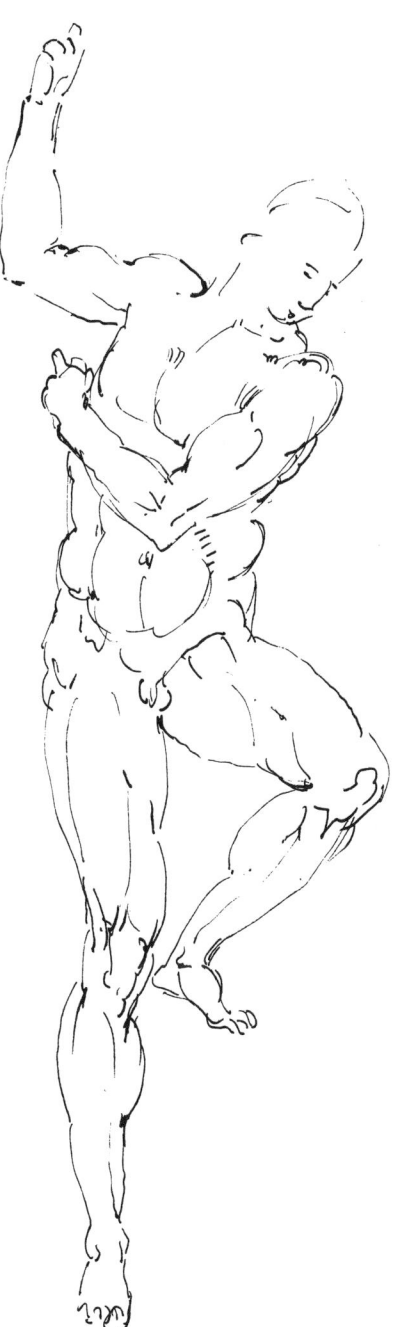

*a Michelangelo sketch
simplified*

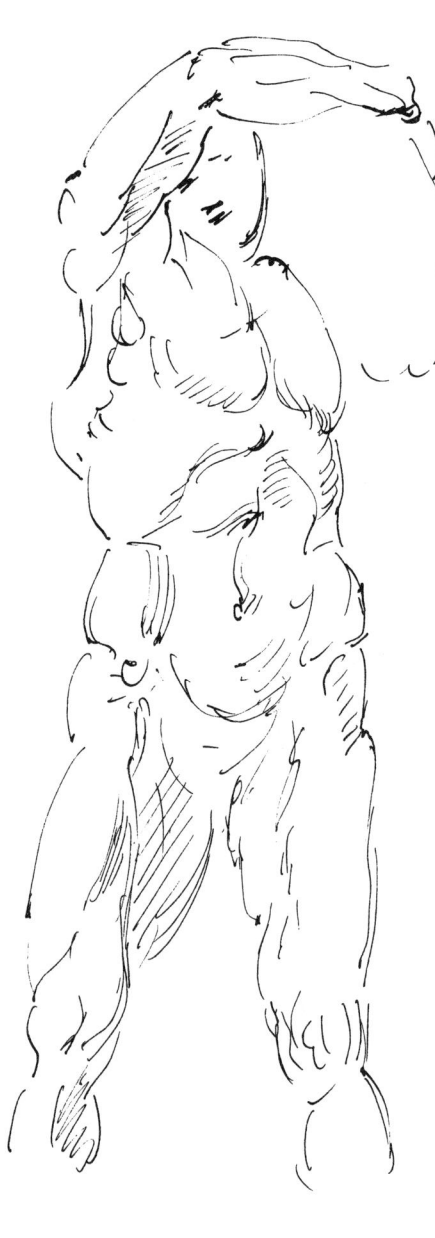
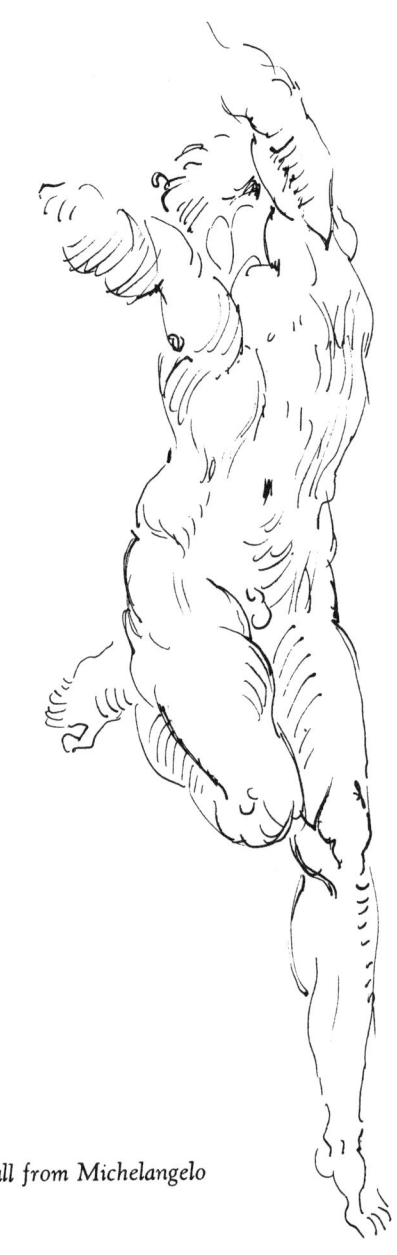

all from Michelangelo

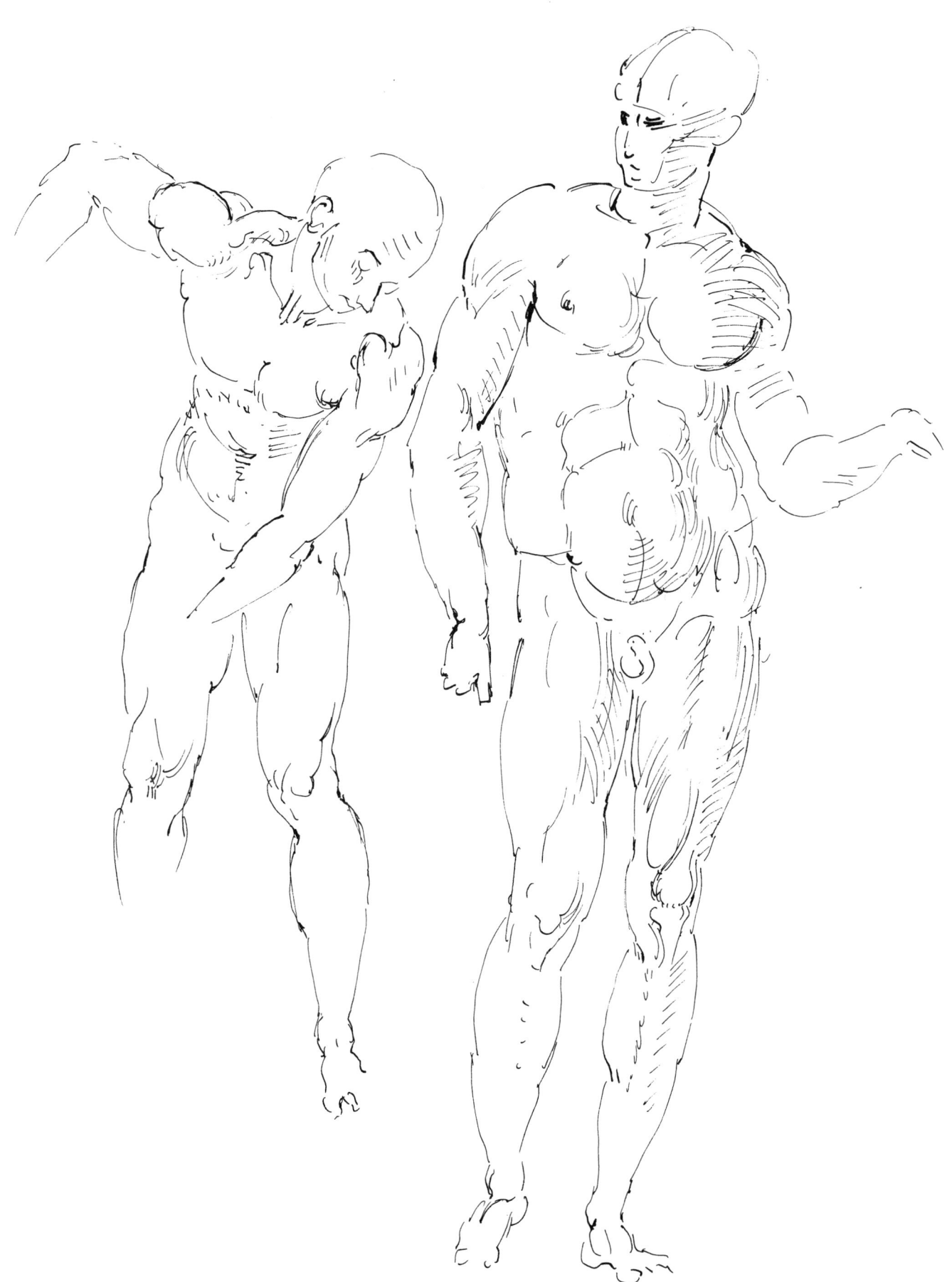

II

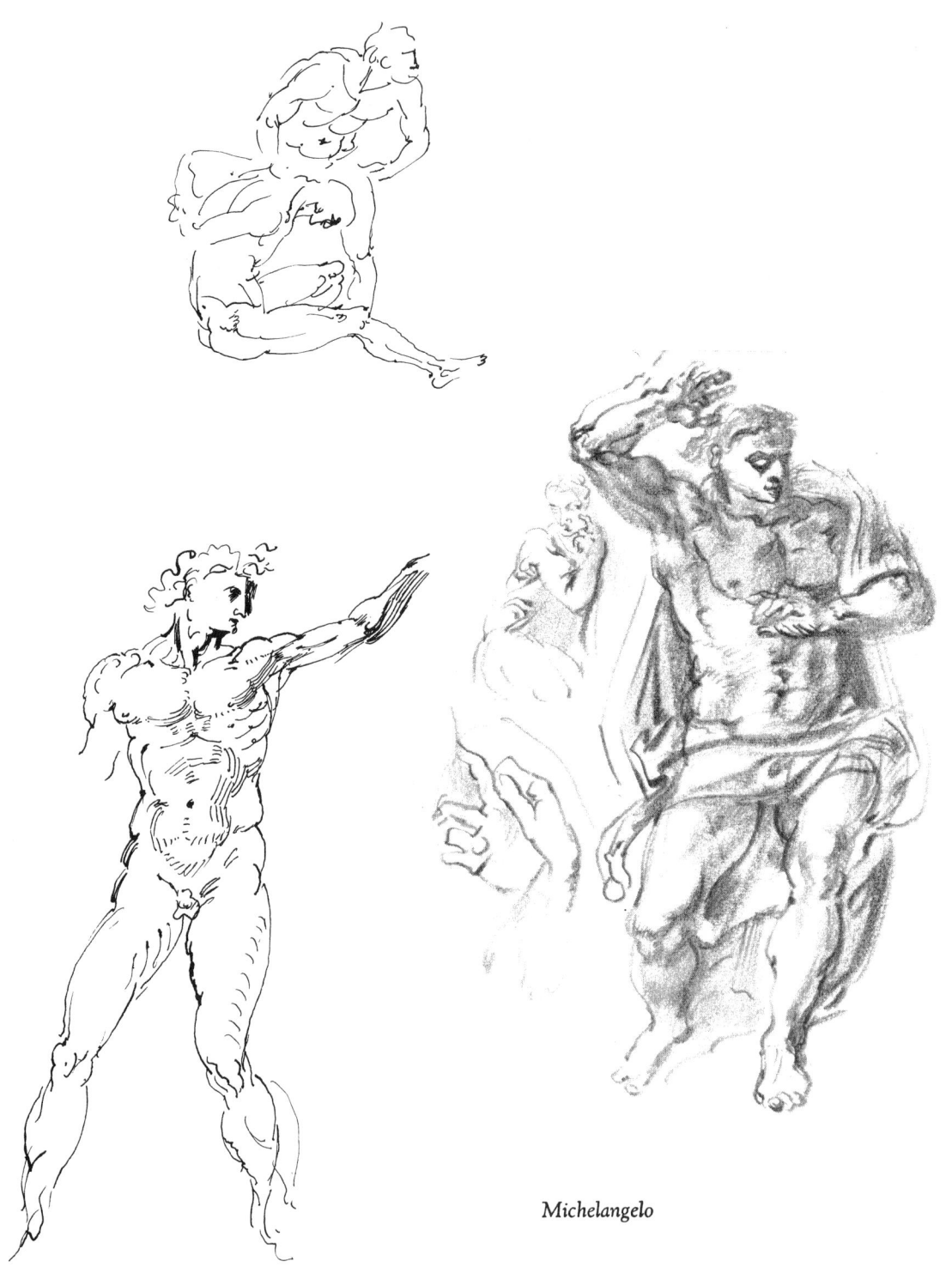

Michelangelo

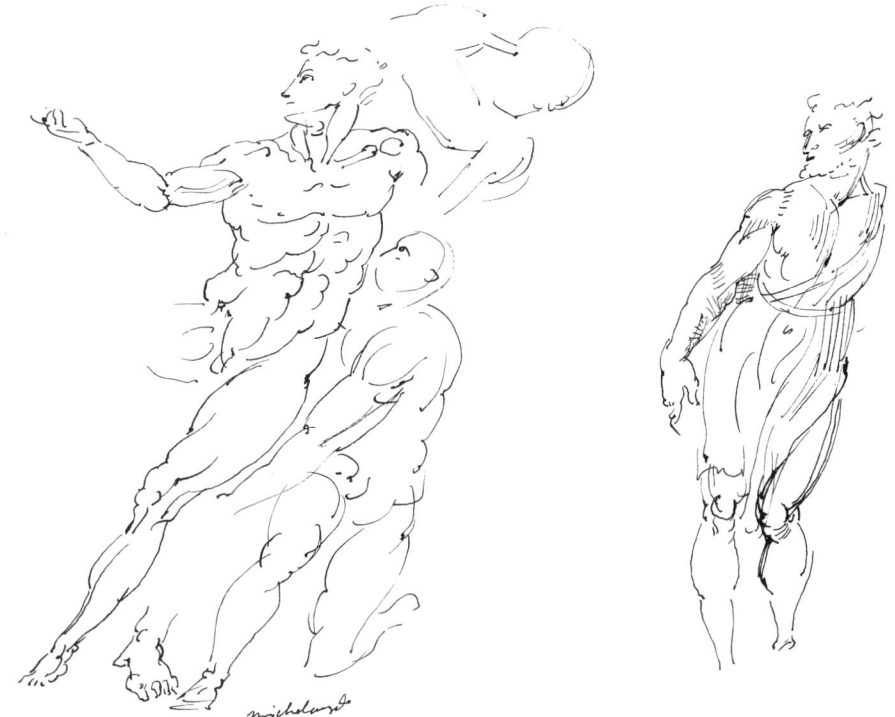

Raphael

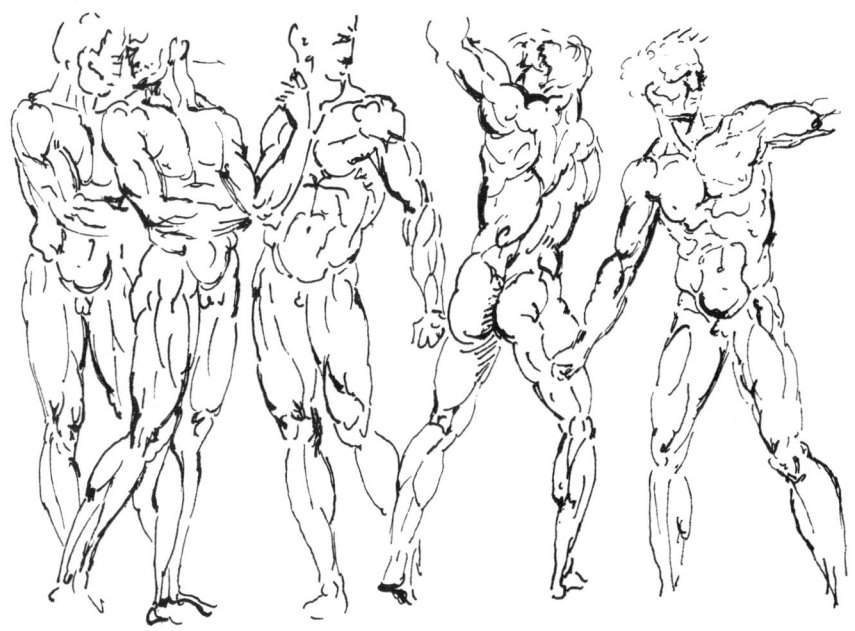

Michelangelo

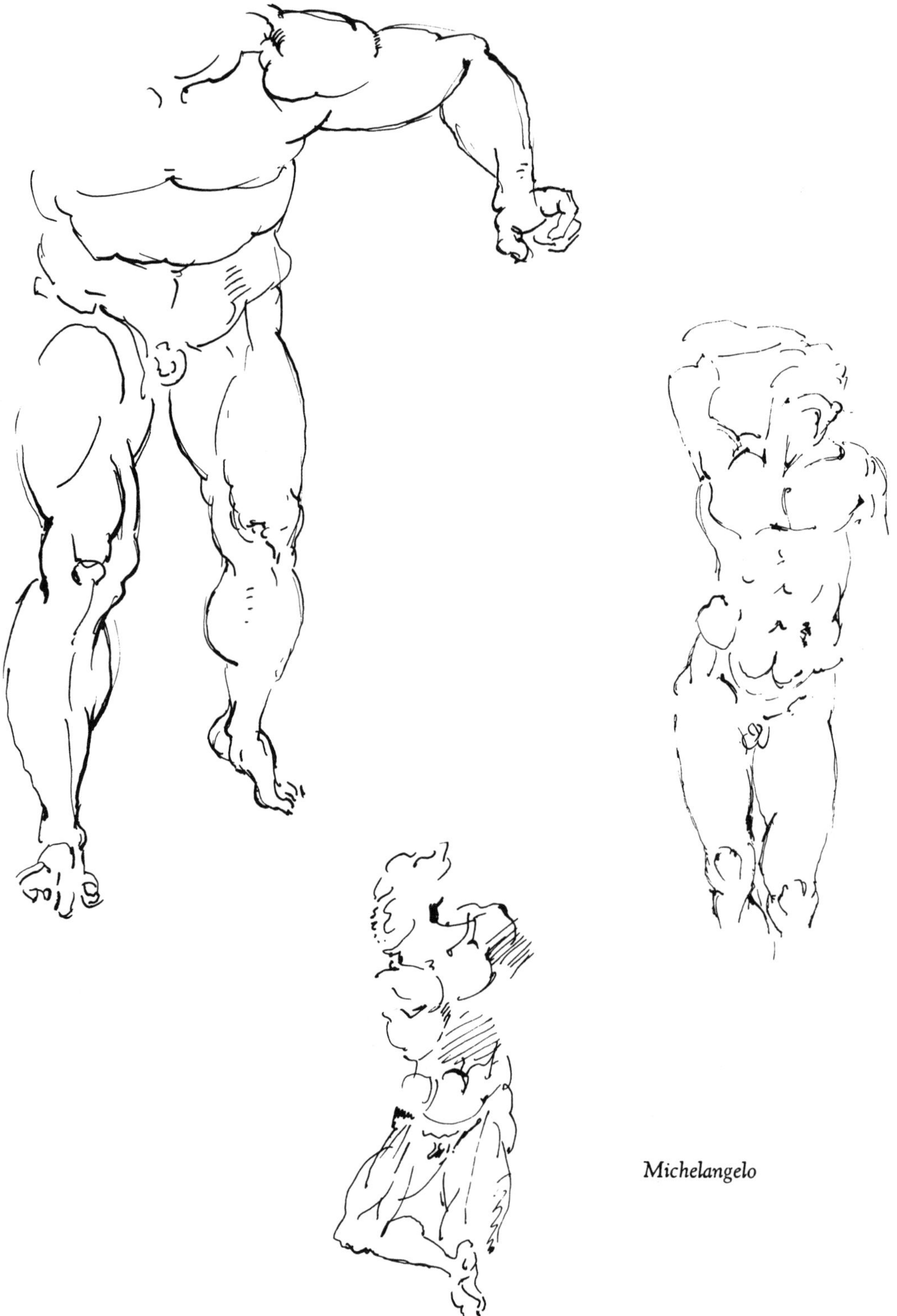

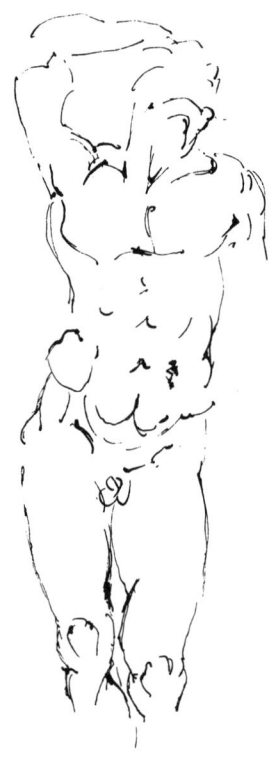

Michelangelo

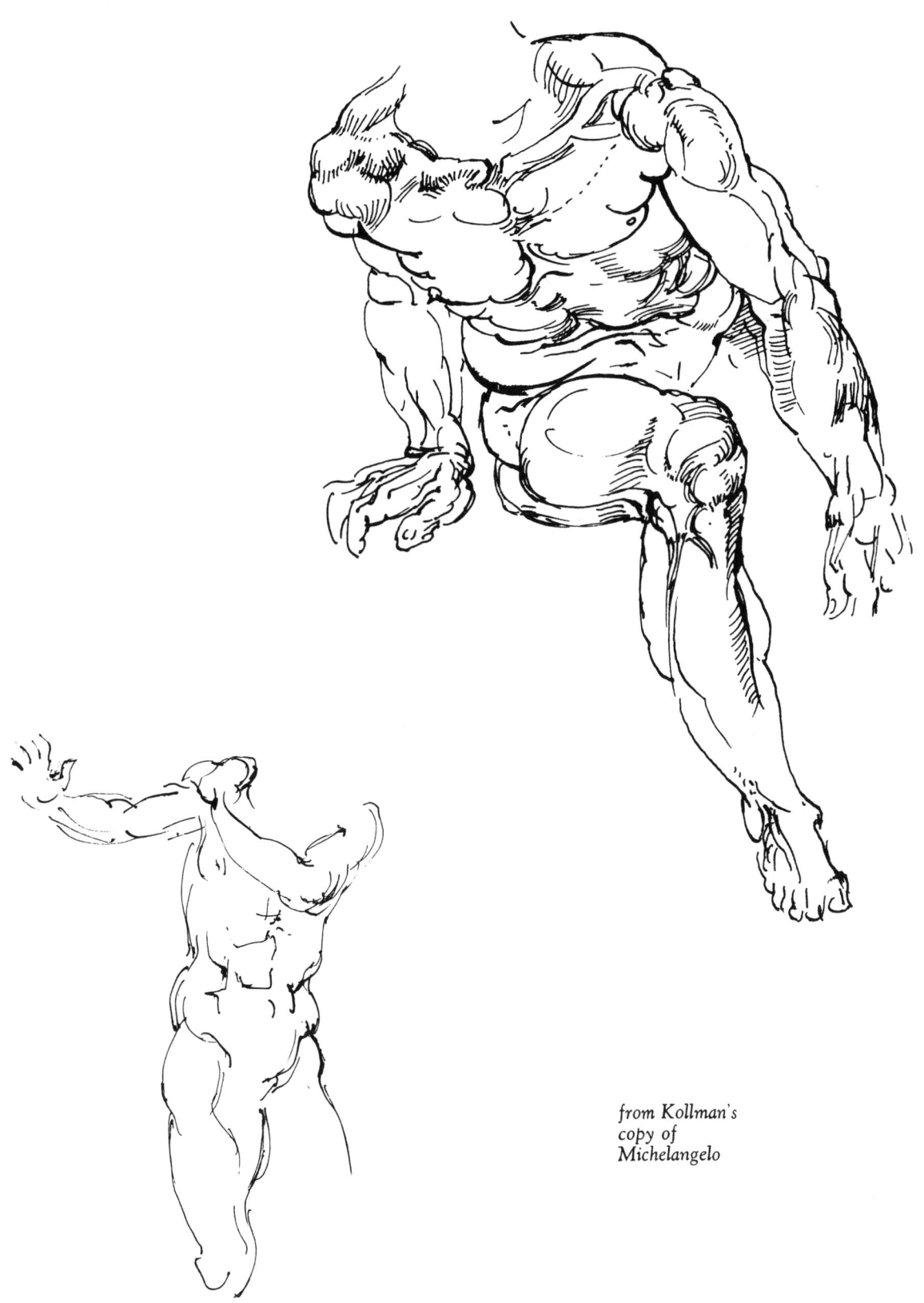

*from Kollman's
copy of
Michelangelo*

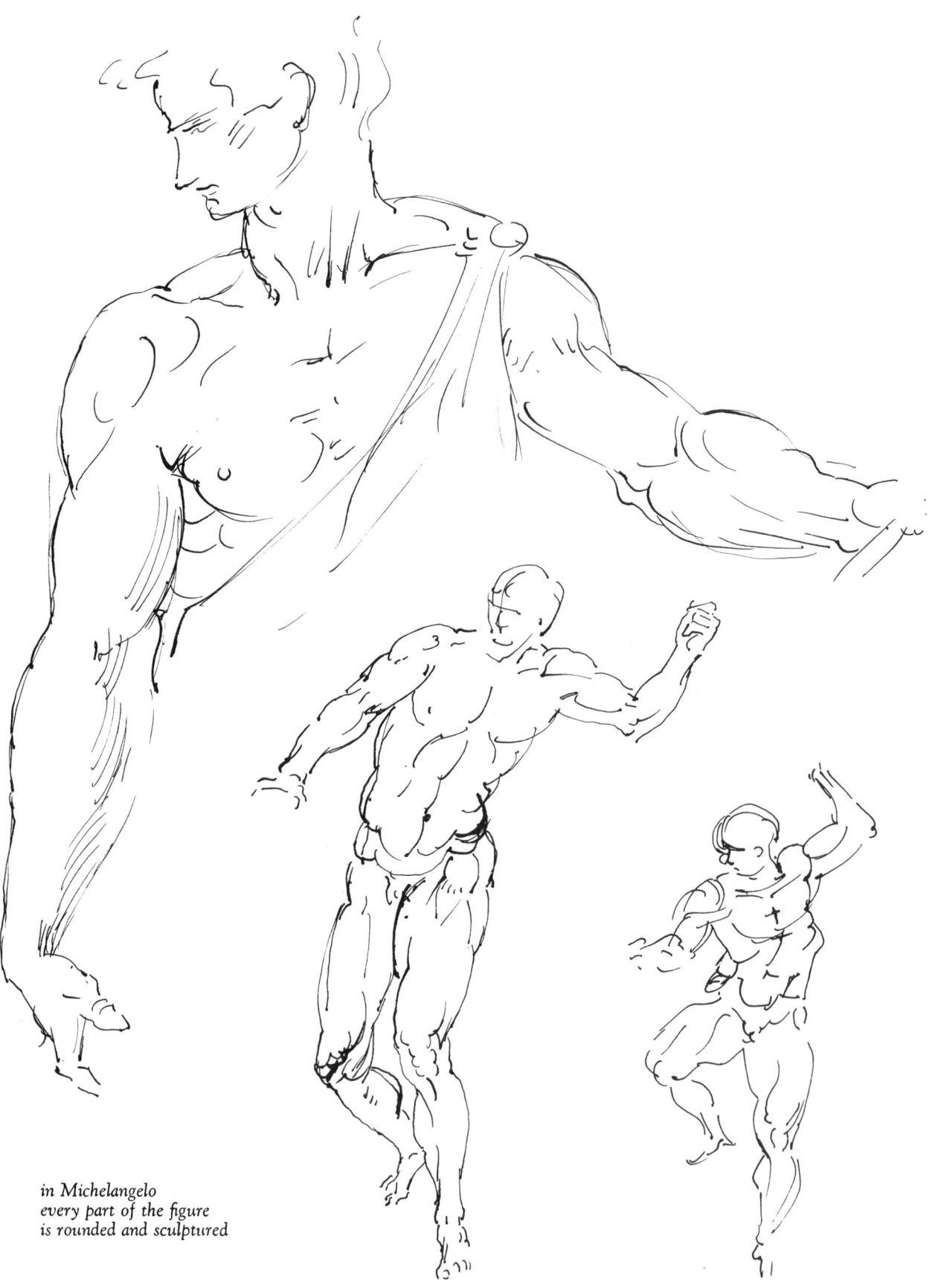

*in Michelangelo
every part of the figure
is rounded and sculptured*

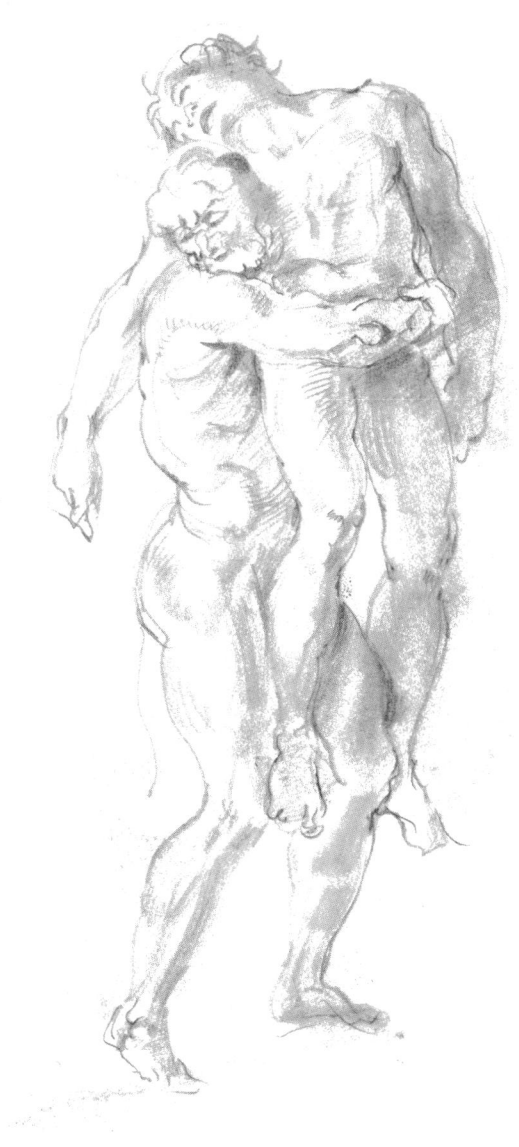

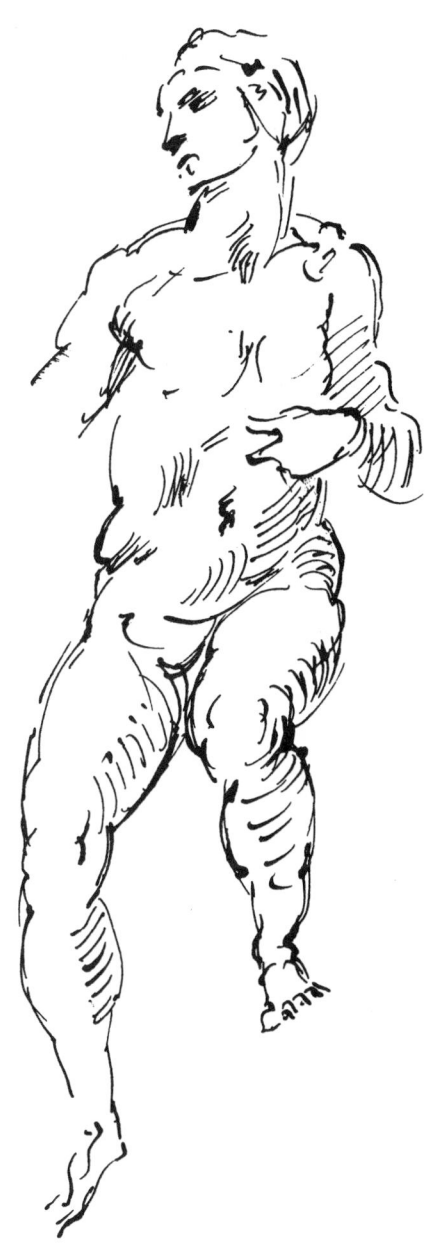

from Michelangelo
Note the spiralling
of forms, the judicious
and ingenious arrangement
of all the parts to
produce rhythm
and unity

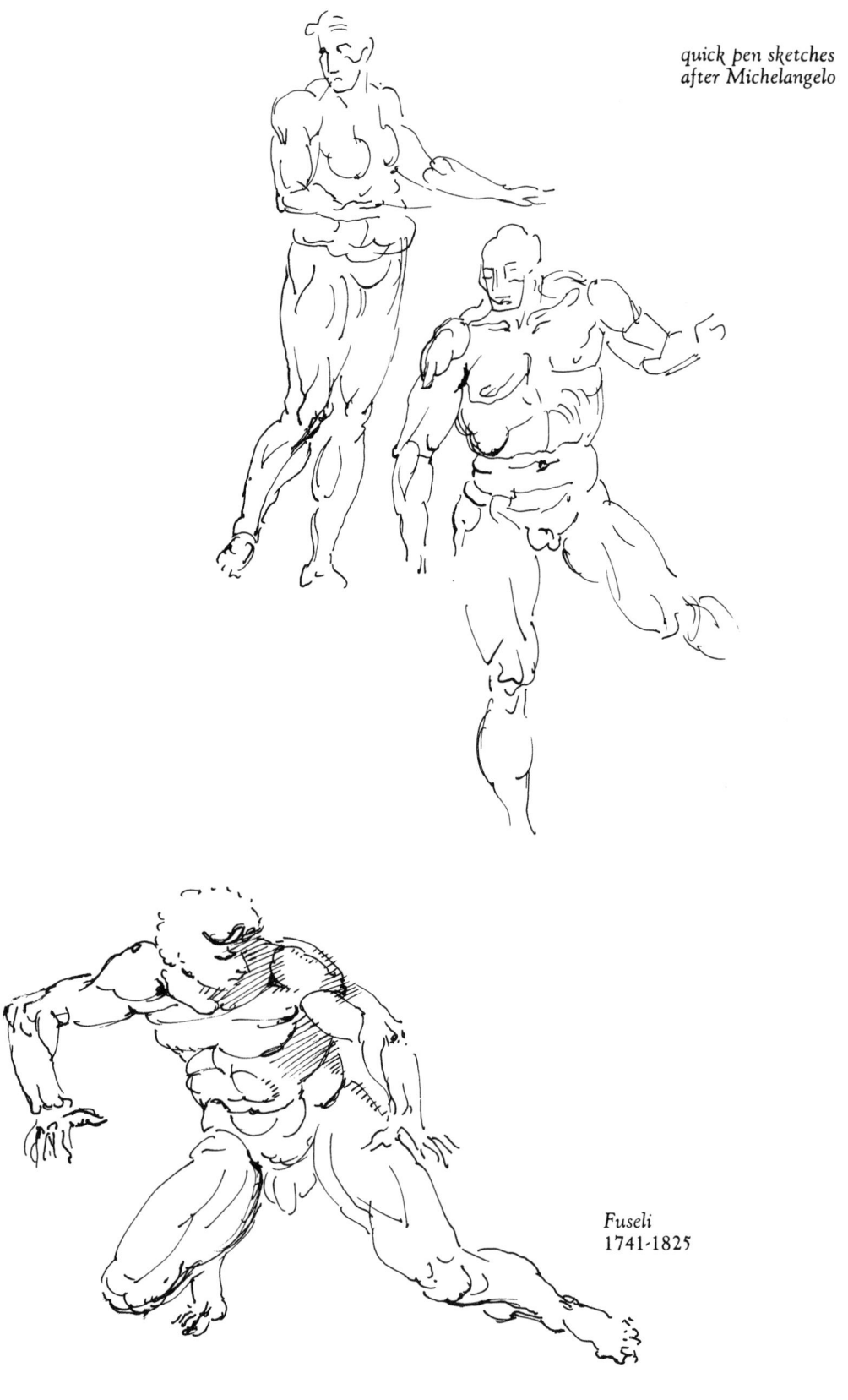

*quick pen sketches
after Michelangelo*

*Fuseli
1741-1825*

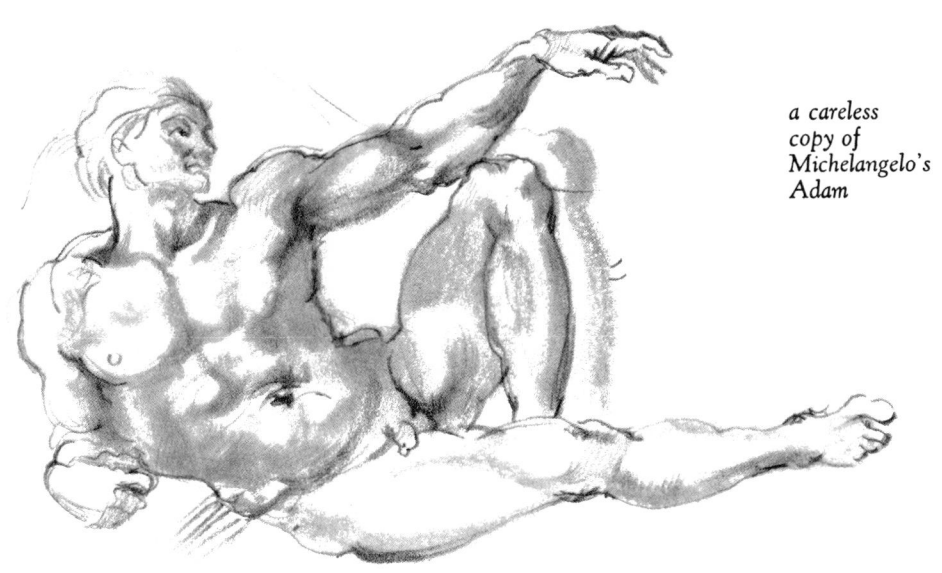

*a careless
copy of
Michelangelo's
Adam*

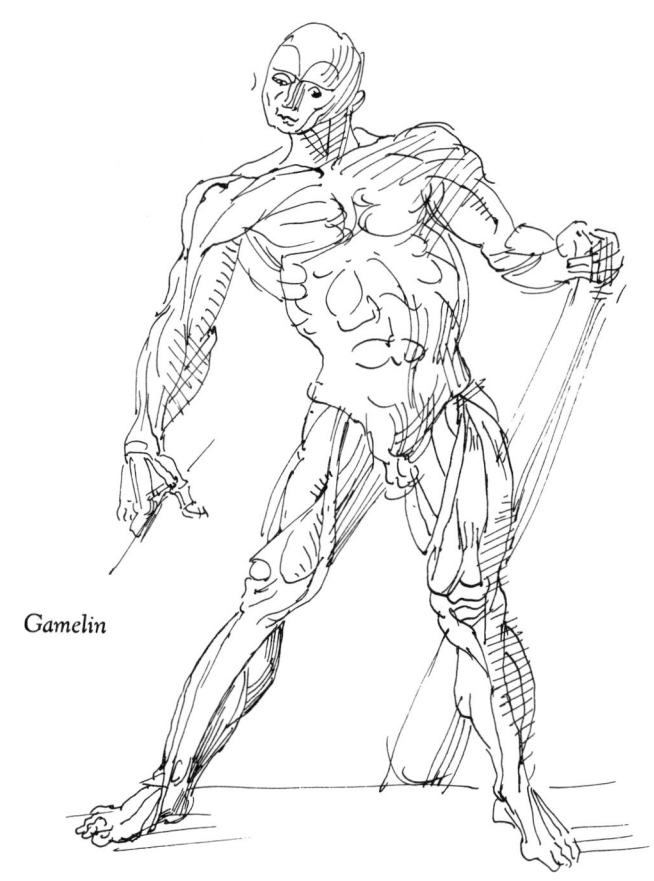

Gamelin

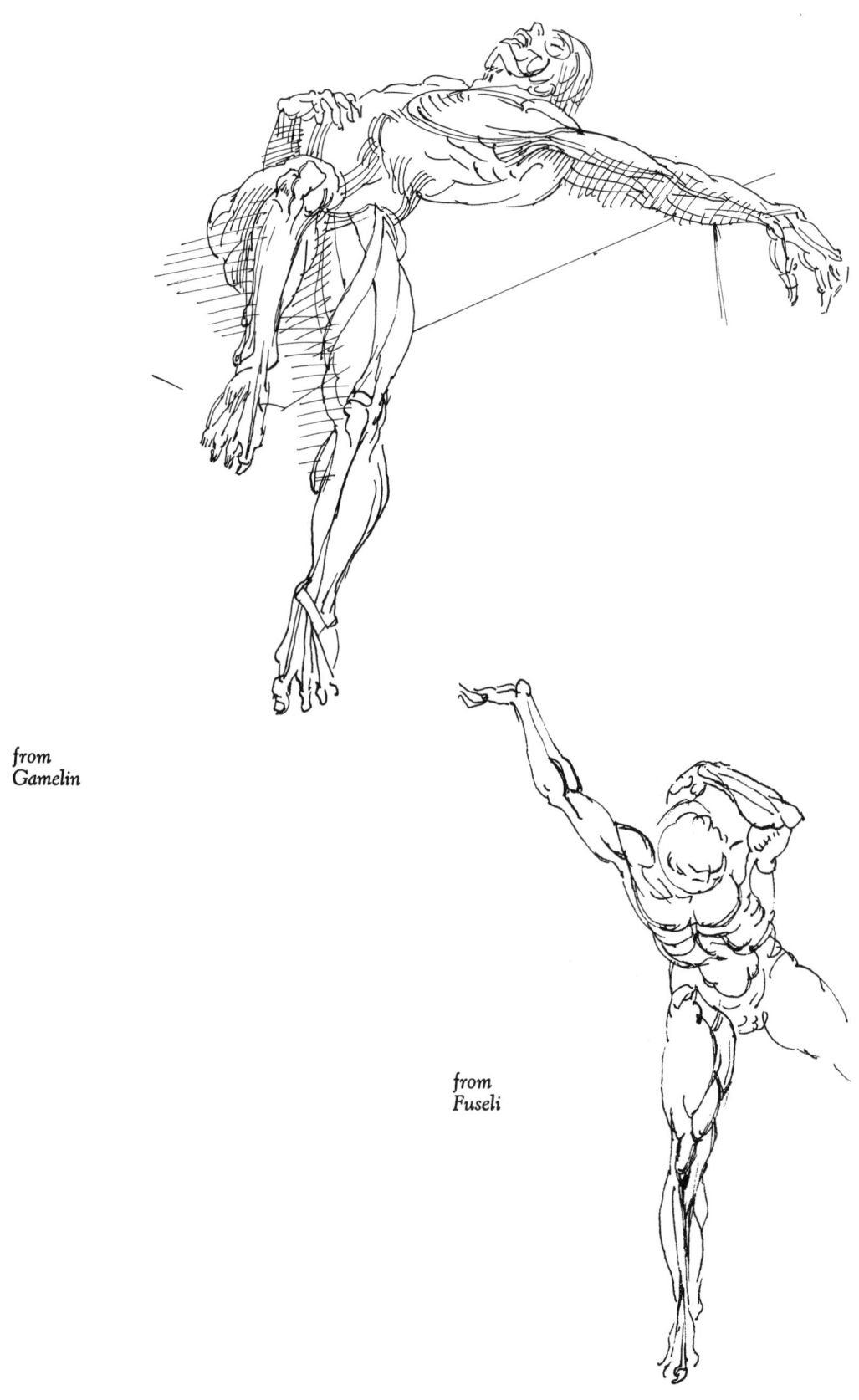

from
Gamelin

from
Fuseli

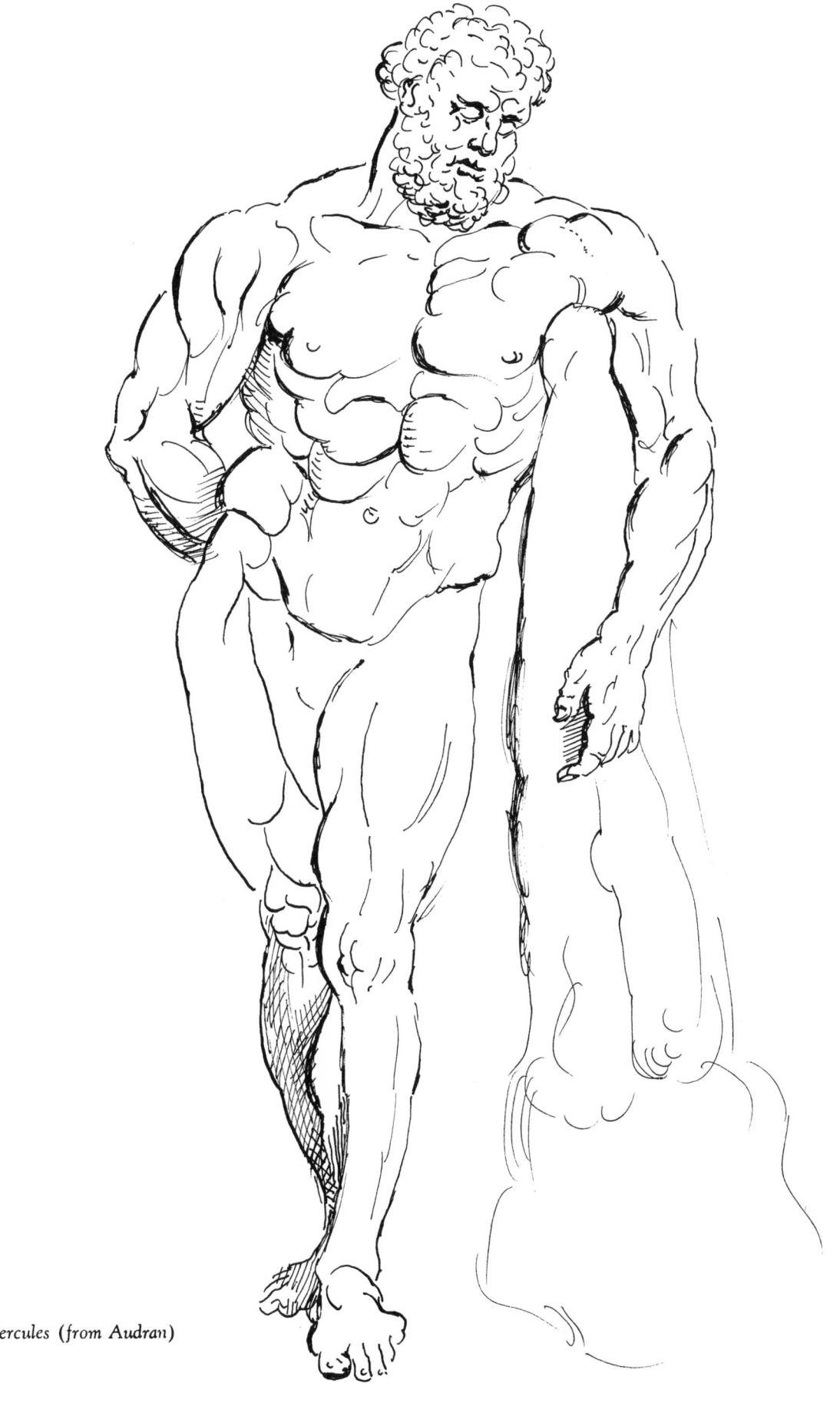

Hercules (from Audran)

21

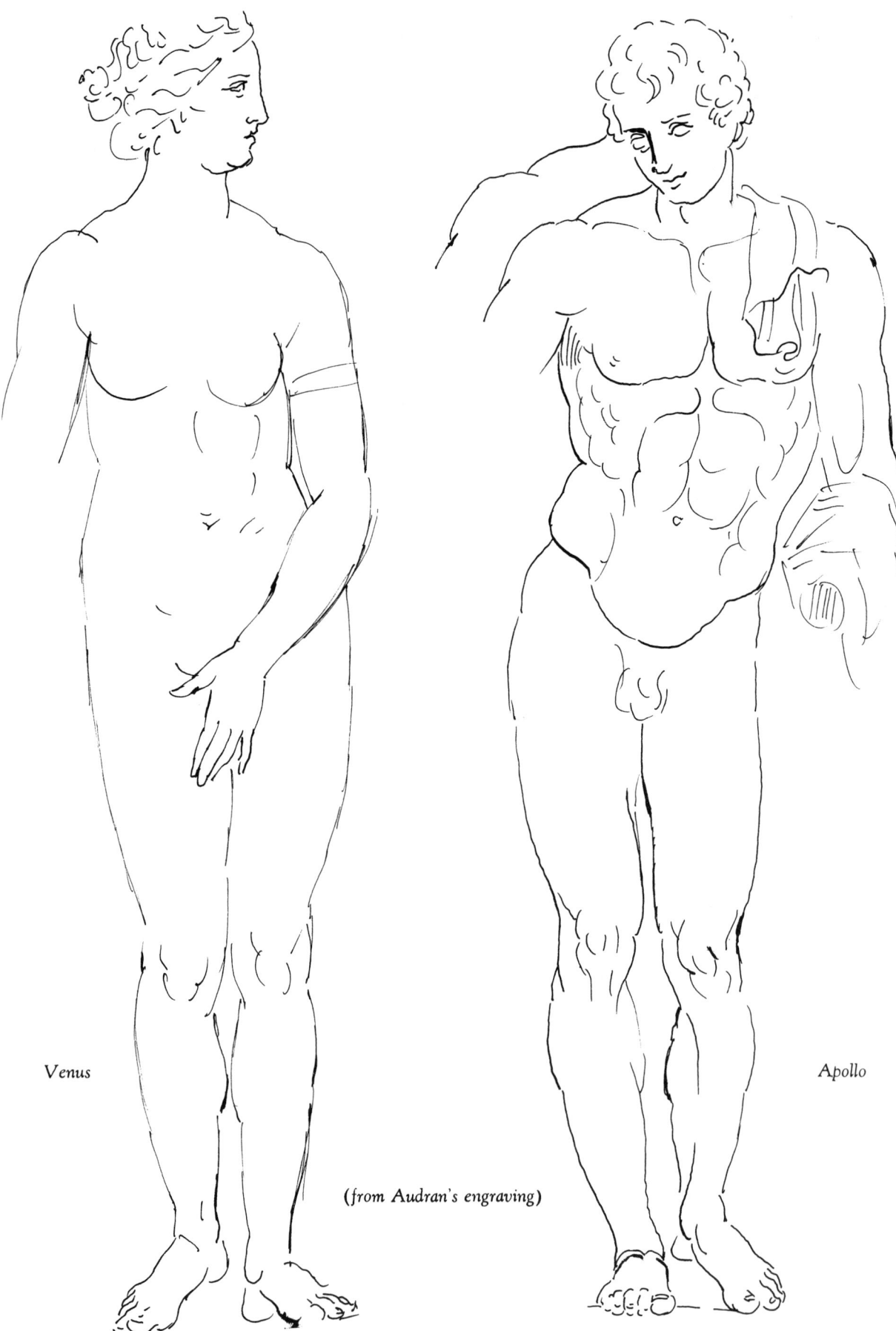

Venus

(from Audran's engraving)

Apollo

22

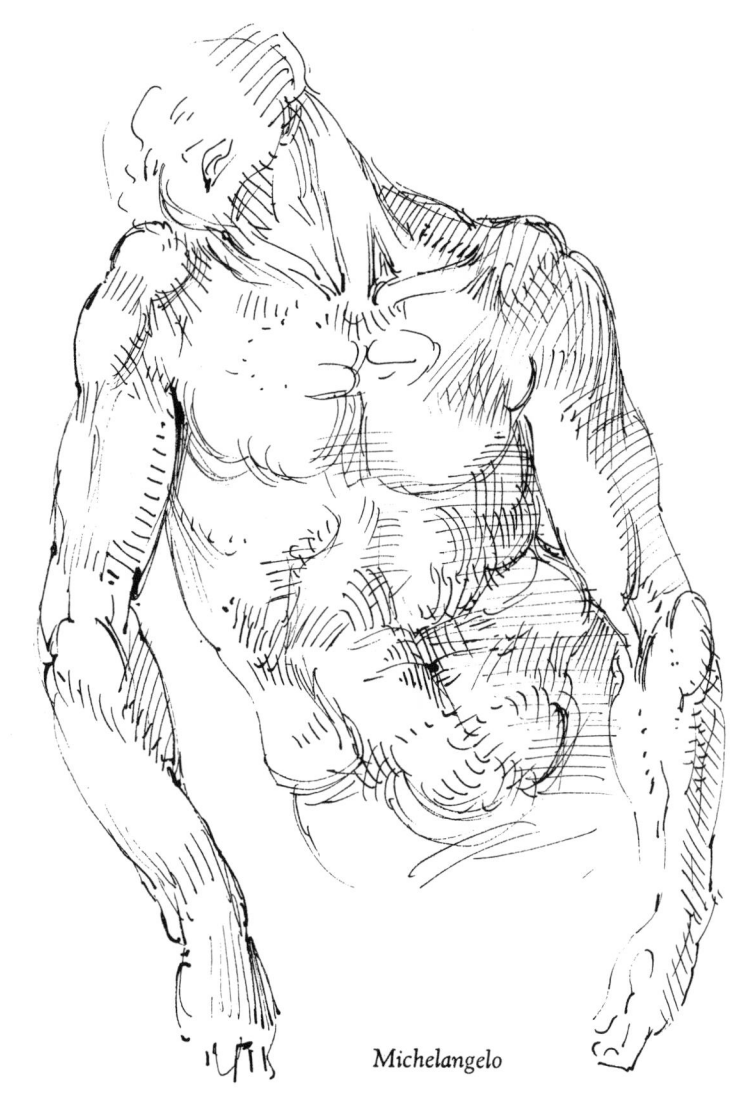

Michelangelo

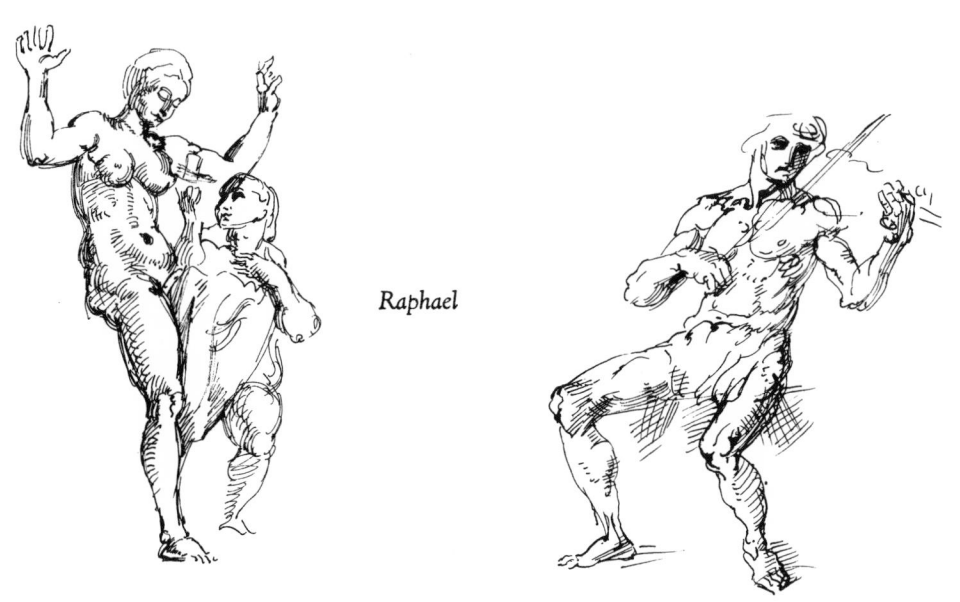

Raphael

23

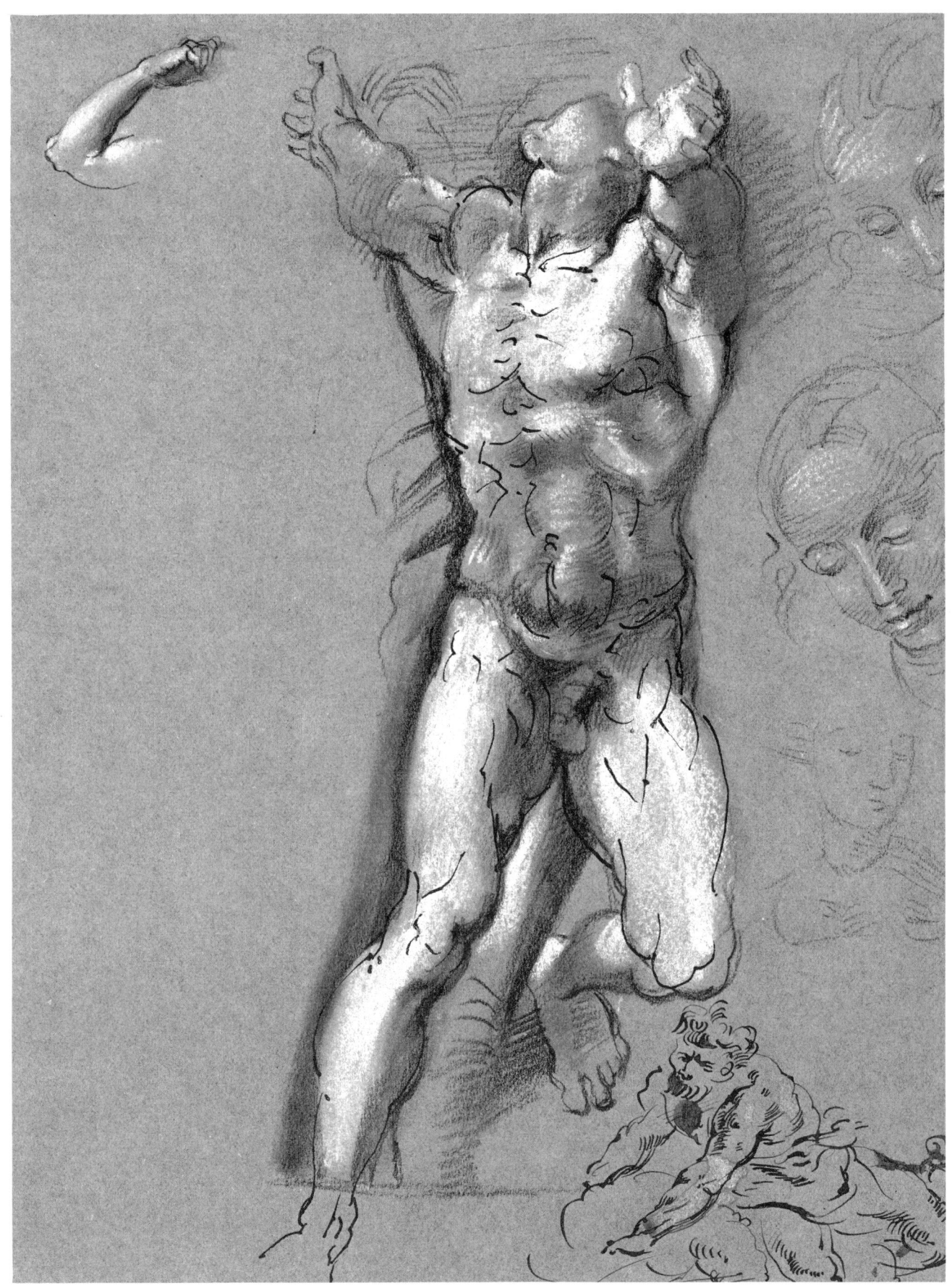

Michelangelo

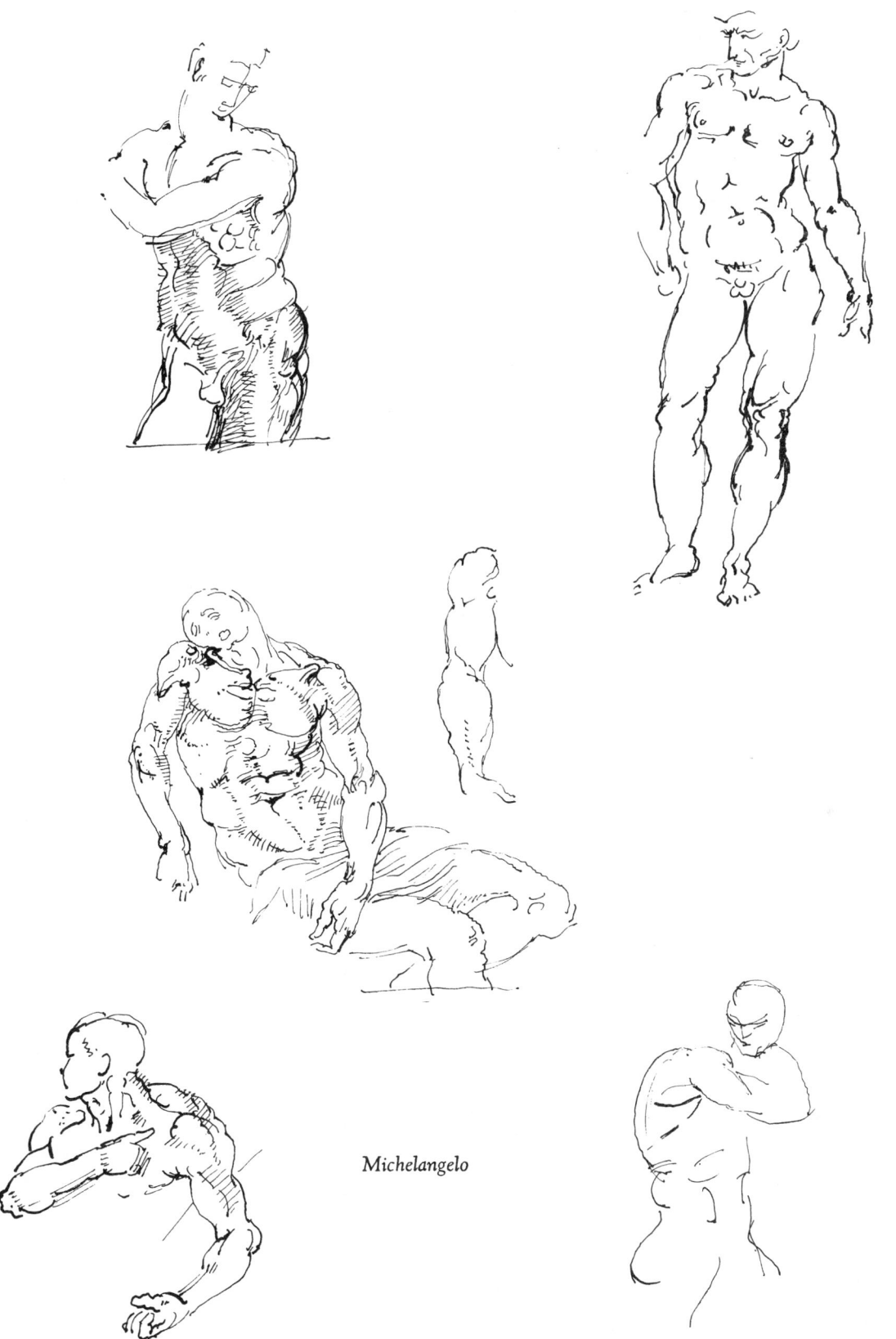

Michelangelo

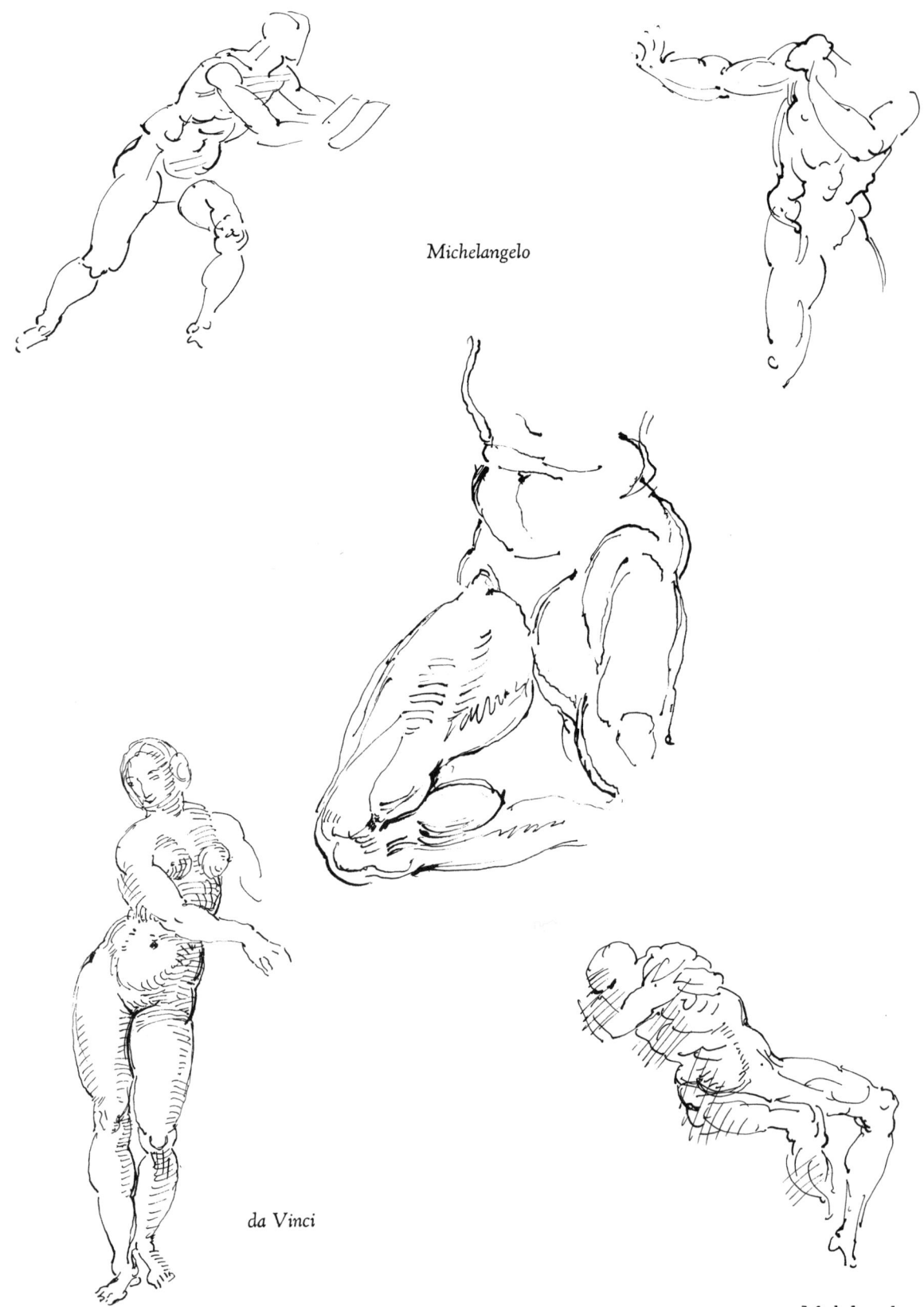

Michelangelo

da Vinci

Michelangelo

26

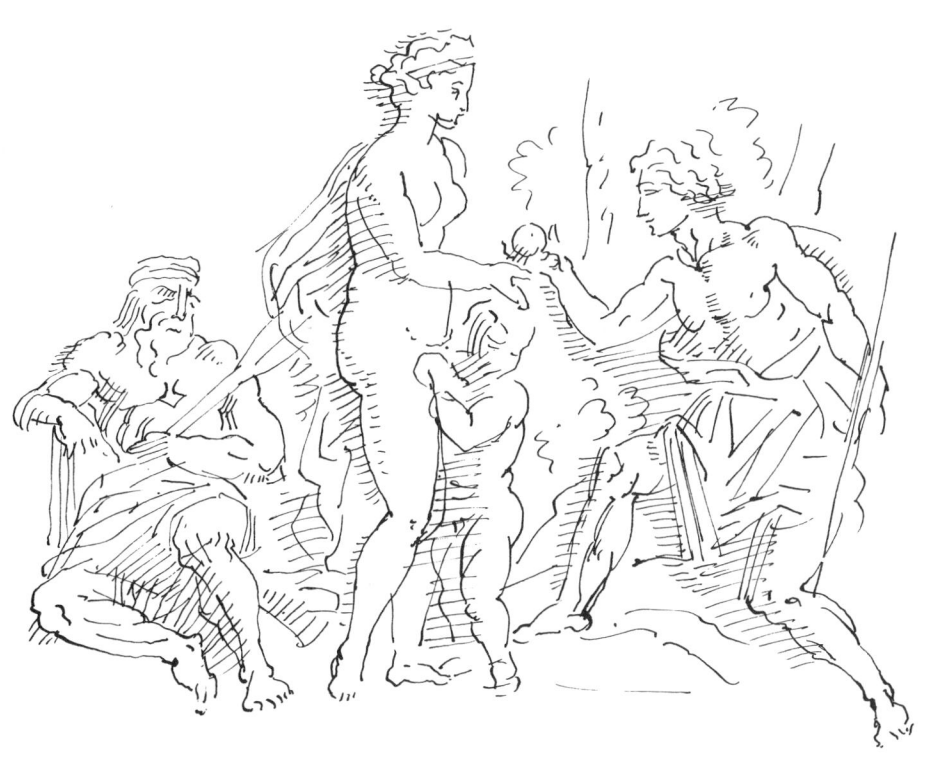

fine pen sketch after washed drawings of Poussin

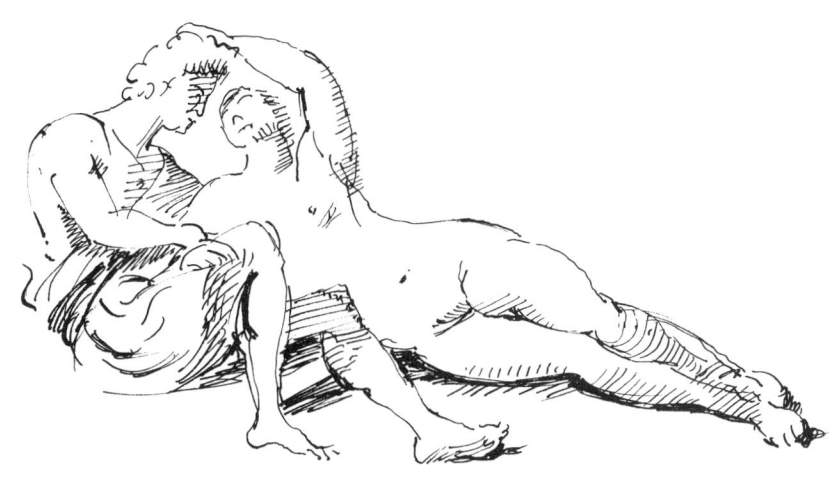

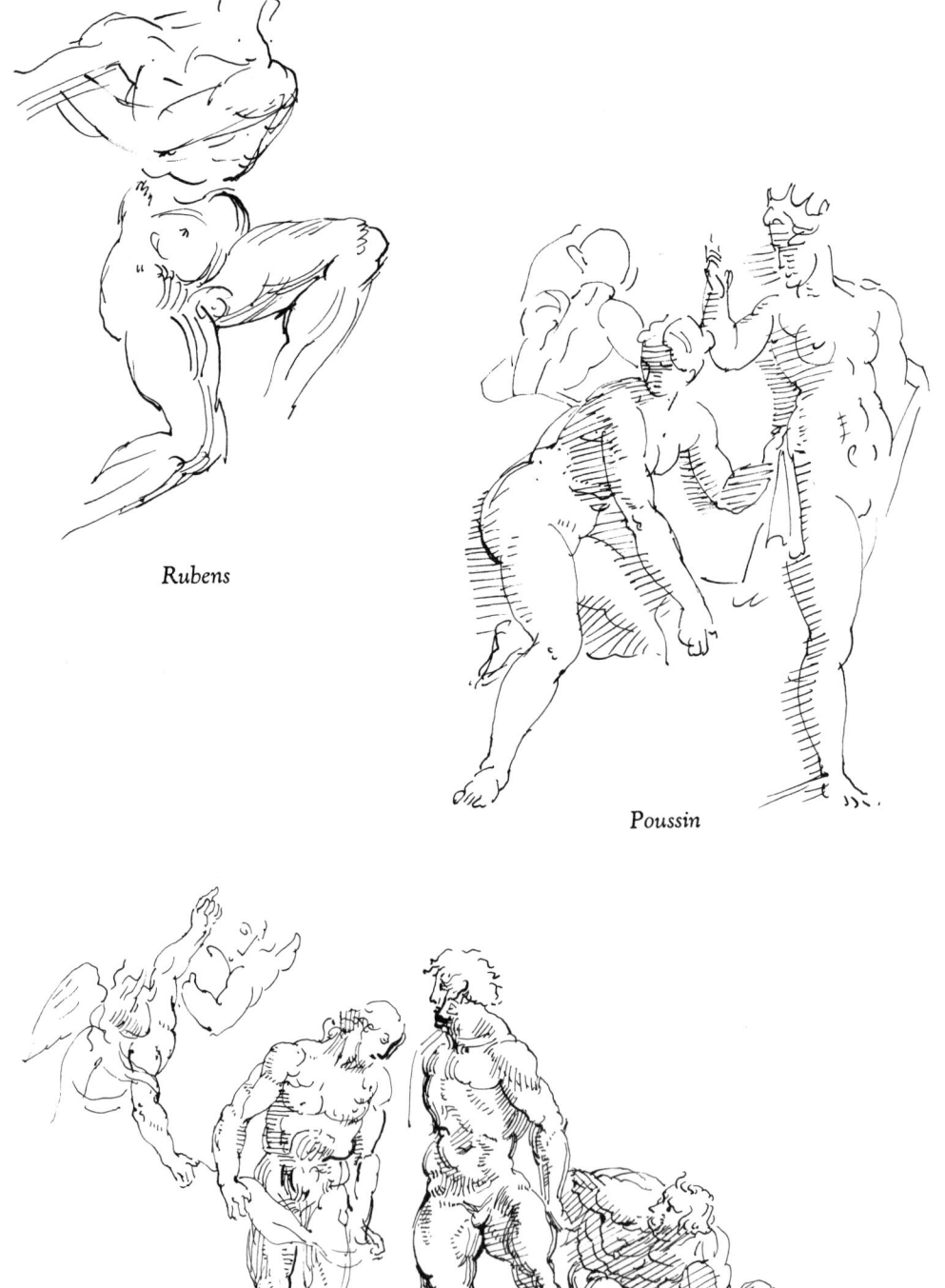

Rubens

Poussin

Rubens

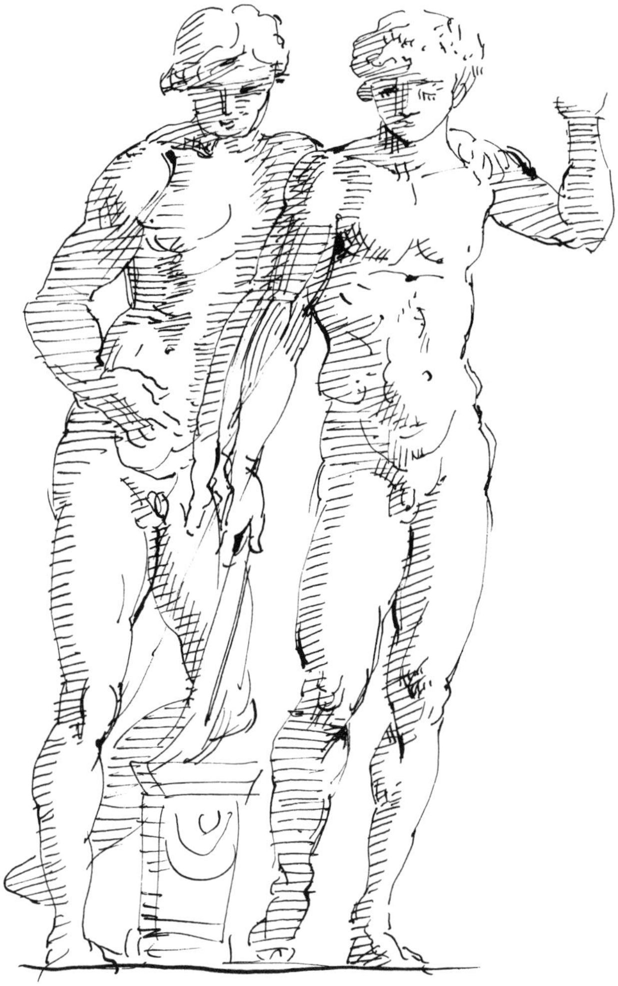

Poussin—study
from the antique

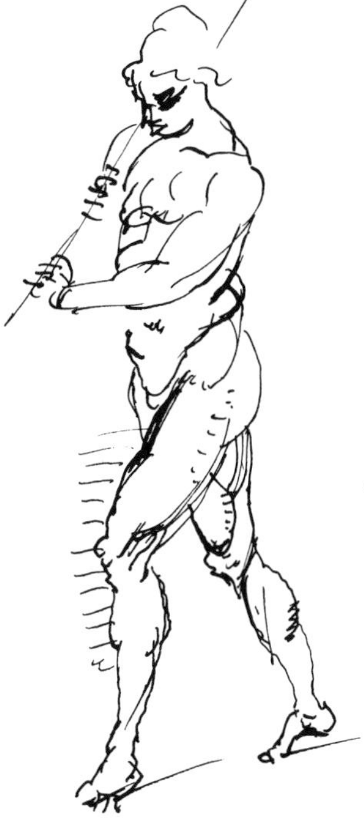

Raphael

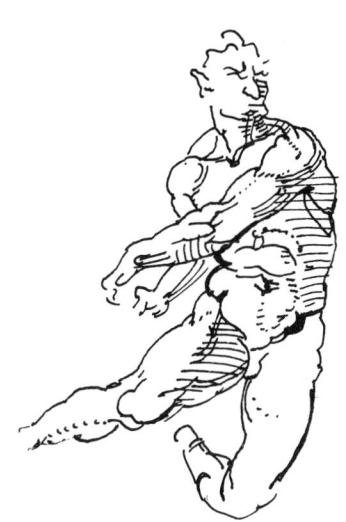

Michelangelo

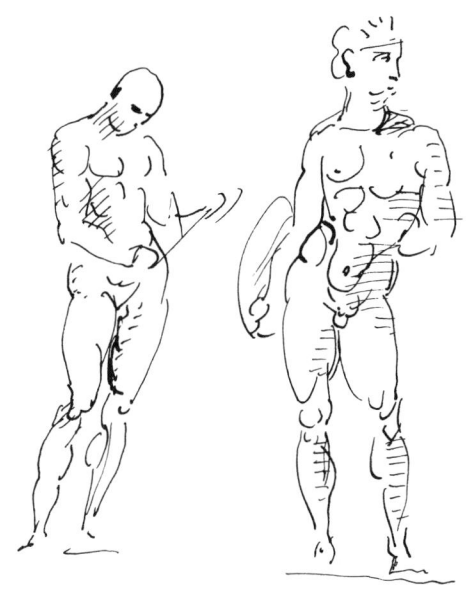

Raphael

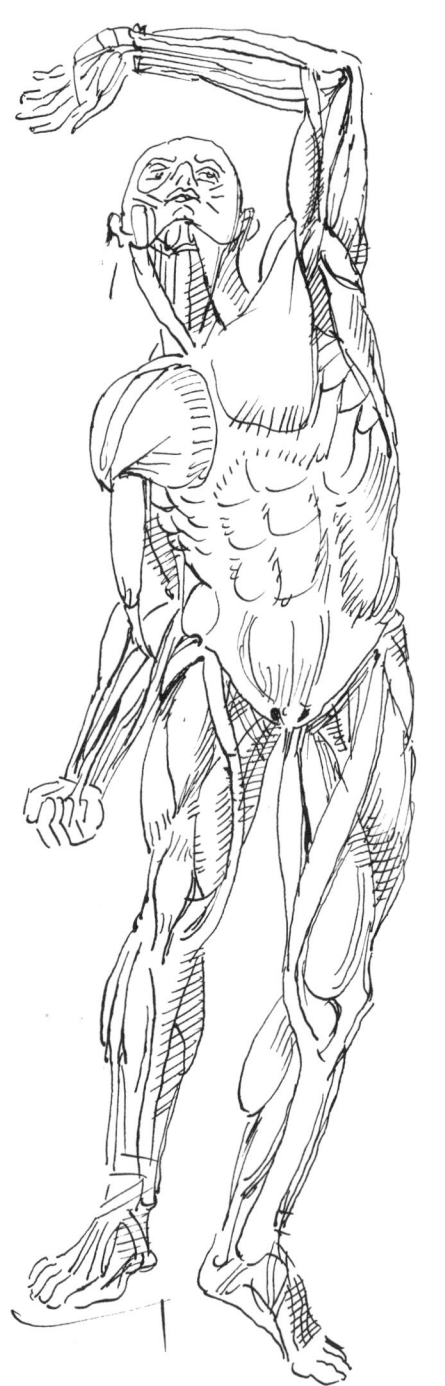

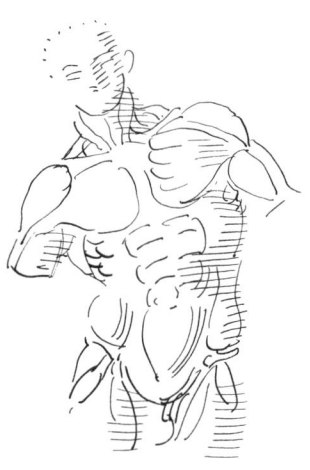

from Richer

from Franz Frohse

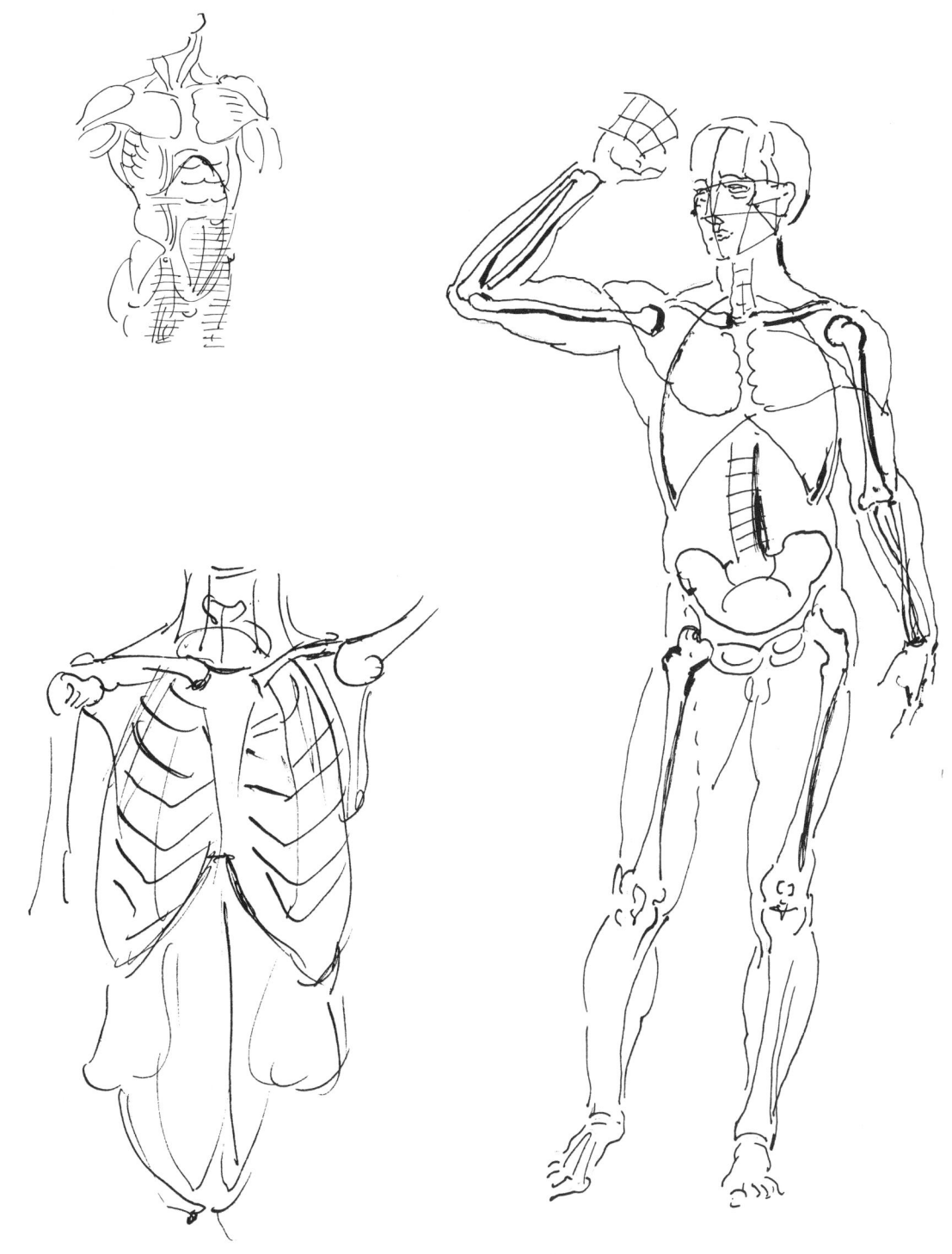

from 19th Century German anatomist

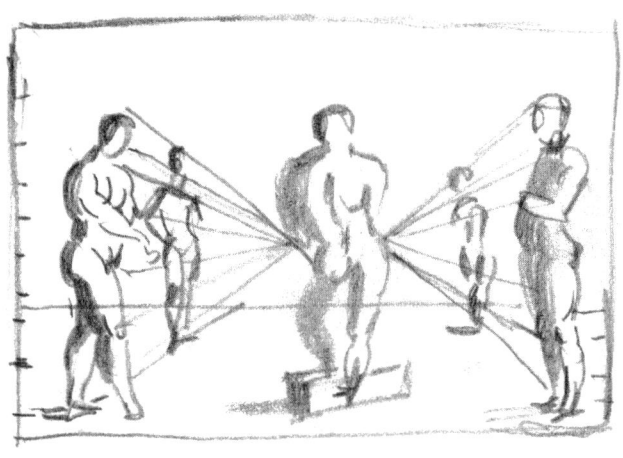

an early perspective

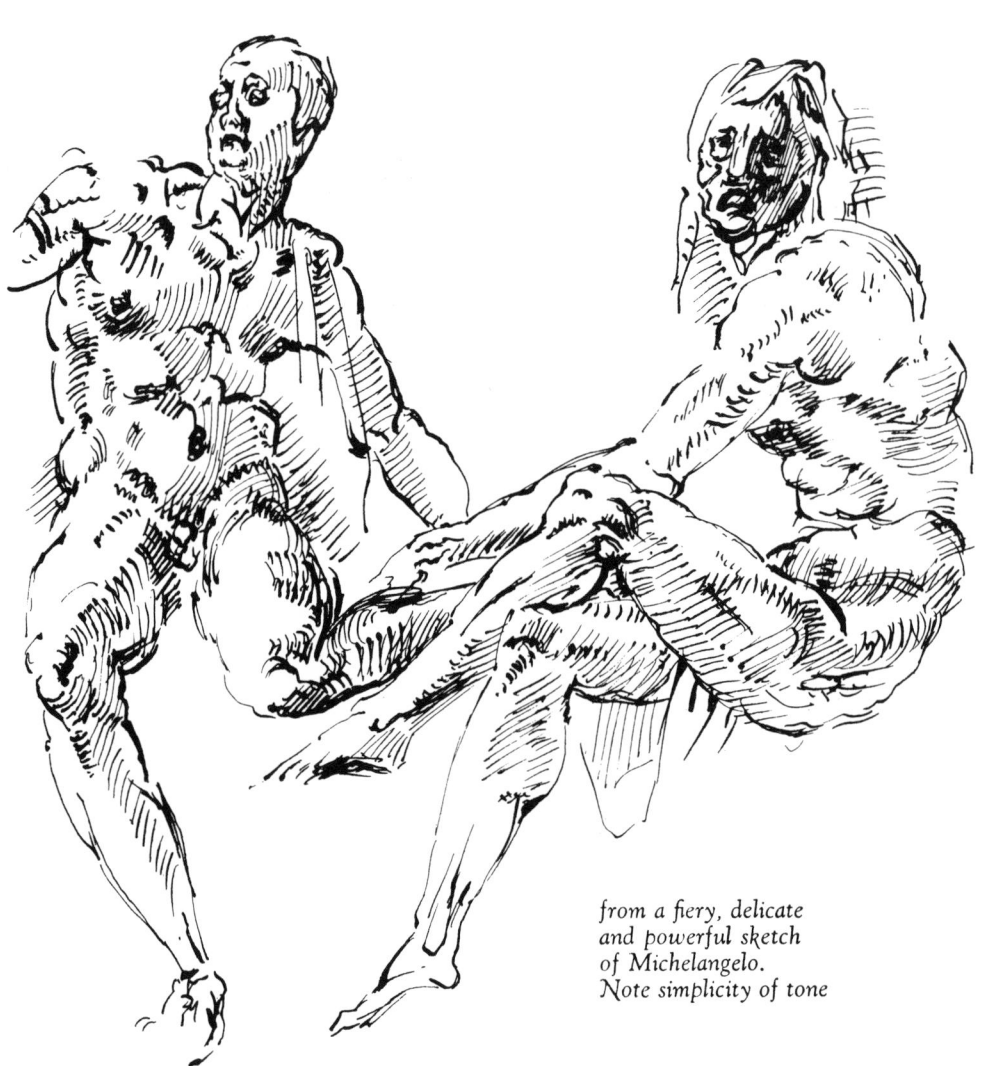

*from a fiery, delicate
and powerful sketch
of Michelangelo.
Note simplicity of tone*

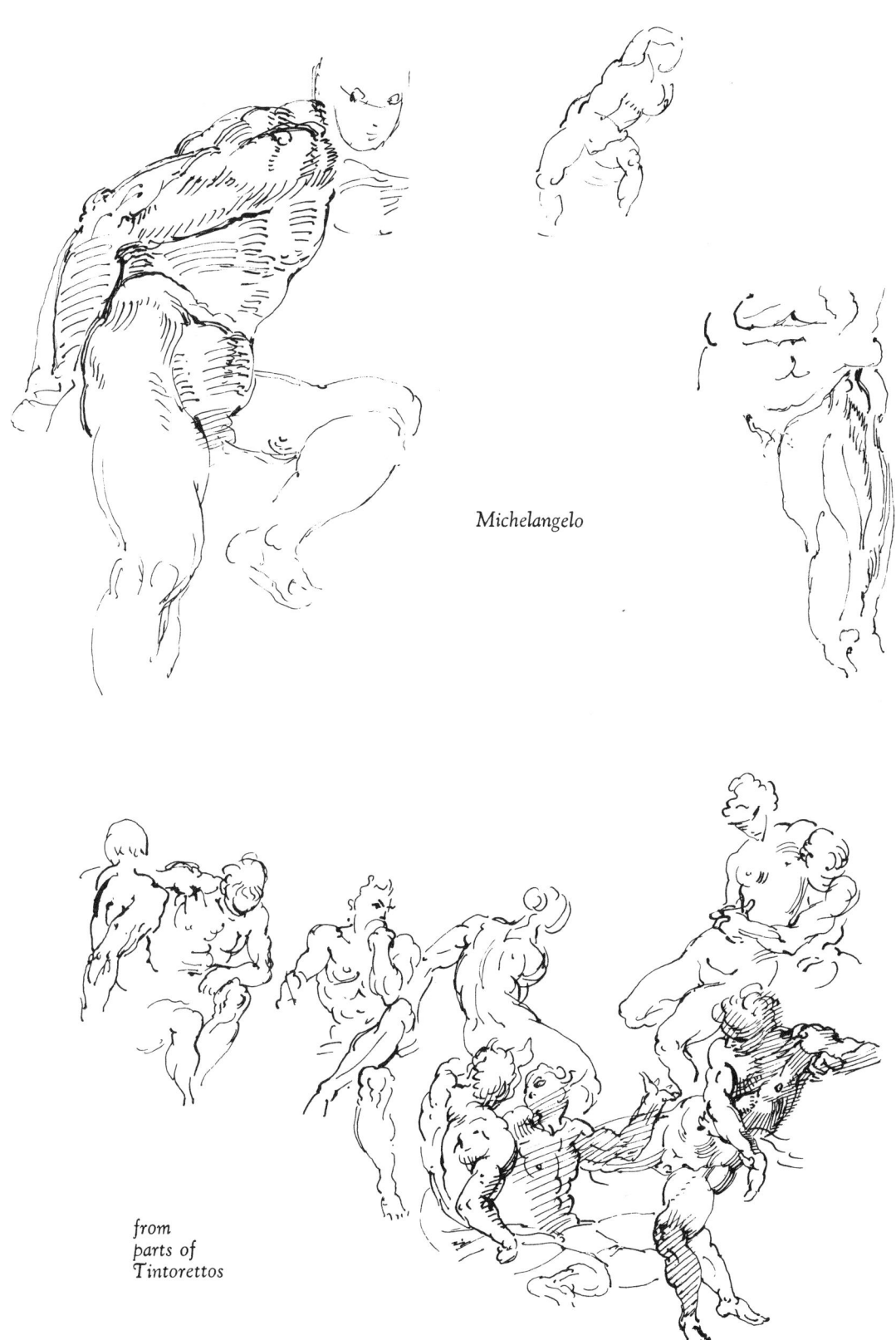

Michelangelo

from
parts of
Tintorettos

33

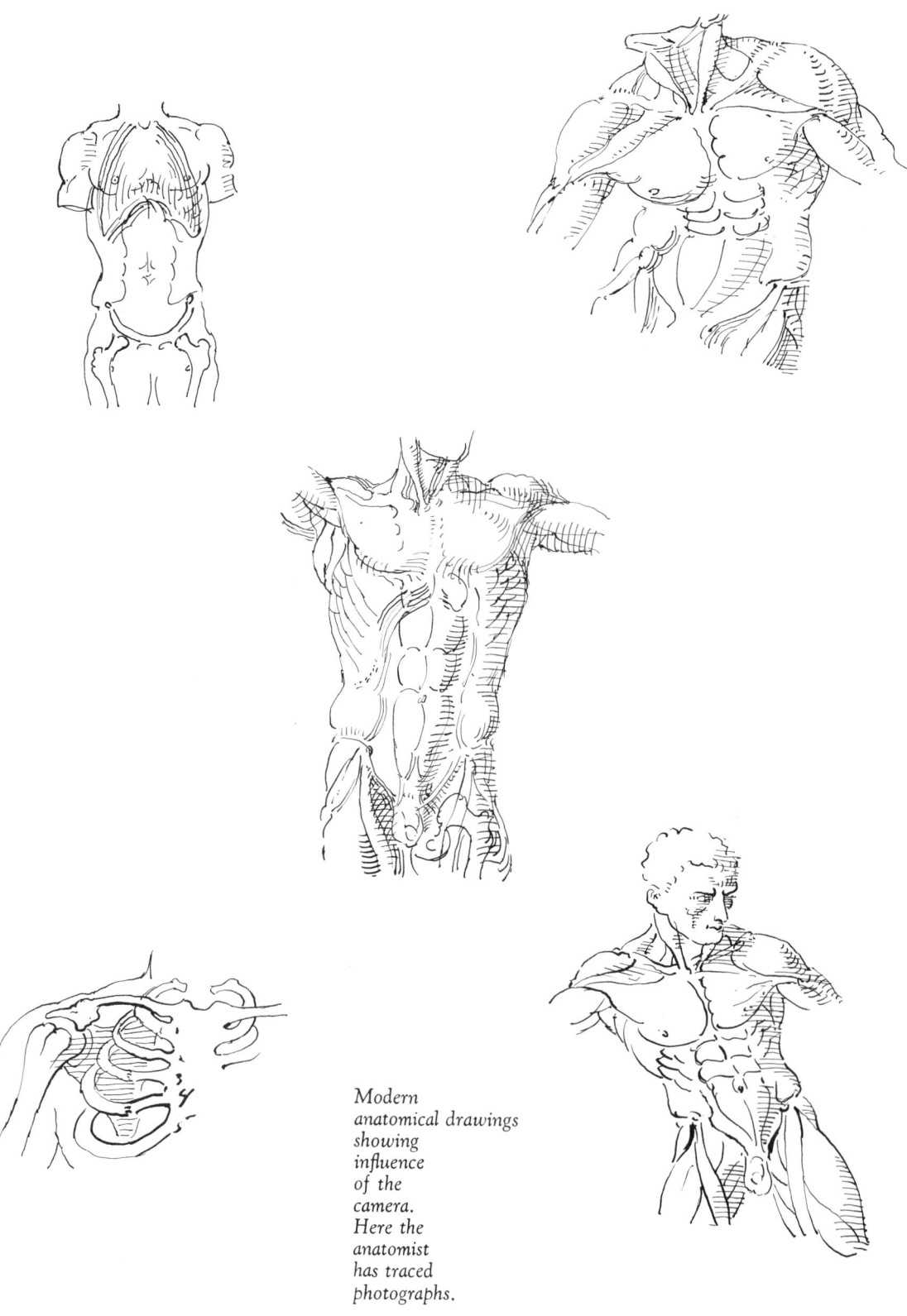

Modern
anatomical drawings
showing
influence
of the
camera.
Here the
anatomist
has traced
photographs.

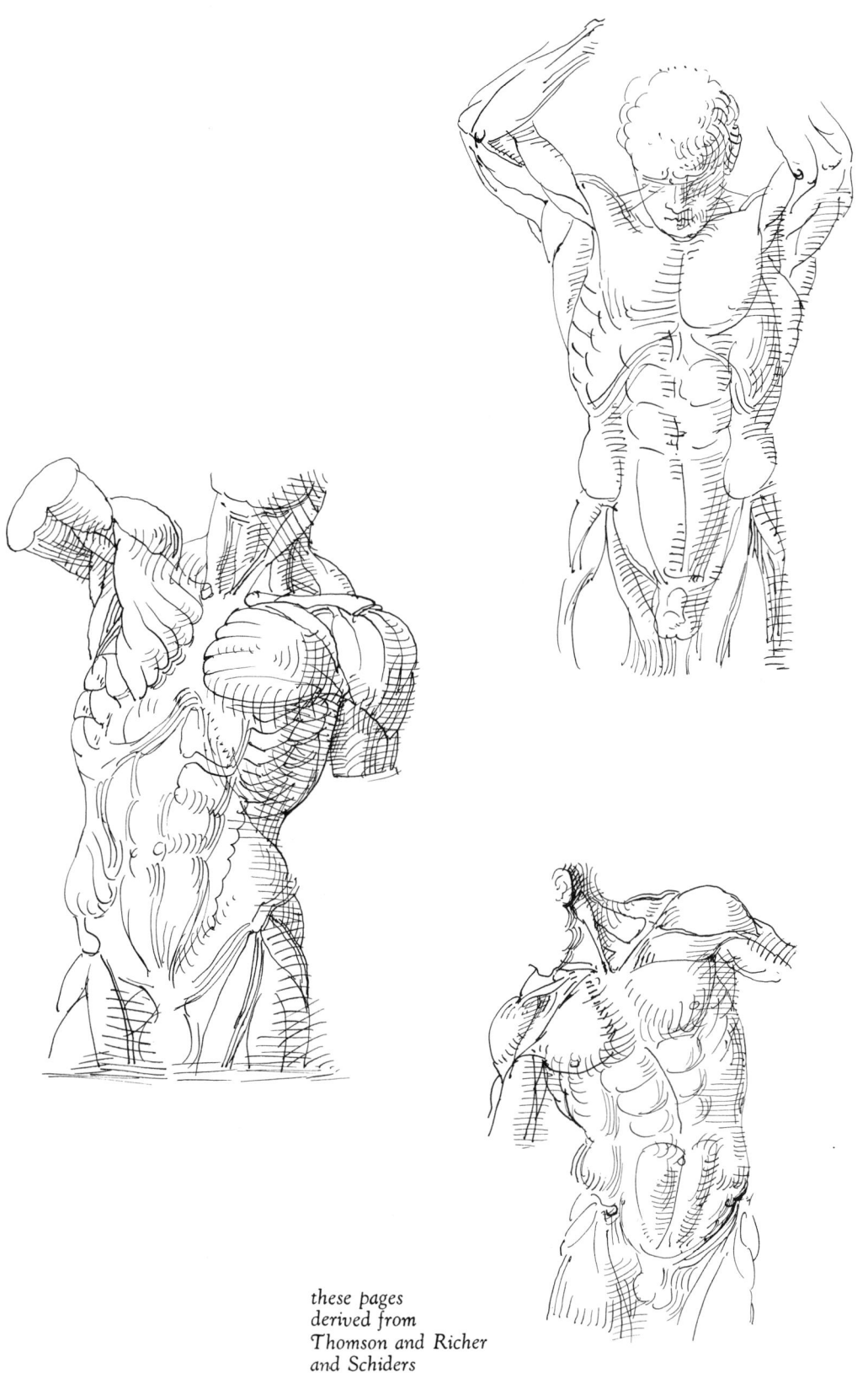

*these pages
derived from
Thomson and Richer
and Schiders*

35

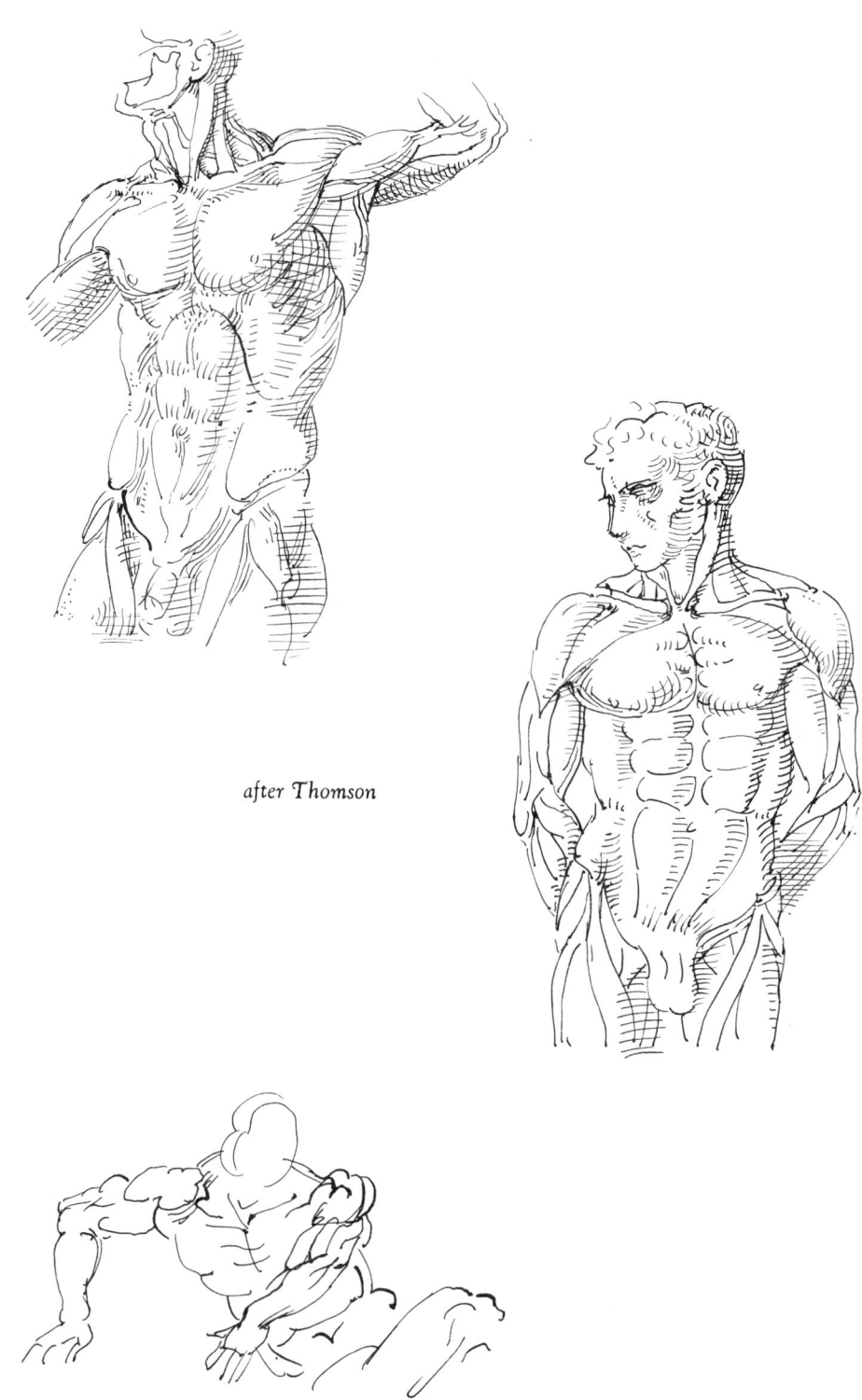

after Thomson

quick sketch after Michelangelo

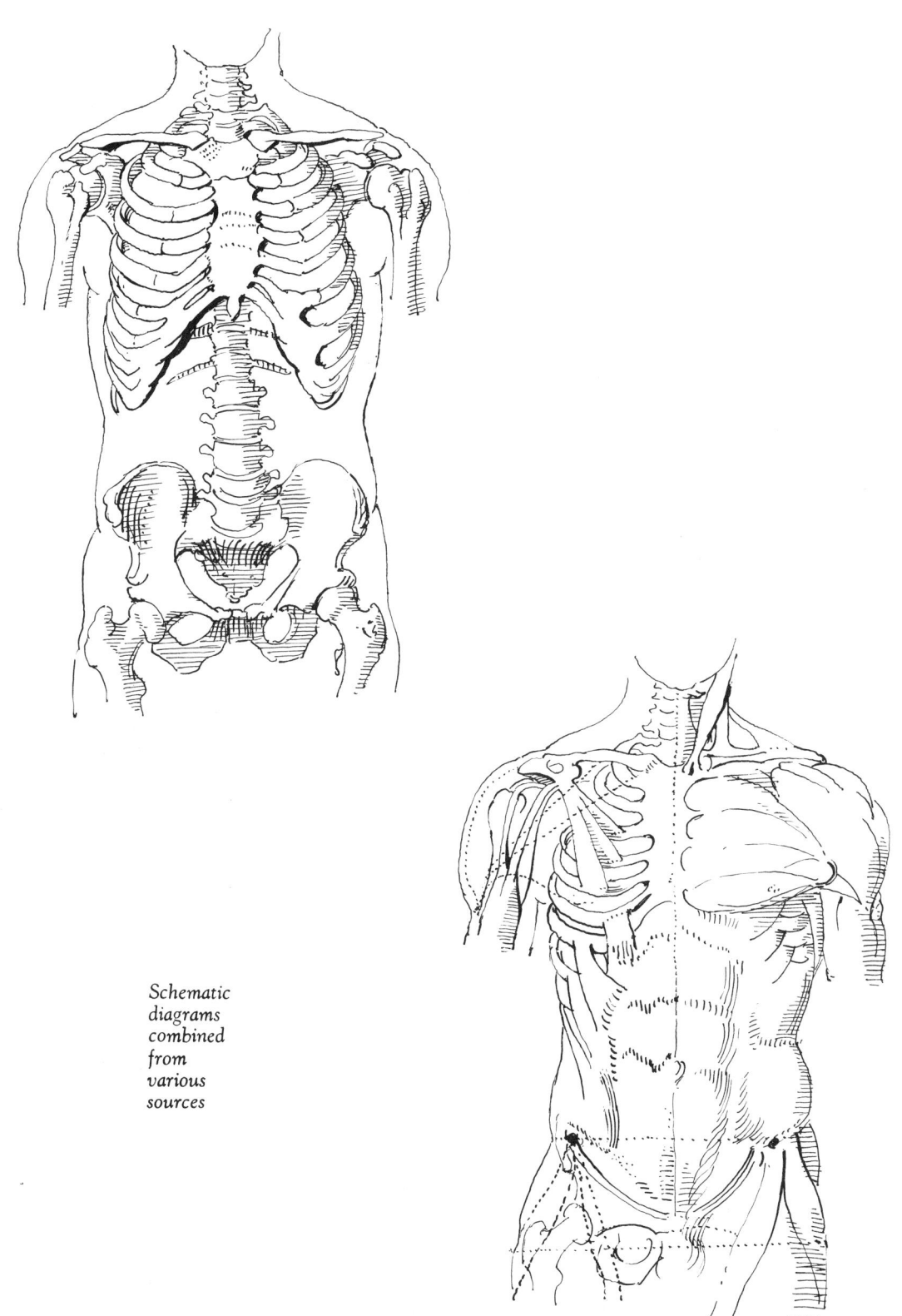

*Schematic
diagrams
combined
from
various
sources*

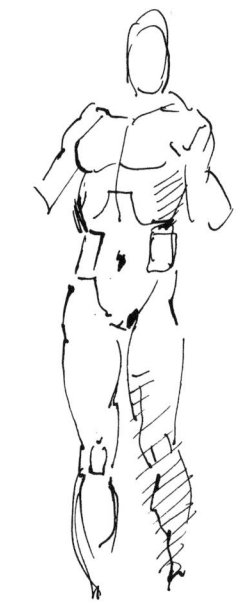

*schematic sketch
from Michelangelo*

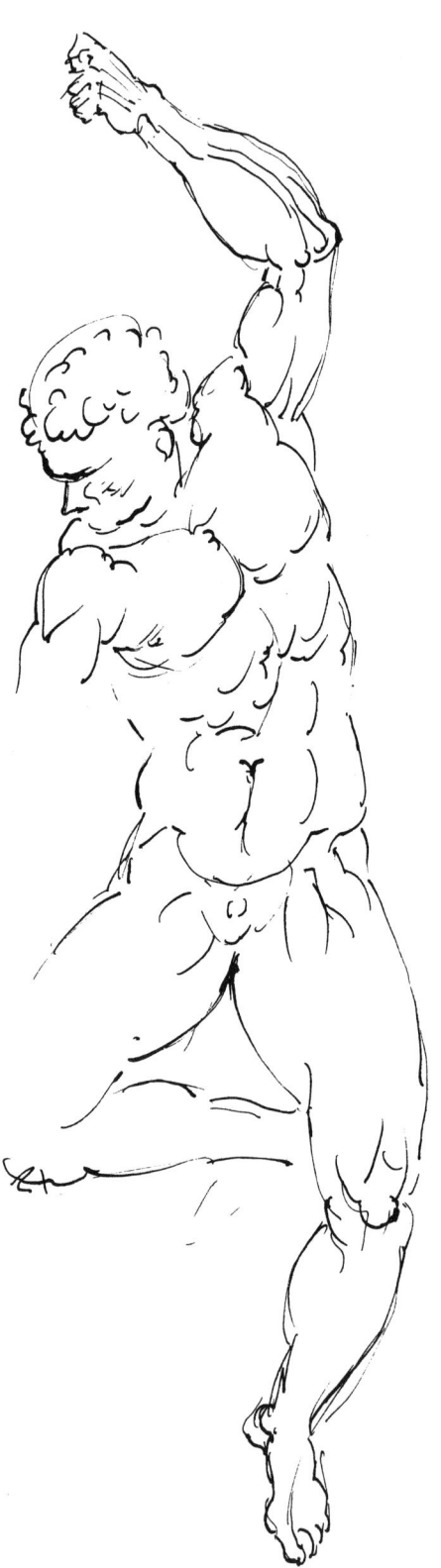

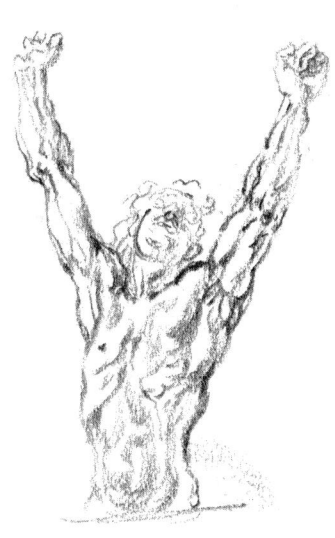

Rubens

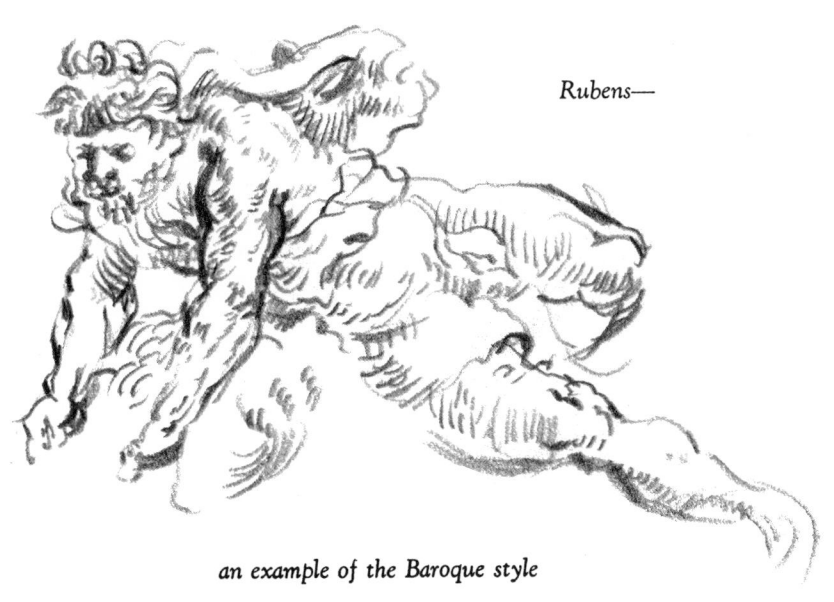

Rubens—

an example of the Baroque style

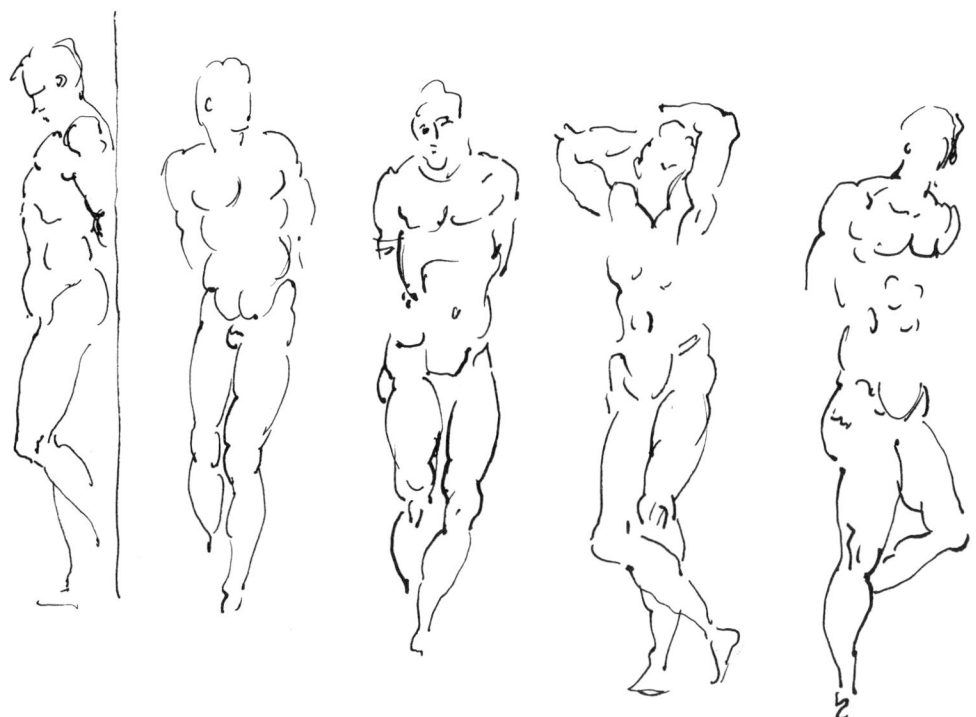

Michelangelo—
Note the contained arrangement of the limbs—
a simple centralized core dominates

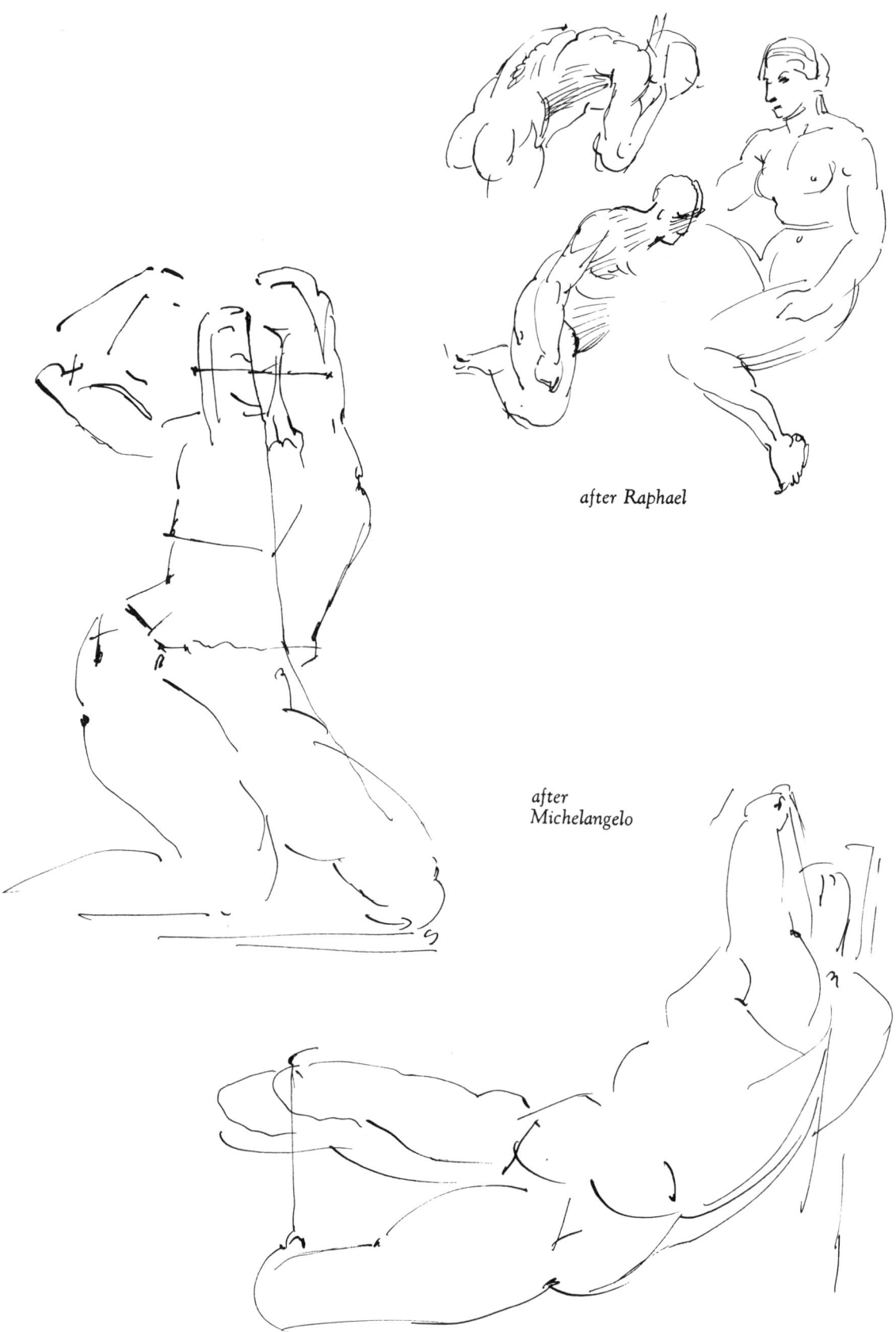

after Raphael

after
Michelangelo

40

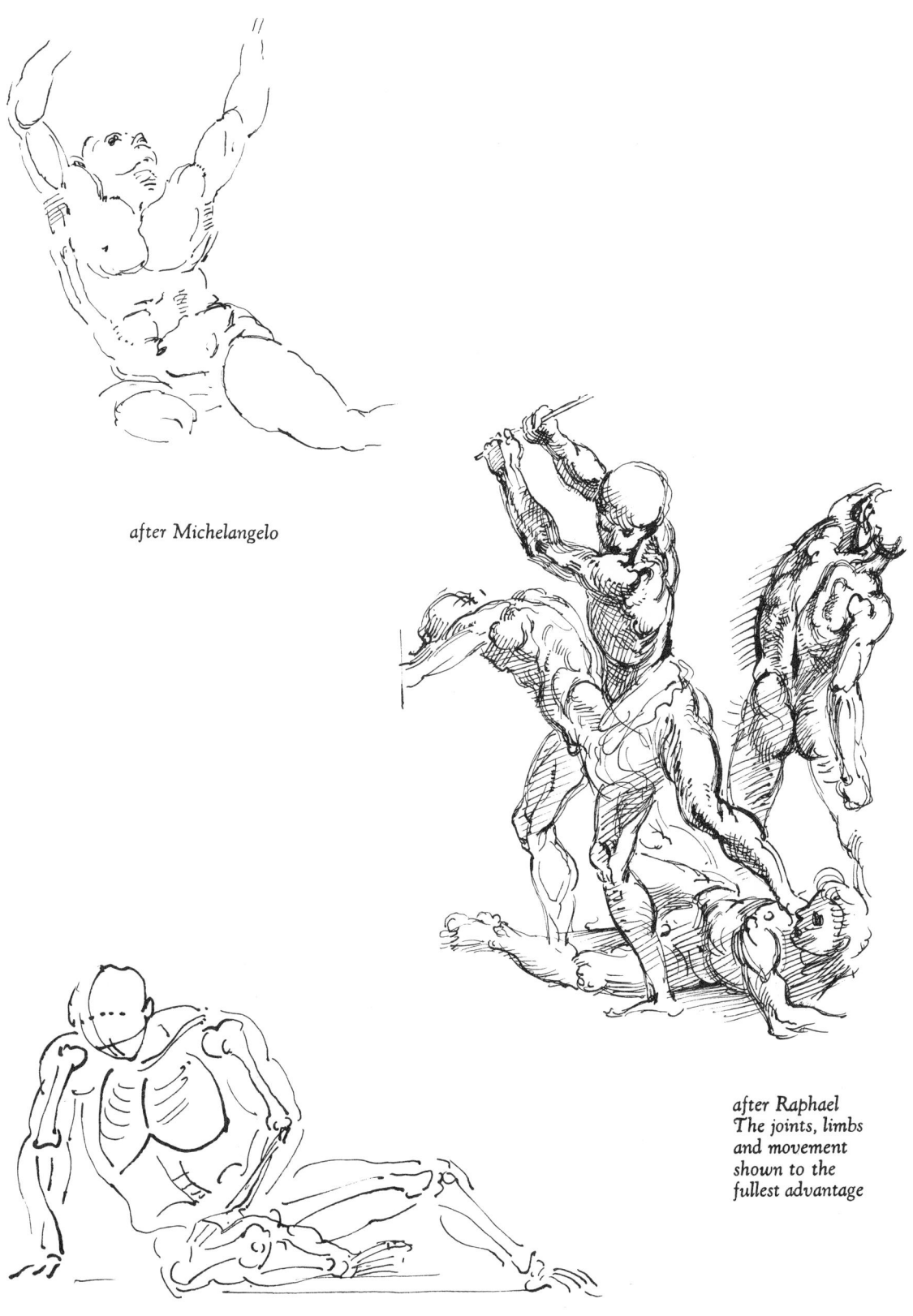

after Michelangelo

after Raphael
The joints, limbs
and movement
shown to the
fullest advantage

from "Choulant." The dying gladiator

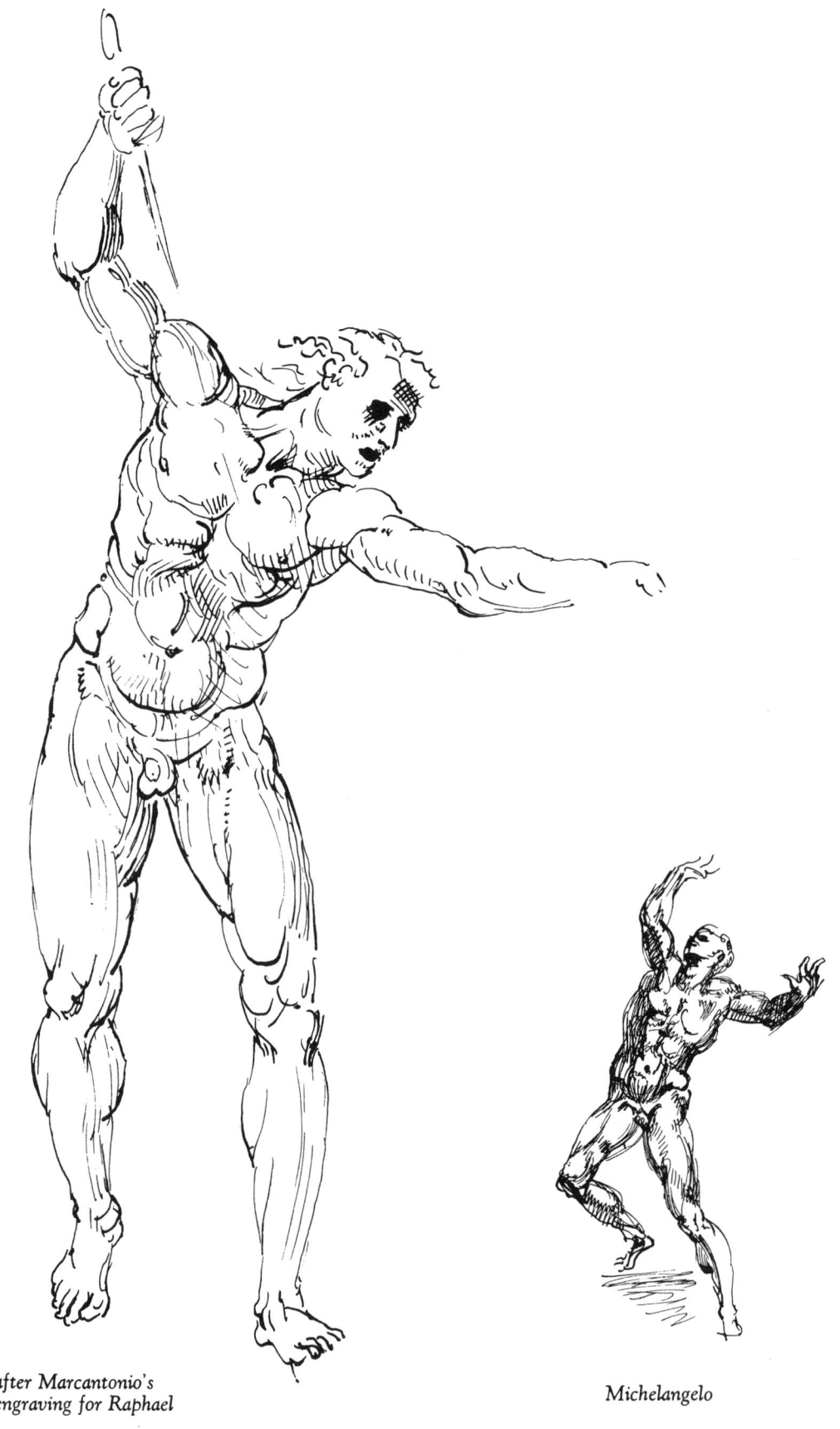

after Marcantonio's
engraving for Raphael

Michelangelo

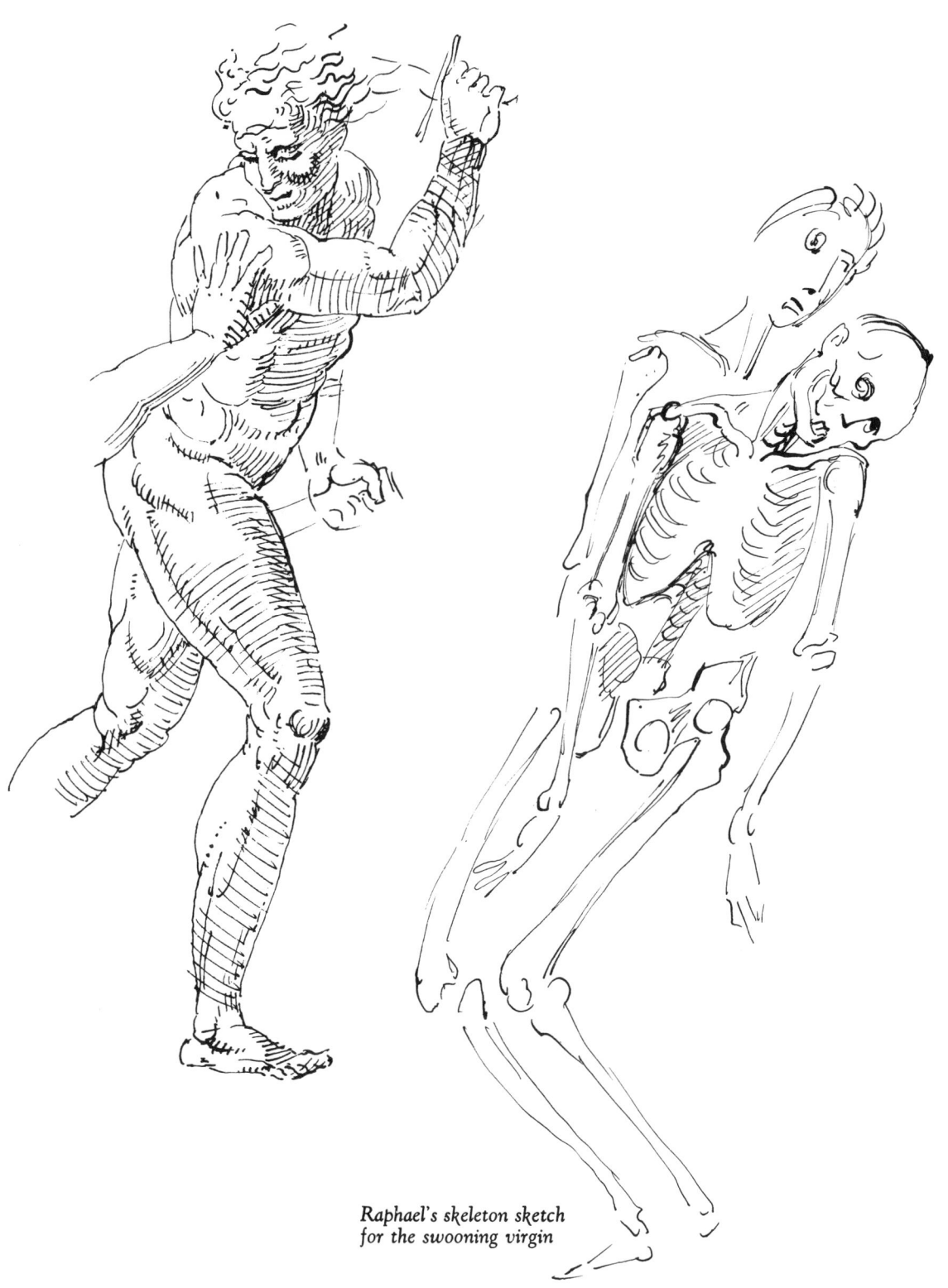

*Raphael's skeleton sketch
for the swooning virgin*

43

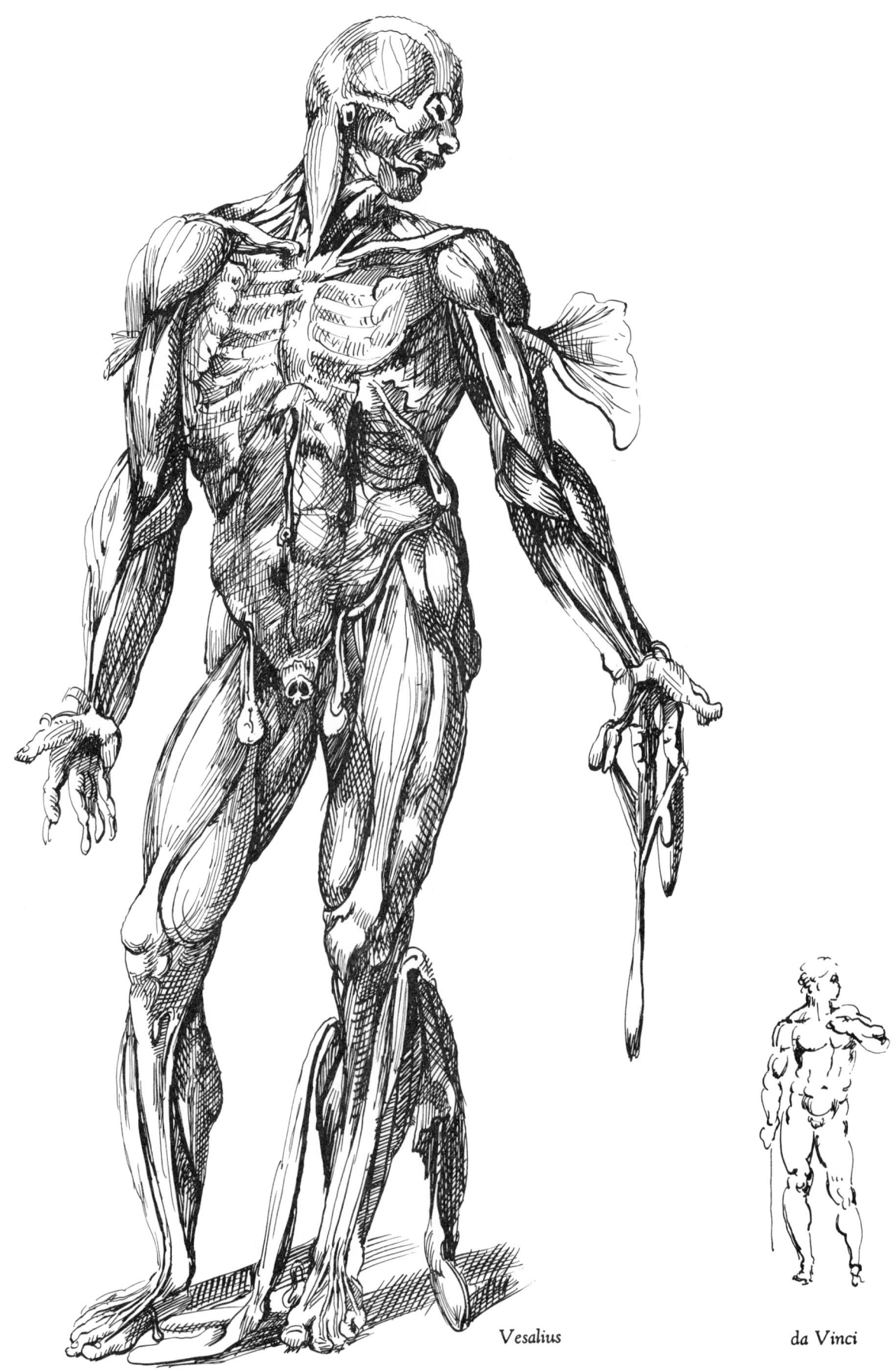

Vesalius

da Vinci

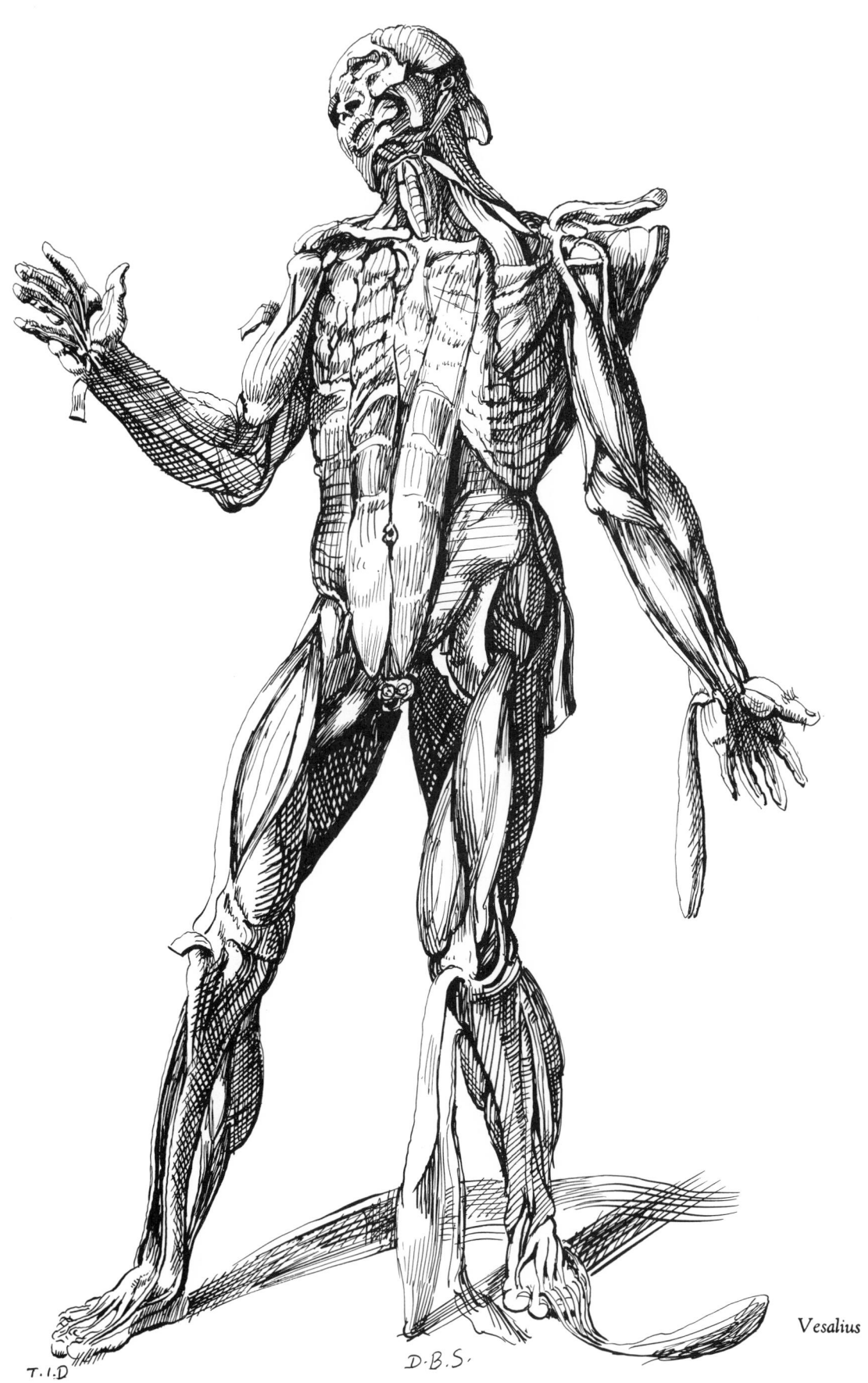

T.I.D

D.B.S.

Vesalius

45

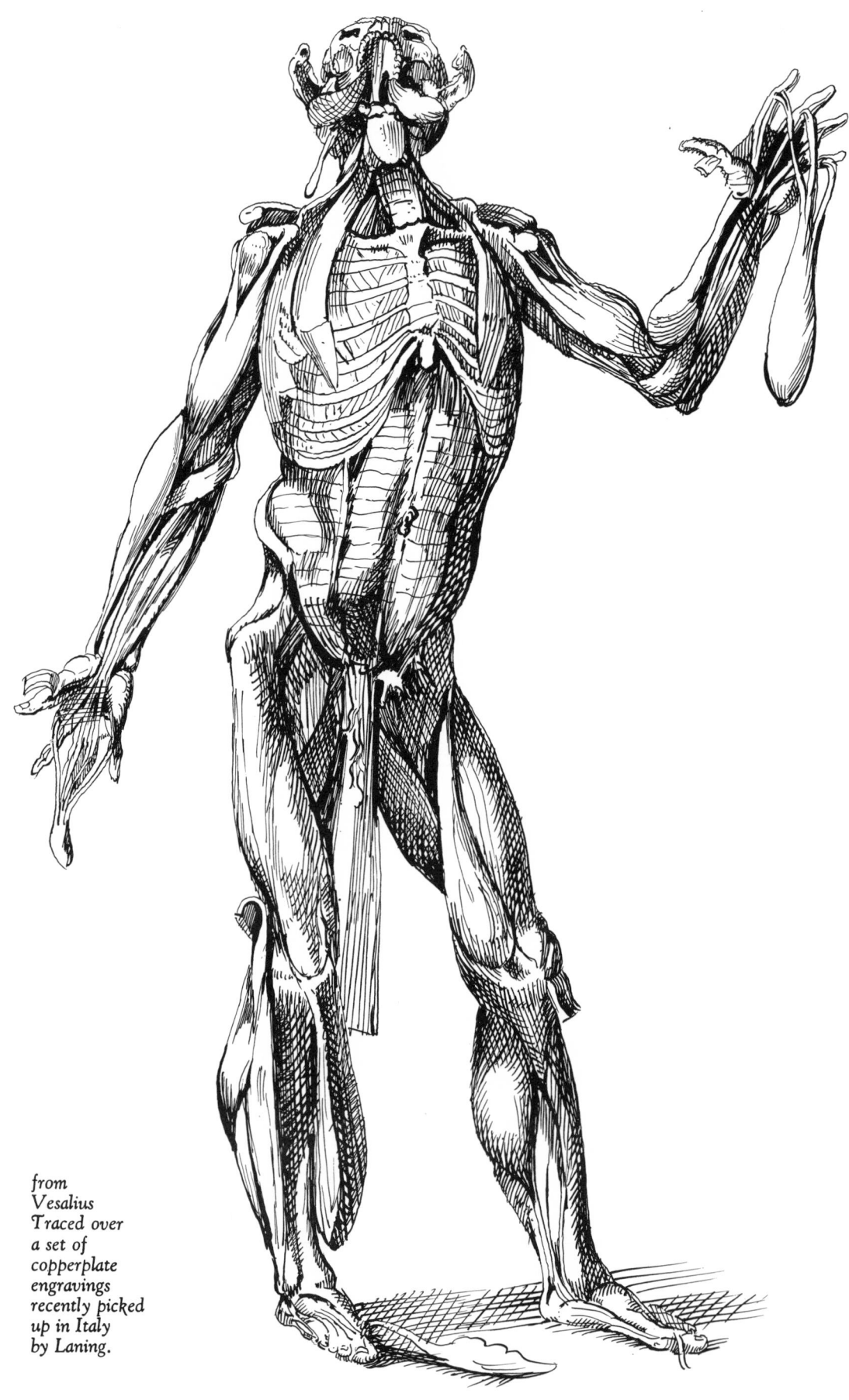

*from
Vesalius
Traced over
a set of
copperplate
engravings
recently picked
up in Italy
by Laning.*

46

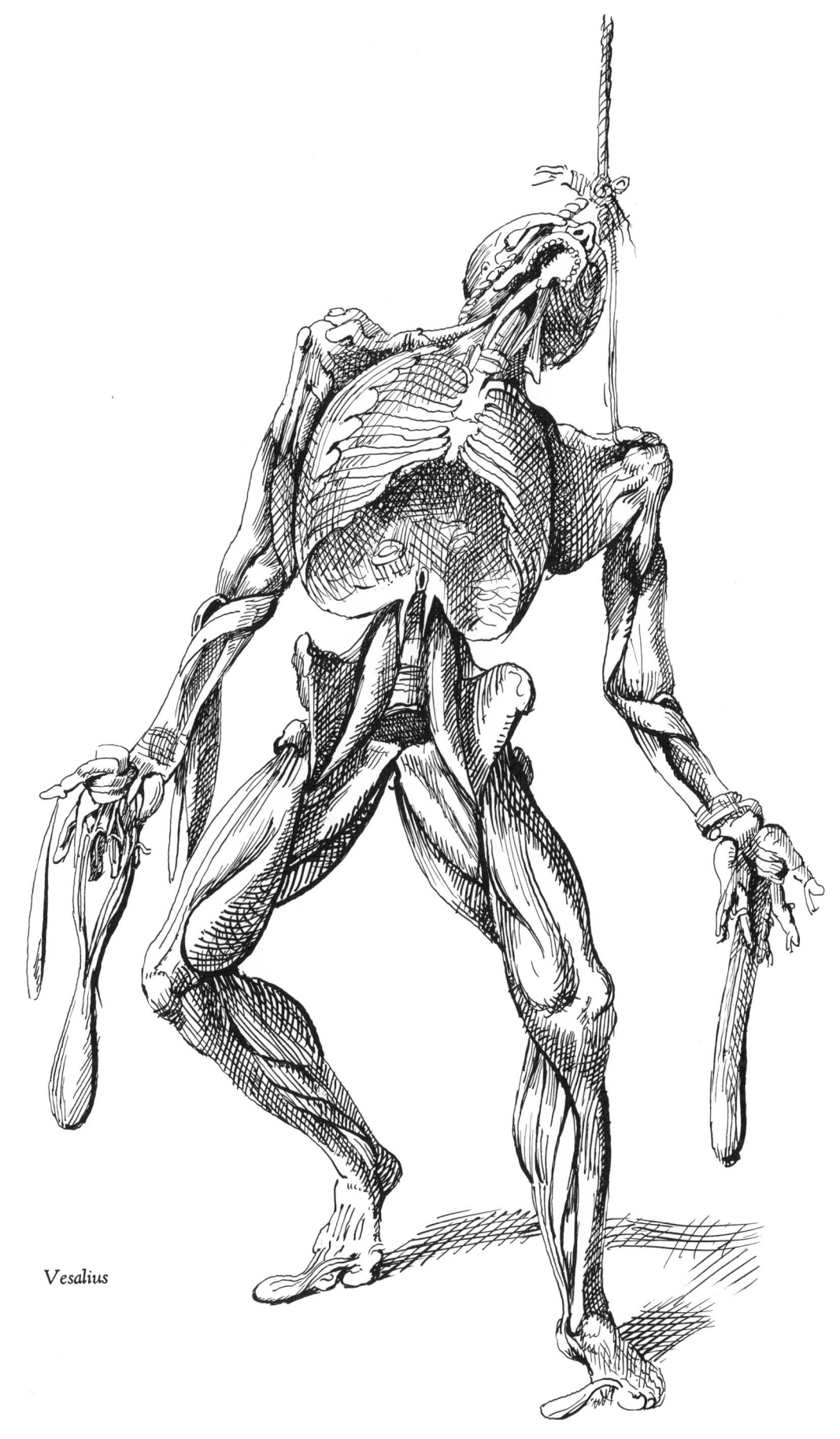

Vesalius

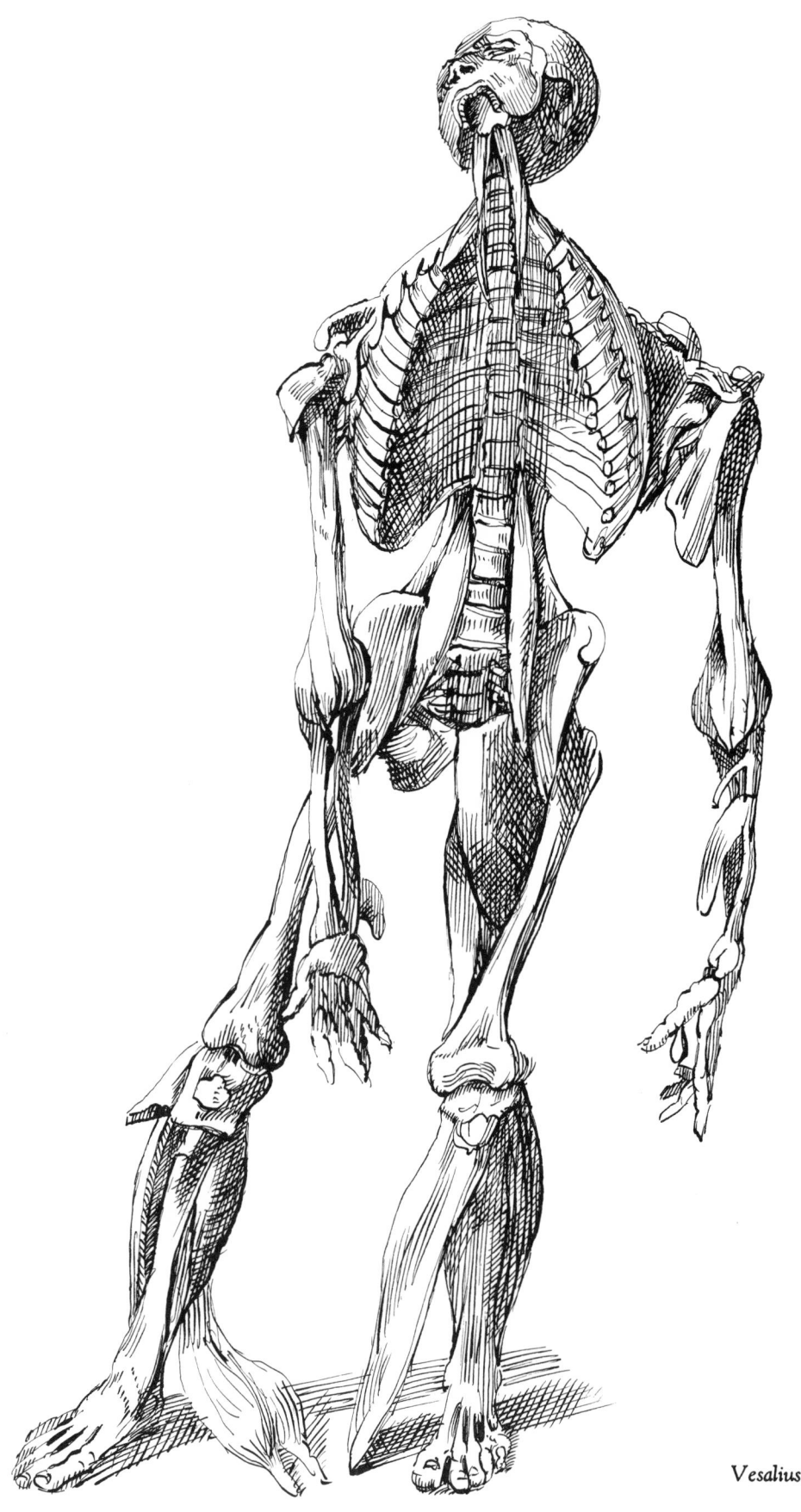

Vesalius

48

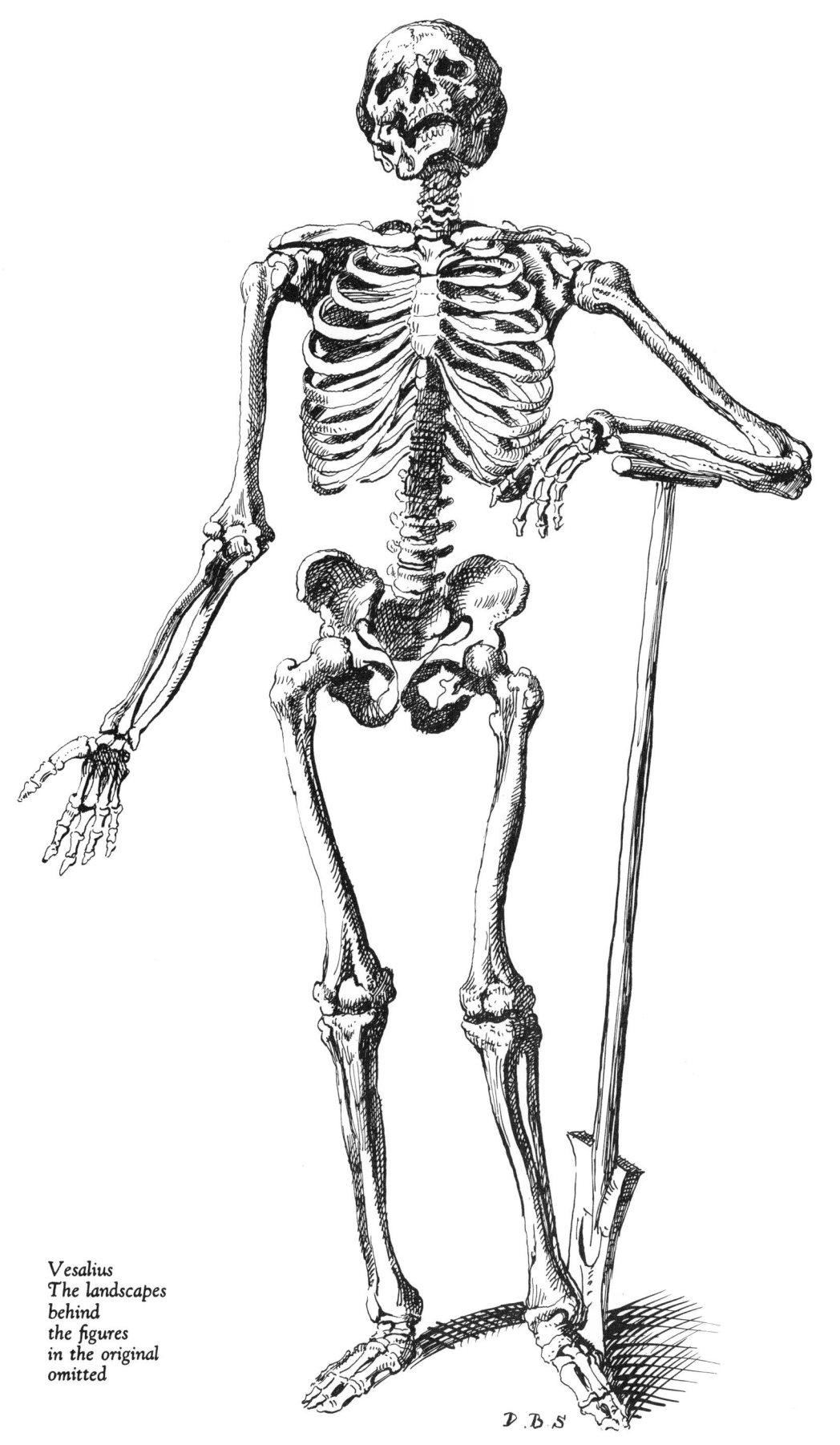

Vesalius
The landscapes
behind
the figures
in the original
omitted

D.B.S

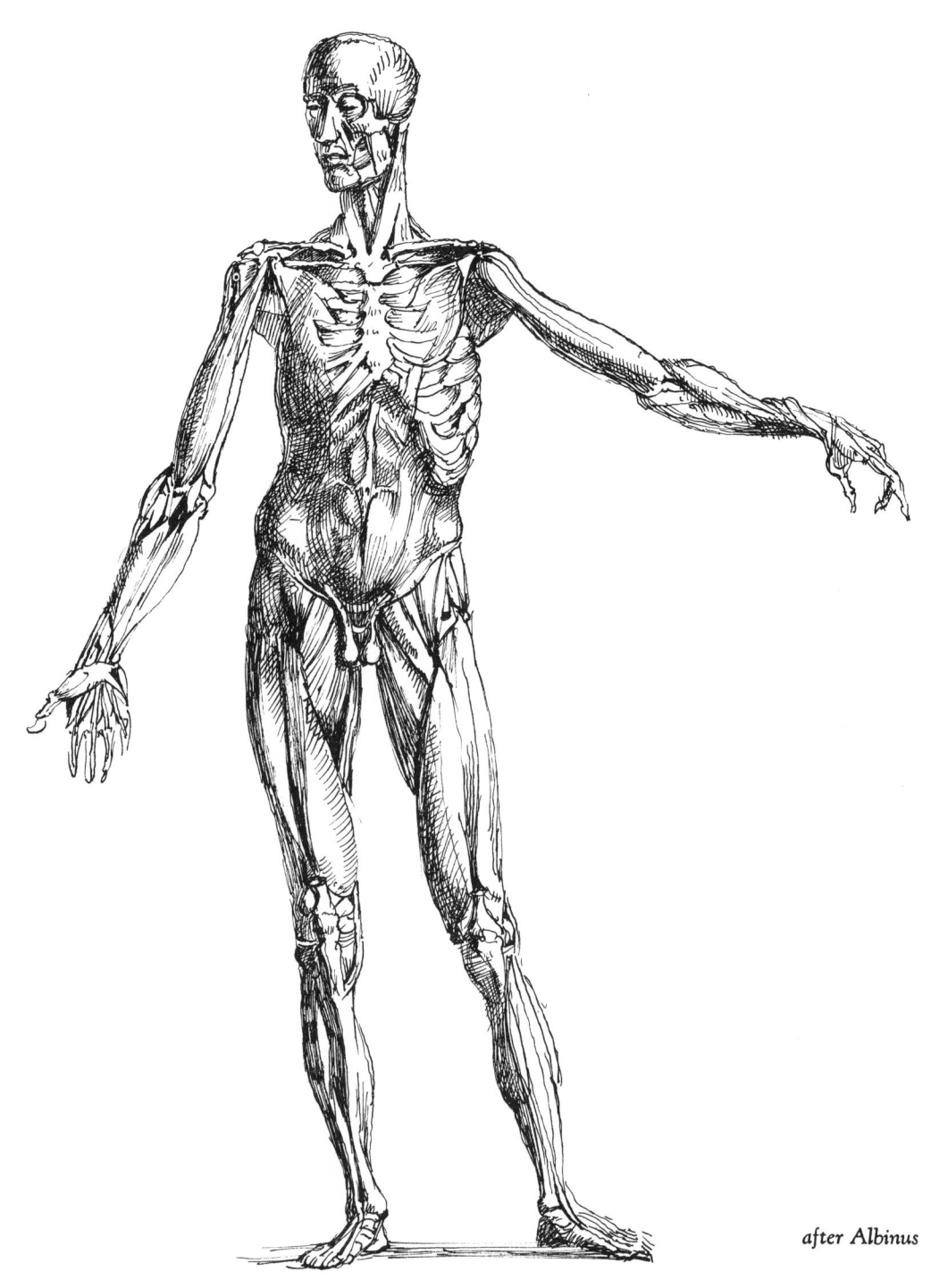

after Albinus

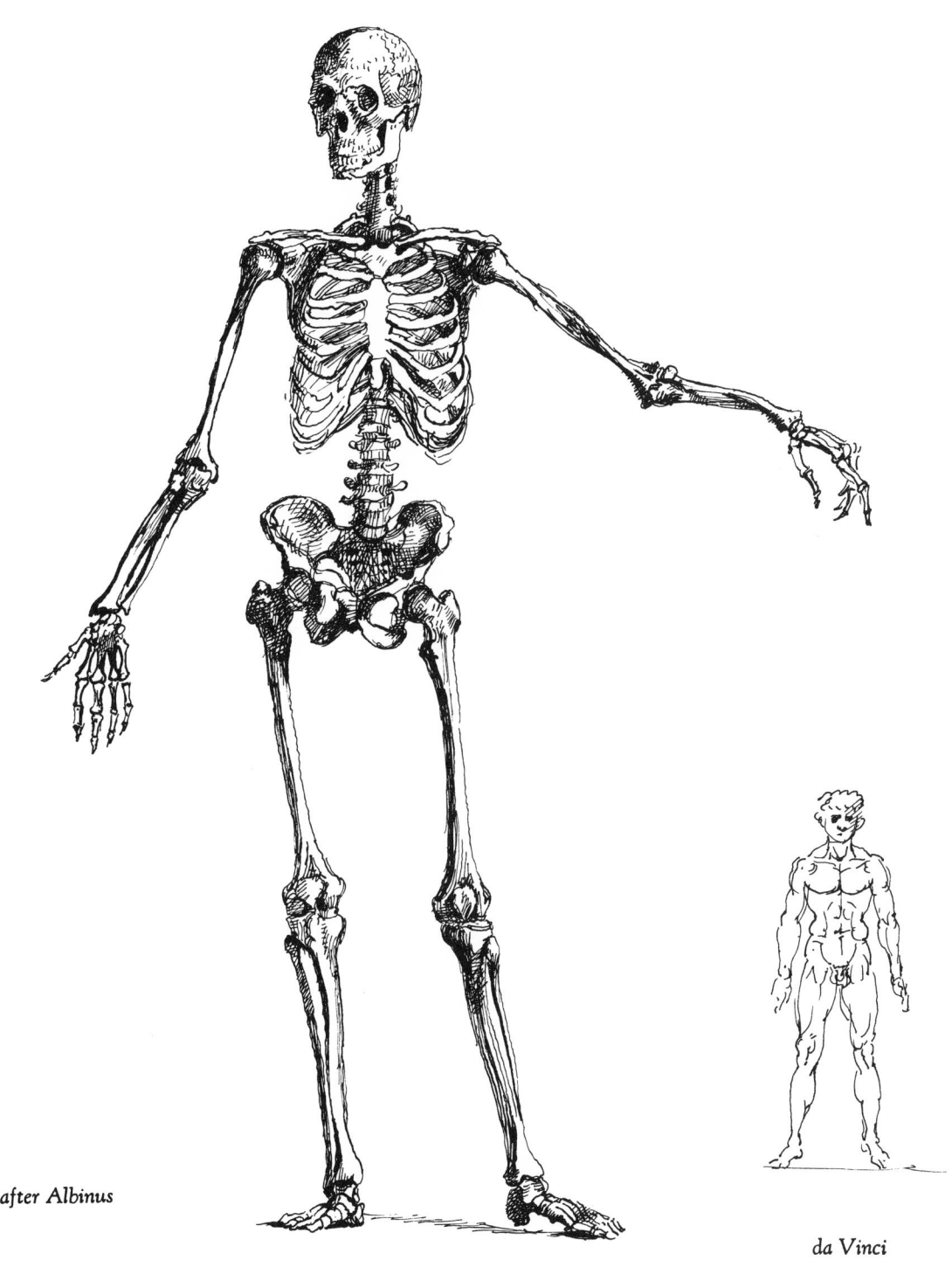

after Albinus

da Vinci

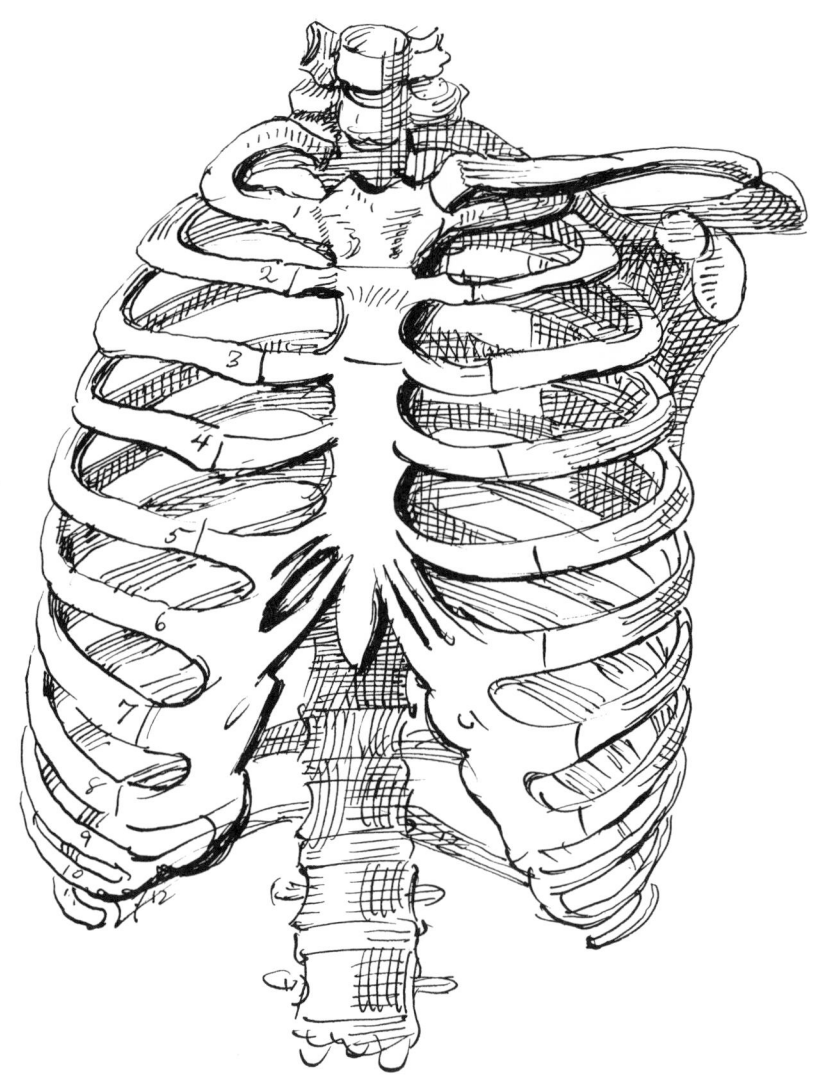

from Sabotta's medical atlas

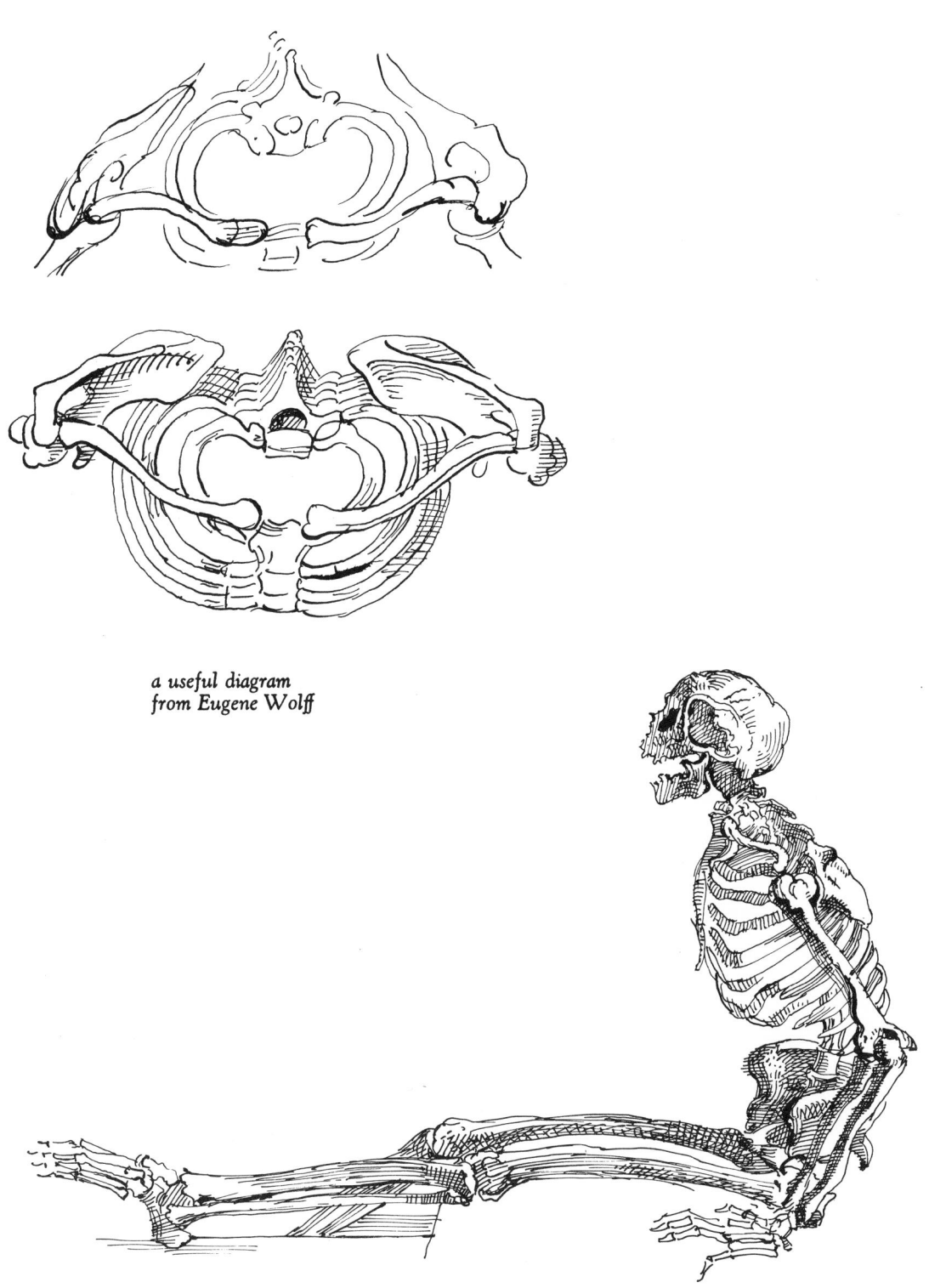

*a useful diagram
from Eugene Wolff*

from Gamelin—the tomb, landscape and Gabriel's bell omitted

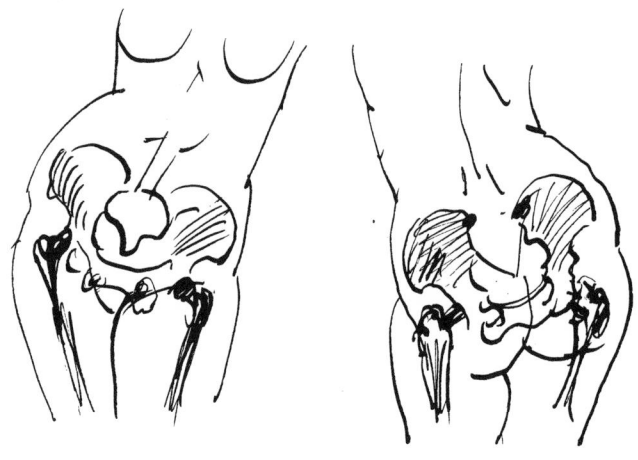

Richer

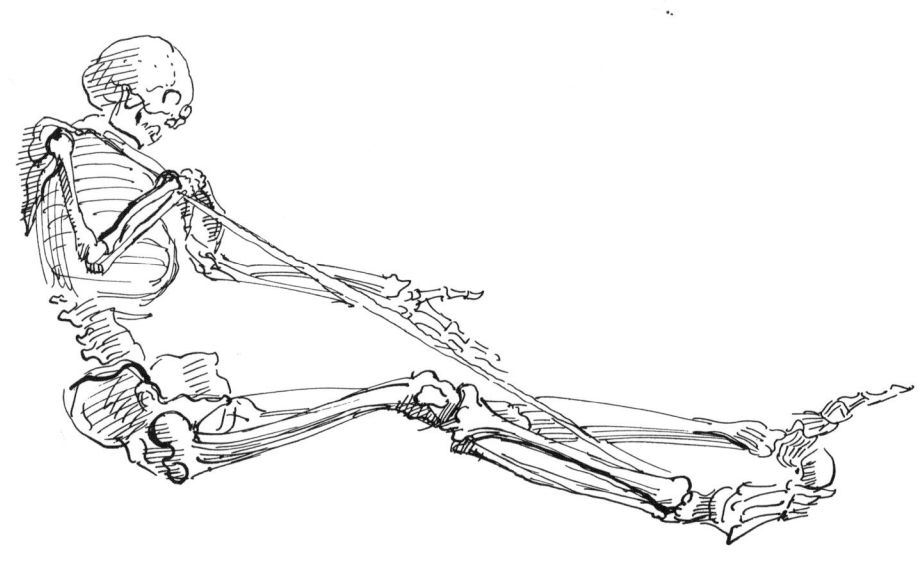

Gamelin

Side

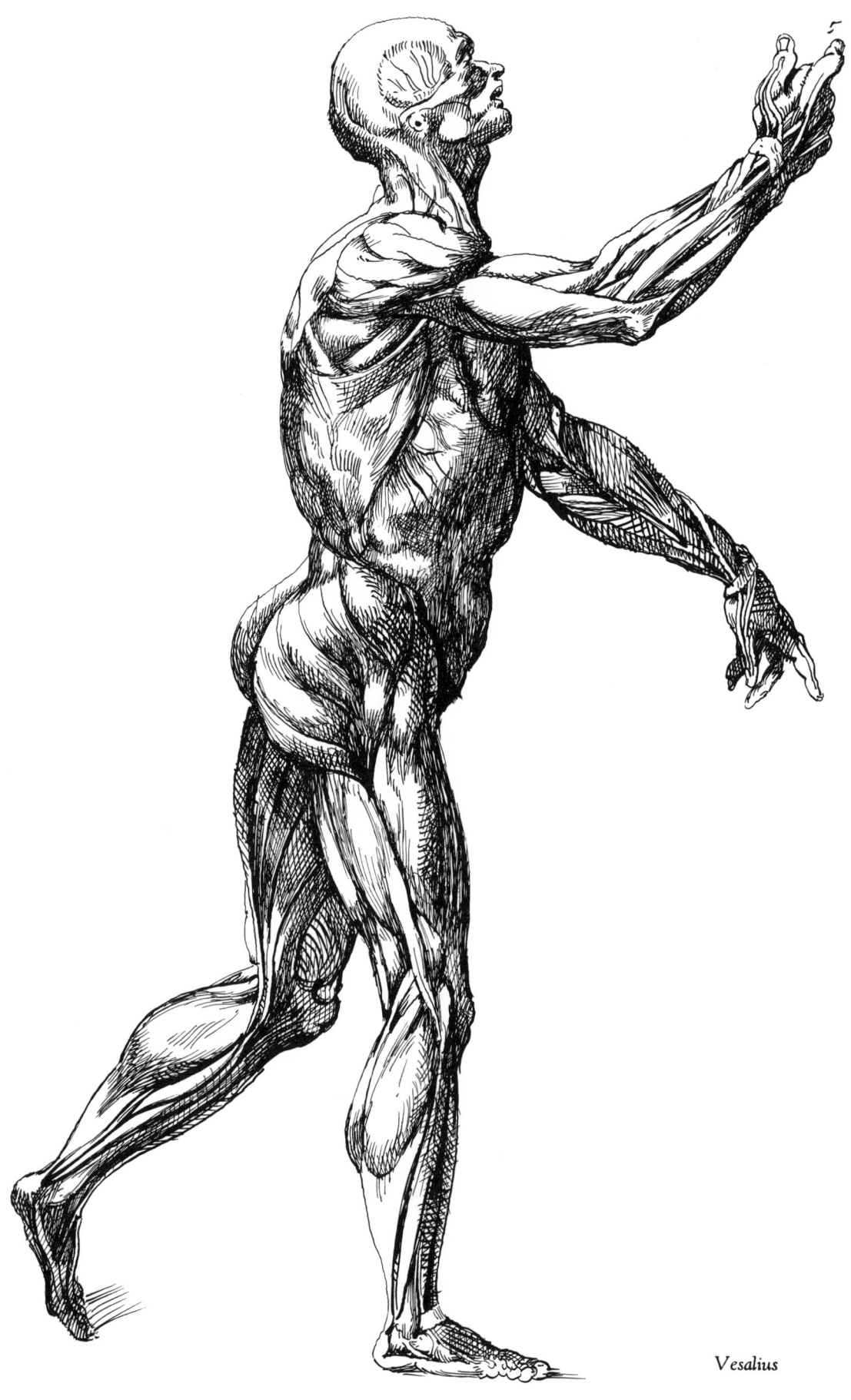

Vesalius

56

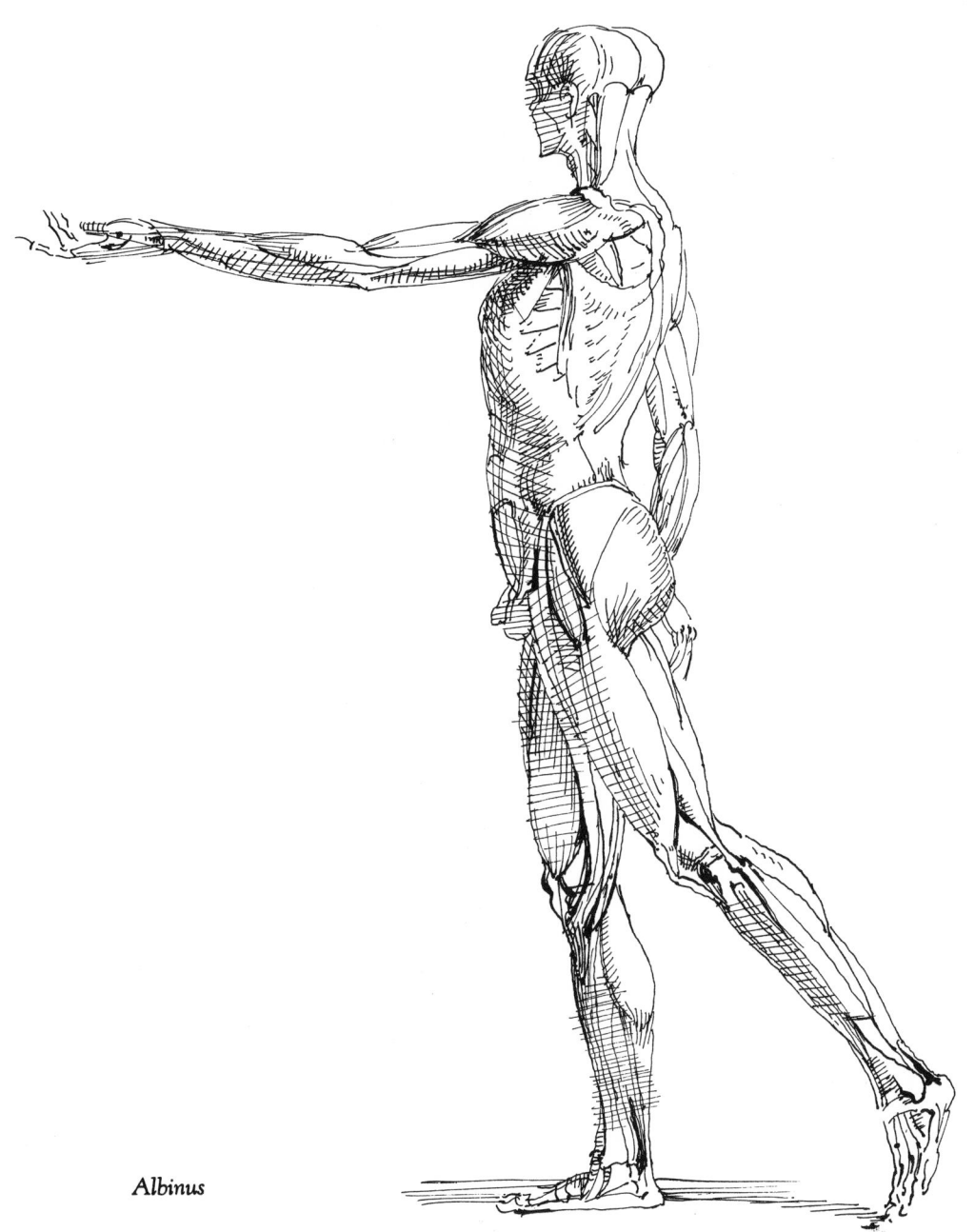

Albinus

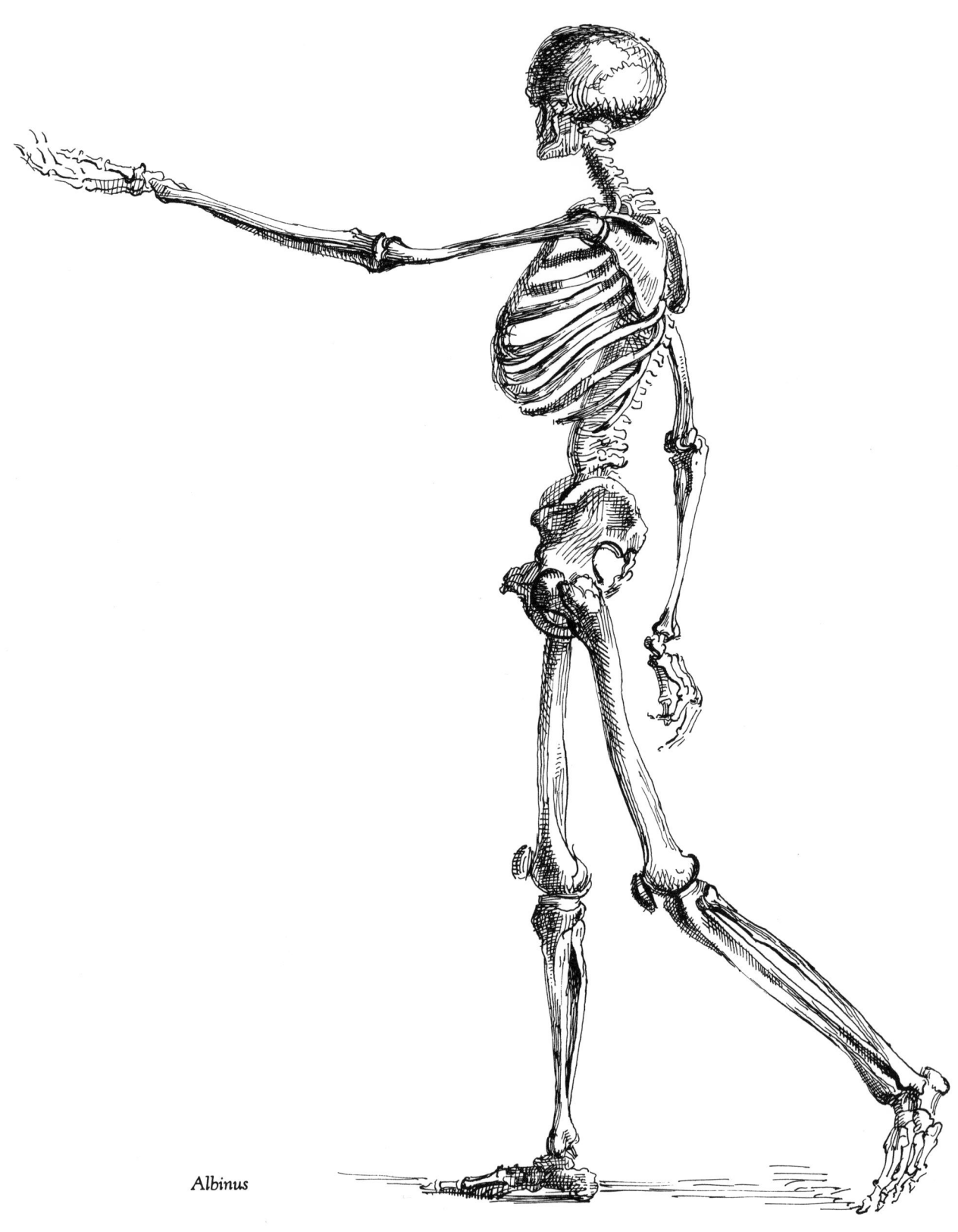

Albinus

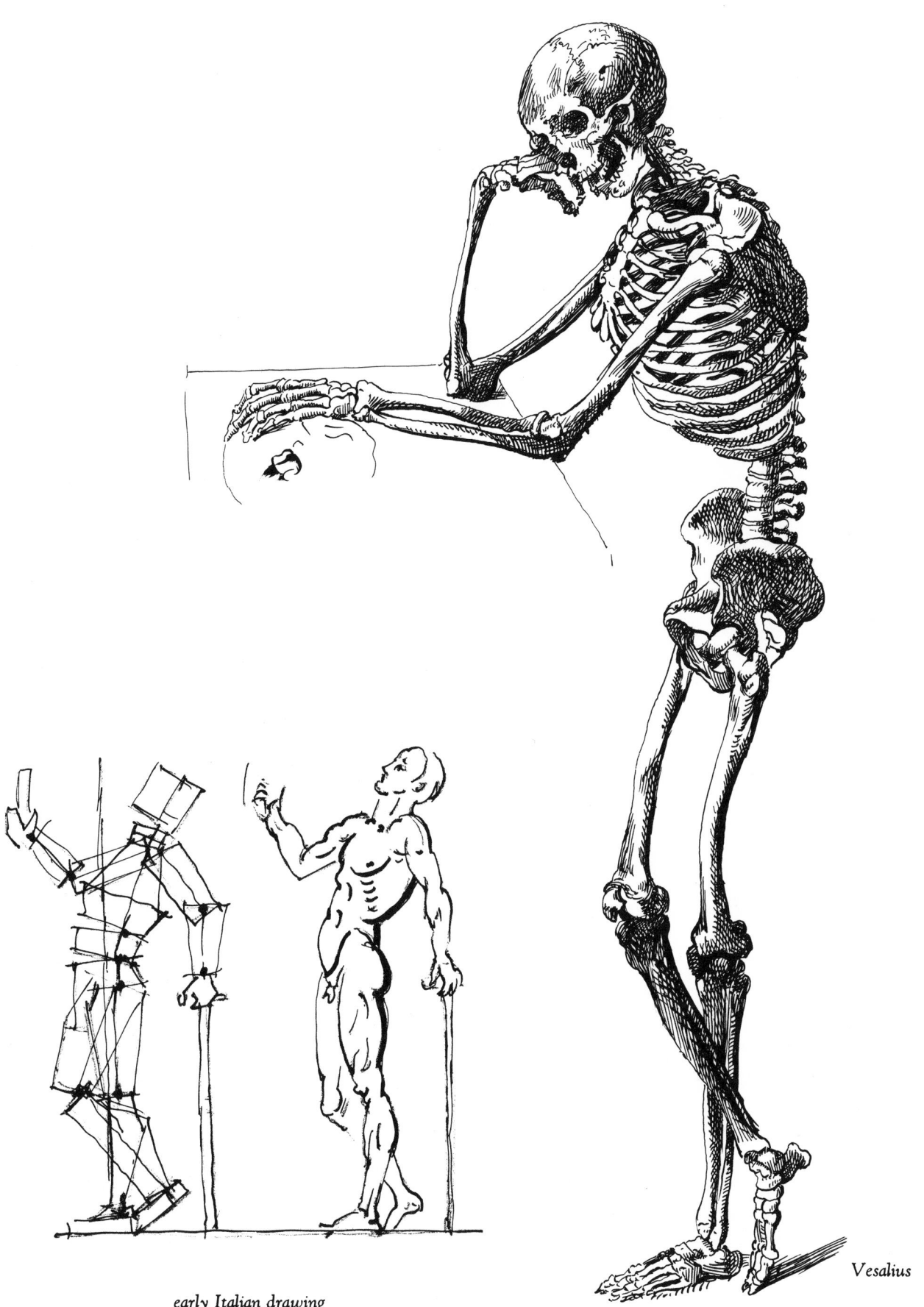

early Italian drawing

Vesalius

59

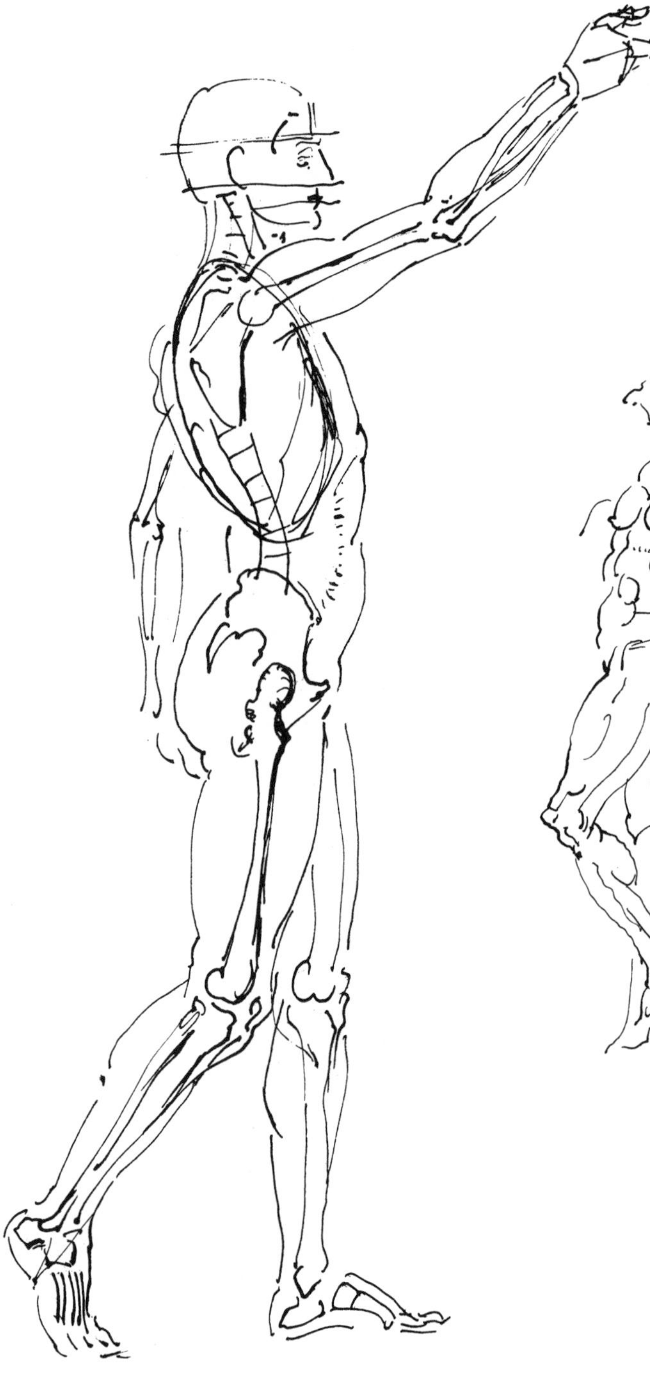

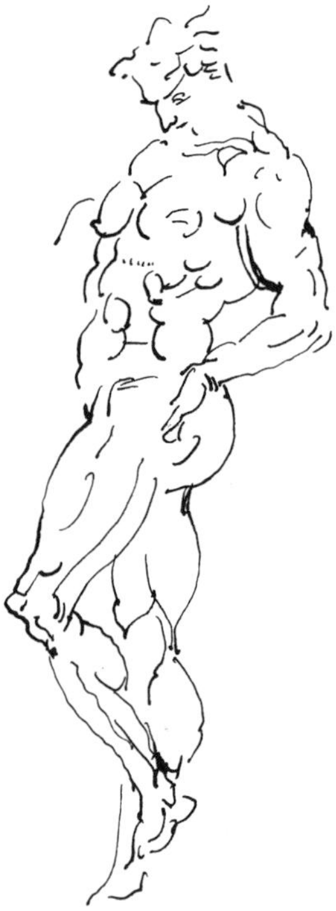

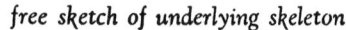

free sketch of underlying skeleton

Michelangelo

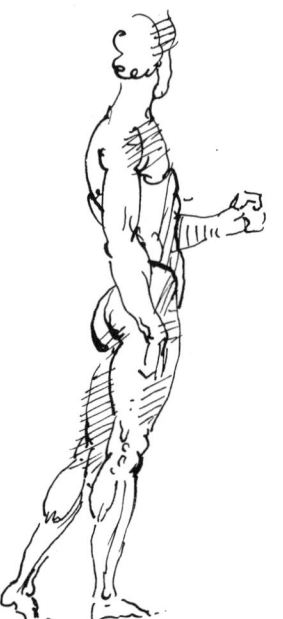

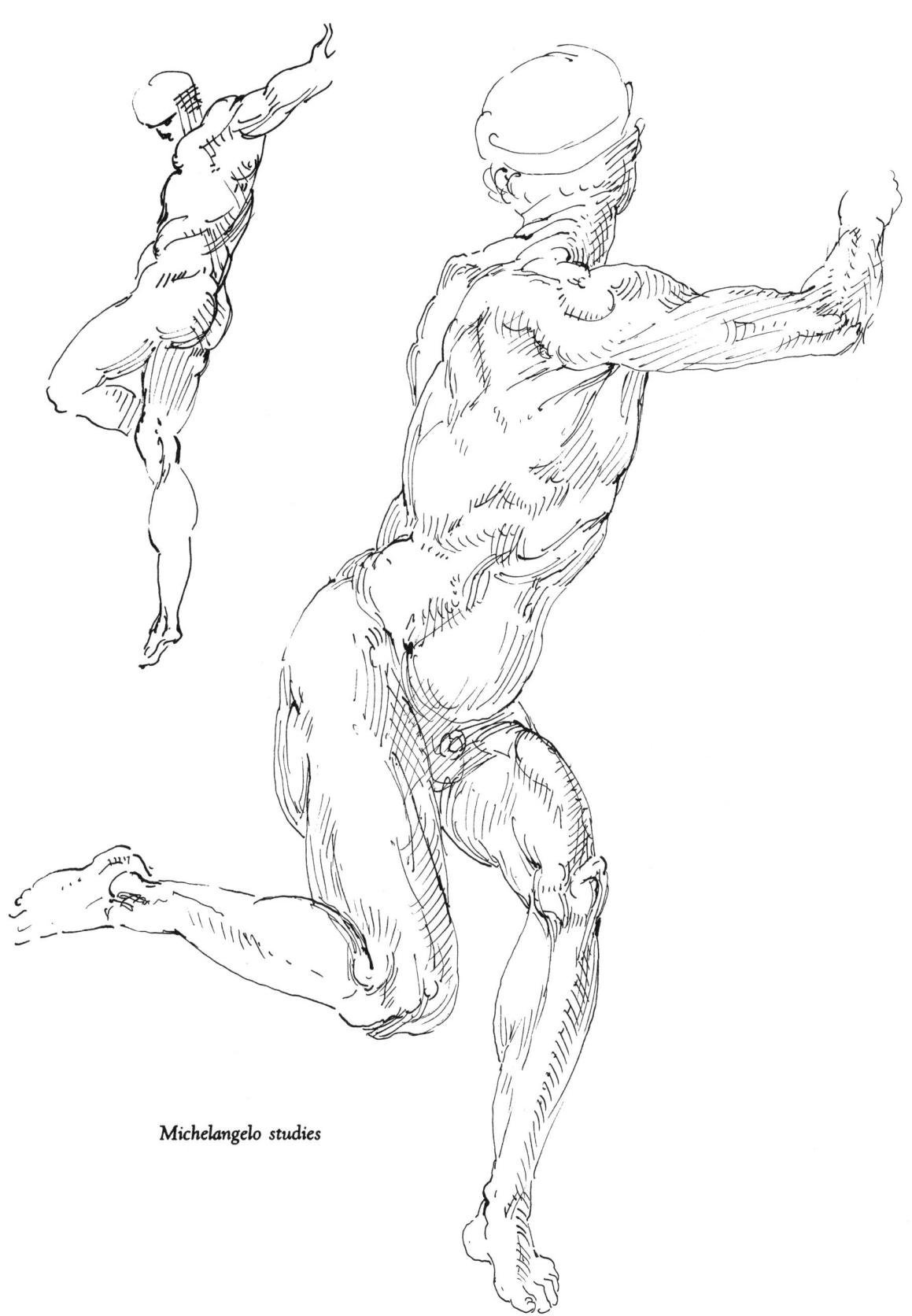

Michelangelo studies

61

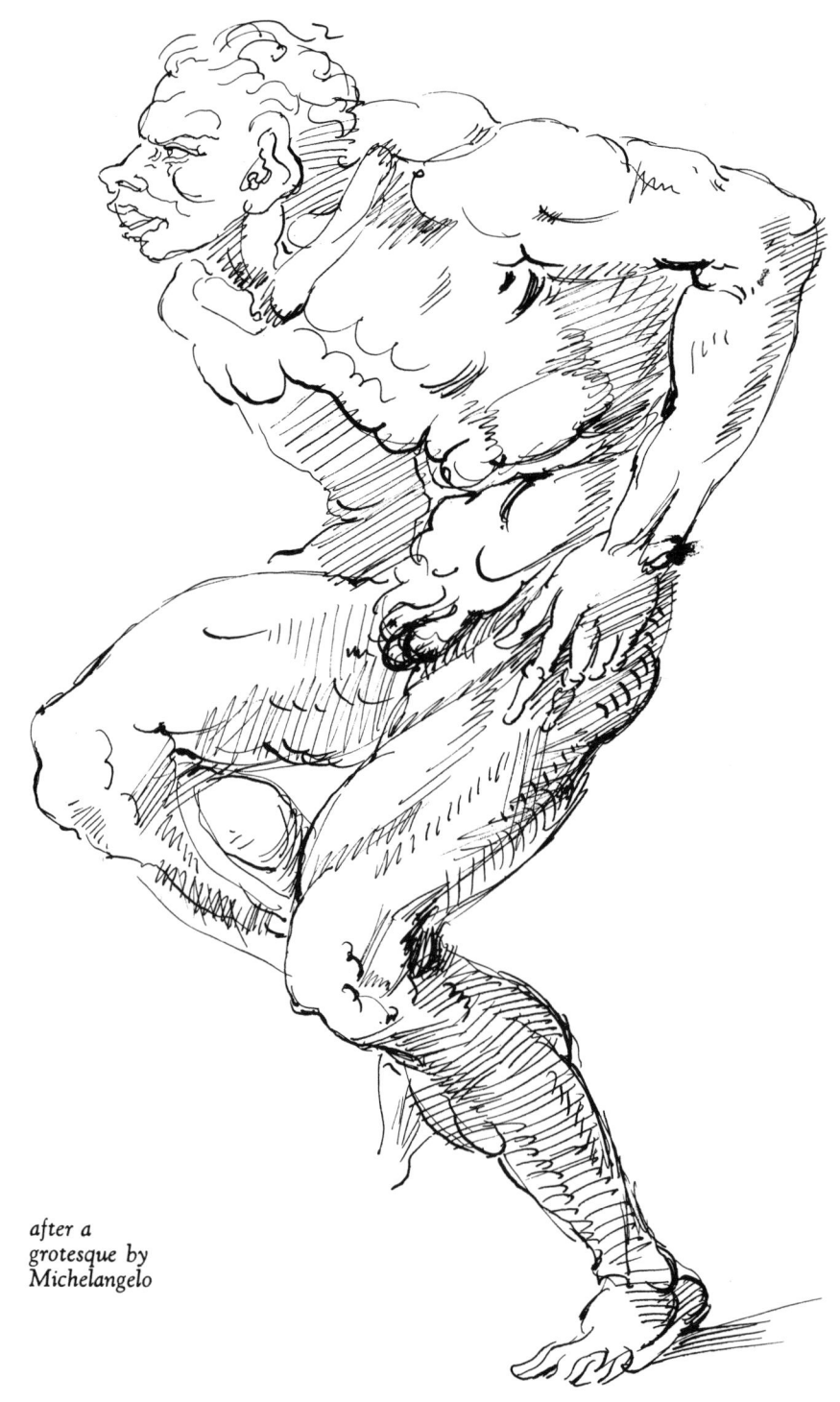

*after a
grotesque by
Michelangelo*

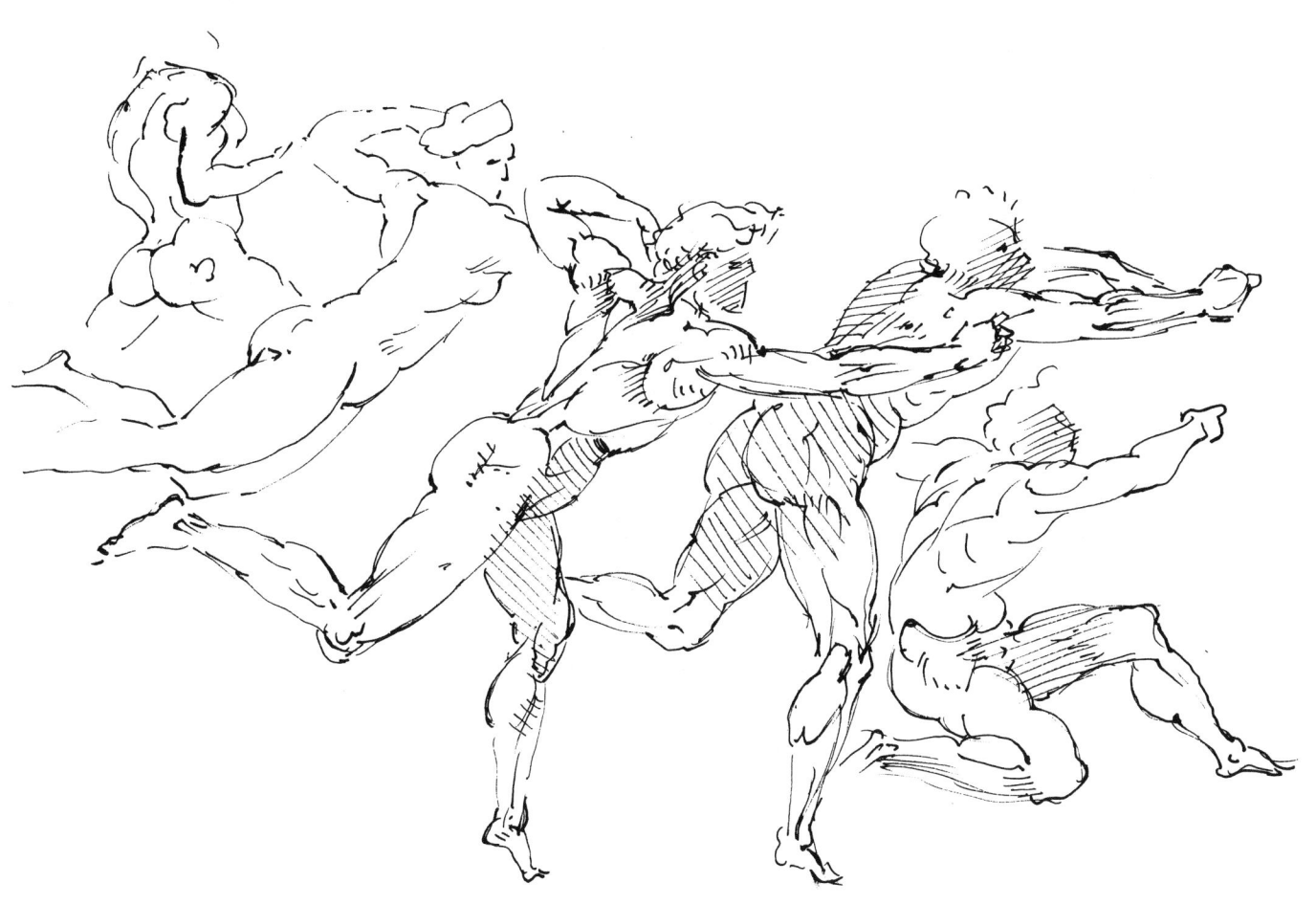

*fragments
from Michelangelo*

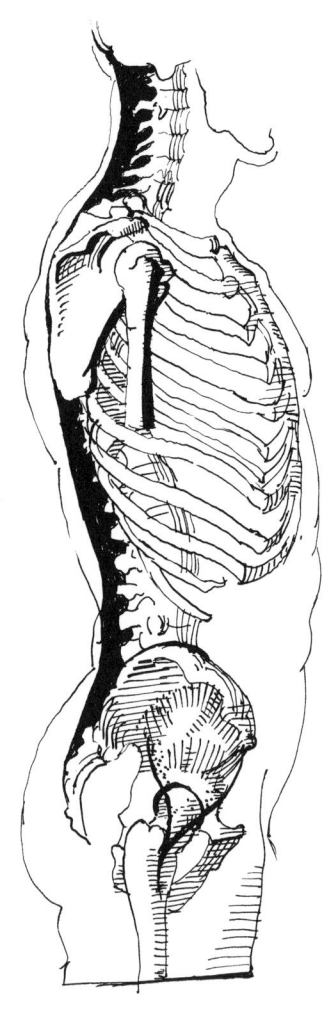

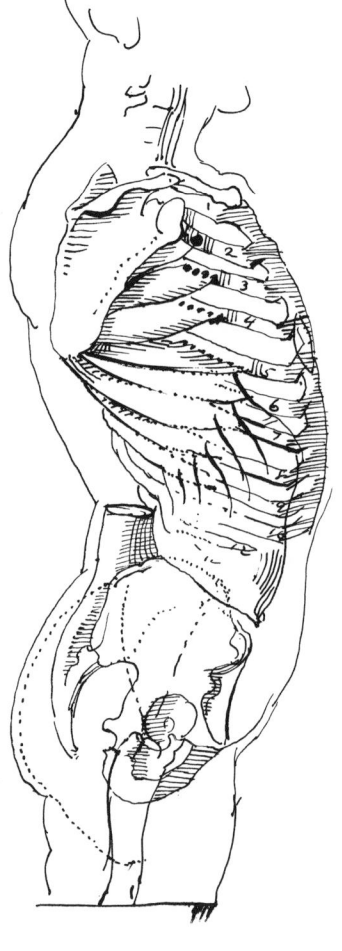

*simplified
diagrams
of the side*

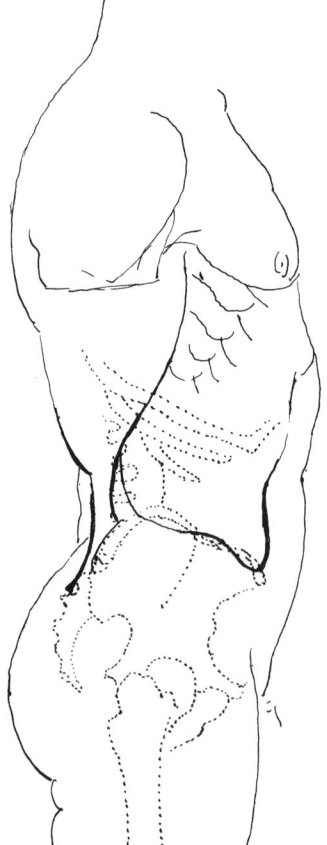

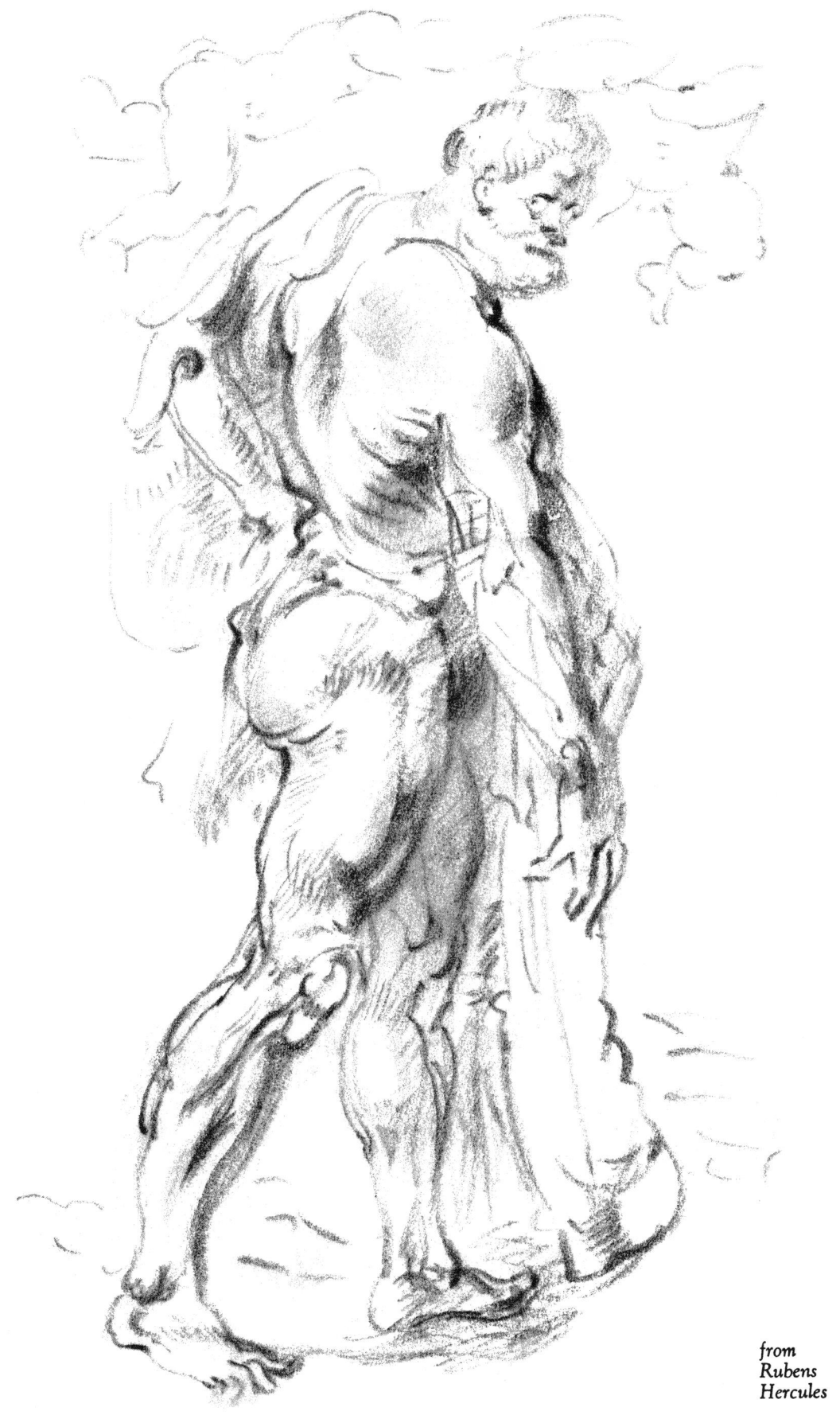

*from
Rubens
Hercules*

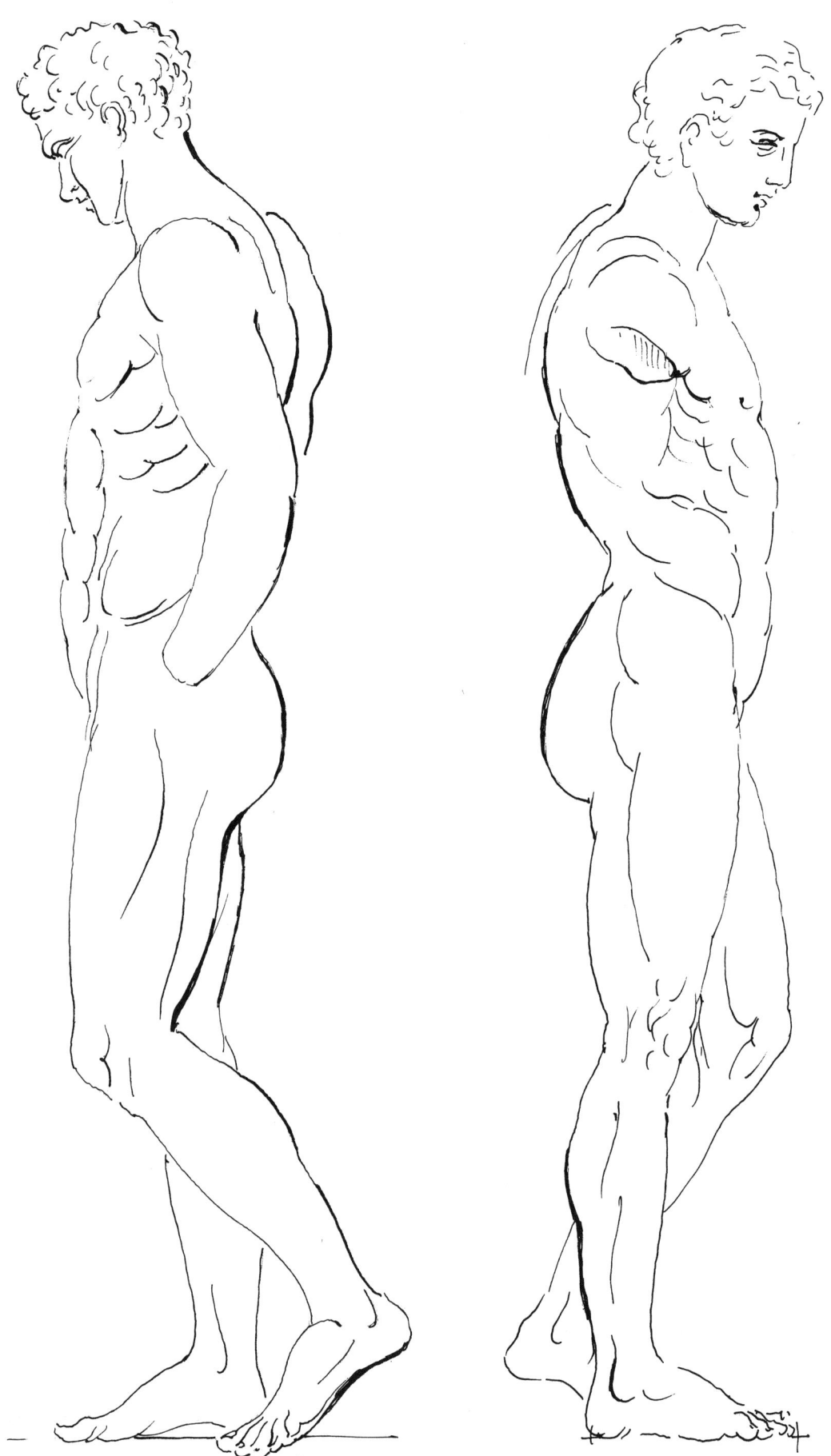

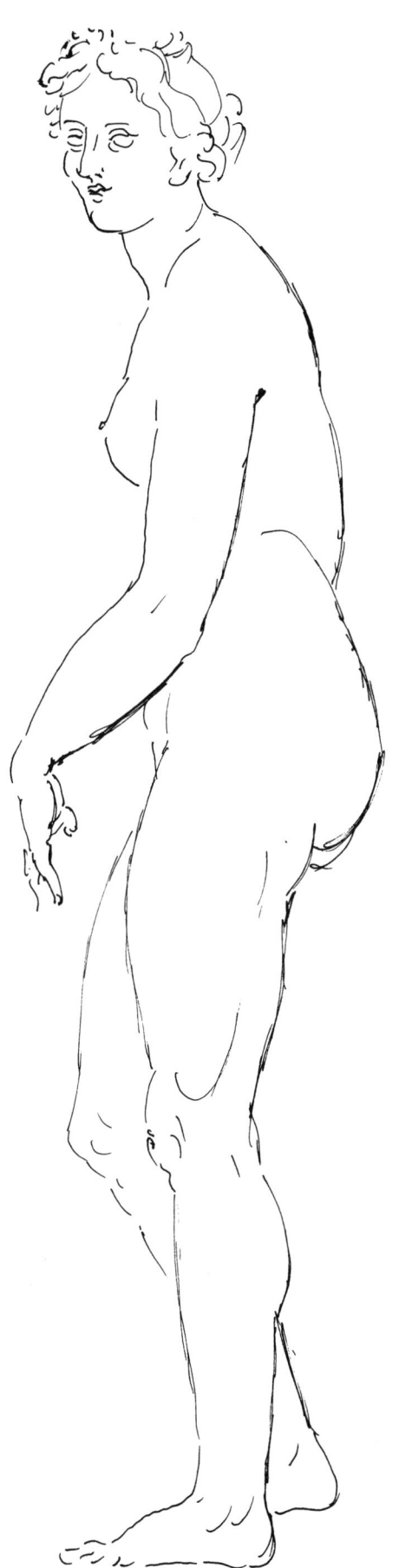
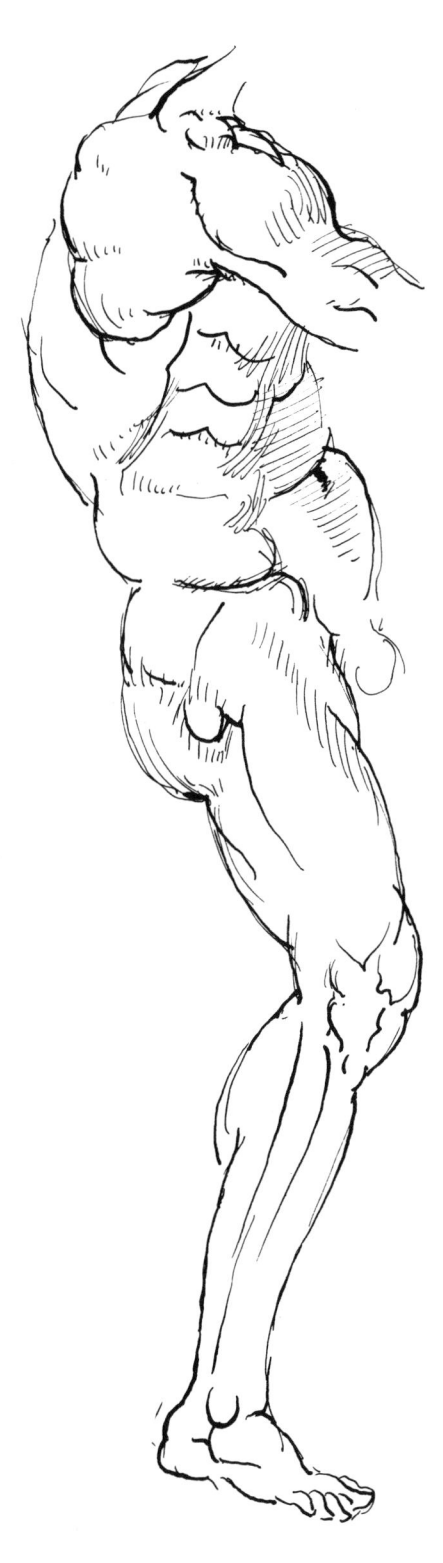

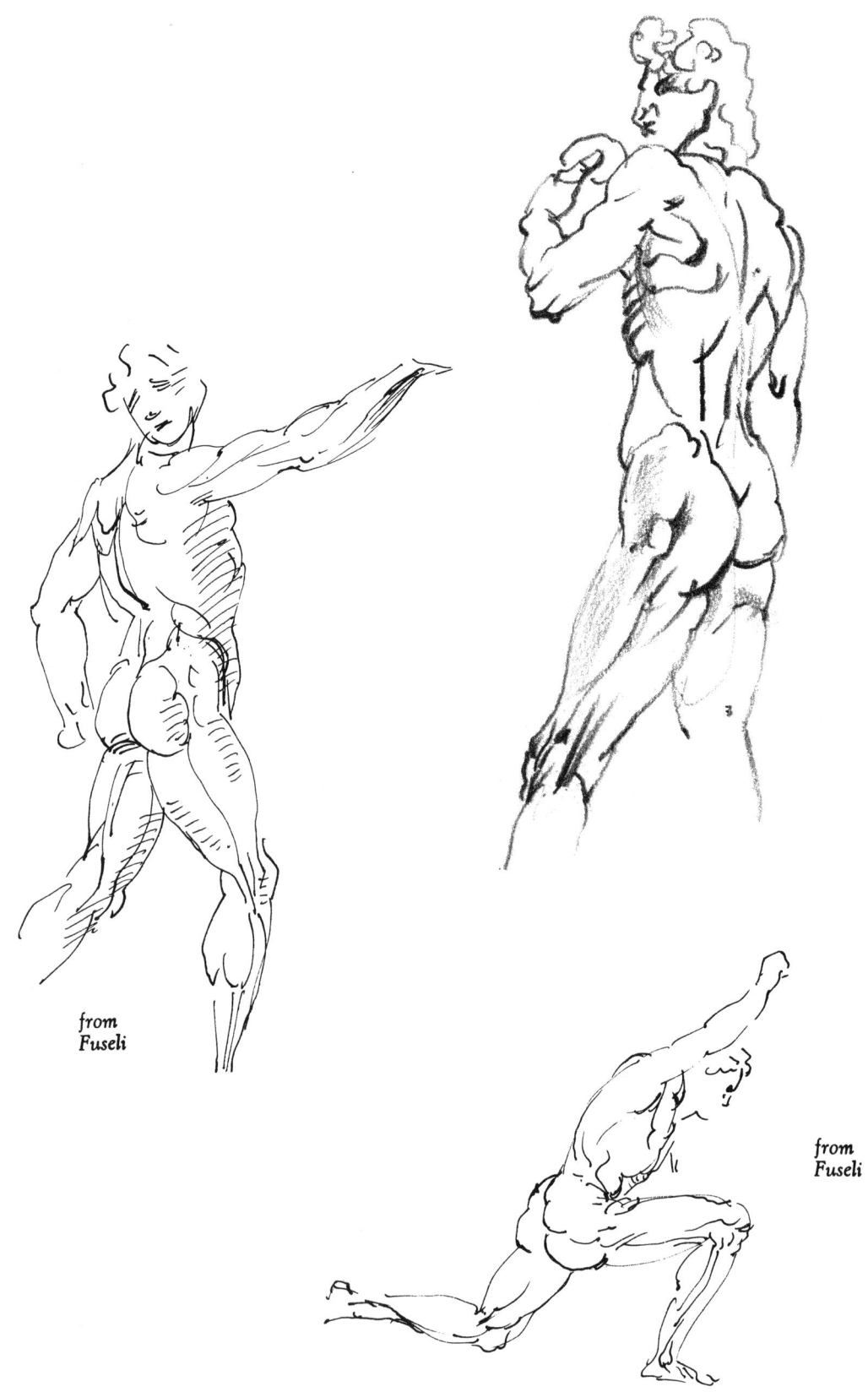

from
Fuseli

from
Fuseli

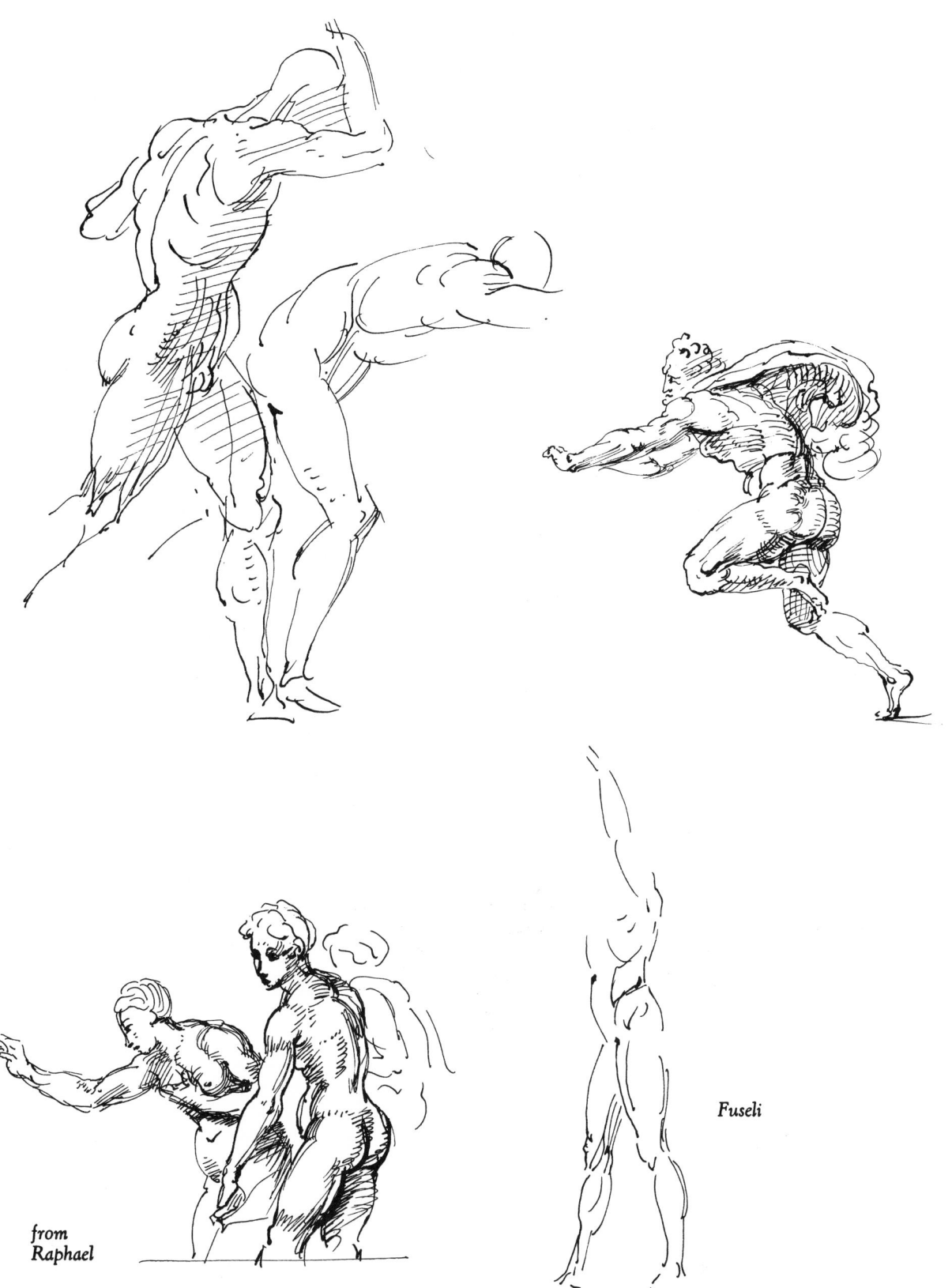

from
Raphael

Fuseli

69

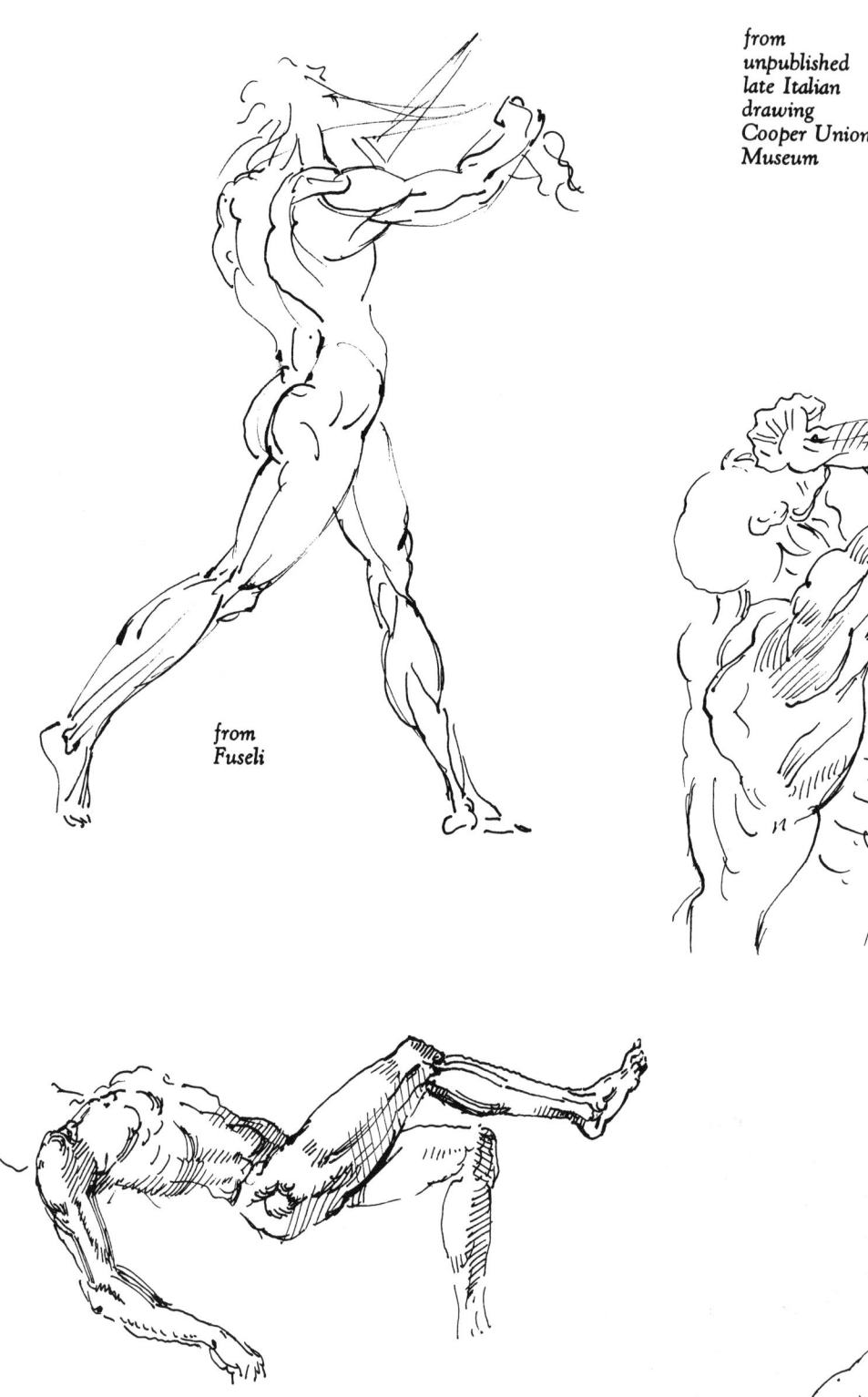

from
unpublished
late Italian
drawing
Cooper Union
Museum

from
Fuseli

from
Michelangelo

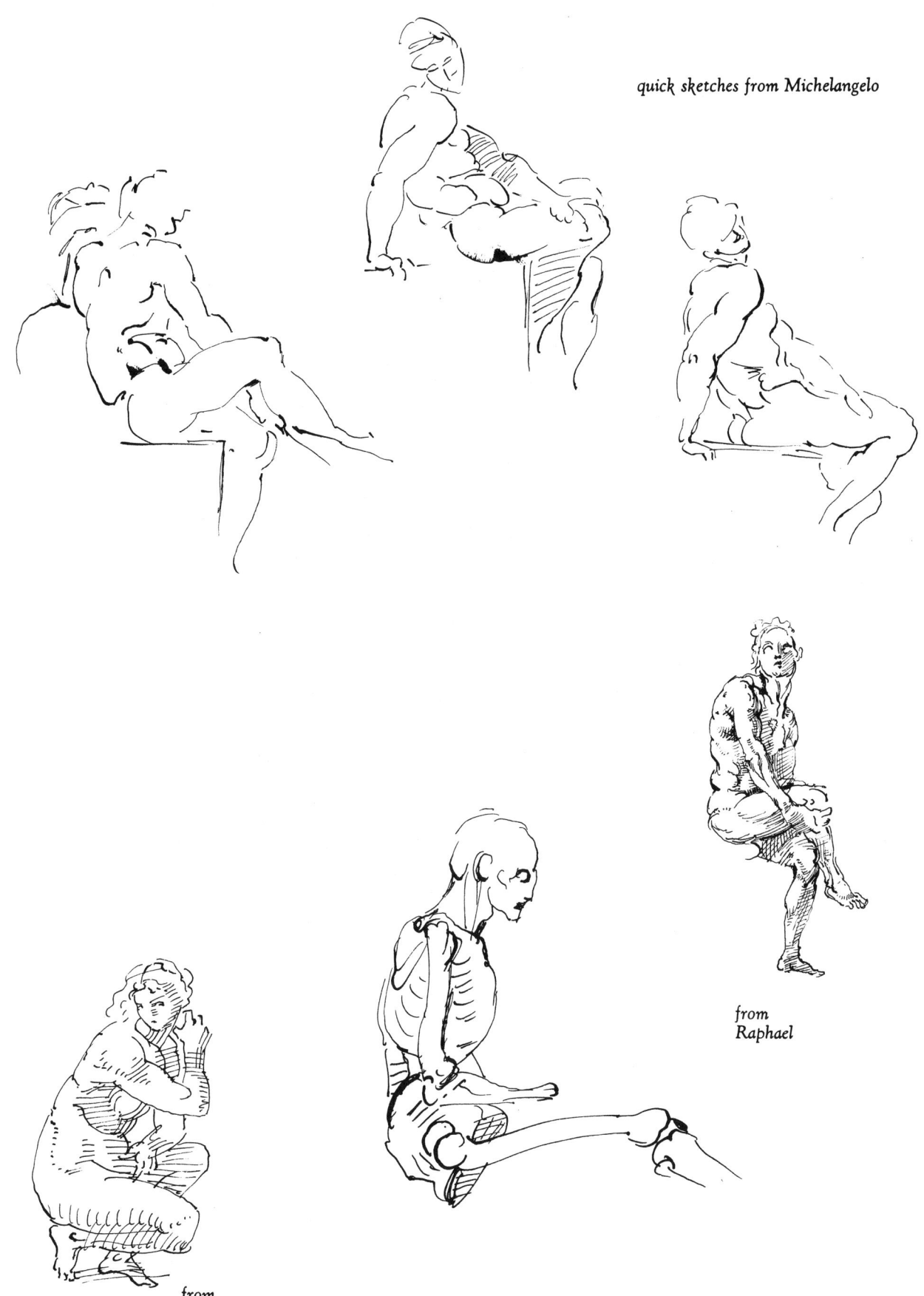

quick sketches from Michelangelo

from
Raphael

from
Poussin

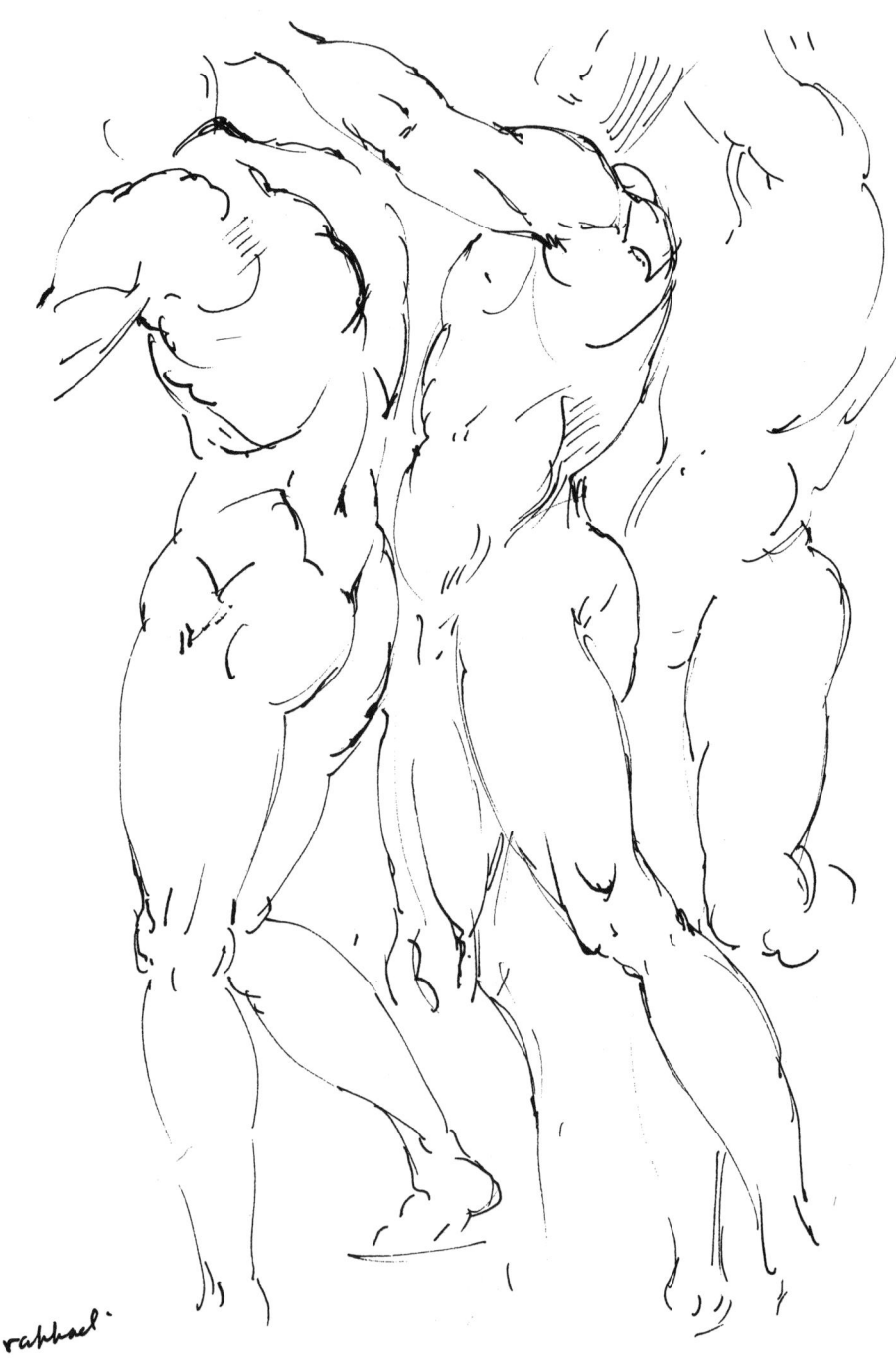

rabbael

72

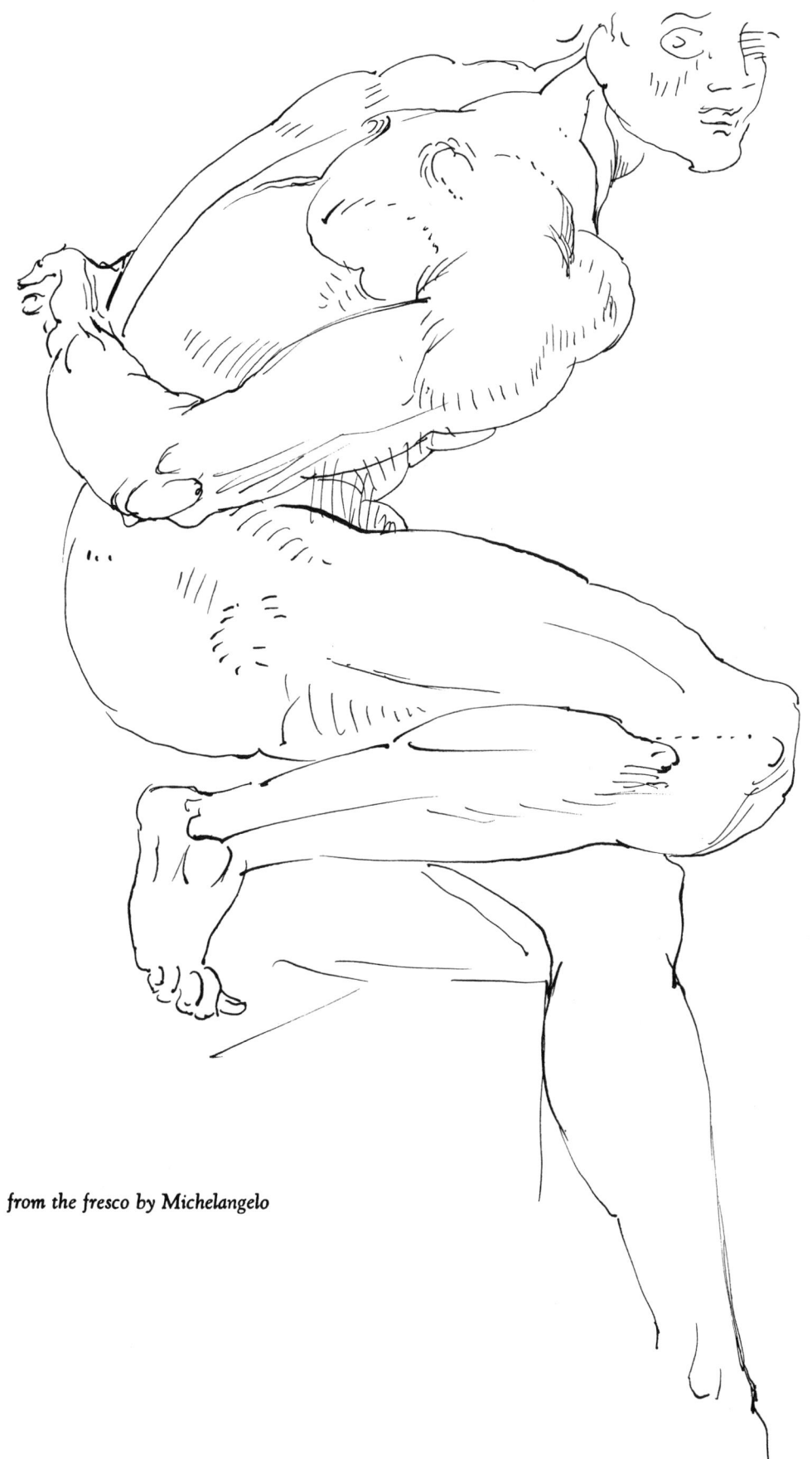

from the fresco by Michelangelo

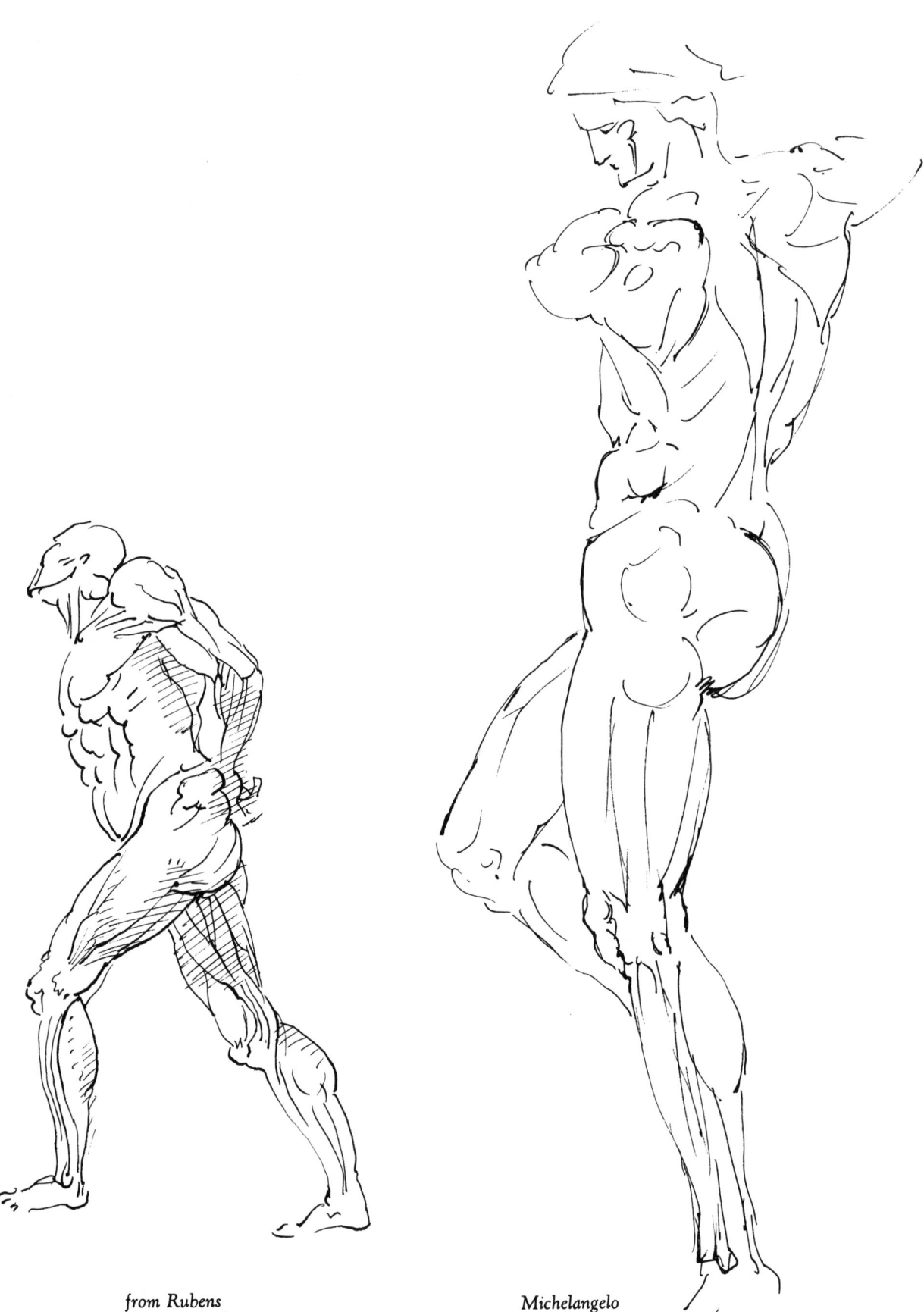

from Rubens
anatomy book

Michelangelo

74

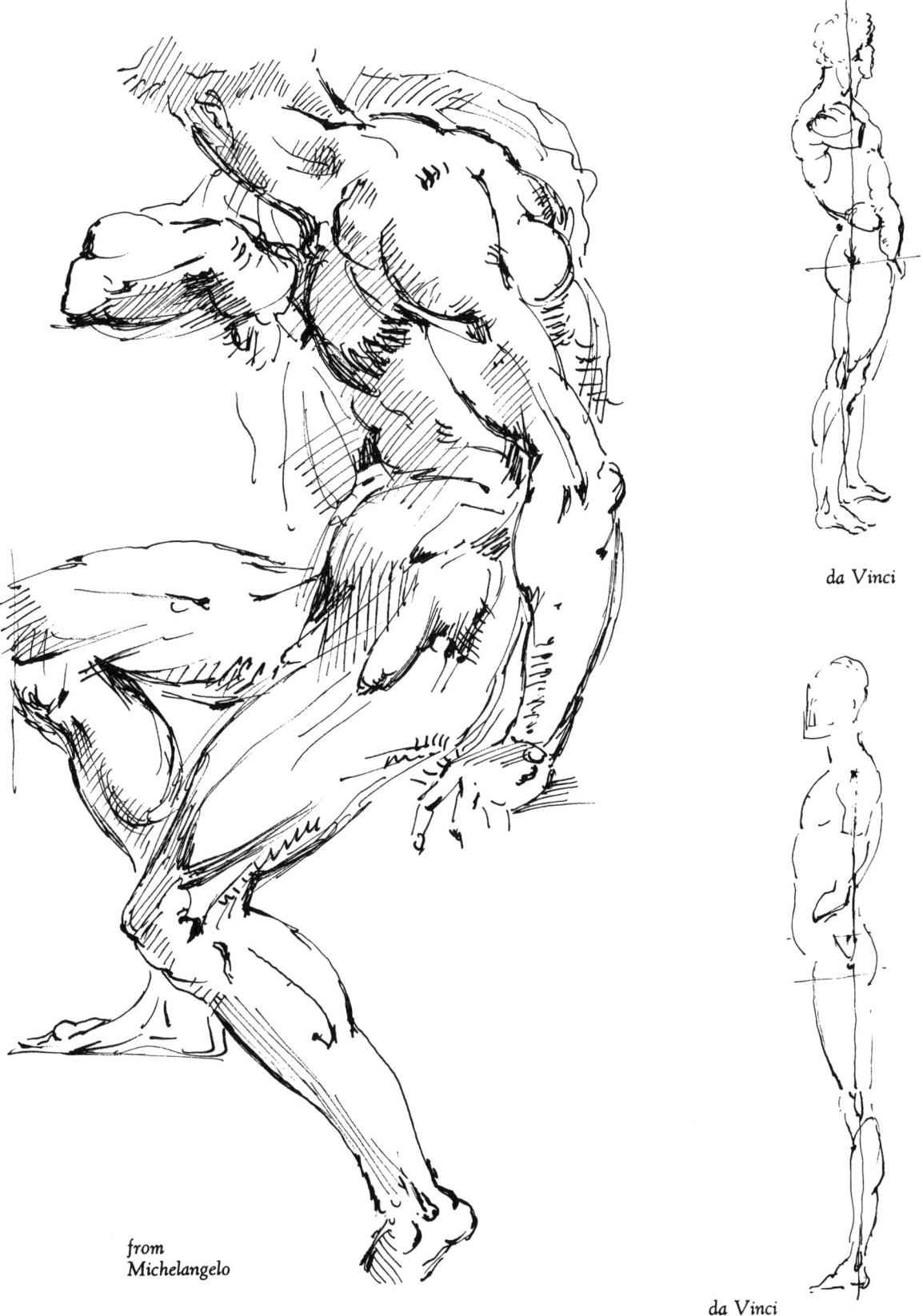

from
Michelangelo

da Vinci

da Vinci

75

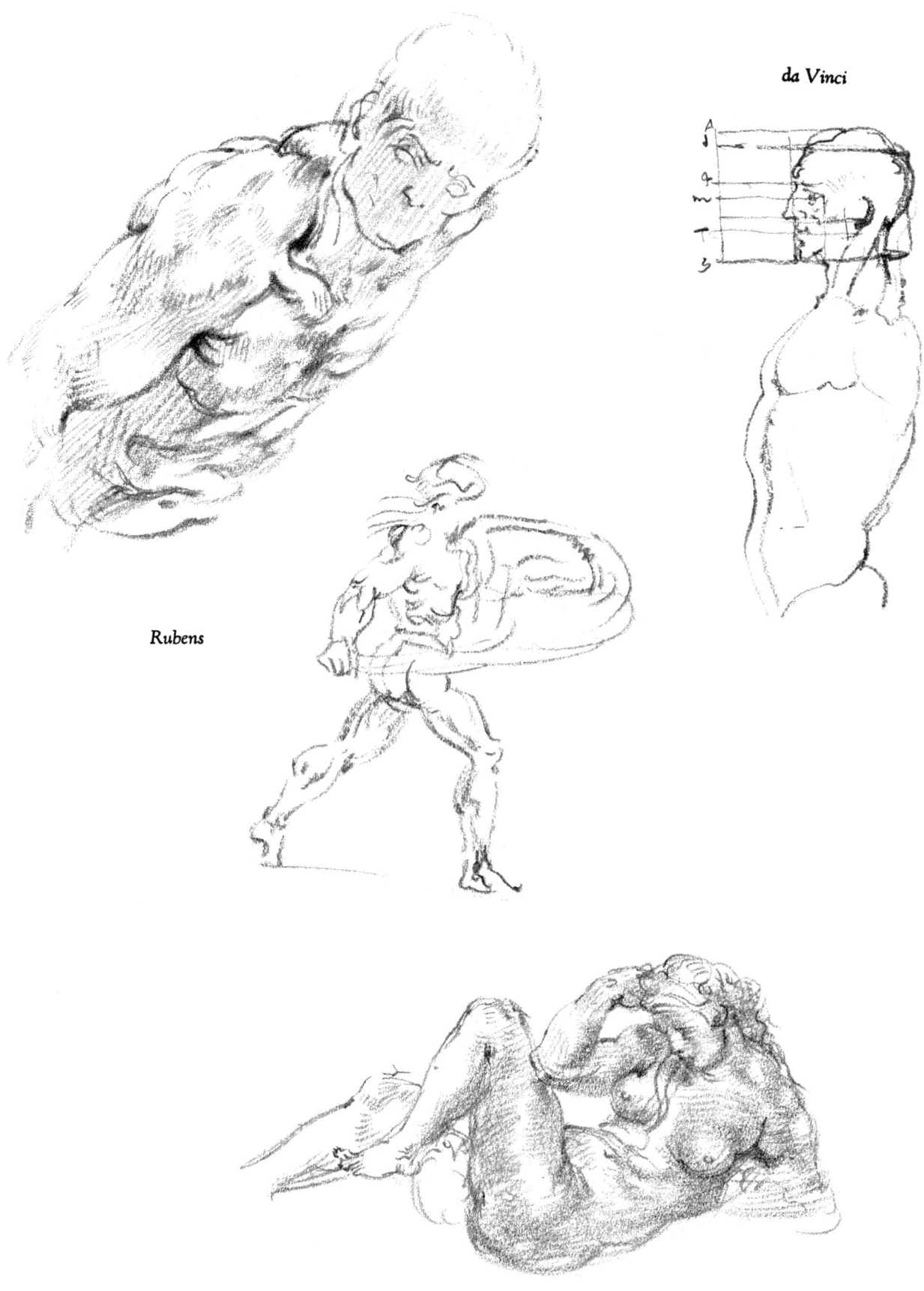

da Vinci

Rubens

Michelangelo

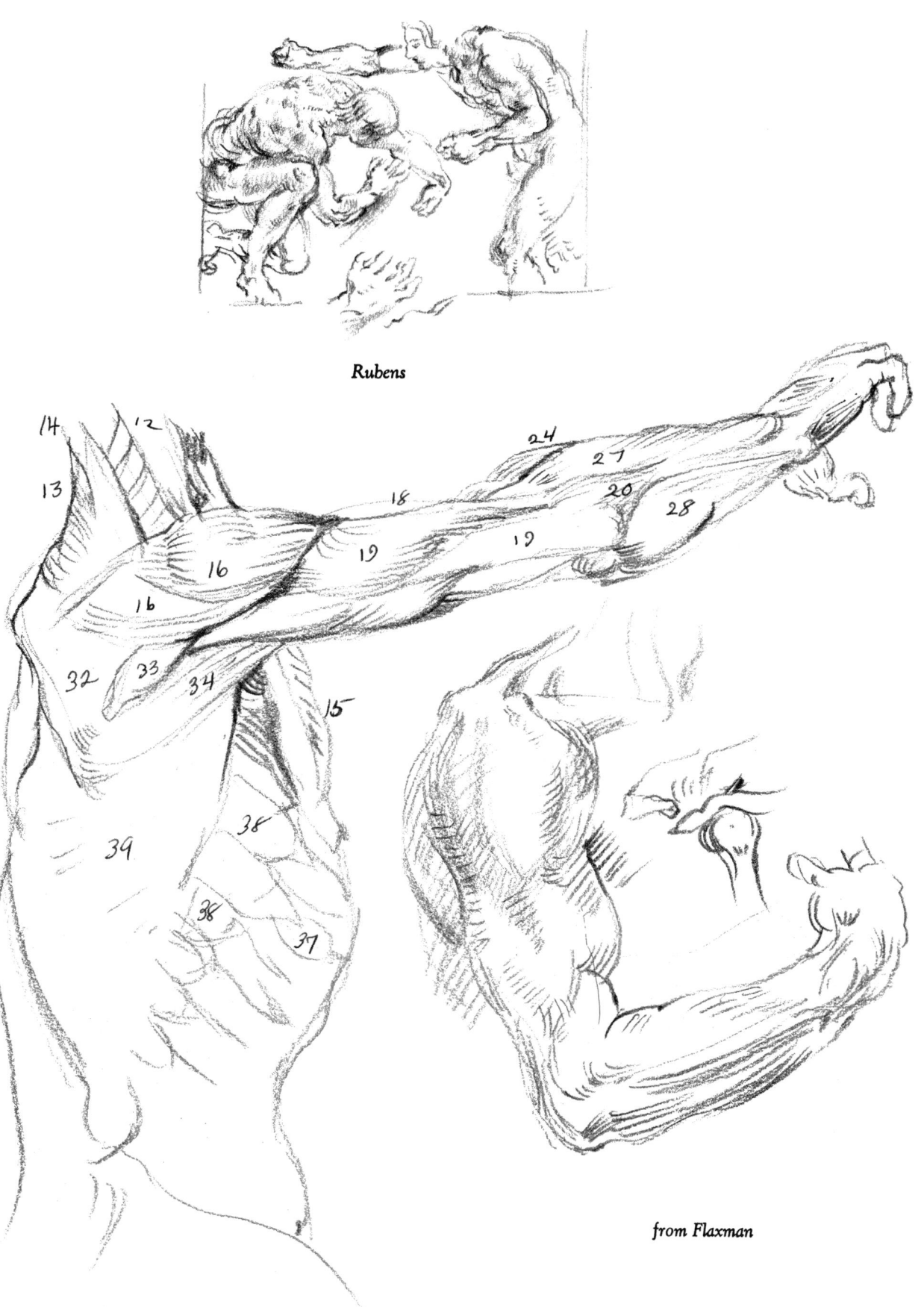

Rubens

14 12

13

24

27

18

20

28

16

19

19

16

32 33

34

15

38

39

38

37

from Flaxman

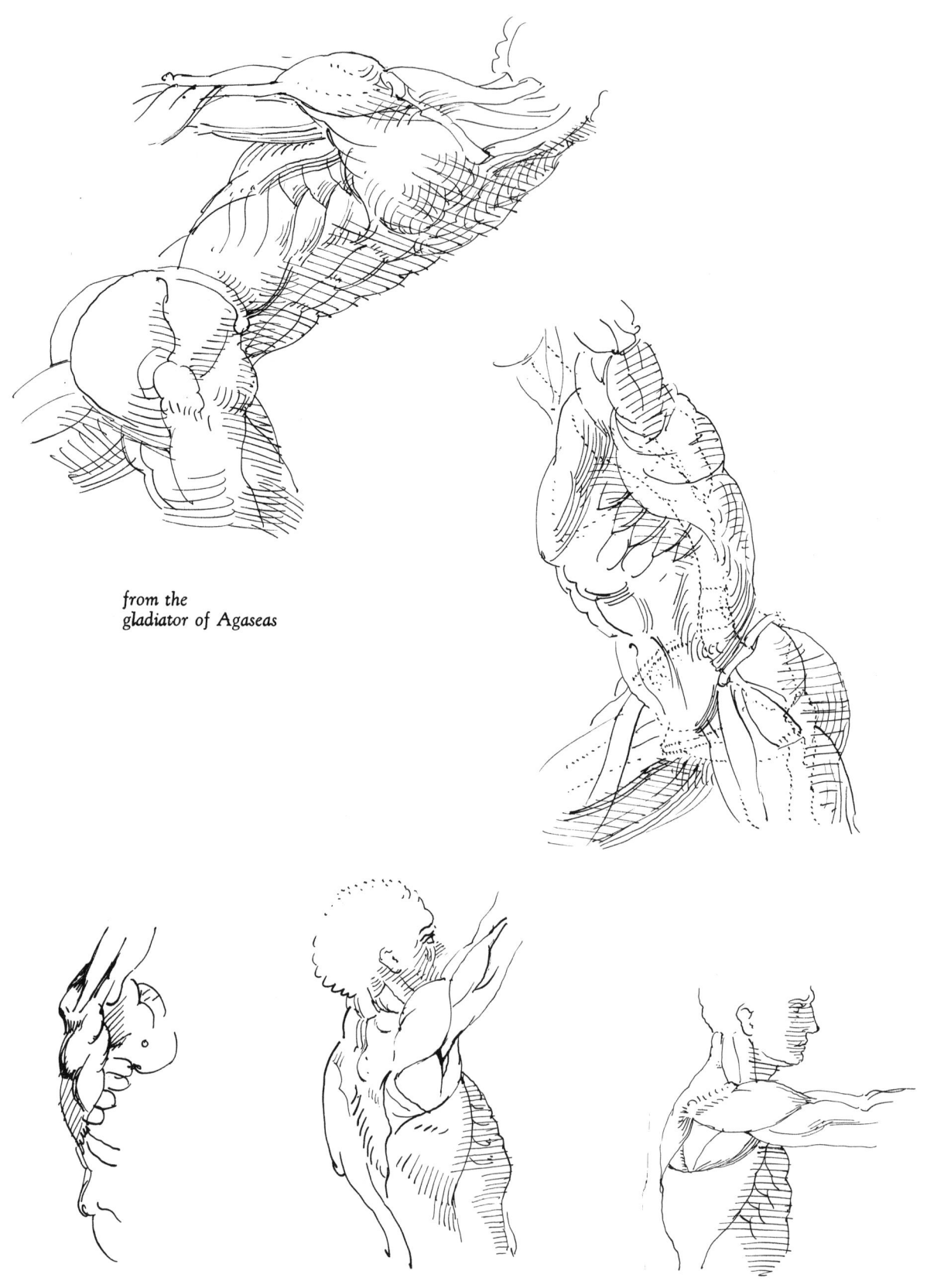

from the
gladiator of Agaseas

derived from modern anatomists

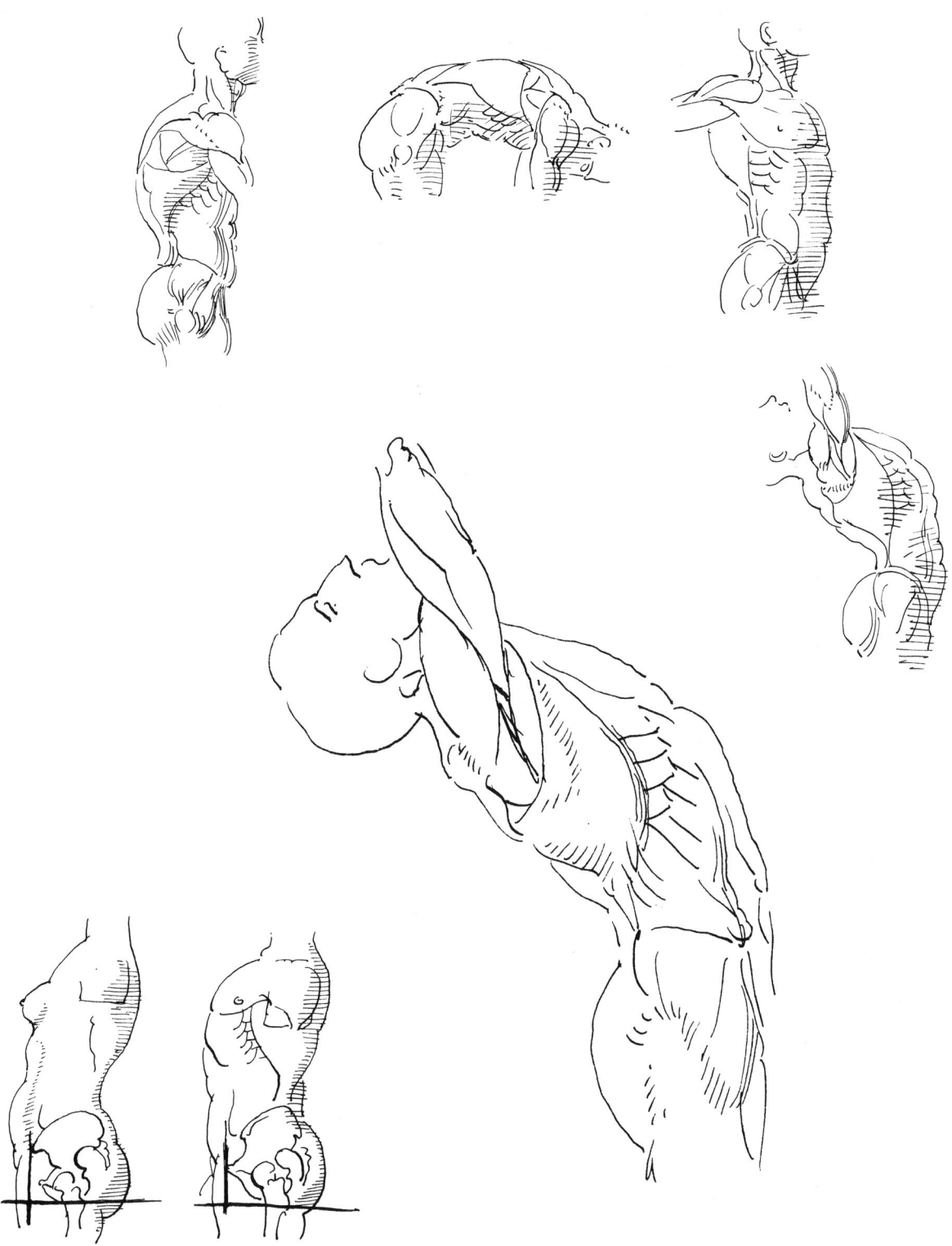

*from Richer
and Schiders*

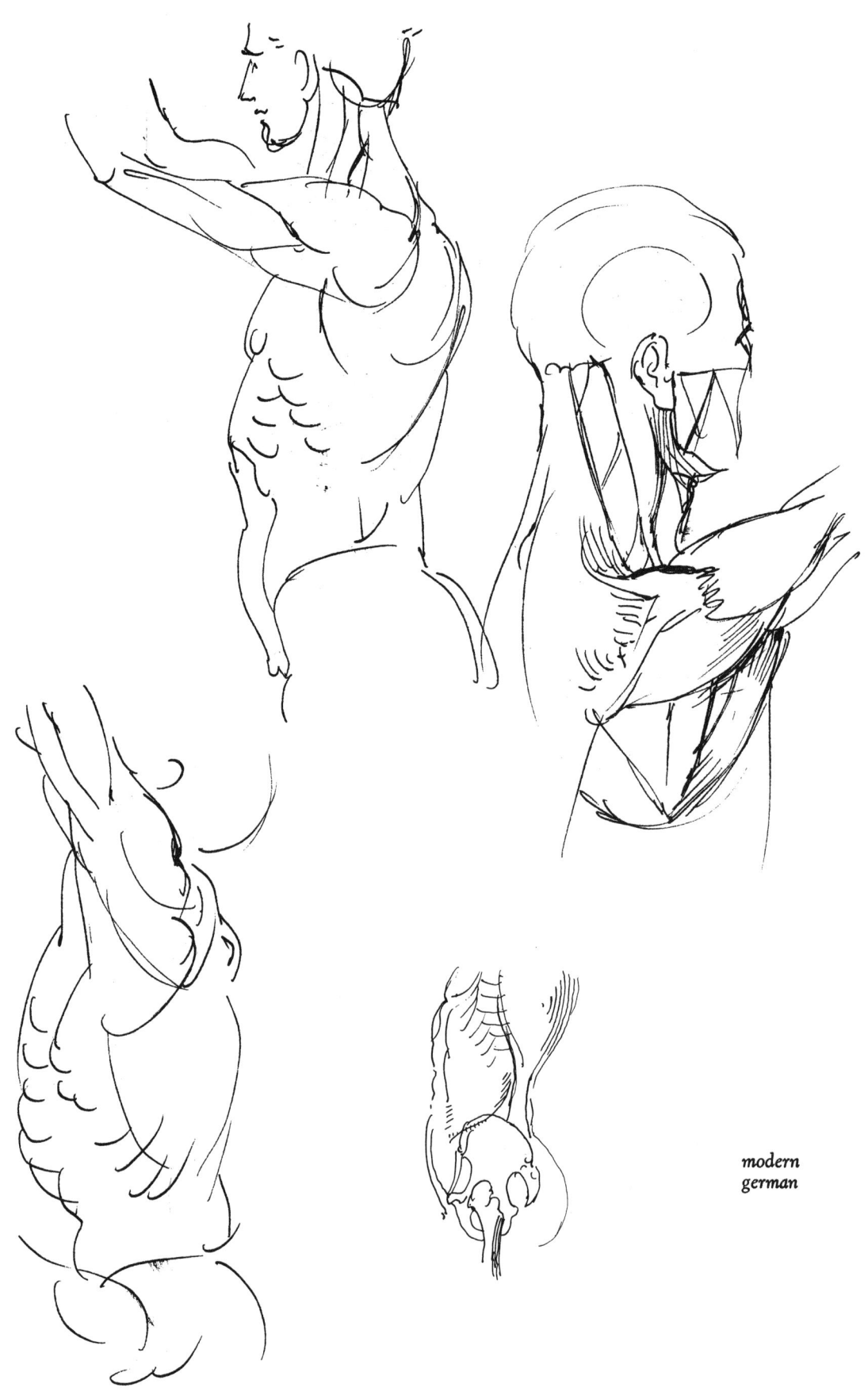

*modern
german*

Back

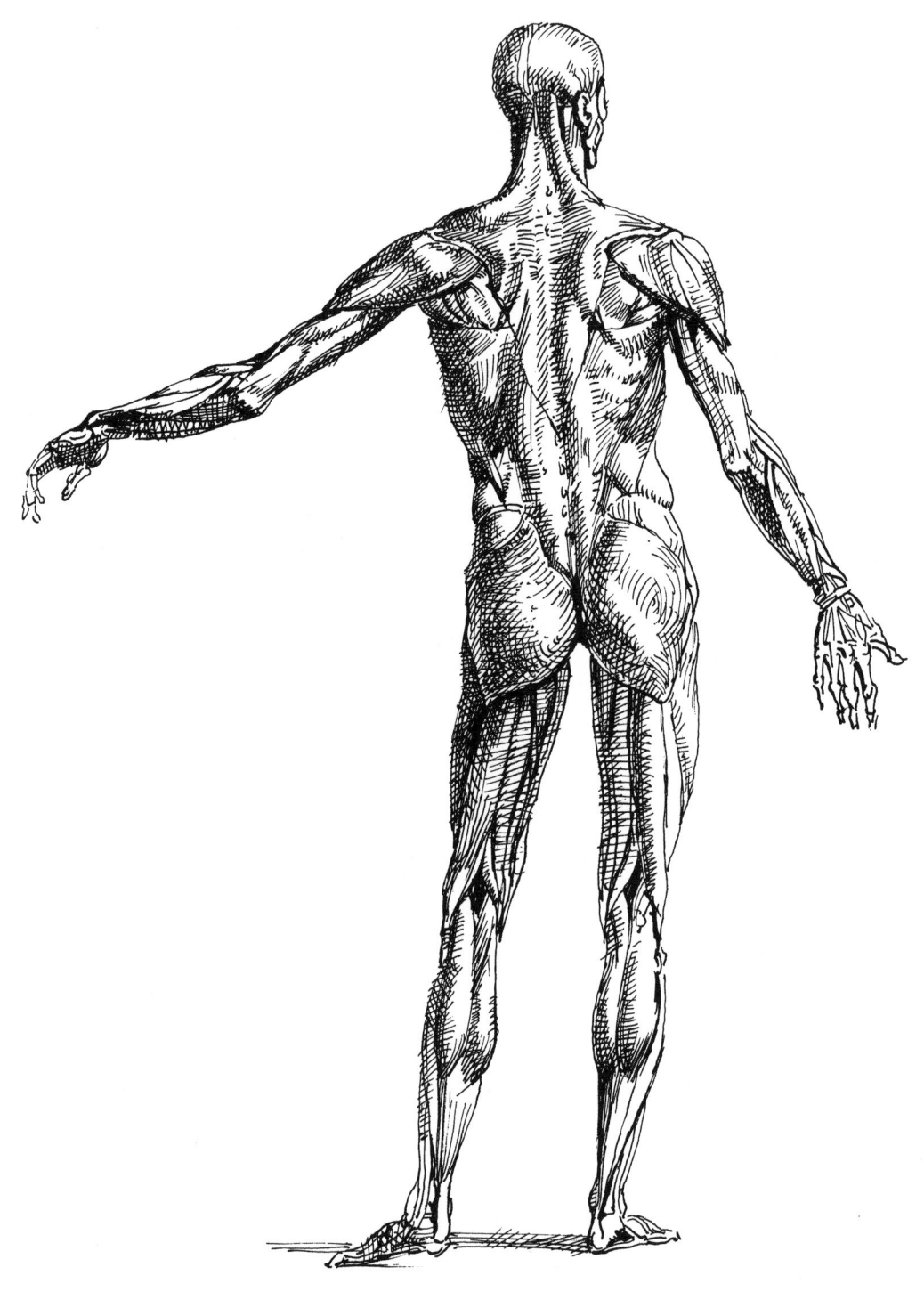

Albinus

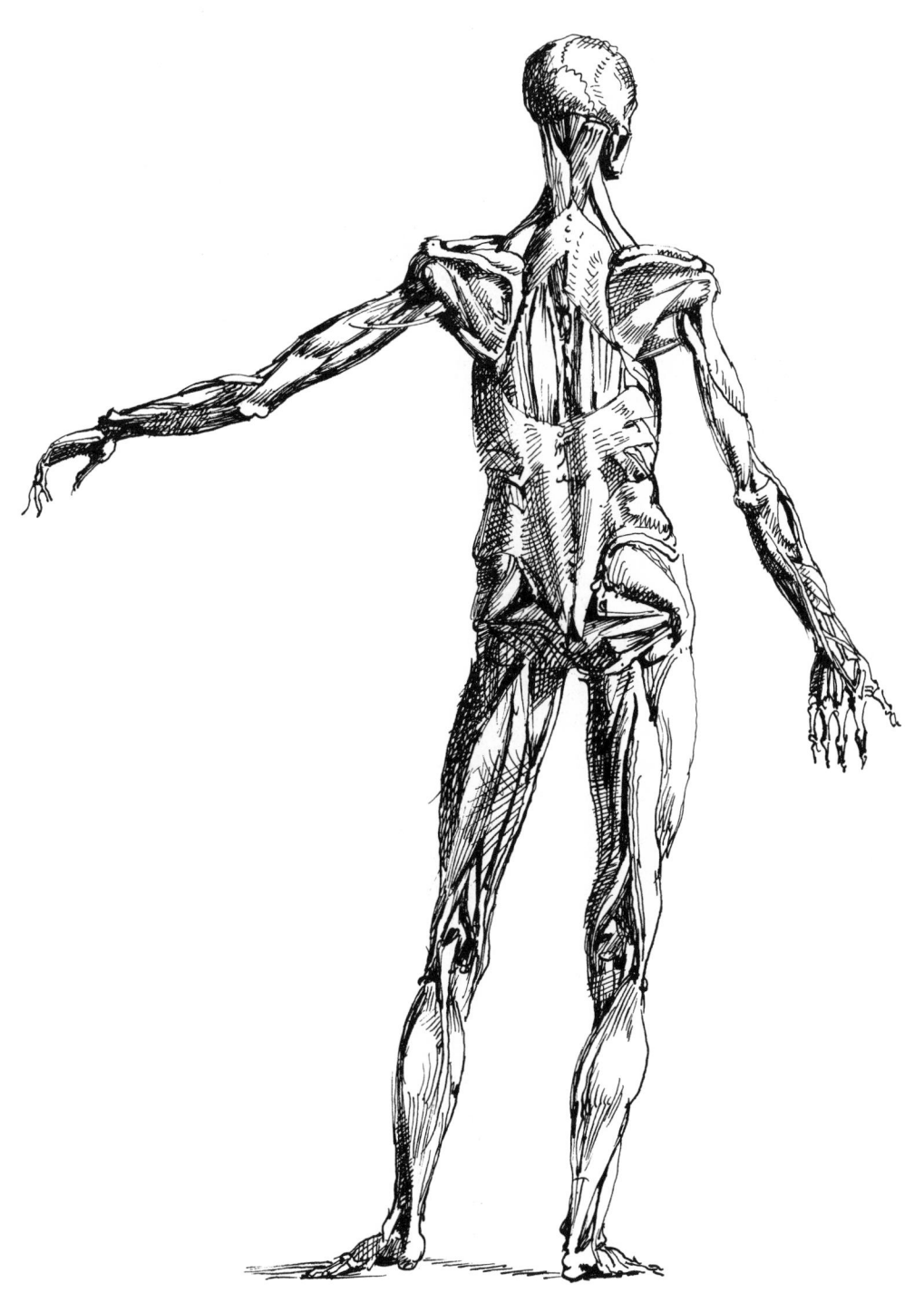

Albinus

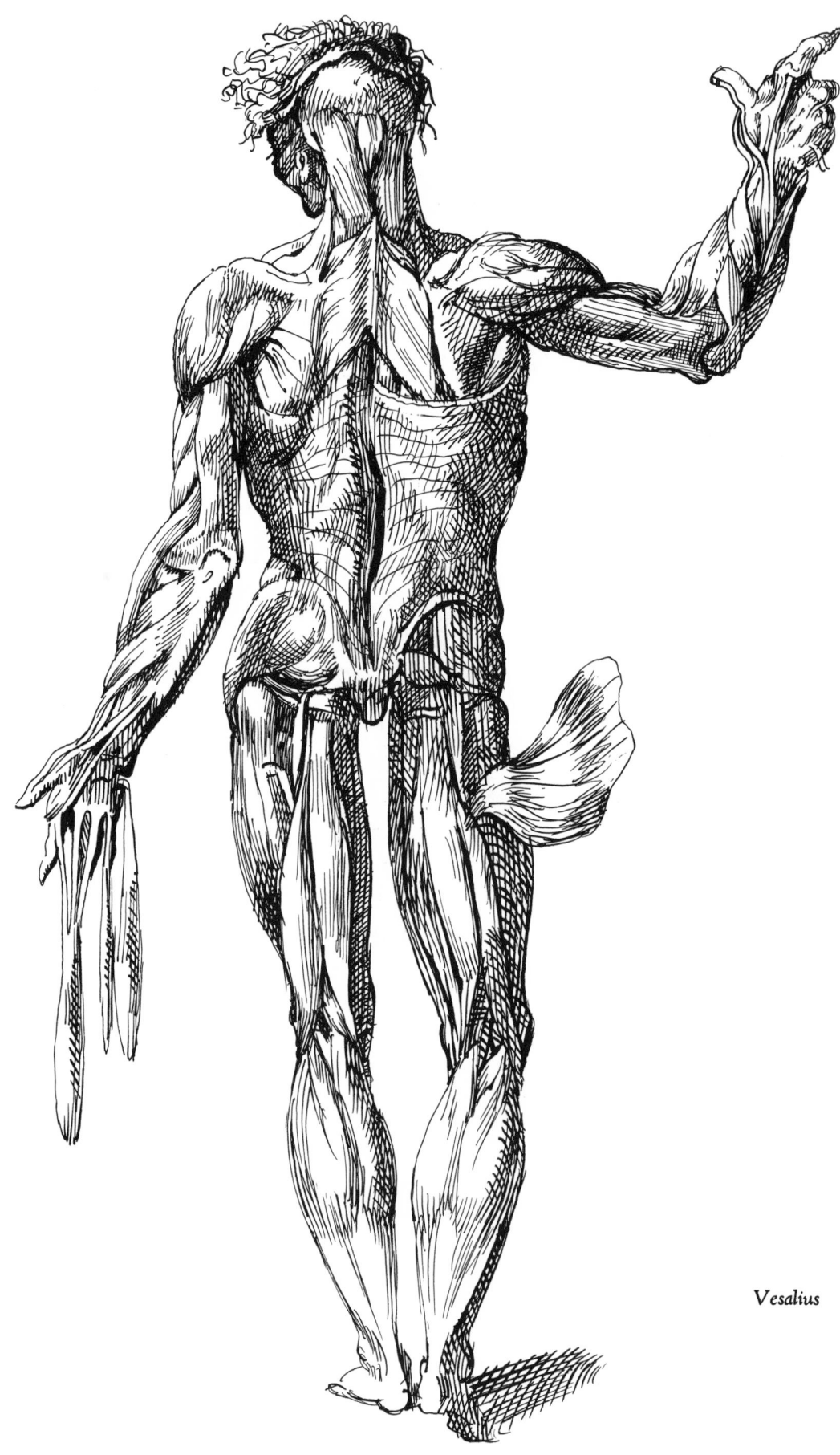

Vesalius

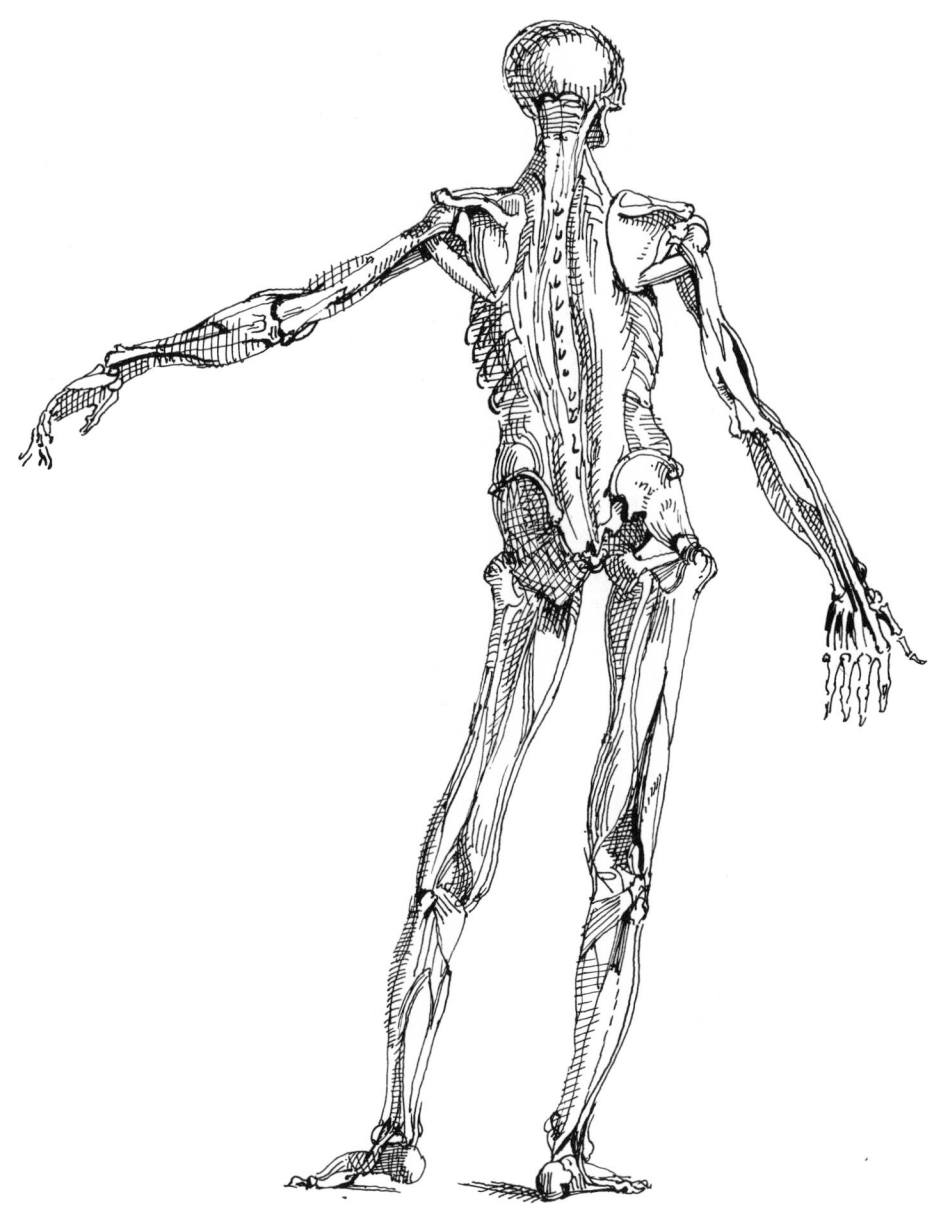

Albinus

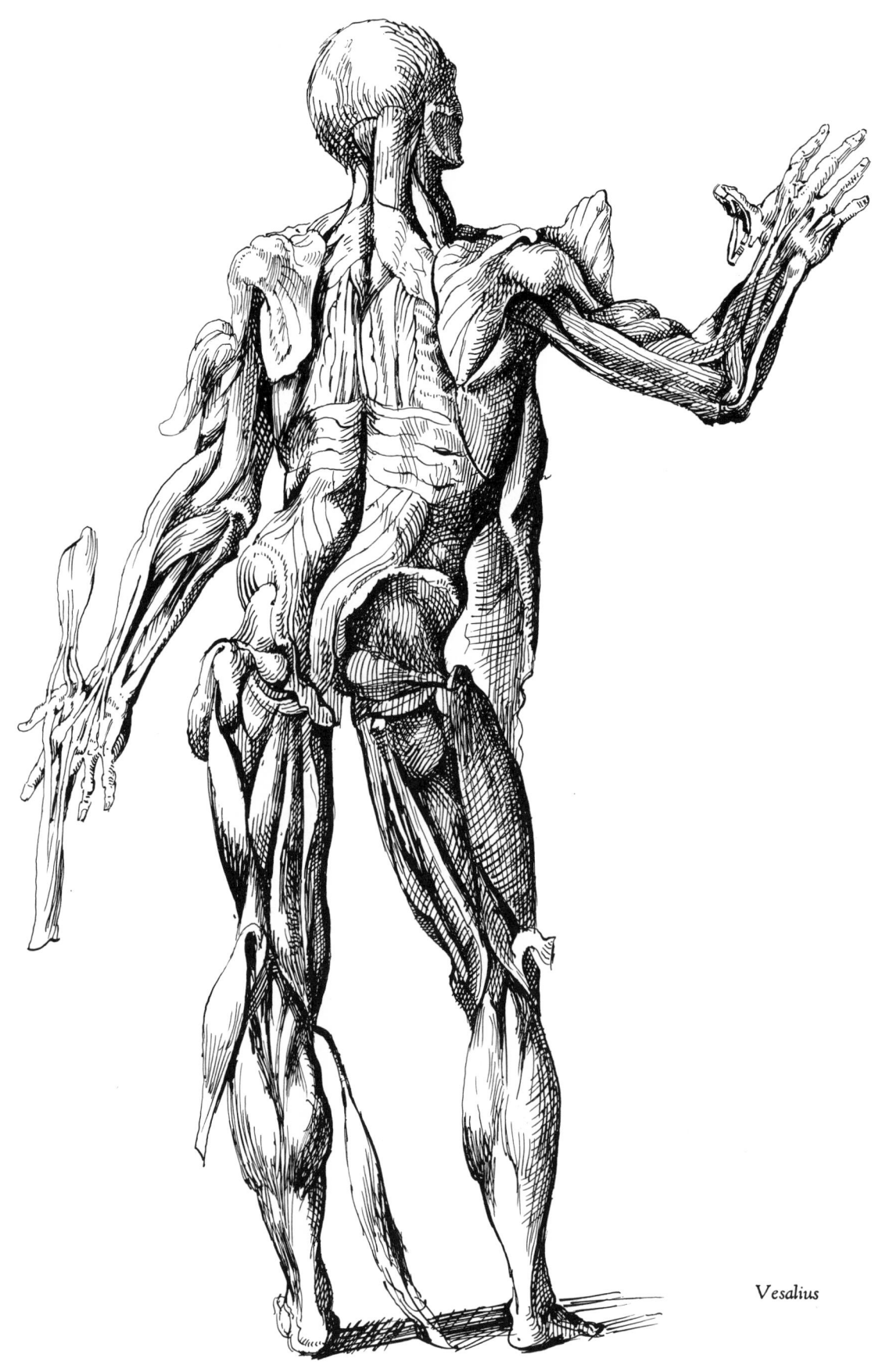

Vesalius

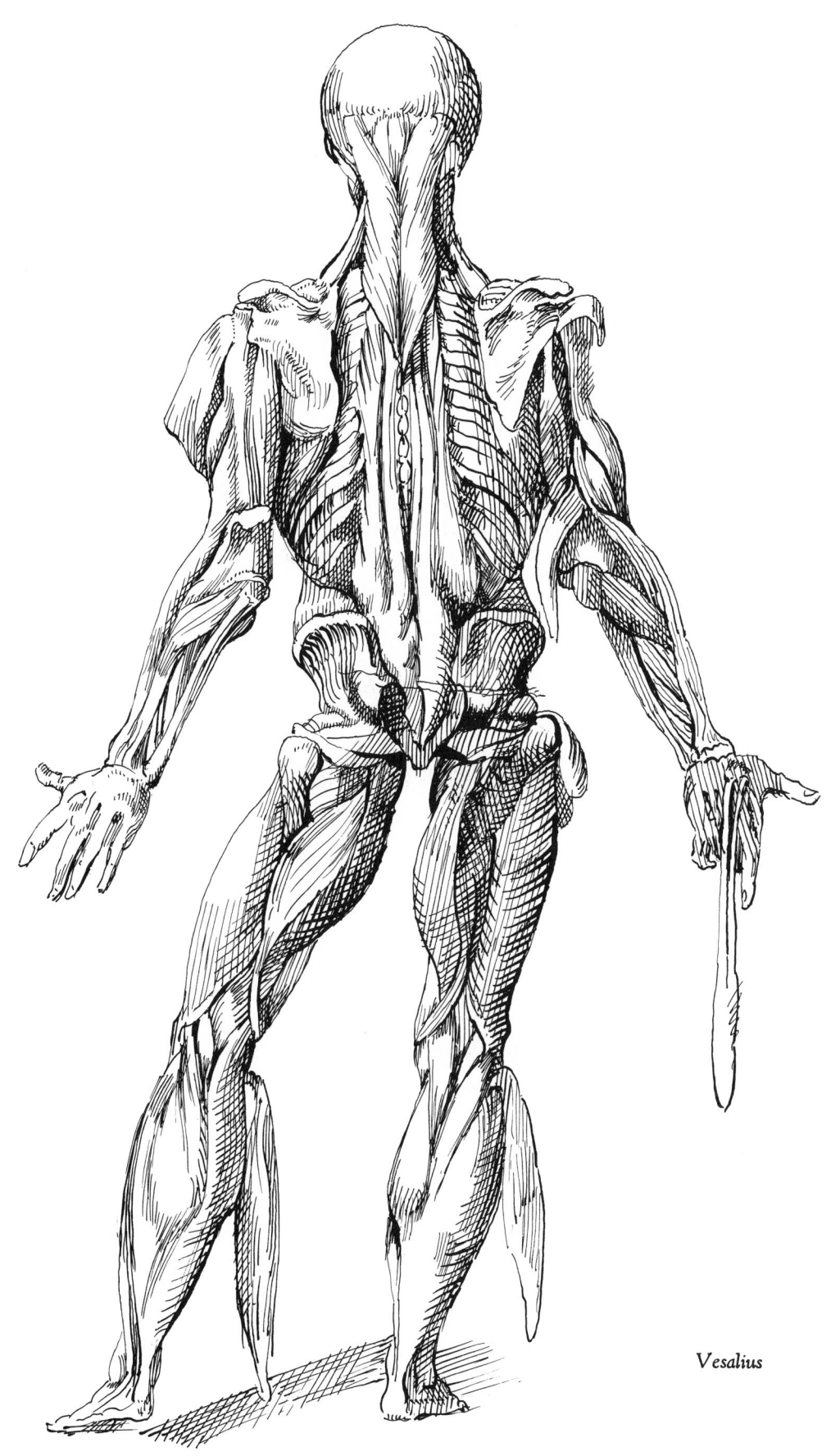

Vesalius

87

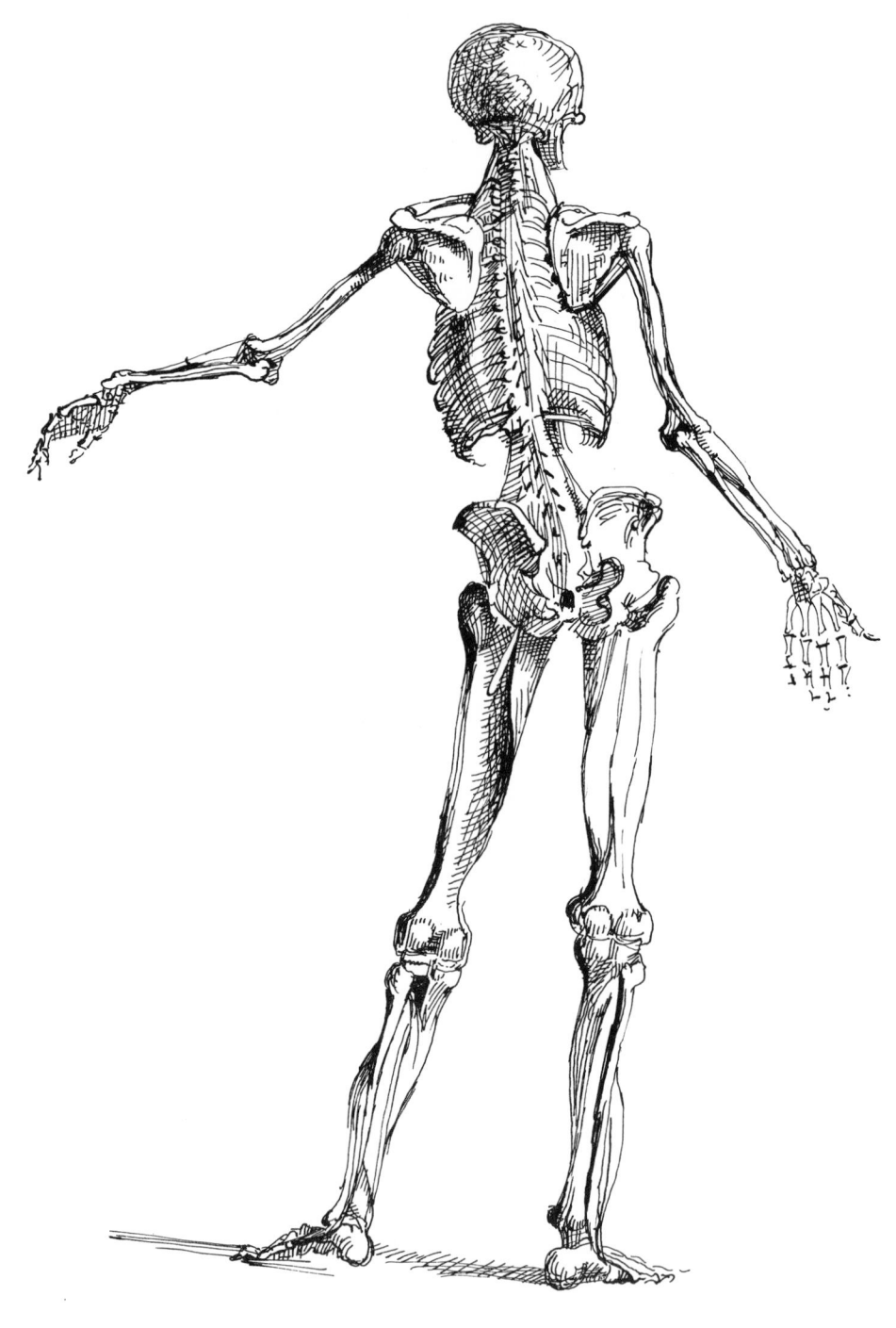

Albinus

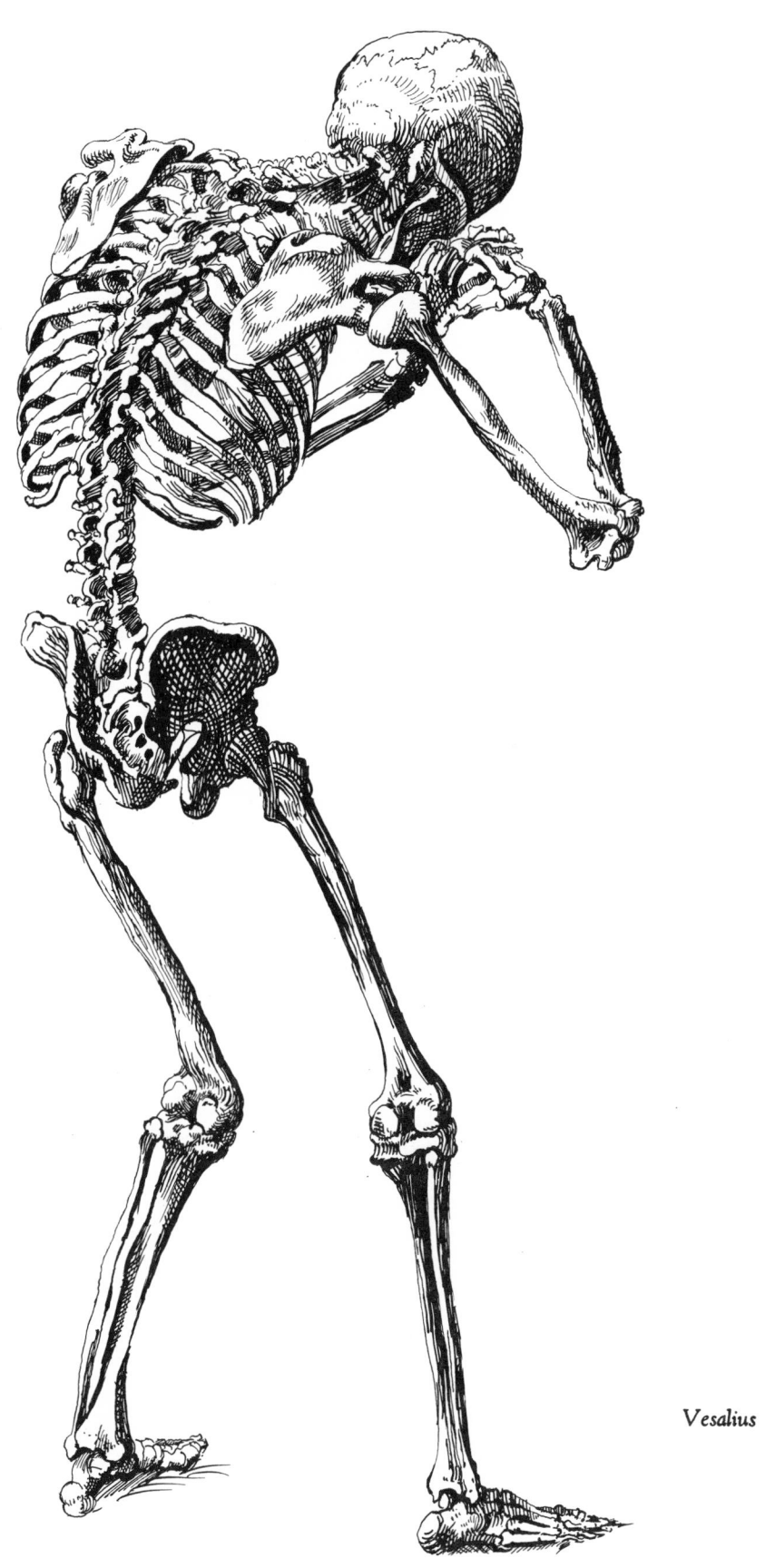

Vesalius

89

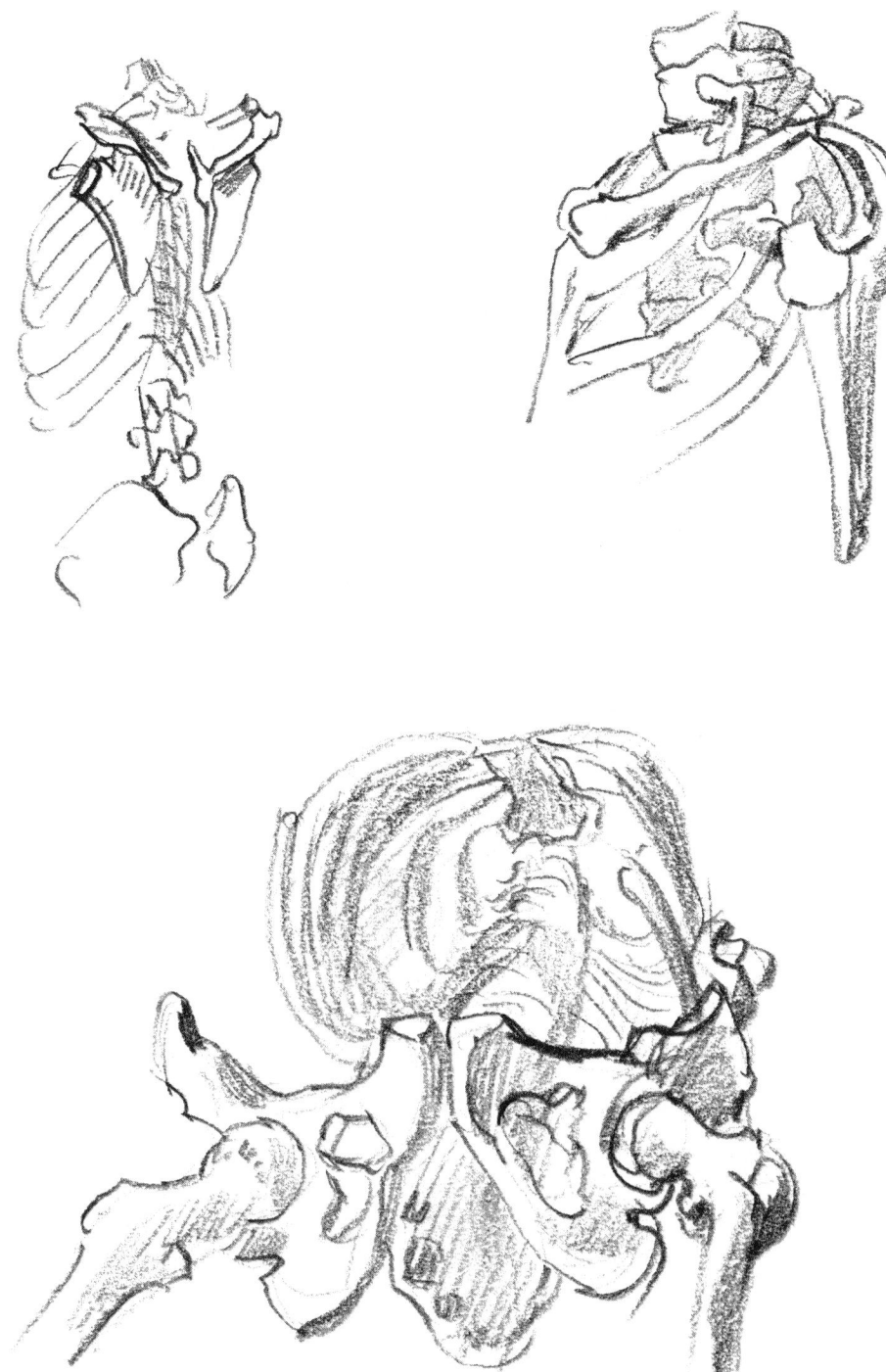

Flaxman

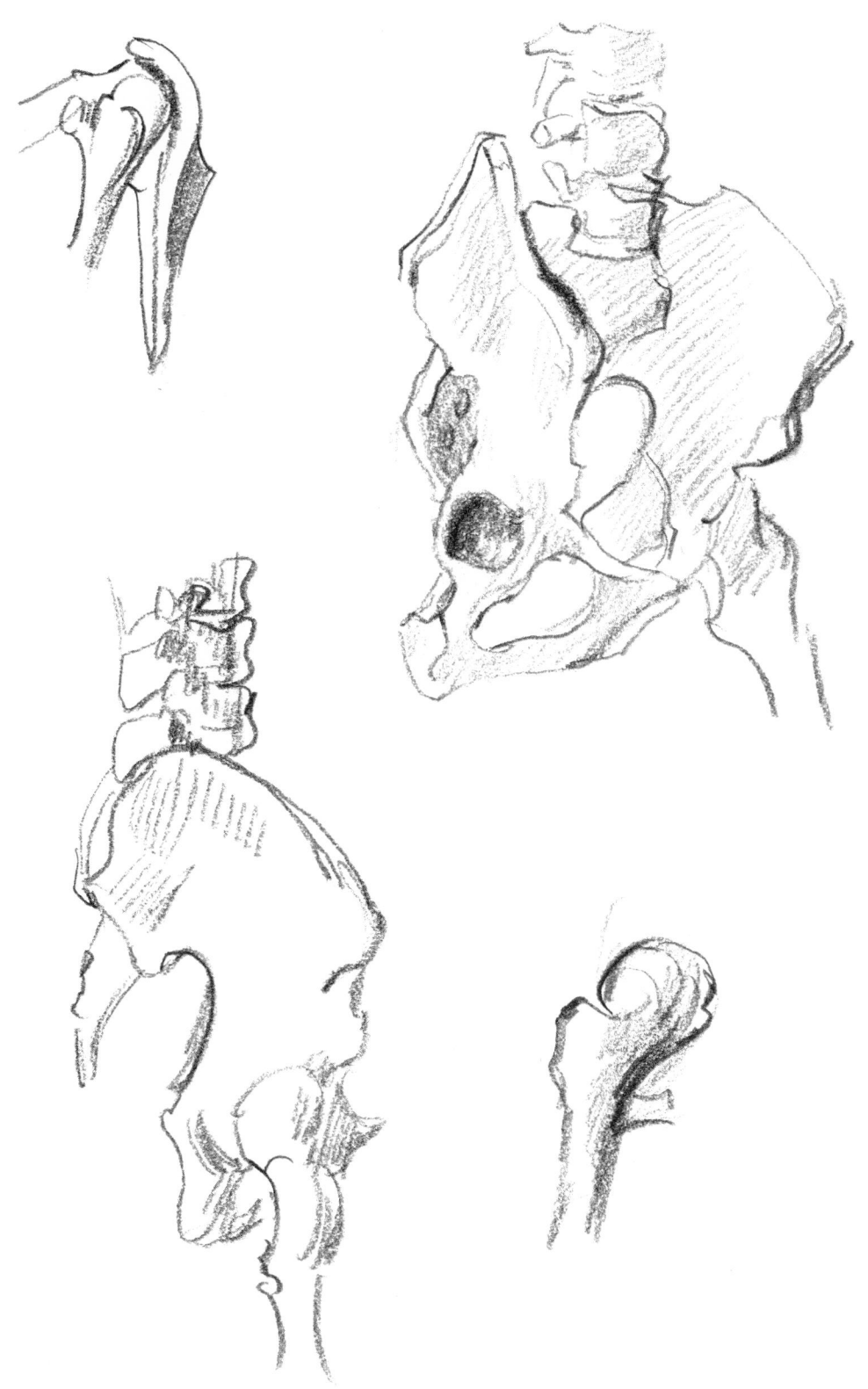

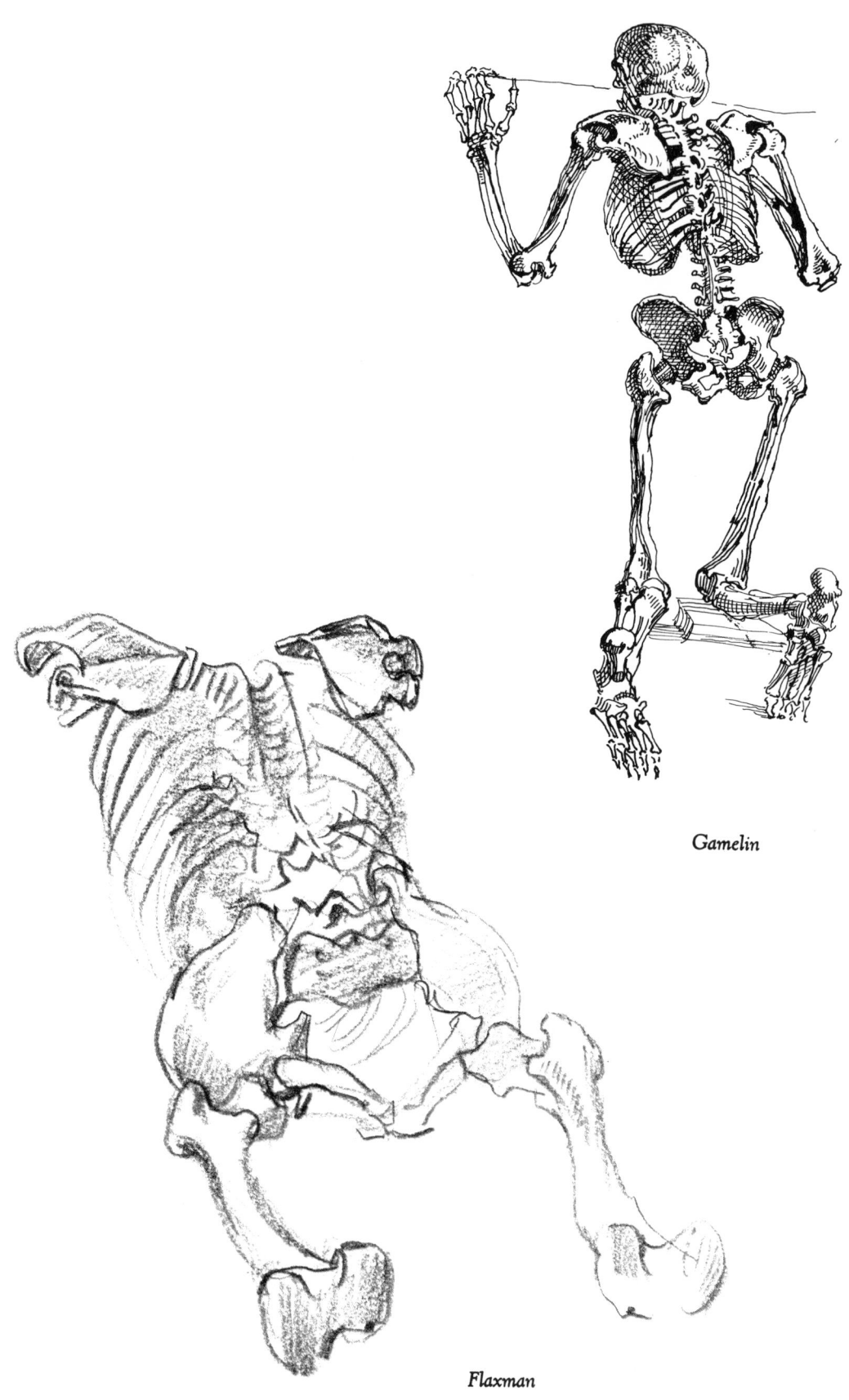

Gamelin

Flaxman

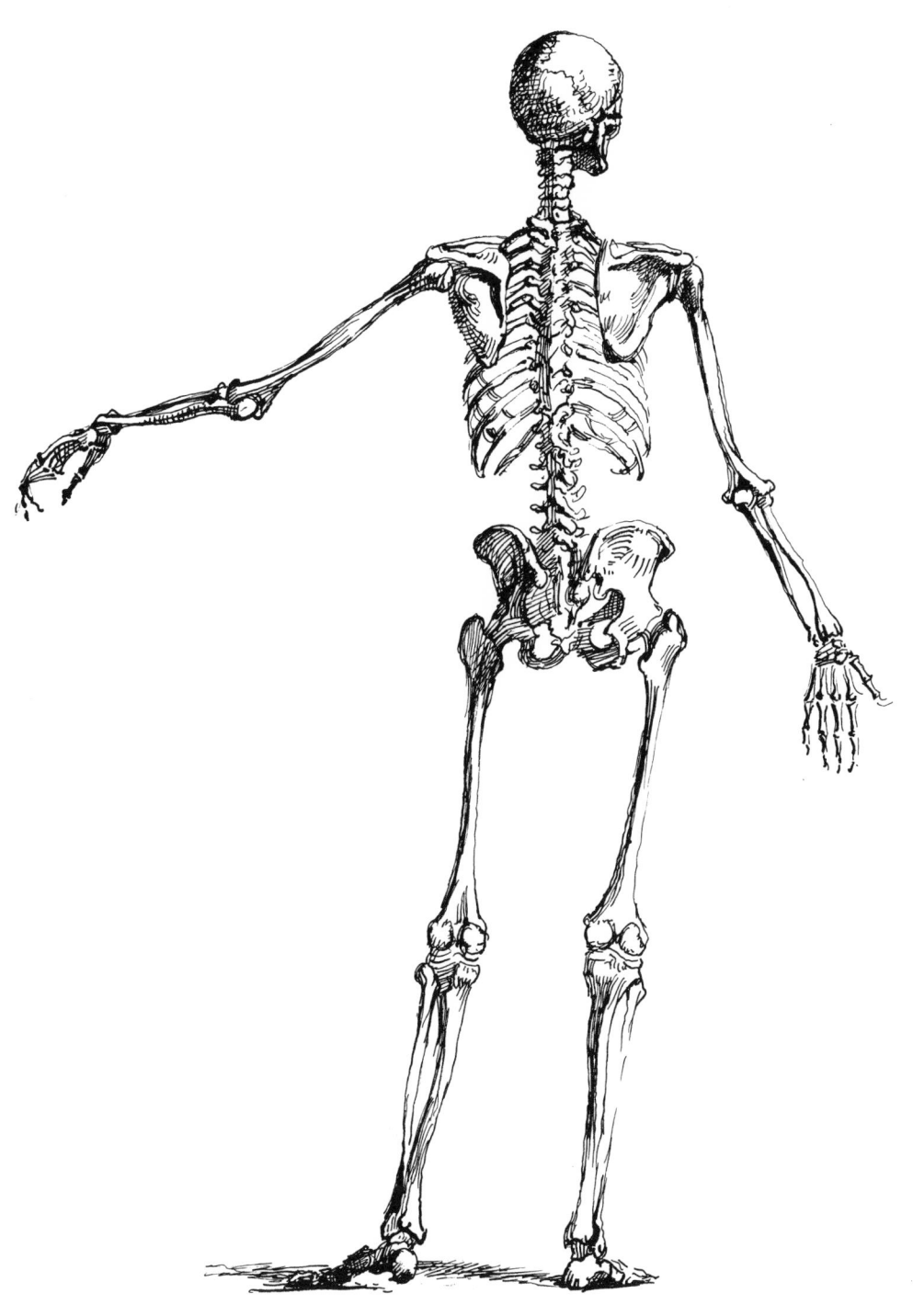

Albinus

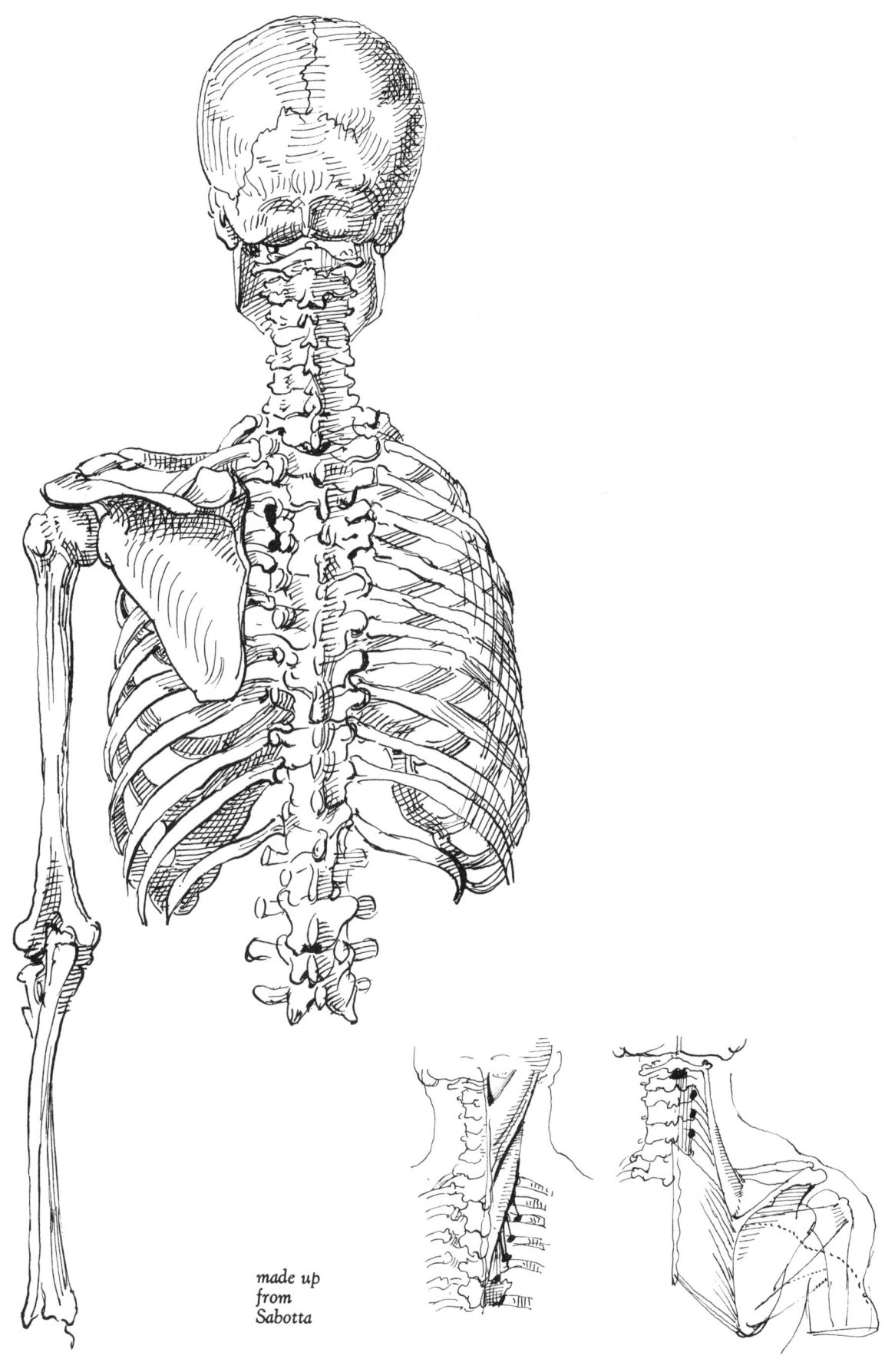

made up
from
Sabotta

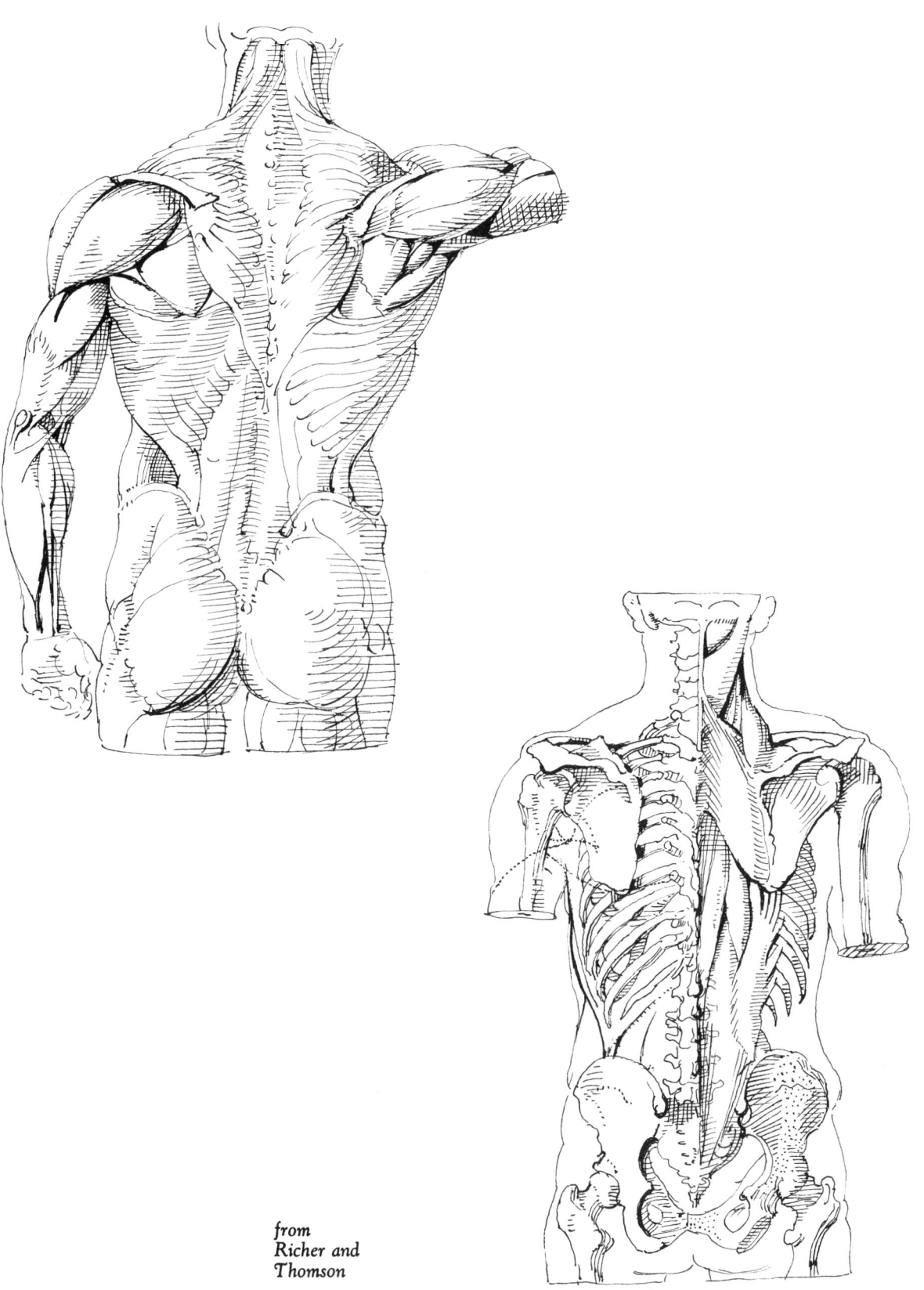

*from
Richer and
Thomson*

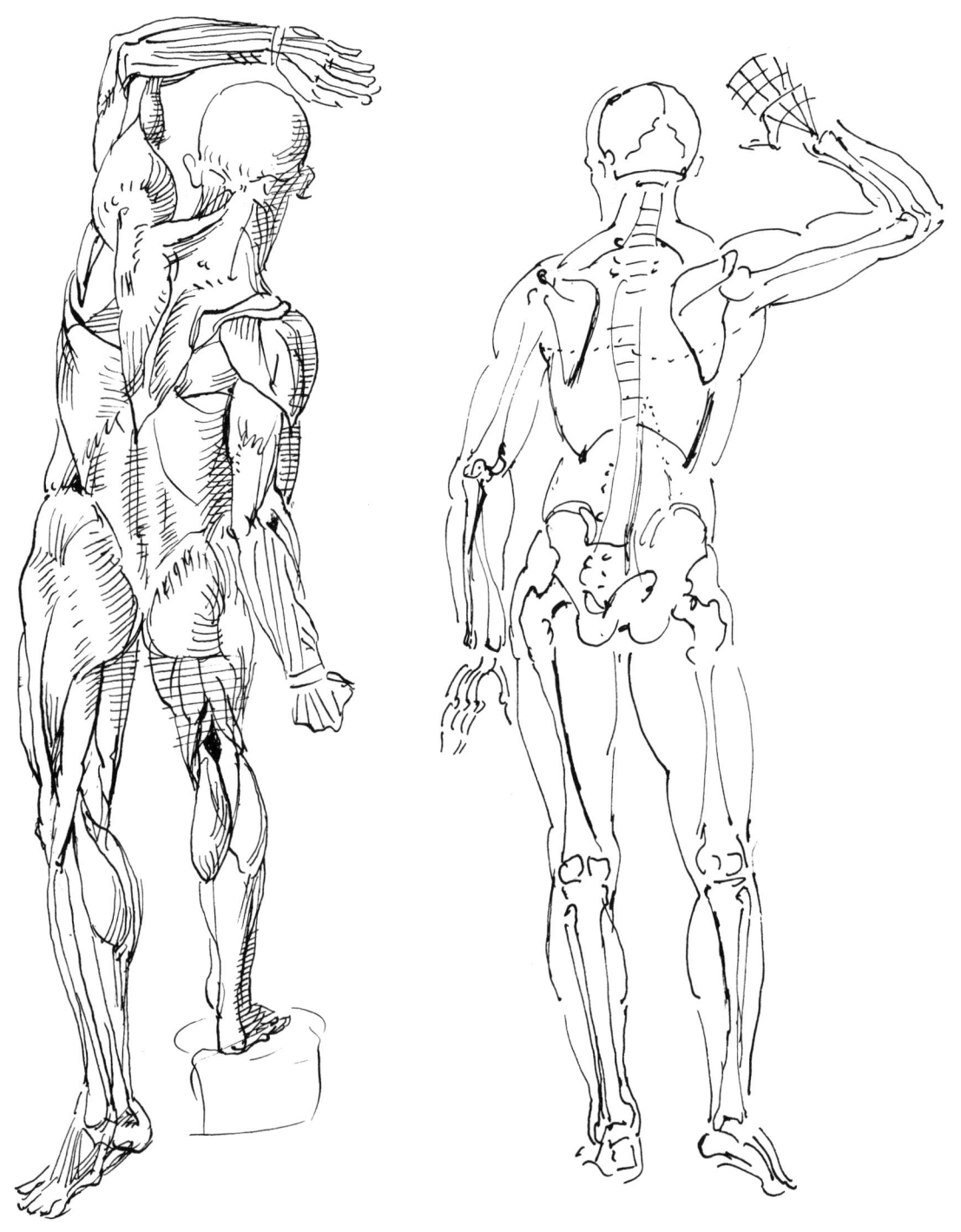

from Franz Frohse

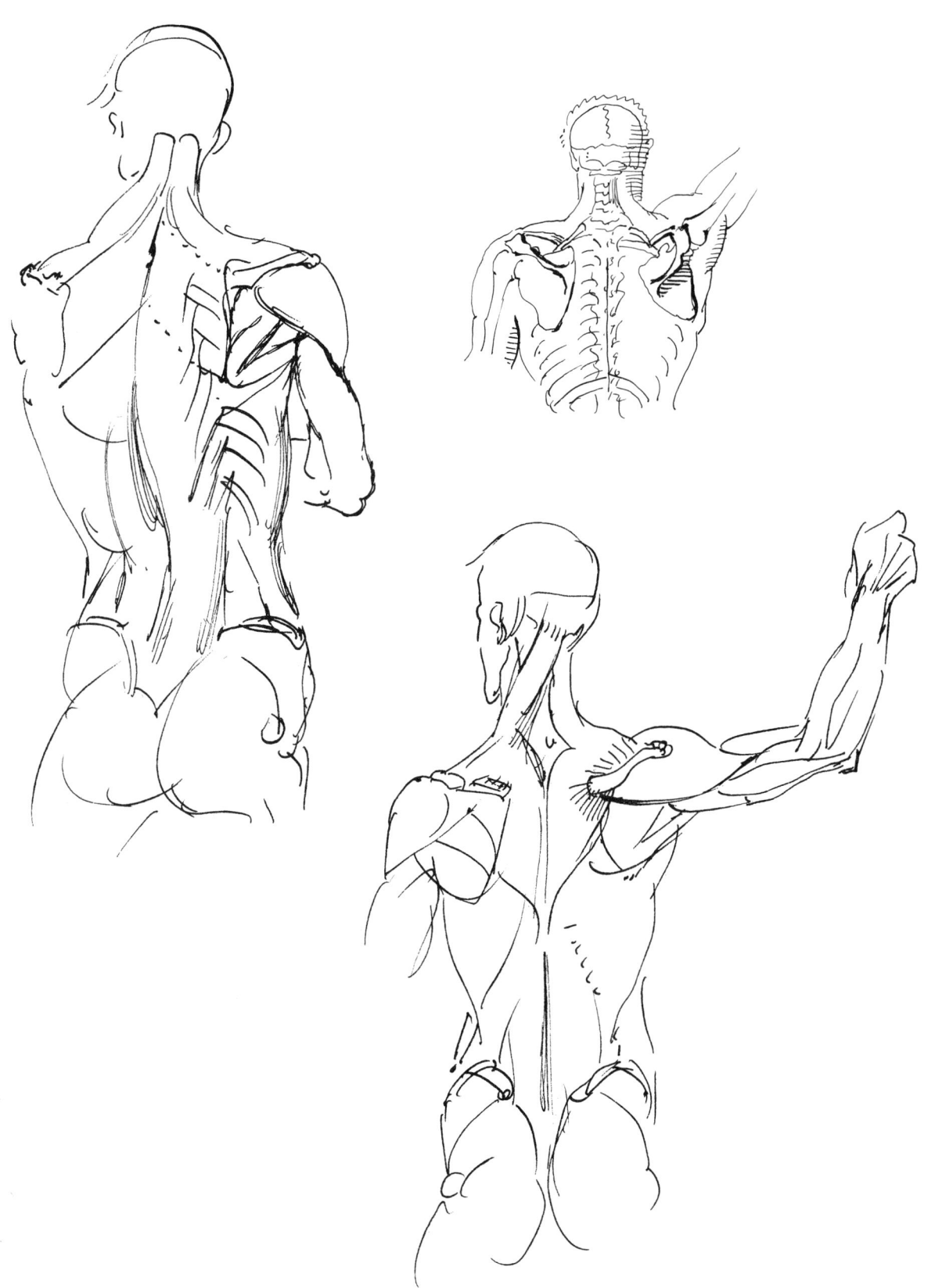

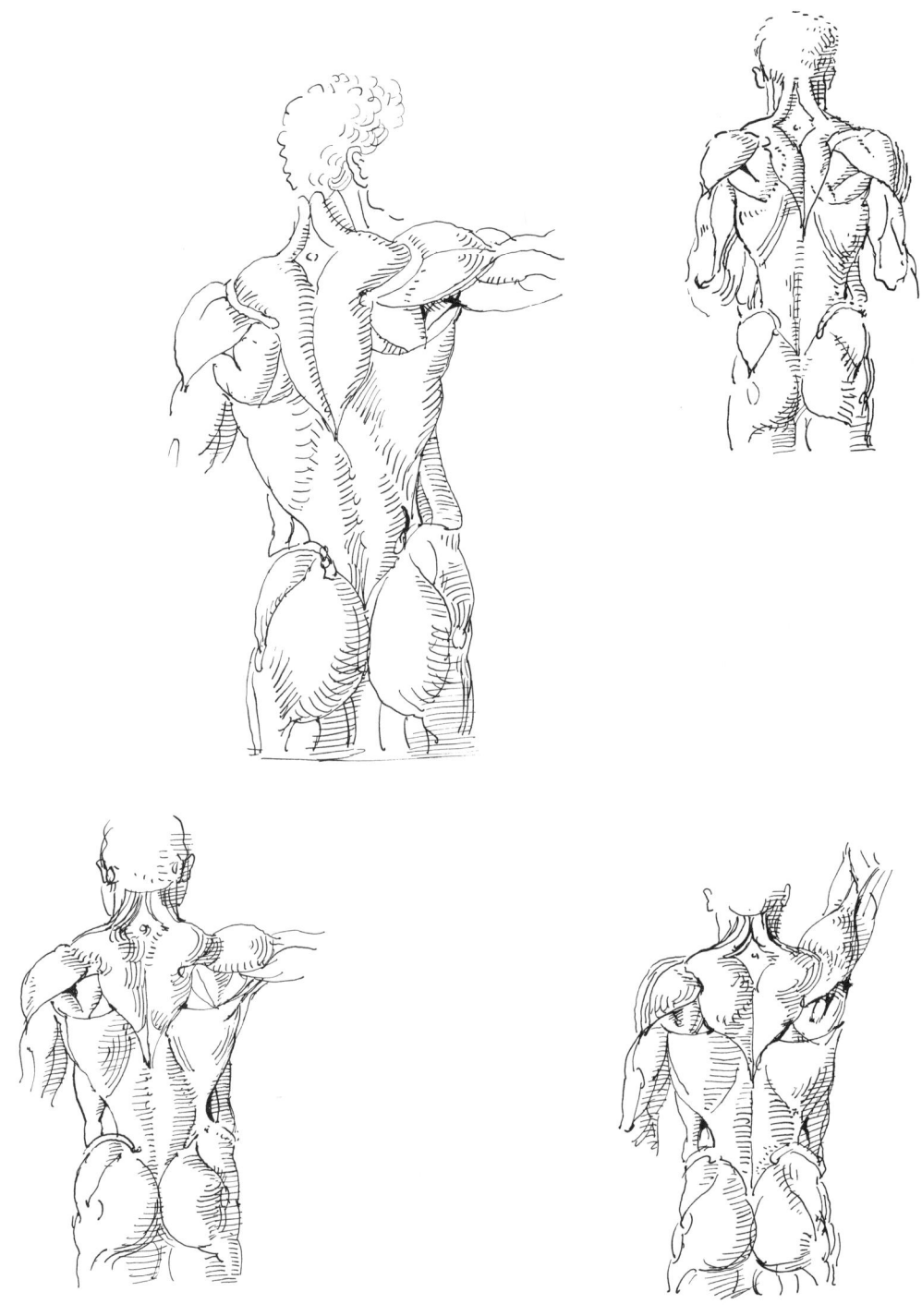

*the following 4 pages derived
from Thomson, Richer and Schiders*

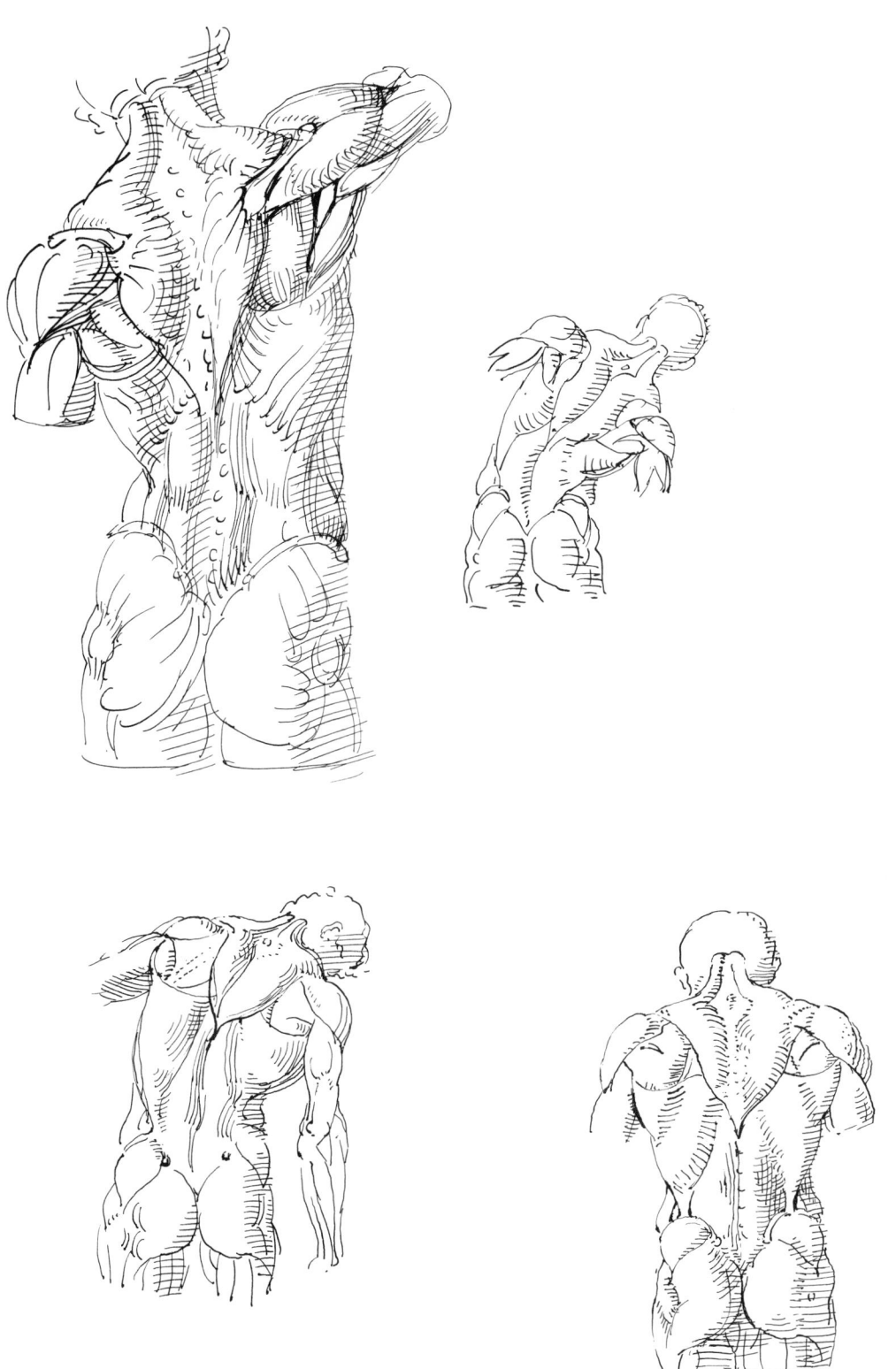

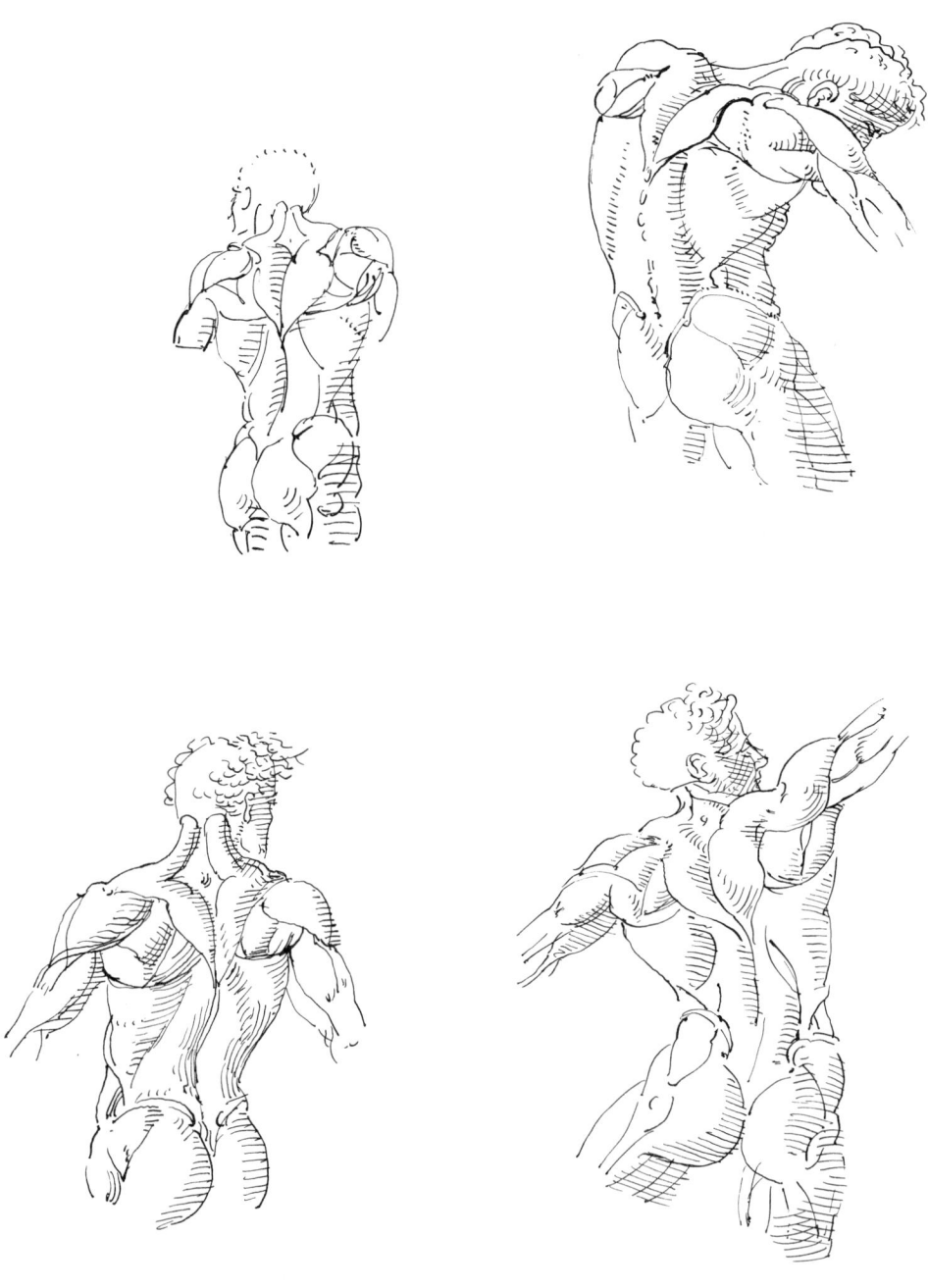

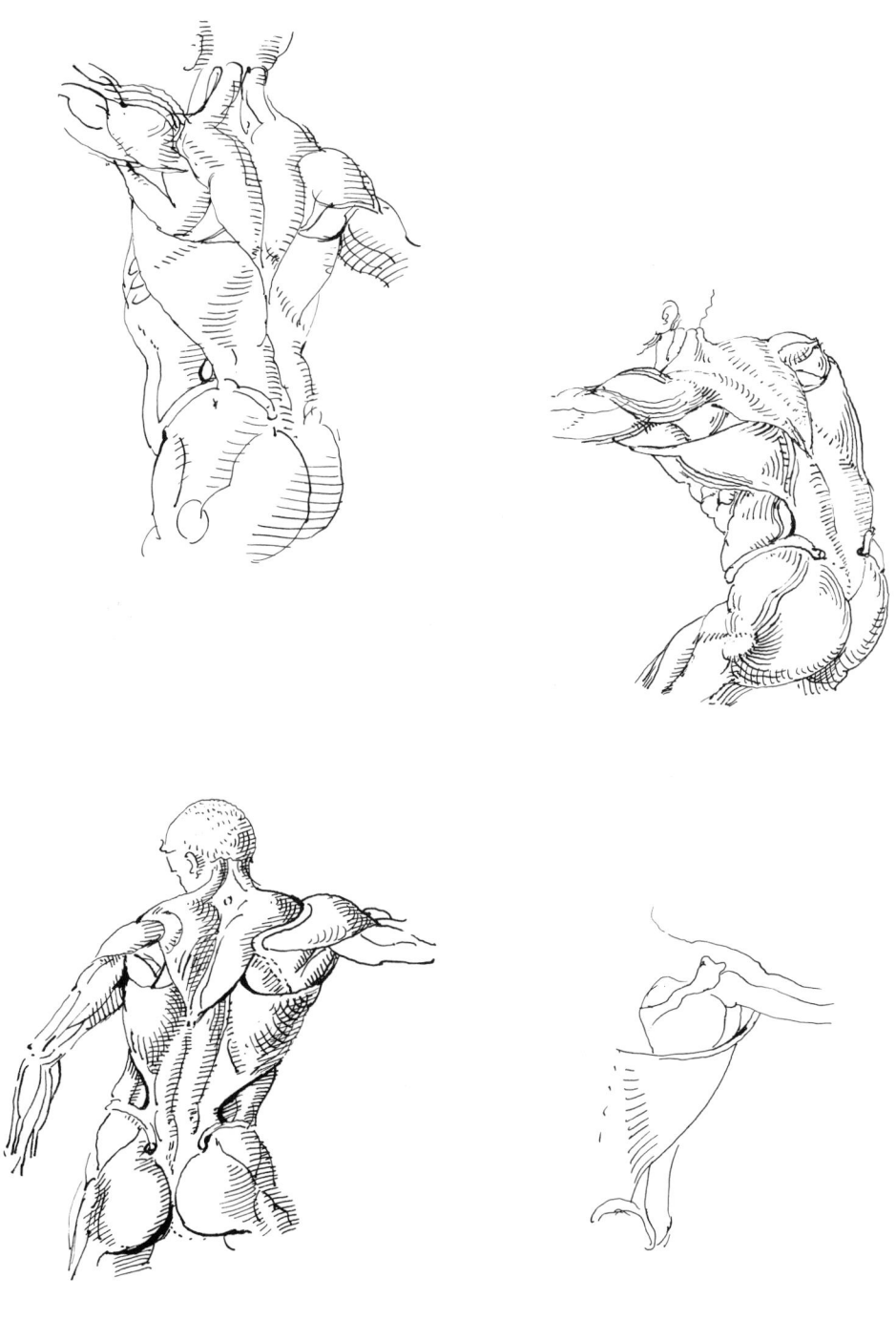

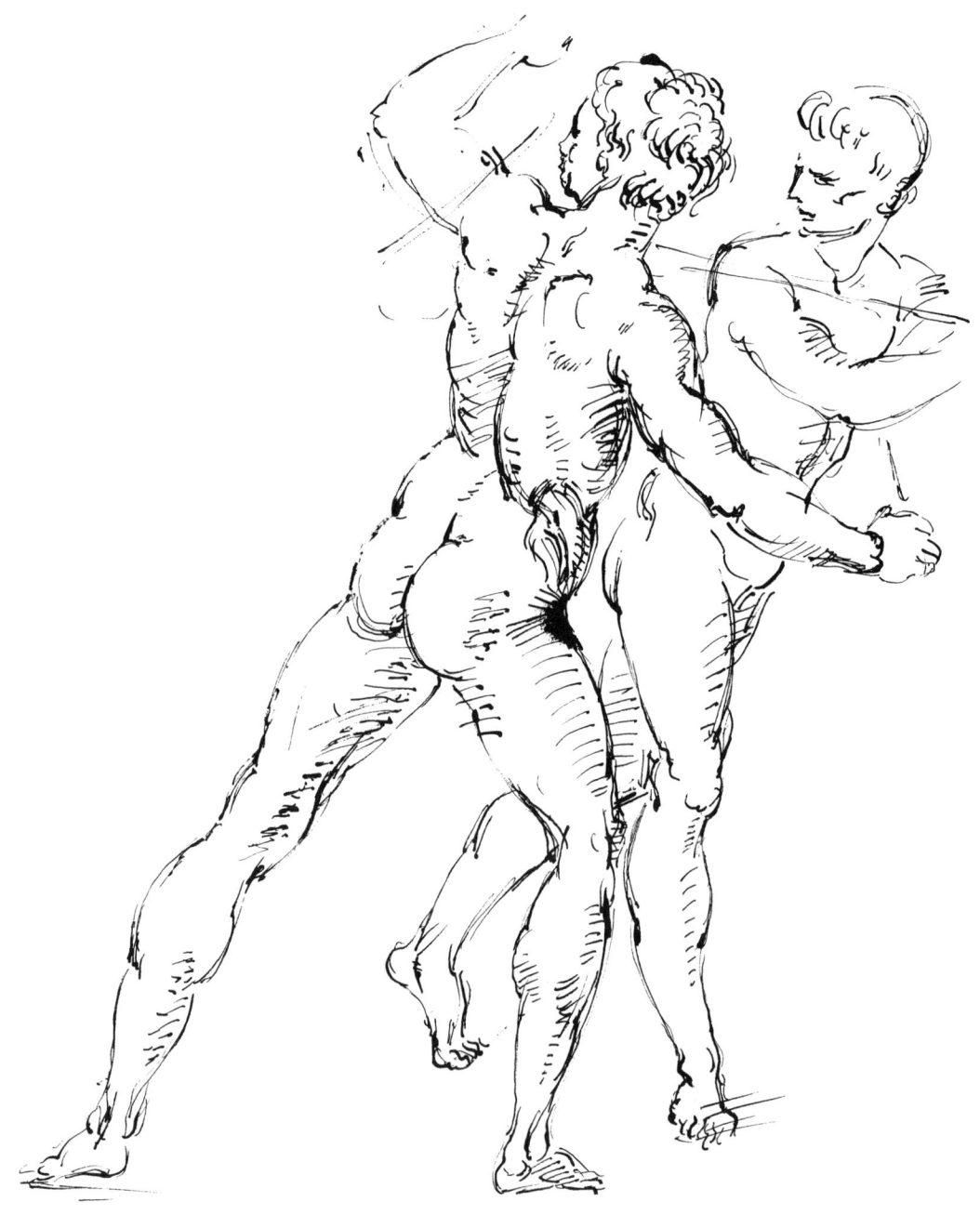

a crude copy of Raphael

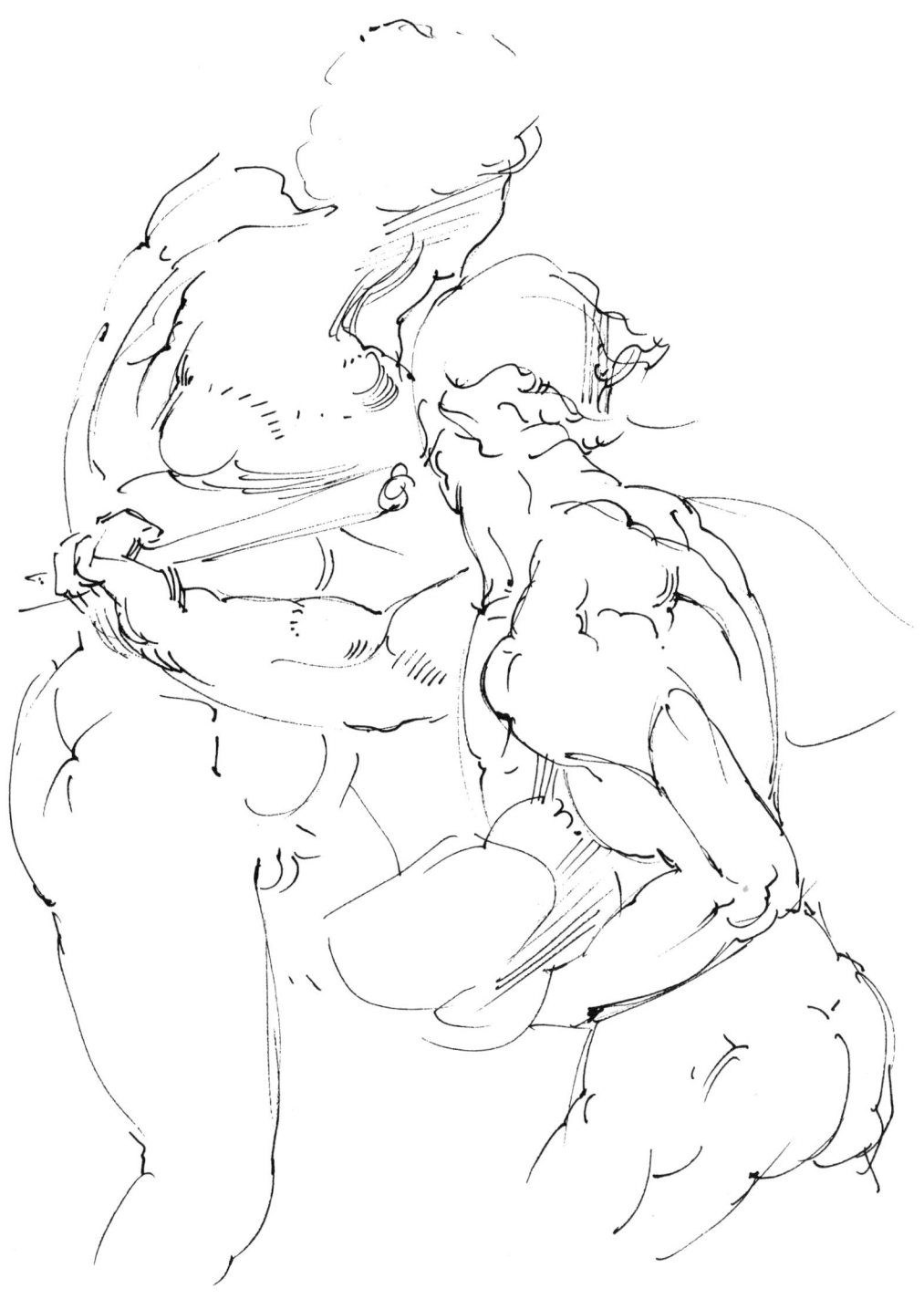

derived from Michelangelo

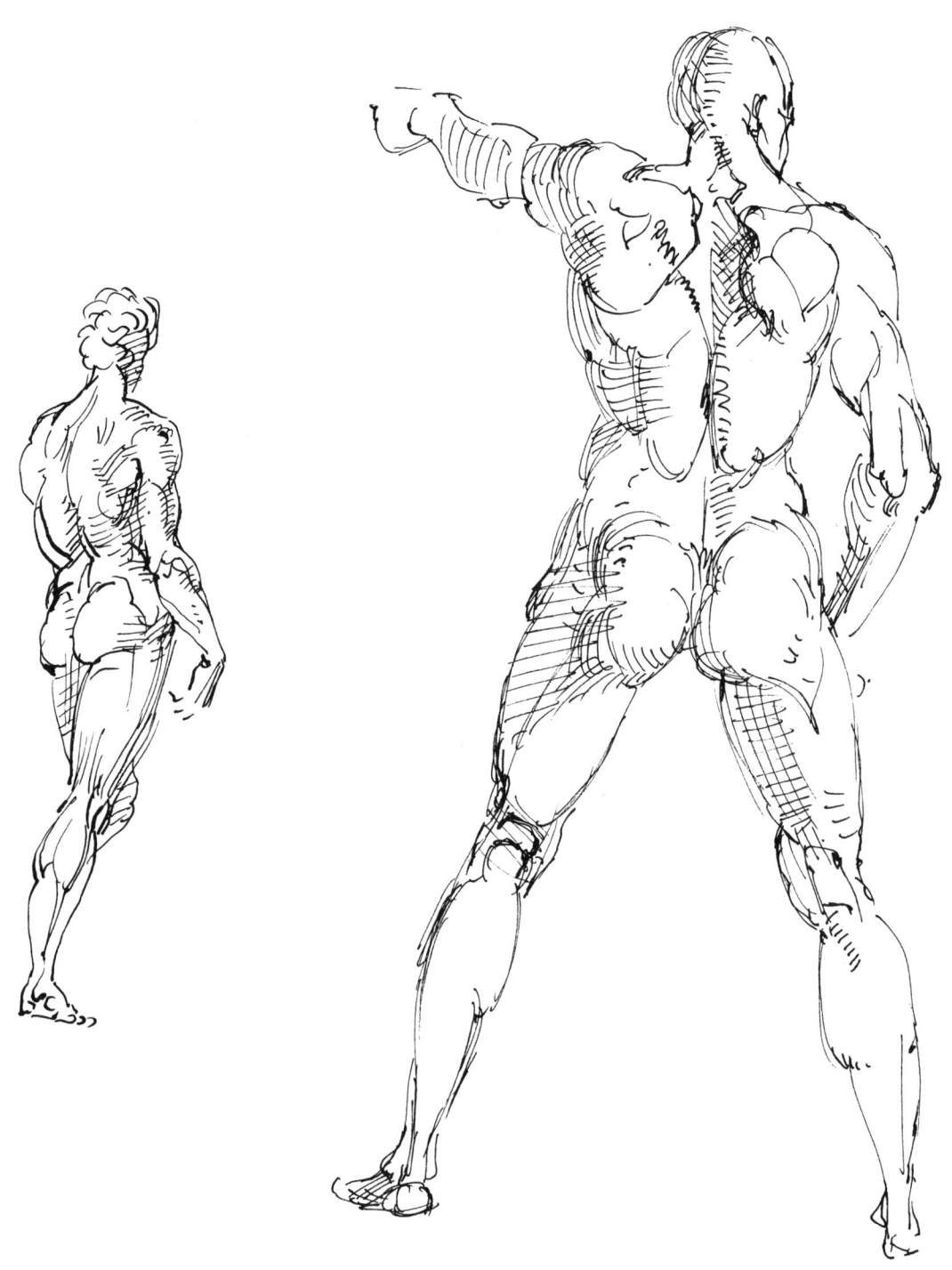

Fuseli

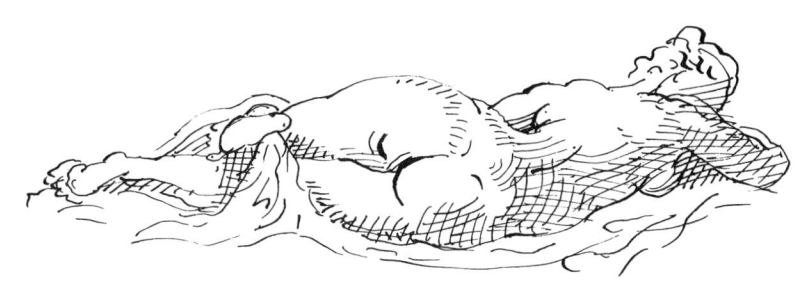

Poussin

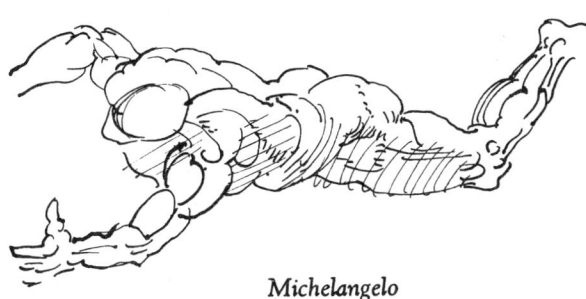

Michelangelo

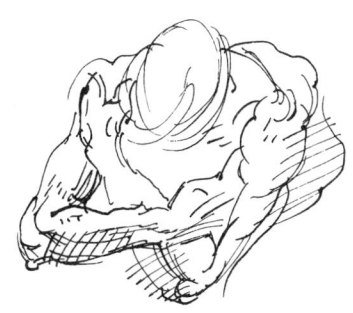

Gamelin

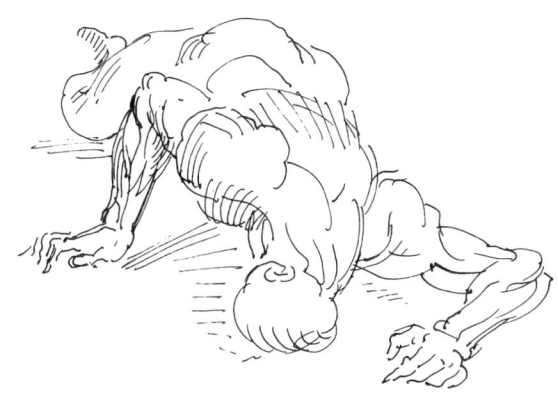

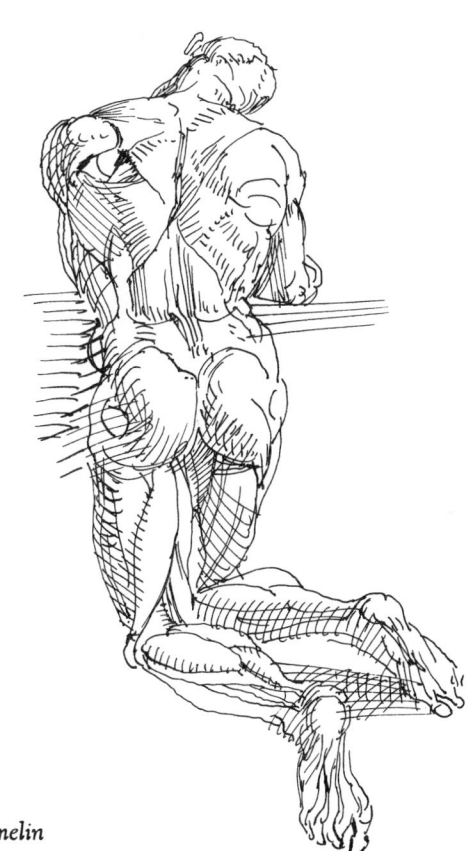

Gamelin

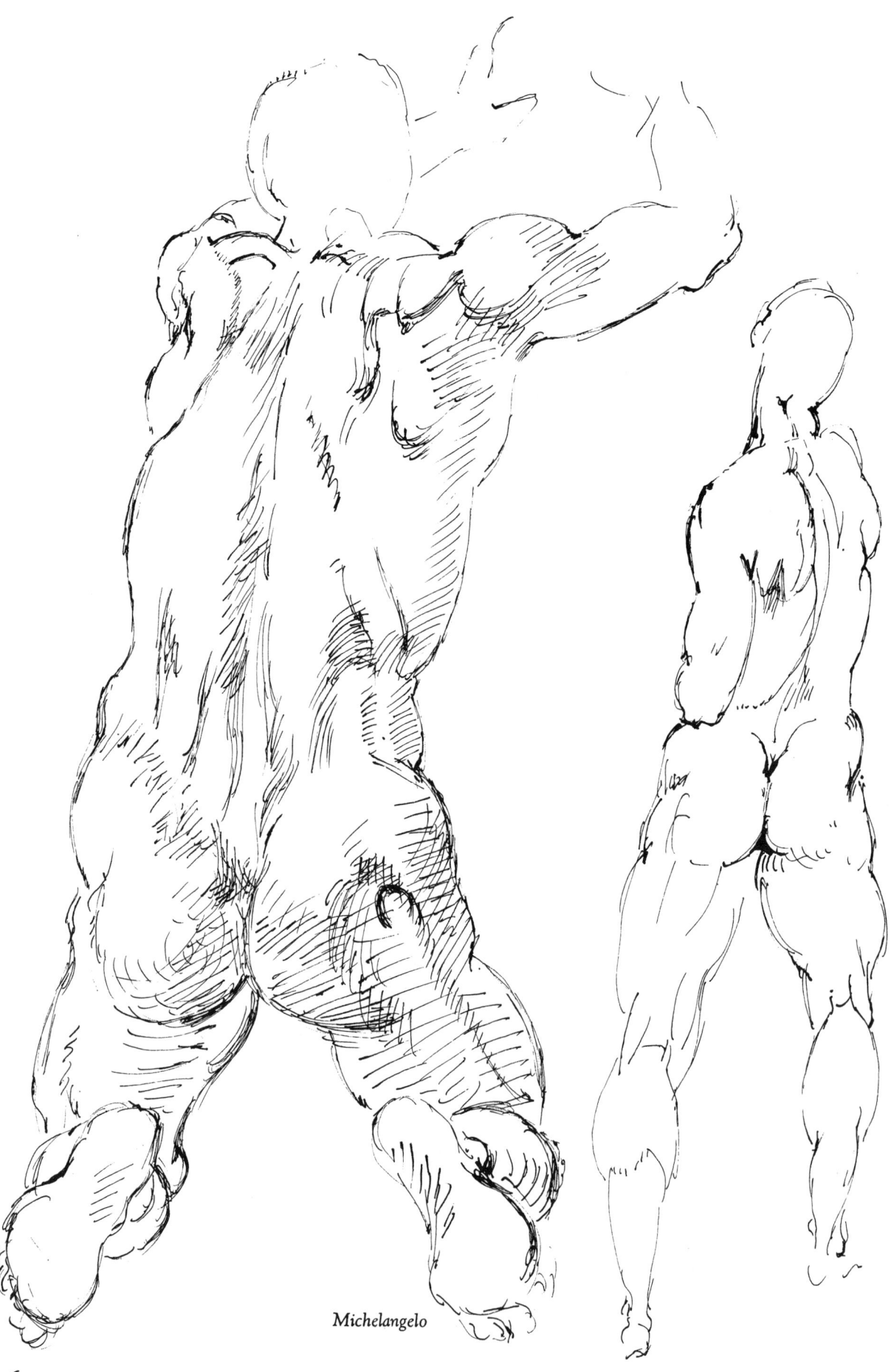

Michelangelo

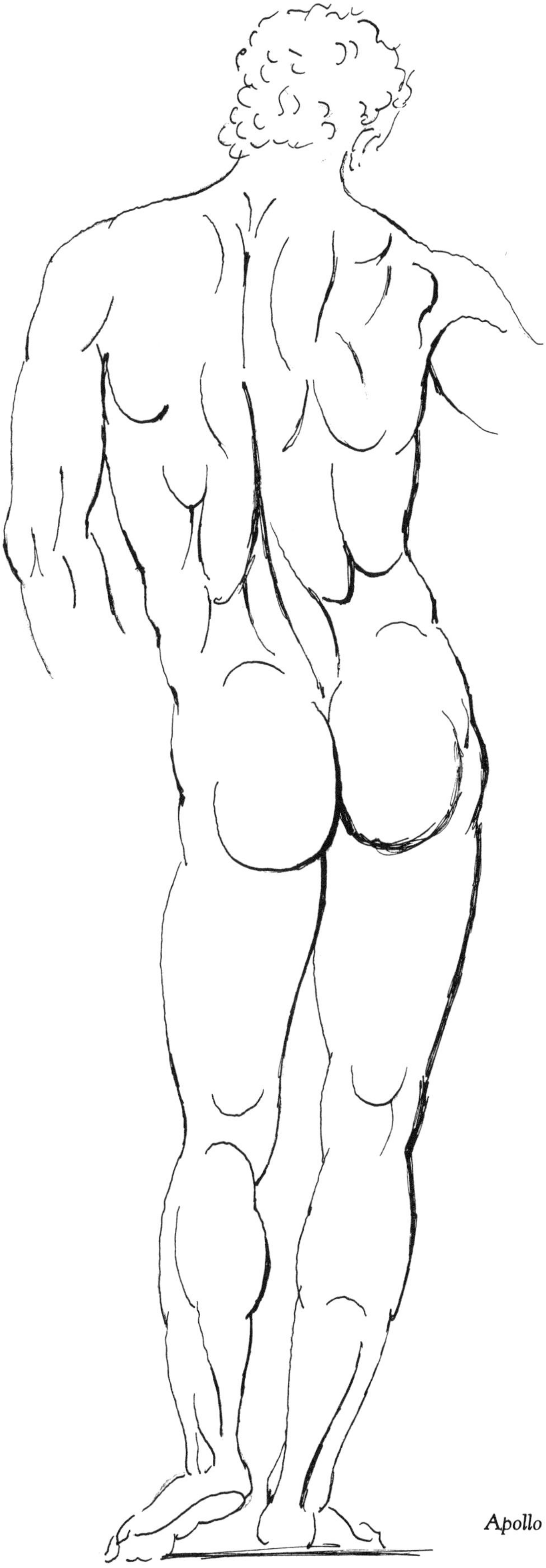

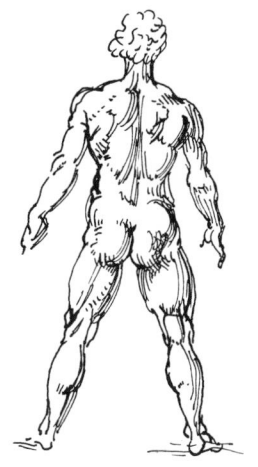

da Vinci

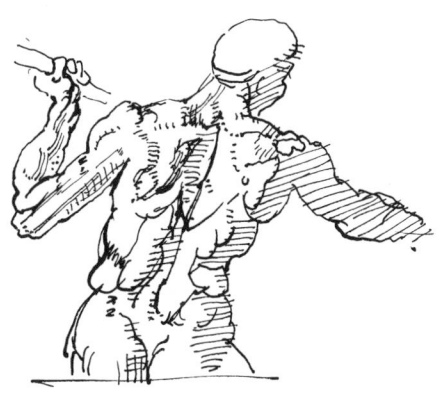

Michelangelo

Apollo

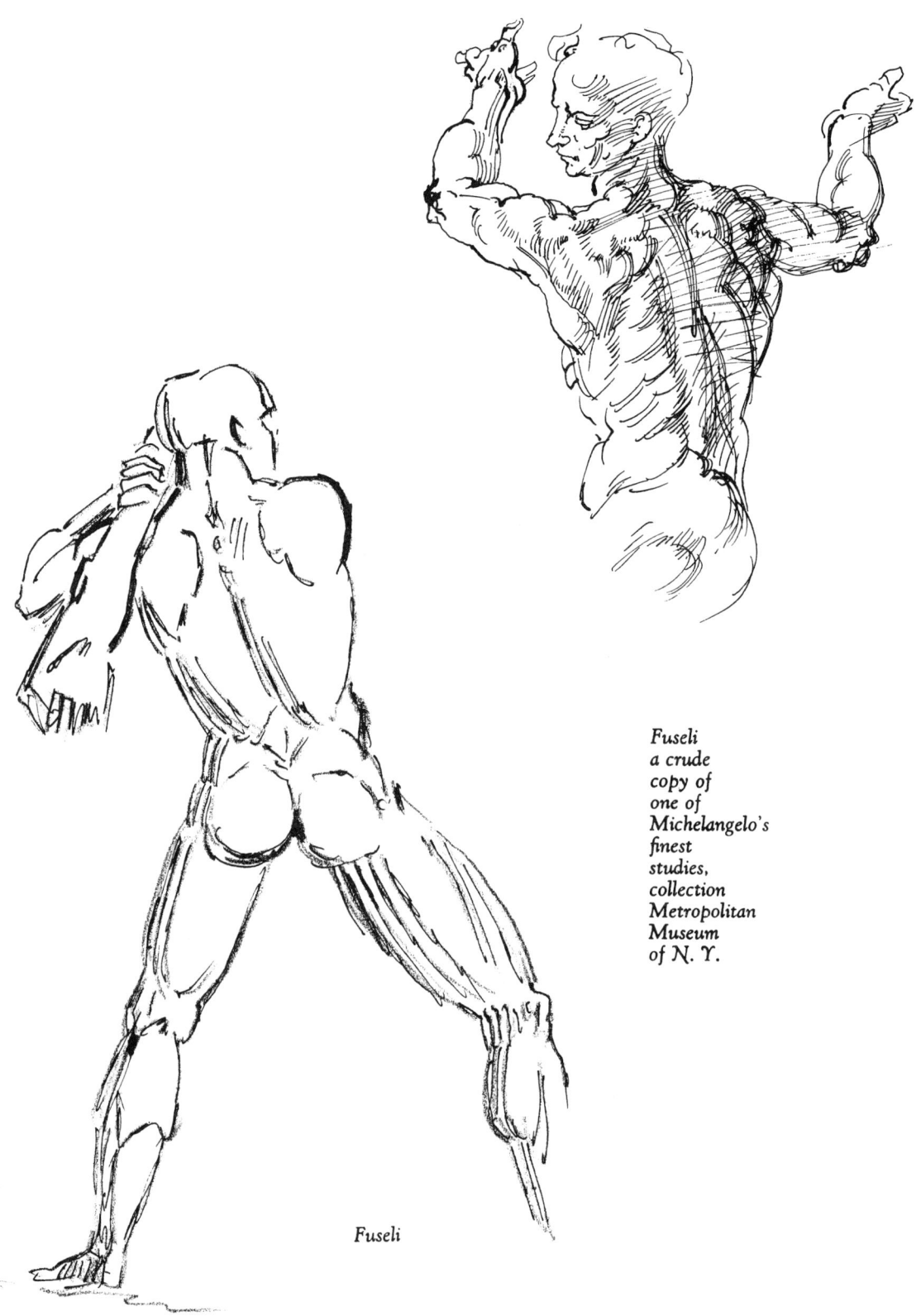

Fuseli
a crude
copy of
one of
Michelangelo's
finest
studies,
collection
Metropolitan
Museum
of N. Y.

Fuseli

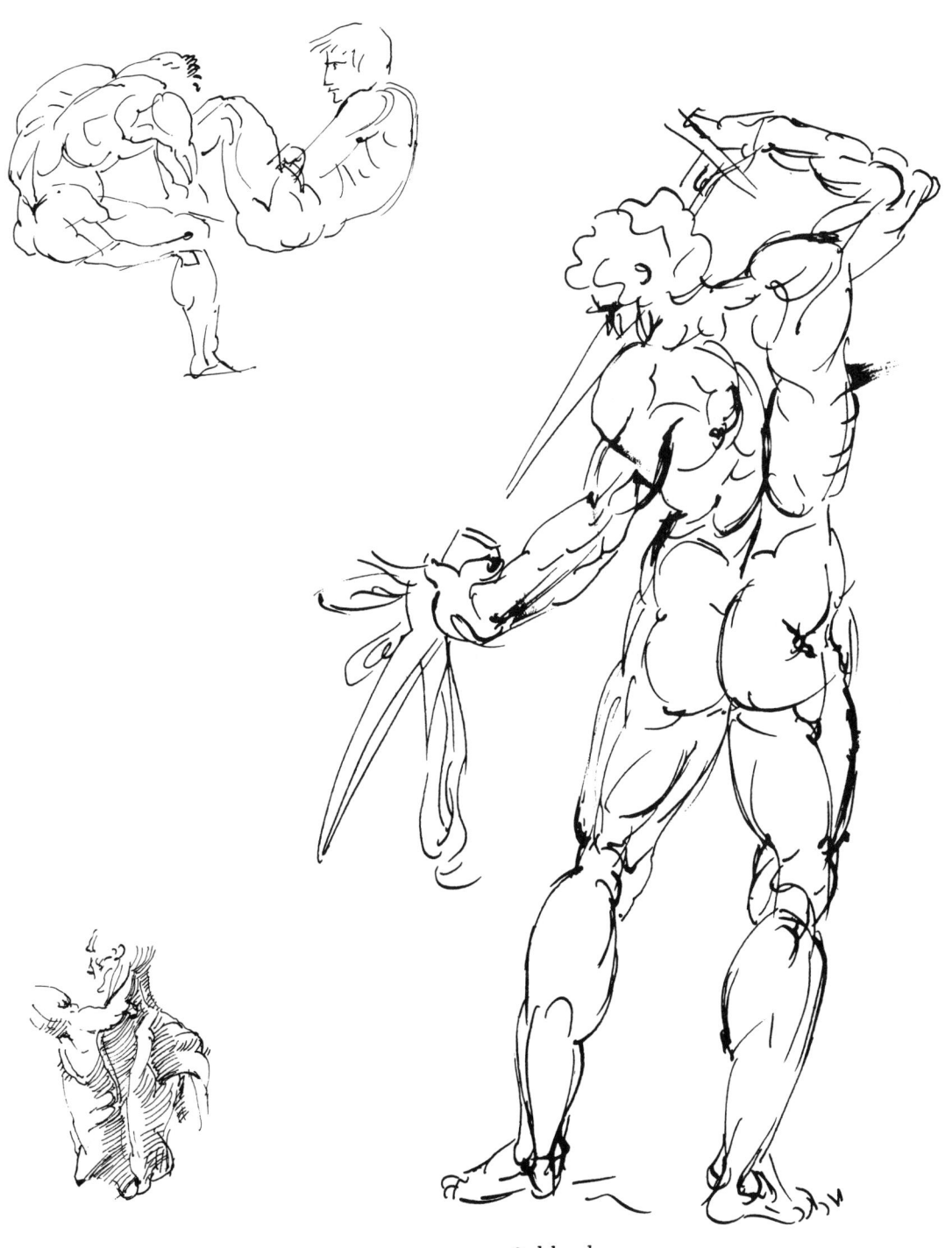

Michelangelo

3rd hand
Copy of Michelangelo

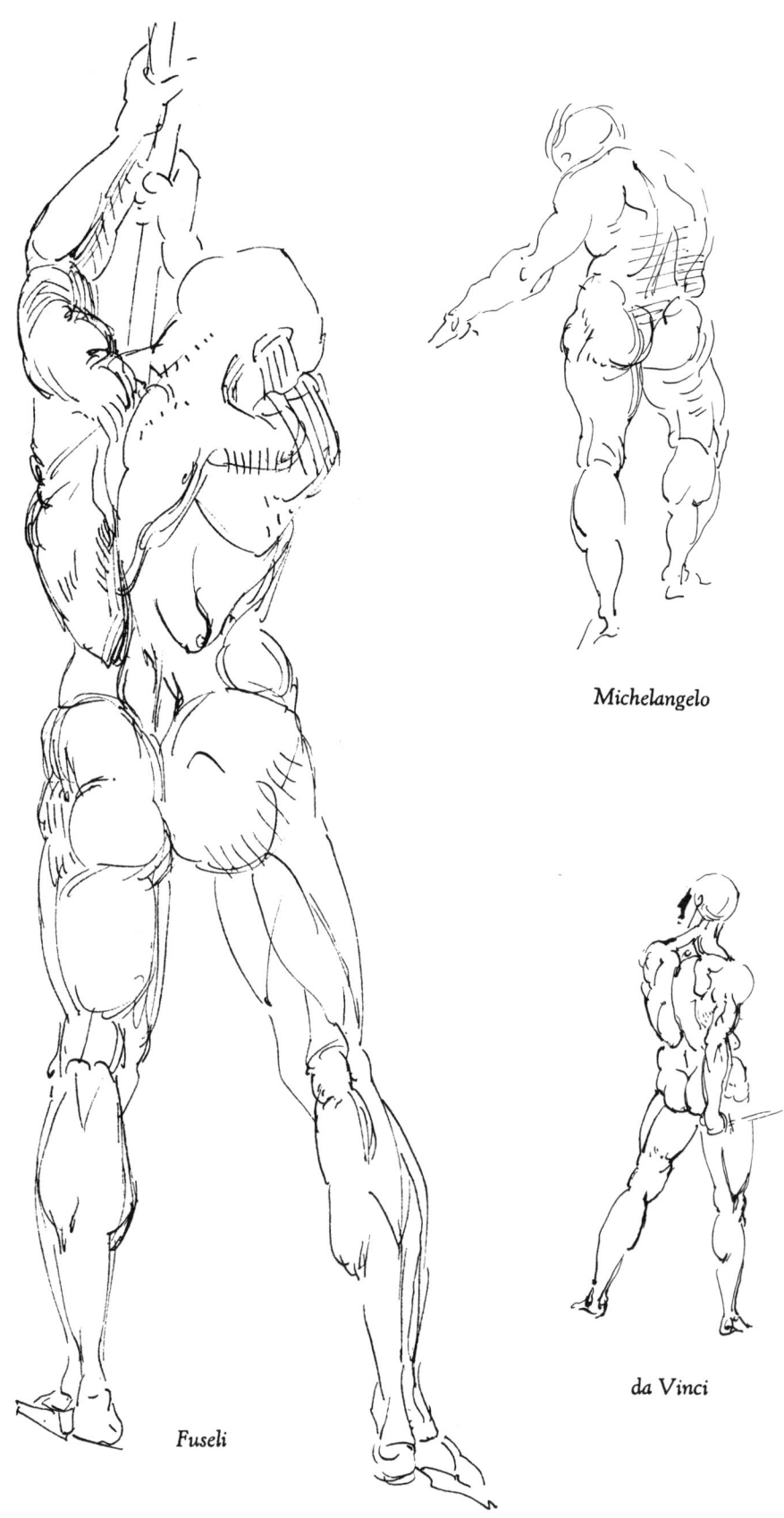

Michelangelo

da Vinci

Fuseli

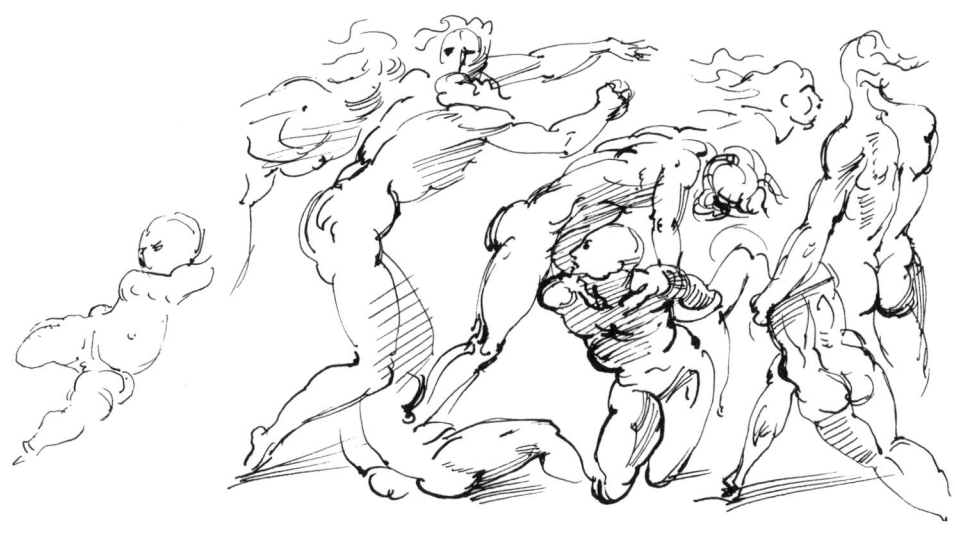

Raphael

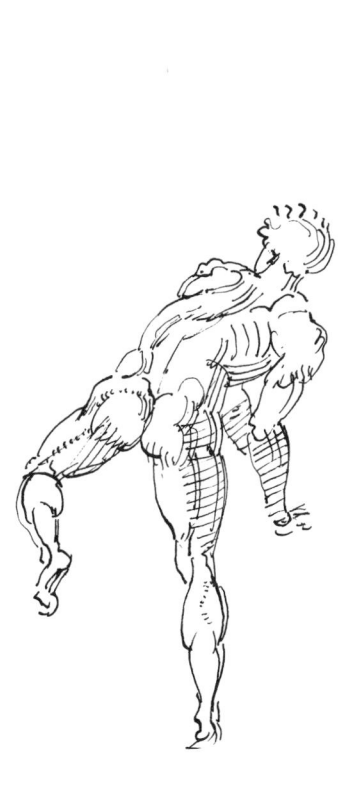

Michelangelo

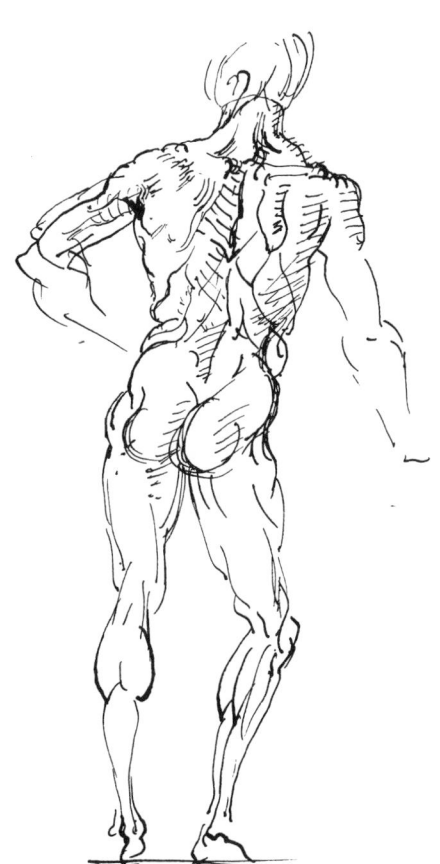

Raphael

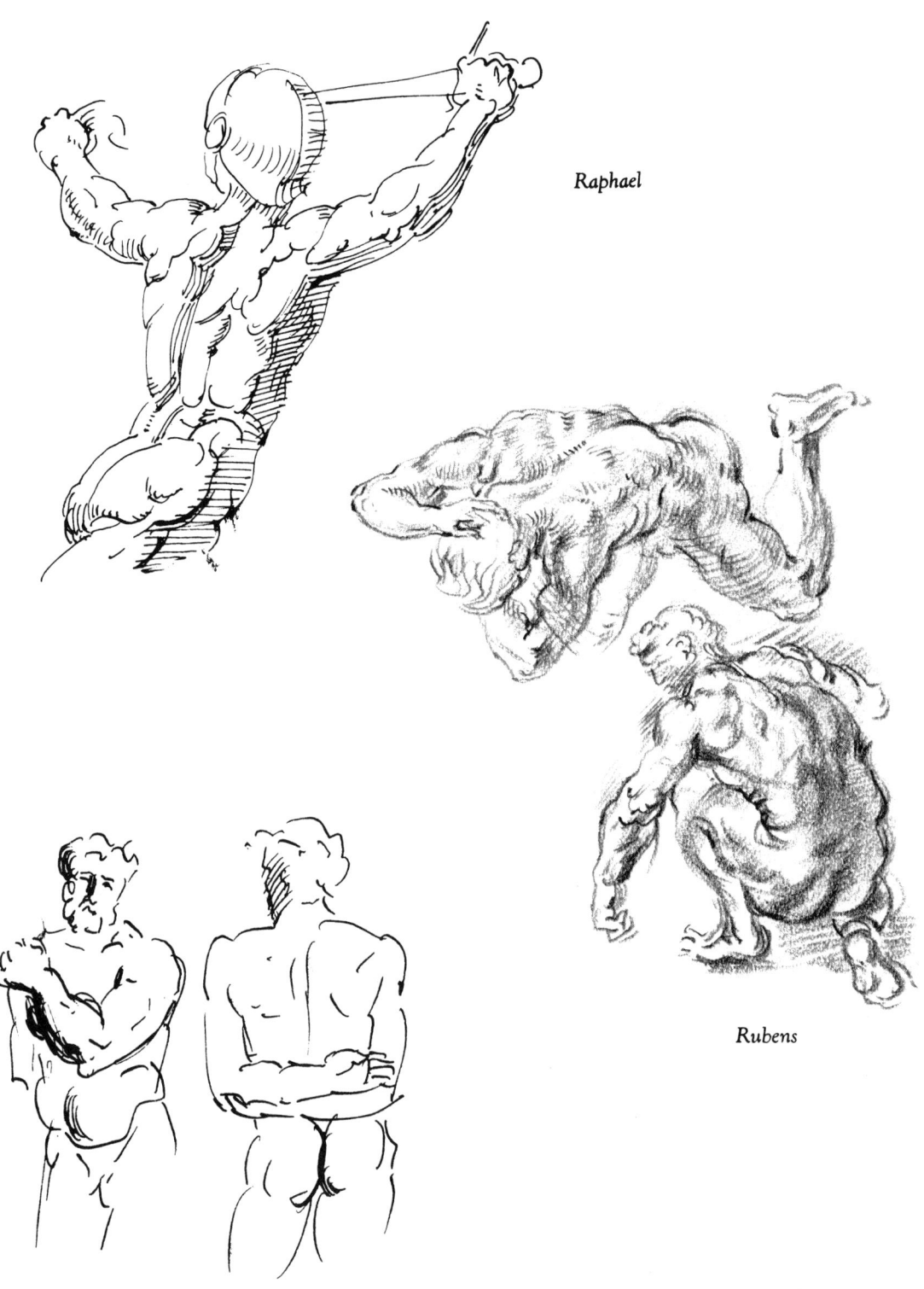

Raphael

Rubens

Richer

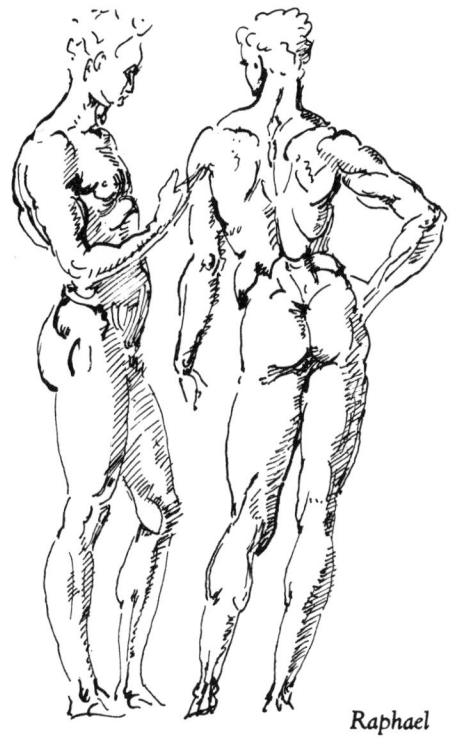

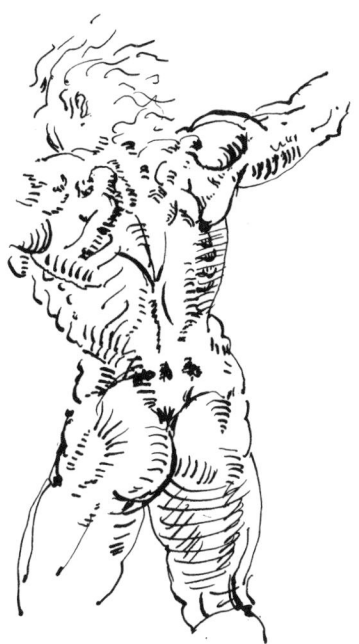

Raphael

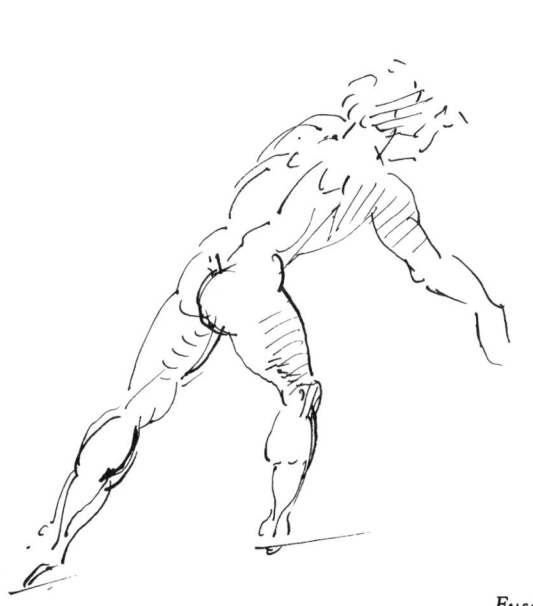

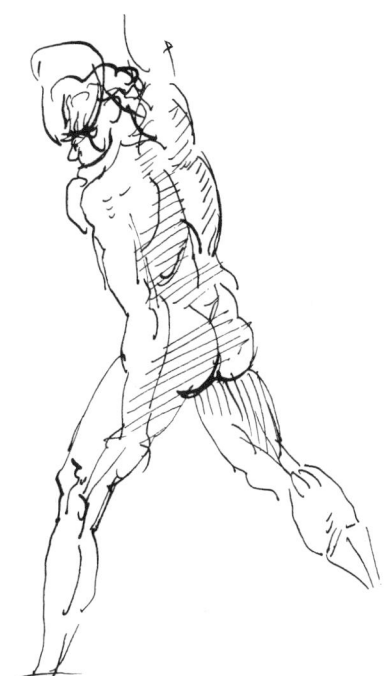

Fuseli

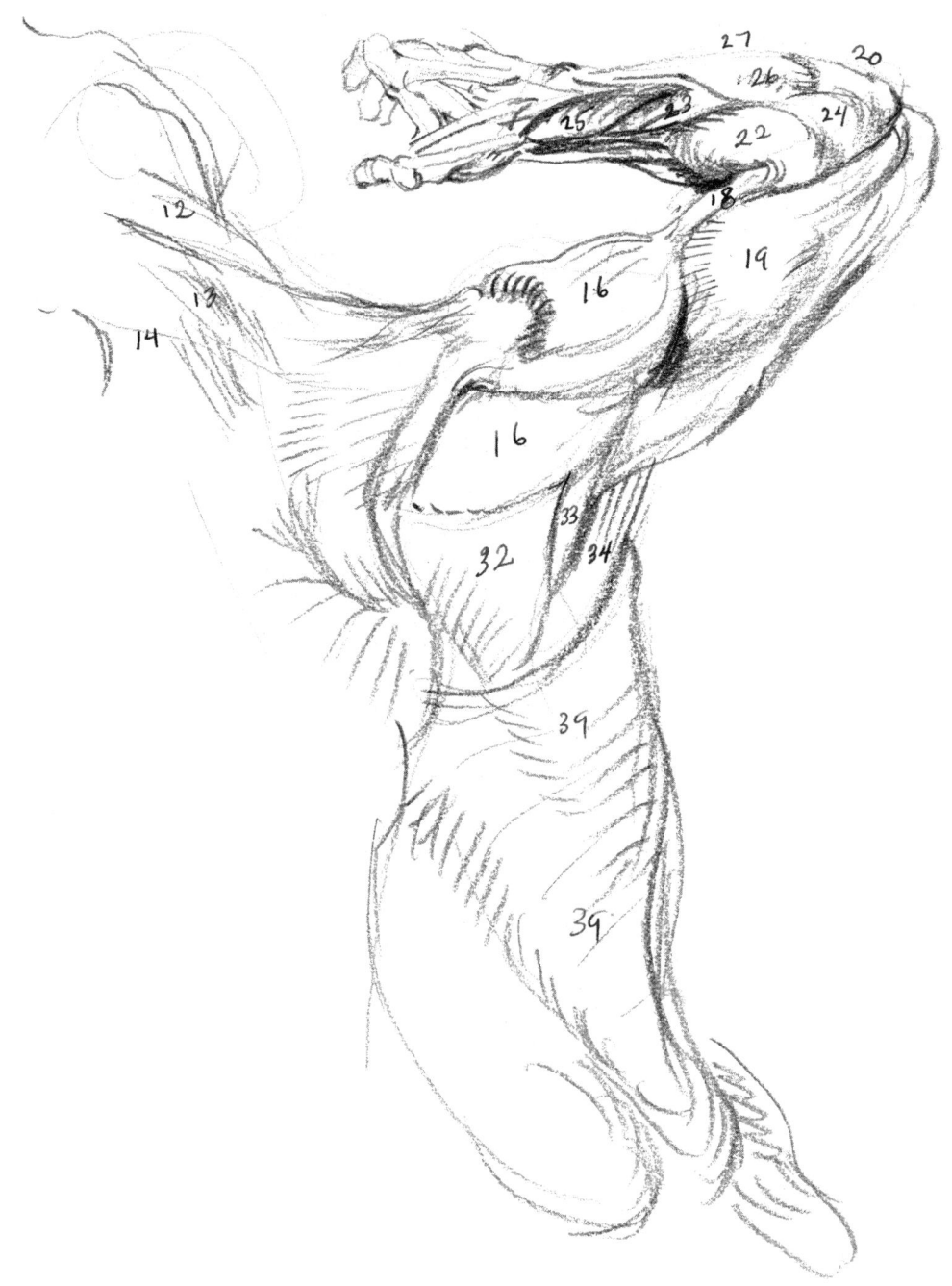

Flaxman

Head

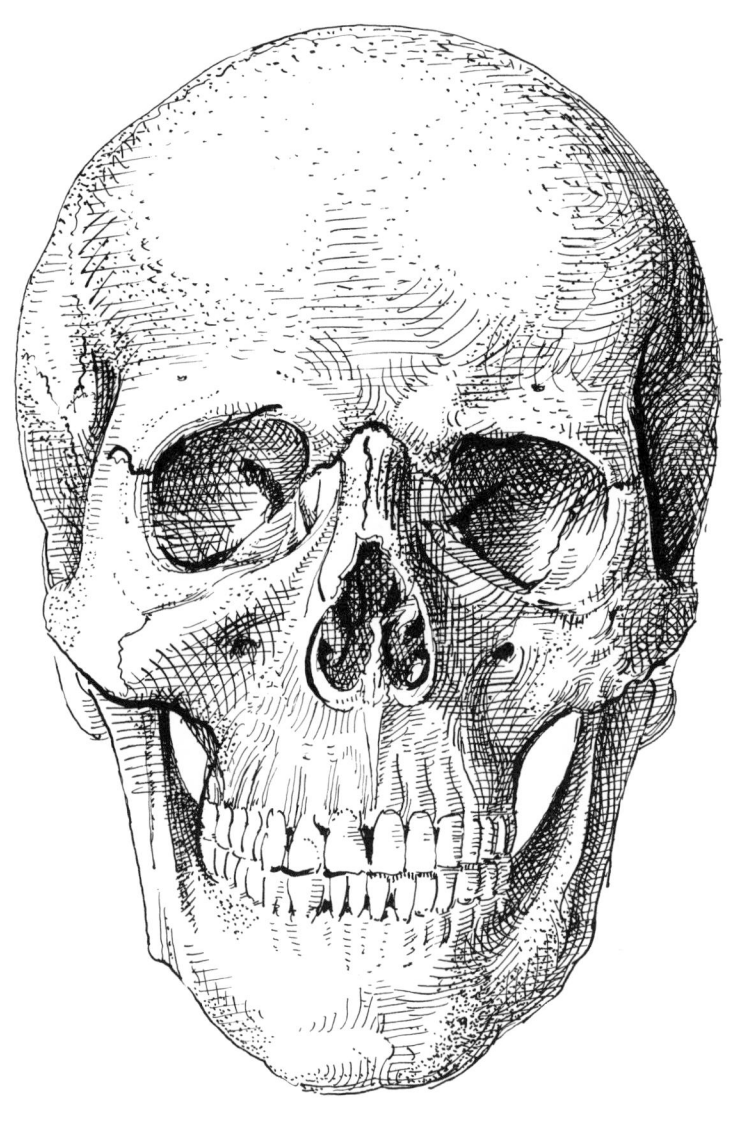

*from a number
of sources*

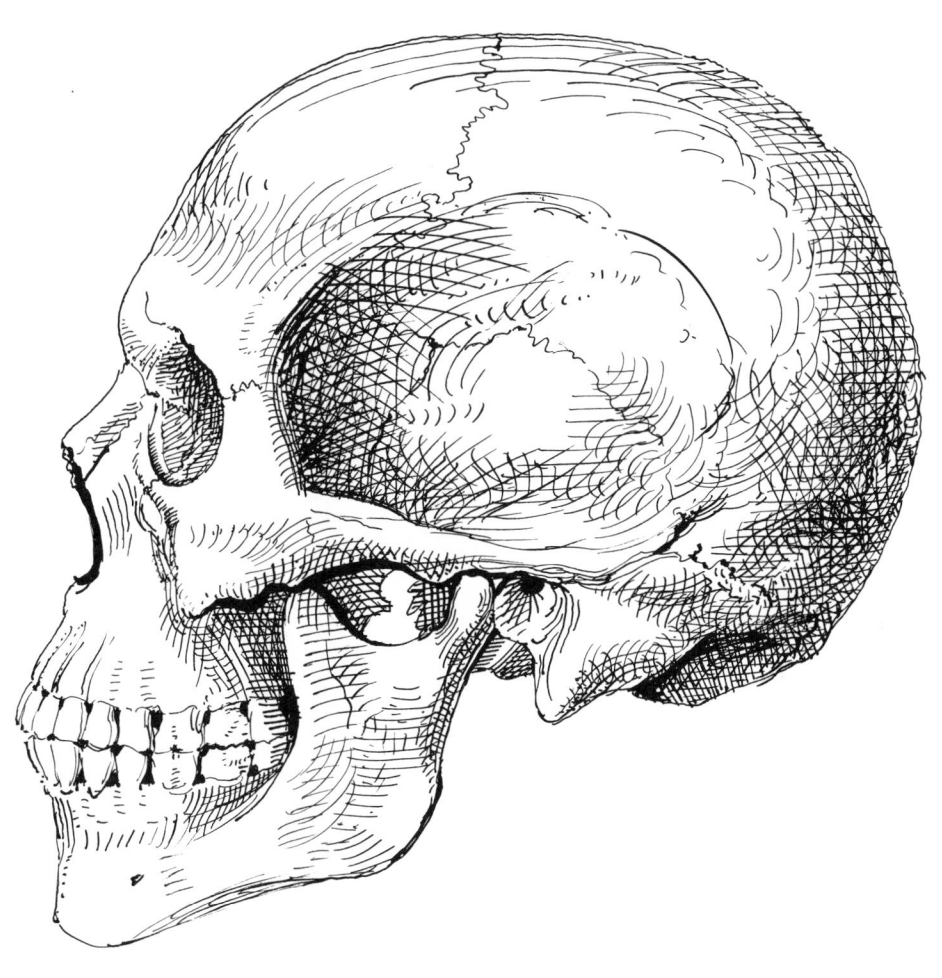

*from a number
of sources*

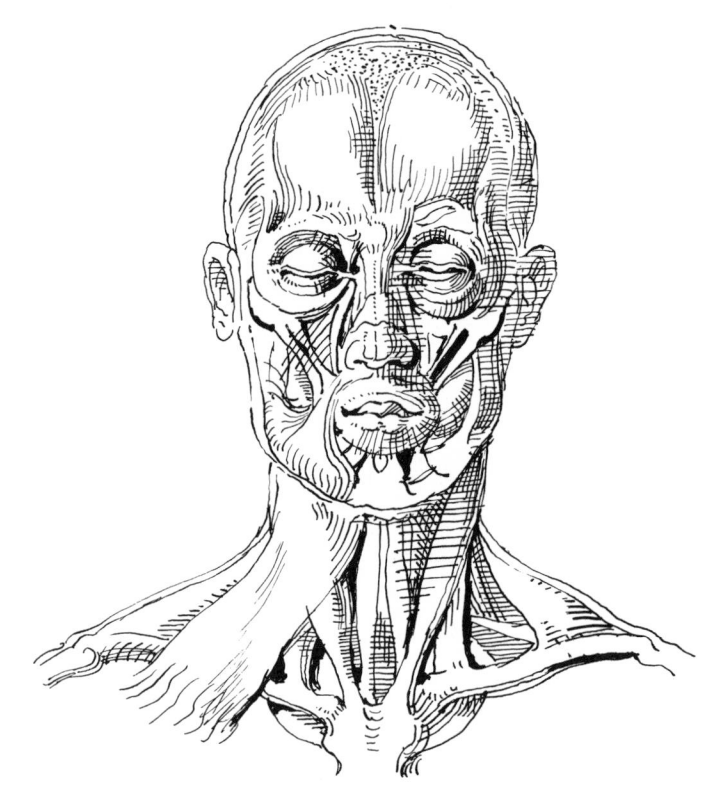

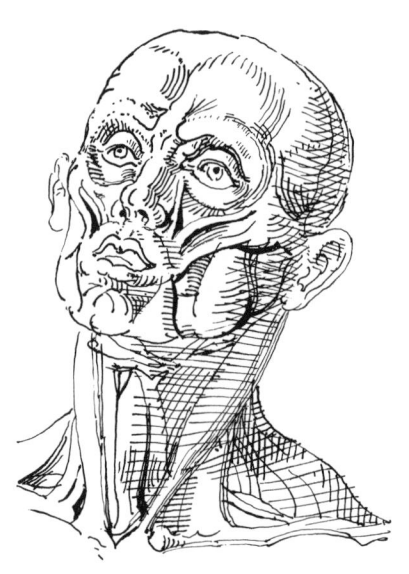

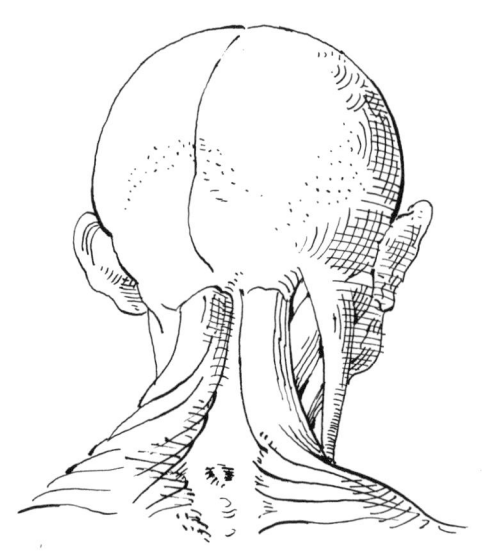

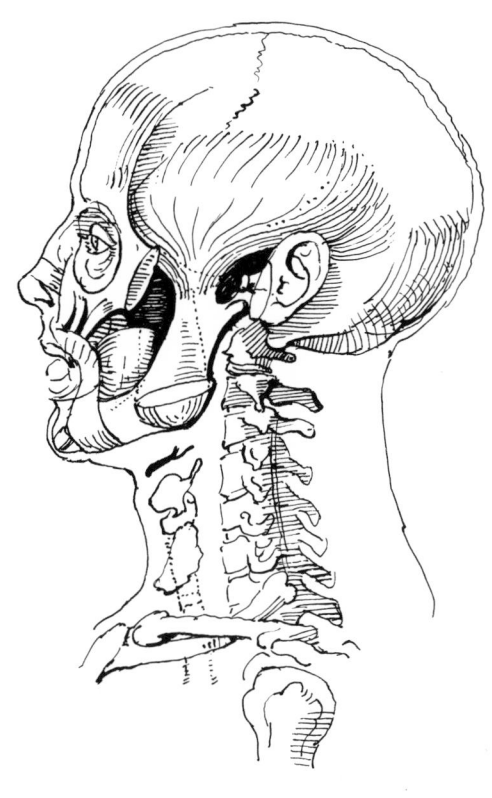

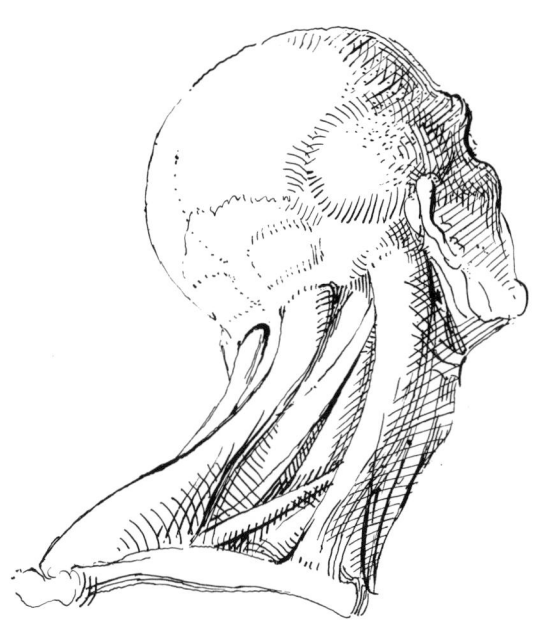

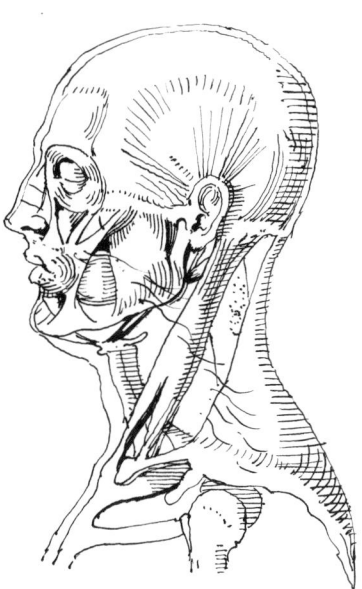

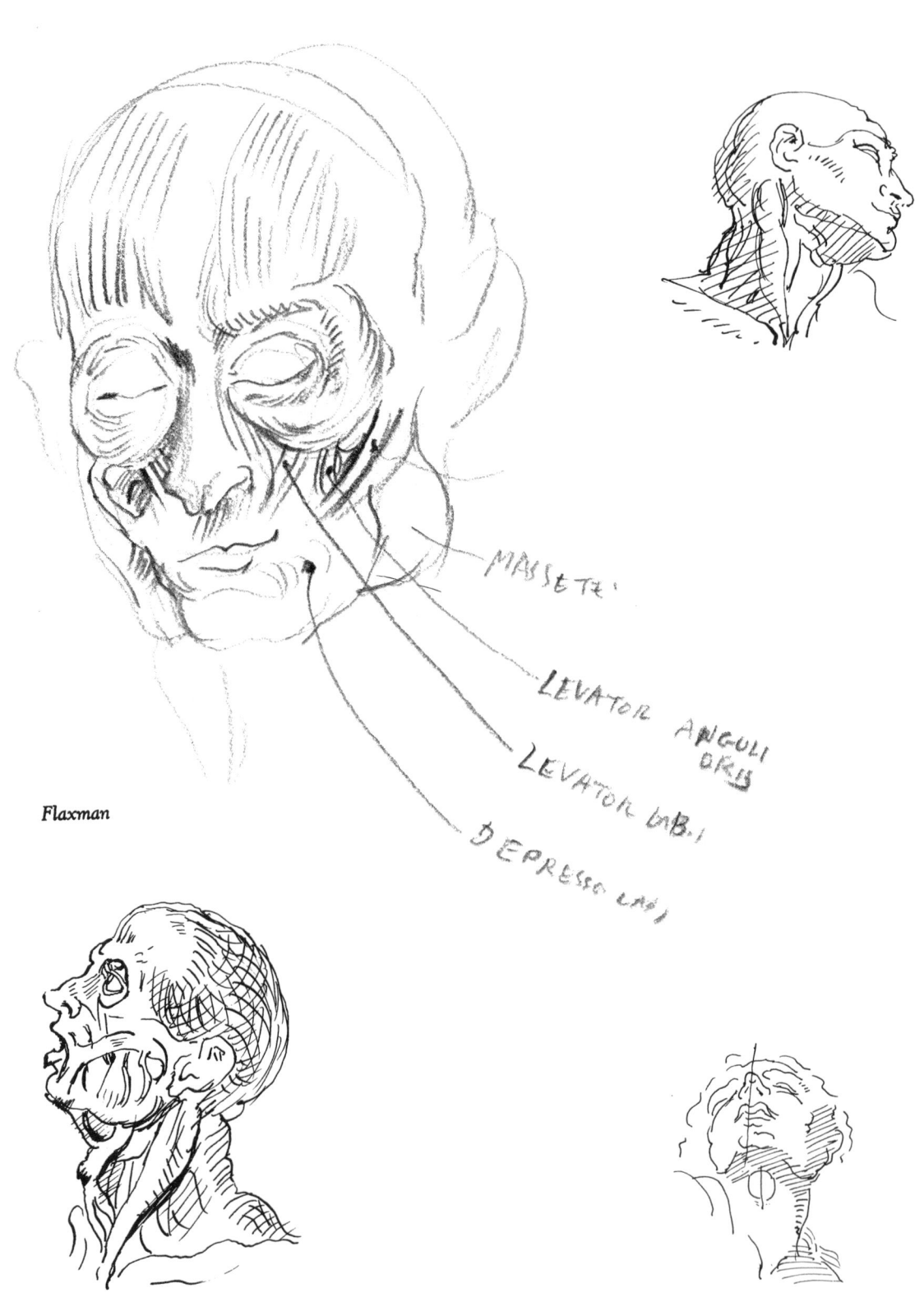

MASSETE'

LEVATOR ANGULI ORIS

LEVATOR LAB.

DEPRESSO LAB.

Flaxman

from an unpublished Italian
drawing—Cooper Union Museum

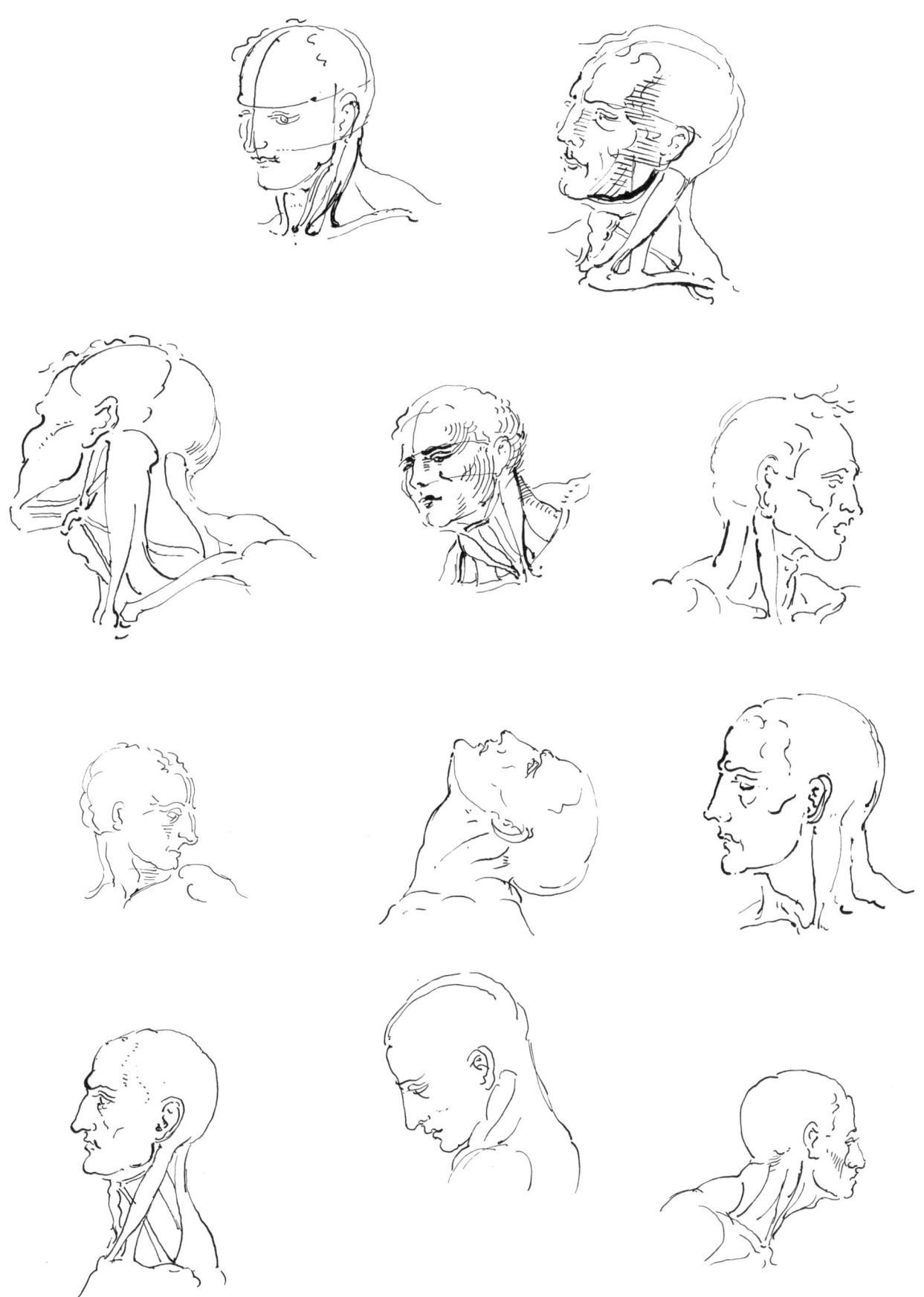

121

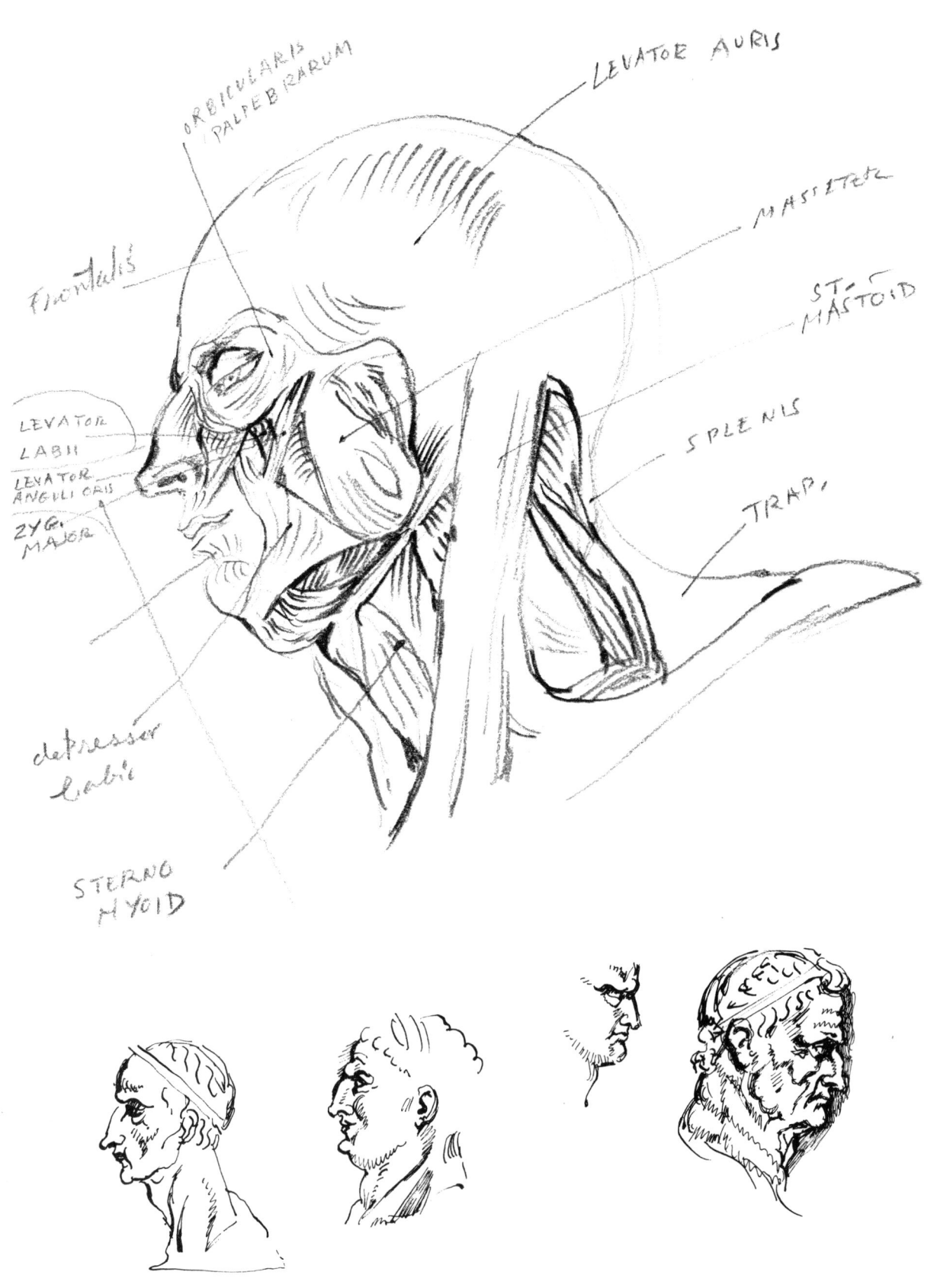

ORBICULARIS
PALPEBRARUM

LEVATOE AURIS

Frontalis

MASSETER

ST-
MASTOID

LEVATOR
LABII

LEVATOR
ANGULI ORIS

ZYG.
MAJOR

SPLENIS

TRAP.

depressor
labii

STERNO
HYOID

after Rubens after antique coins

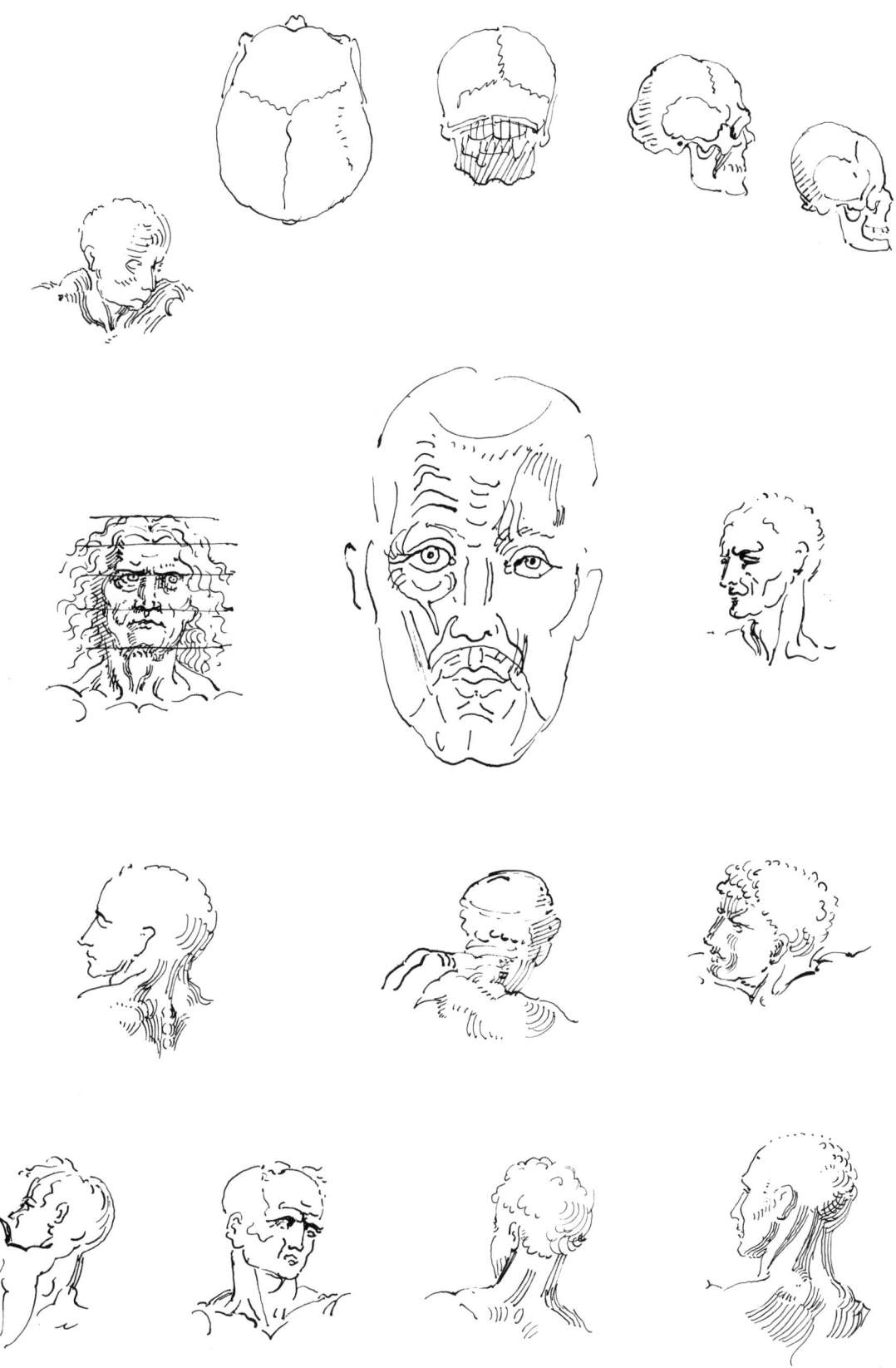

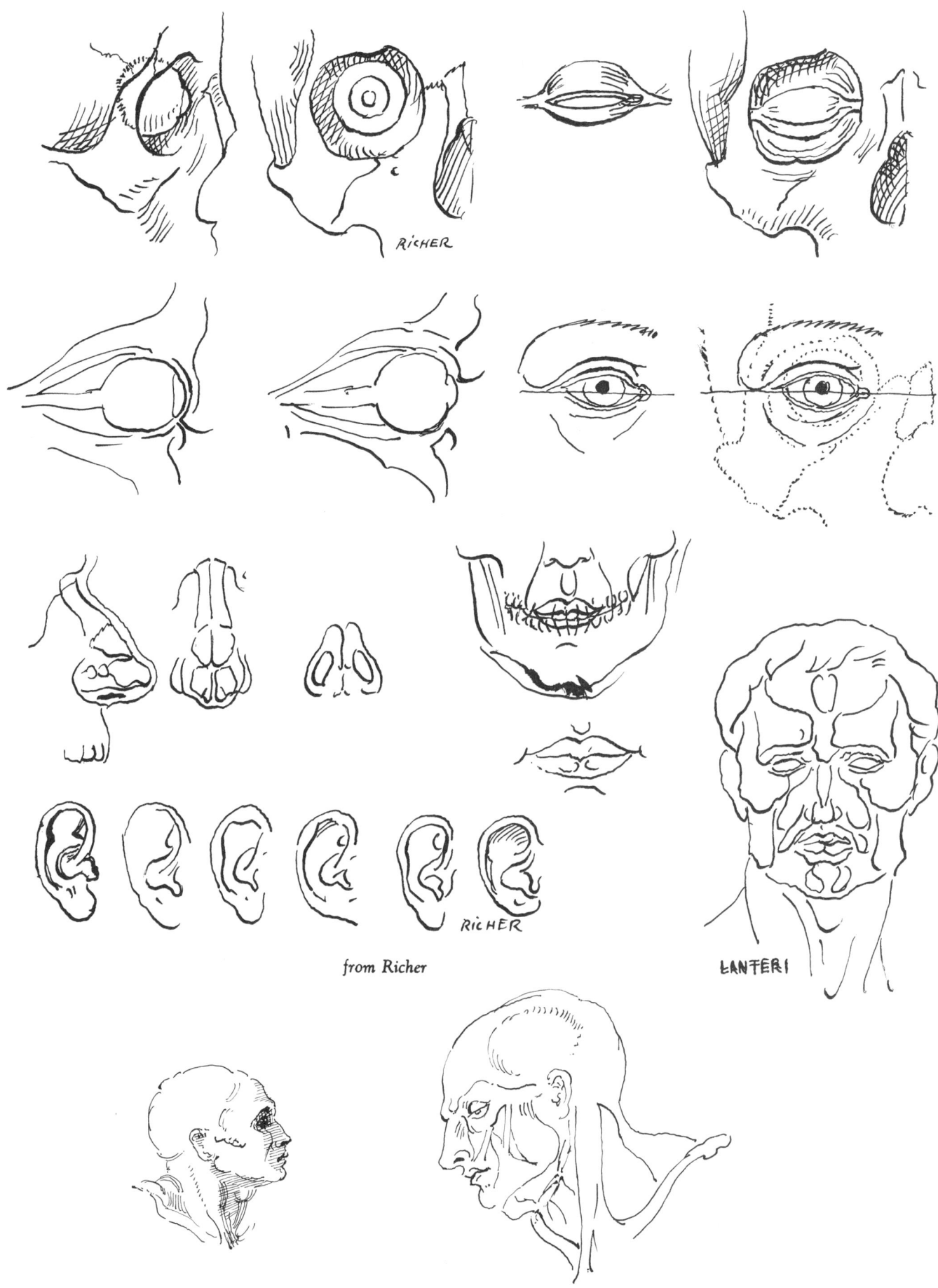

RICHER

from Richer

RICHER

LANTERI

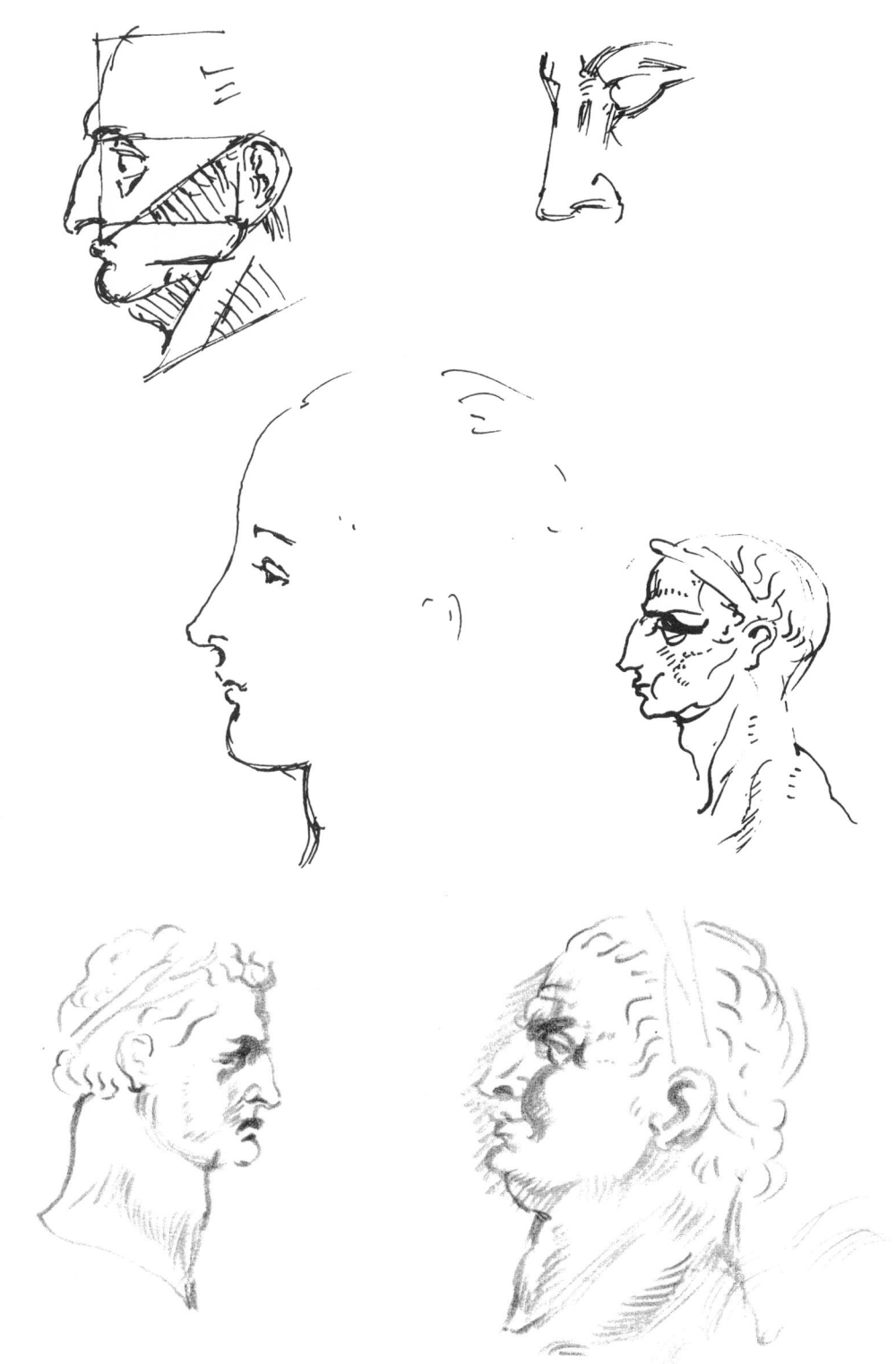

from Rubens

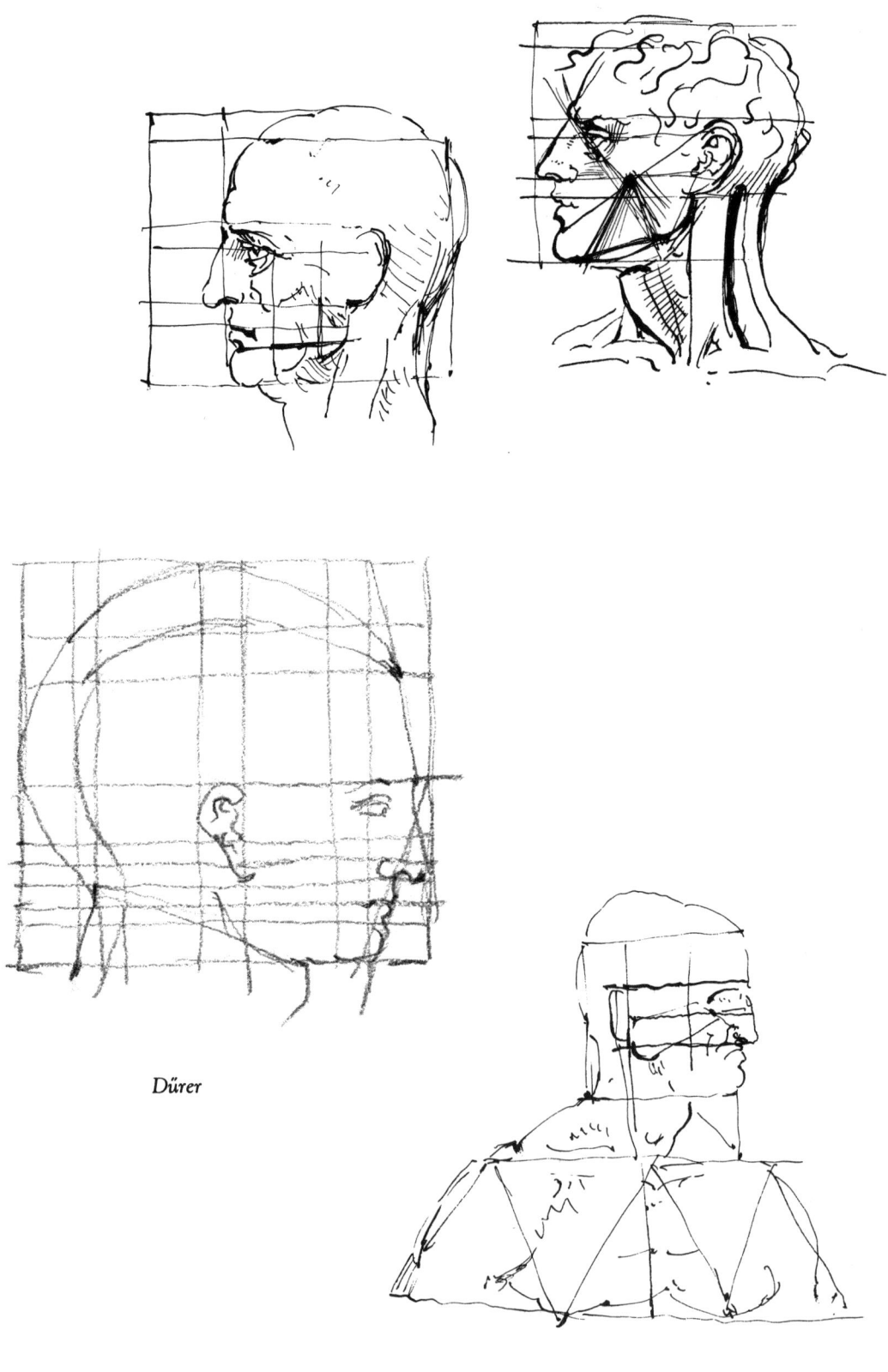

Dürer

da Vinci

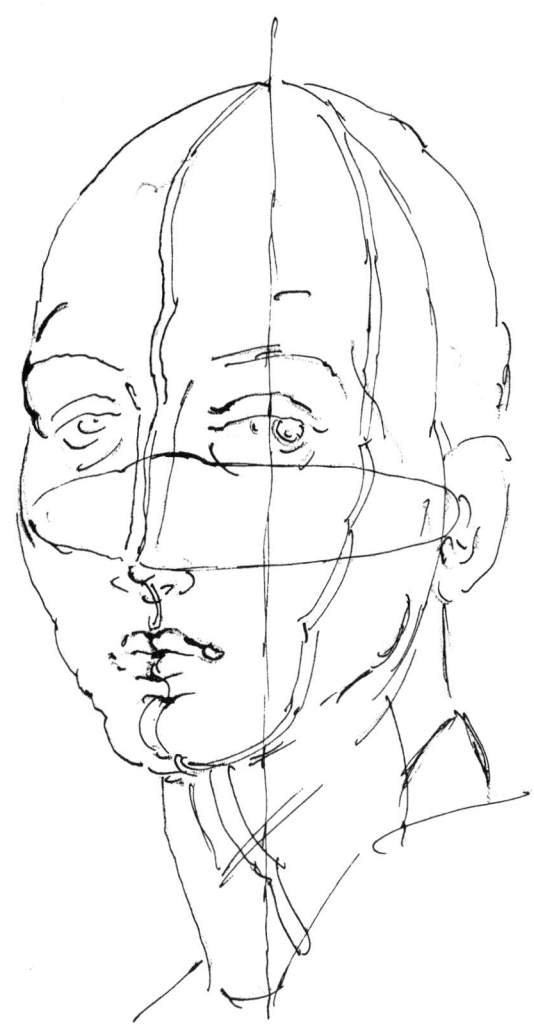

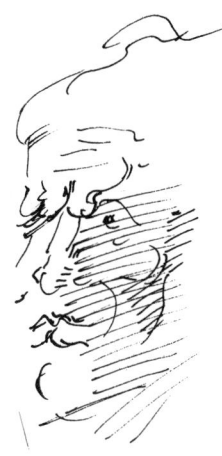

Raphael's drawing
cross sectioned
by Alston

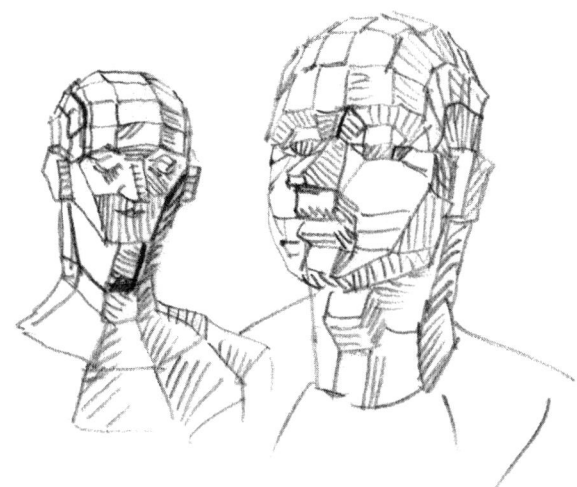

from Dürer

127

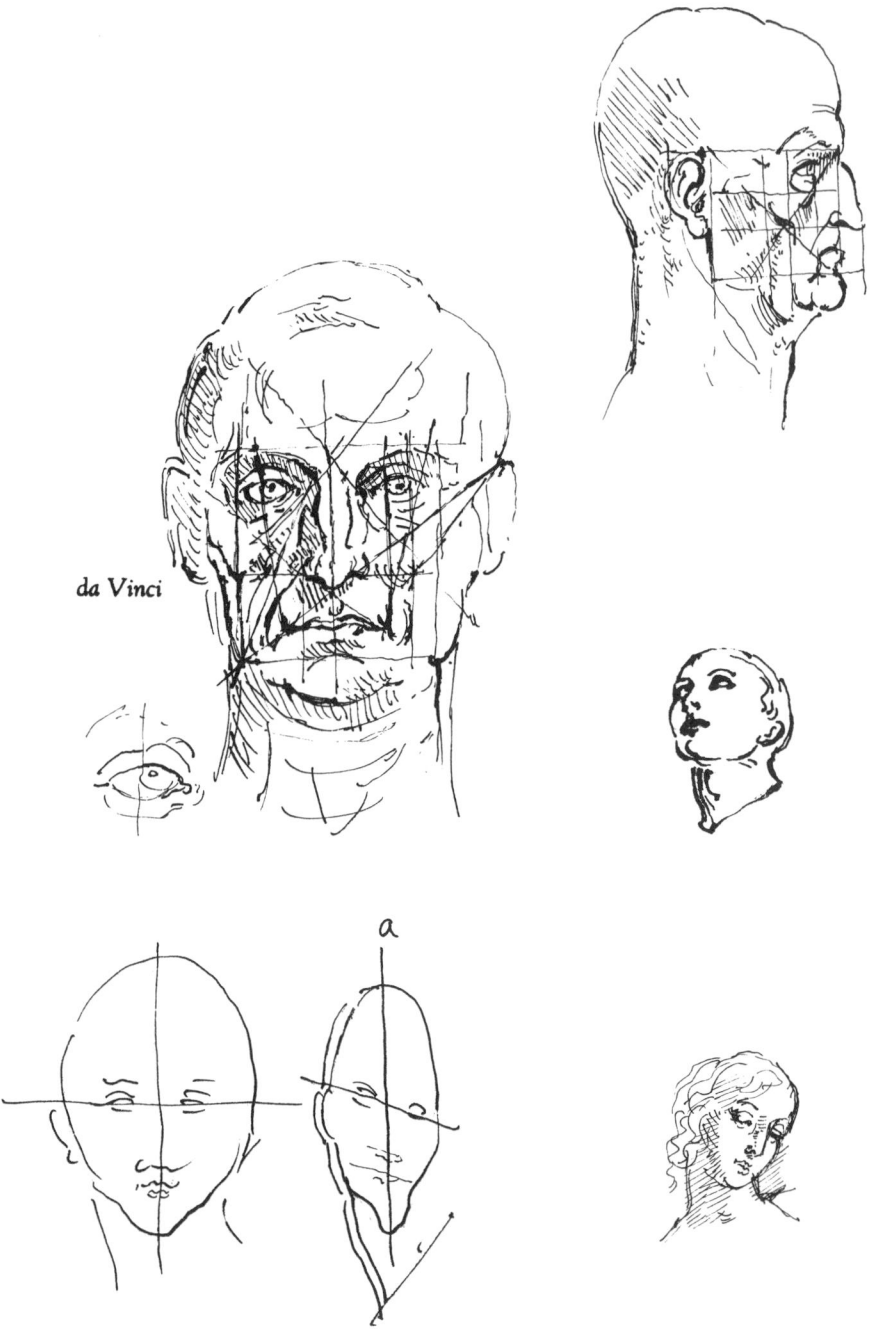

da Vinci

a

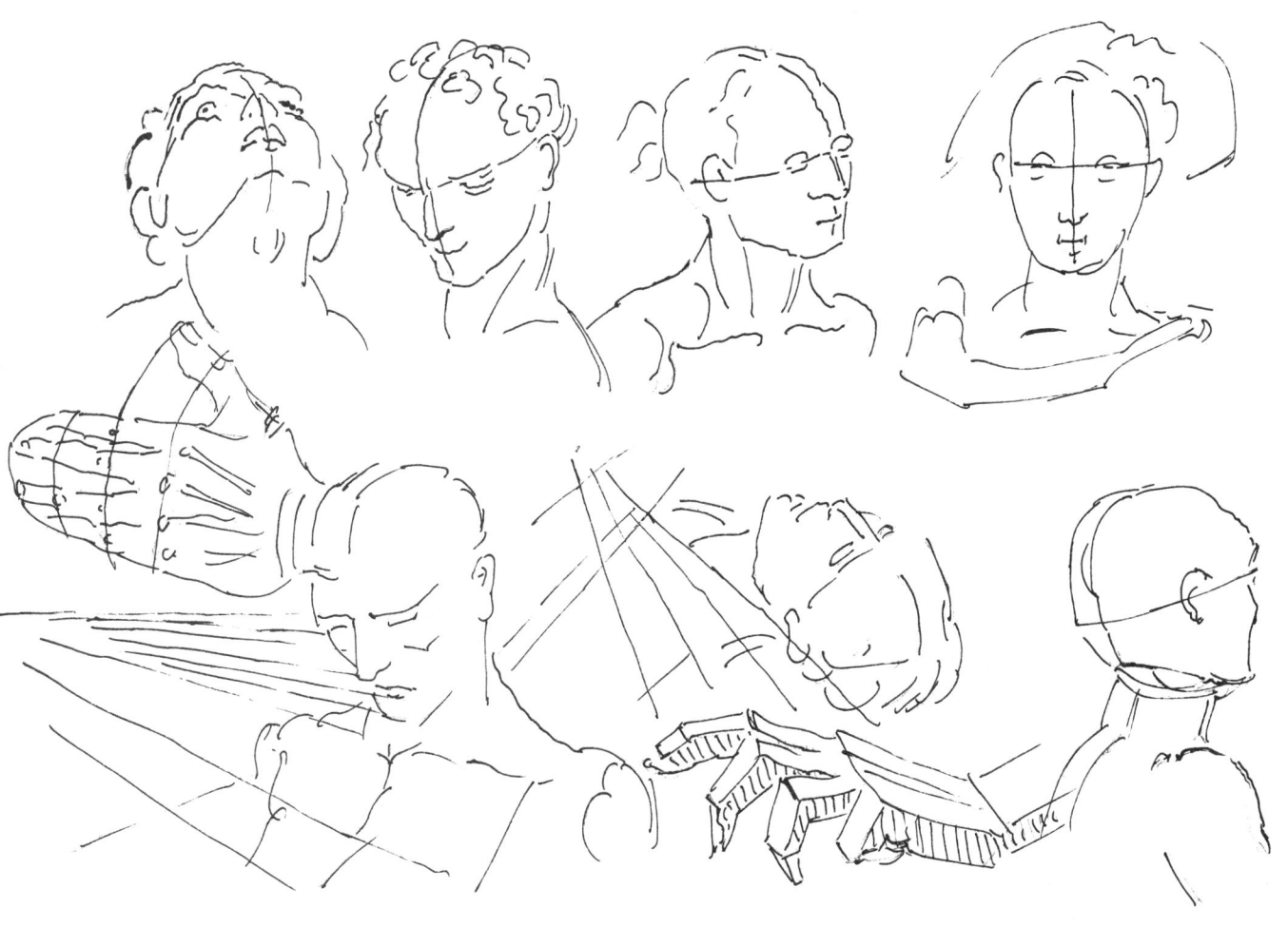

from Holbein

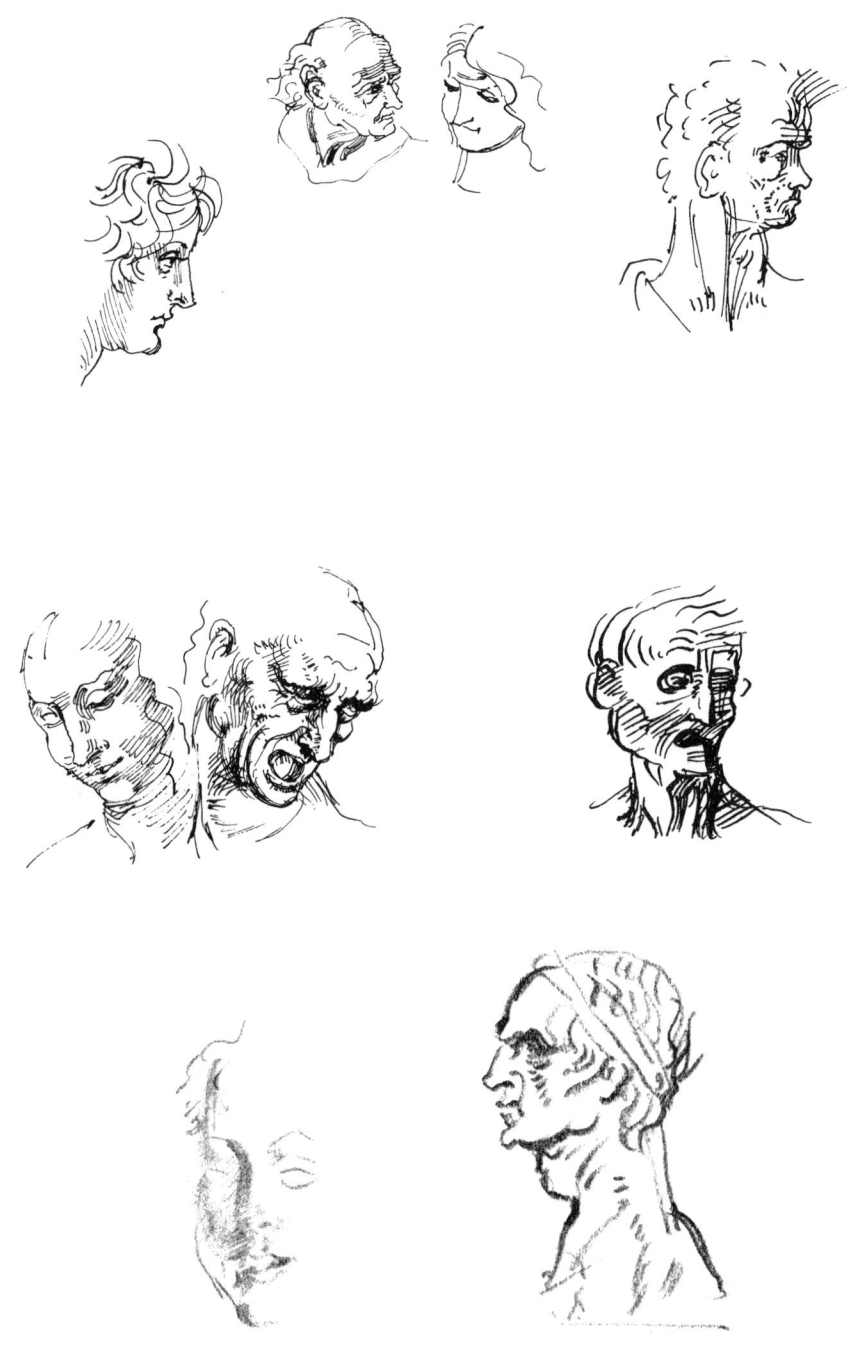

from Michelangelo—da Vinci—Rubens

Arms-Hands

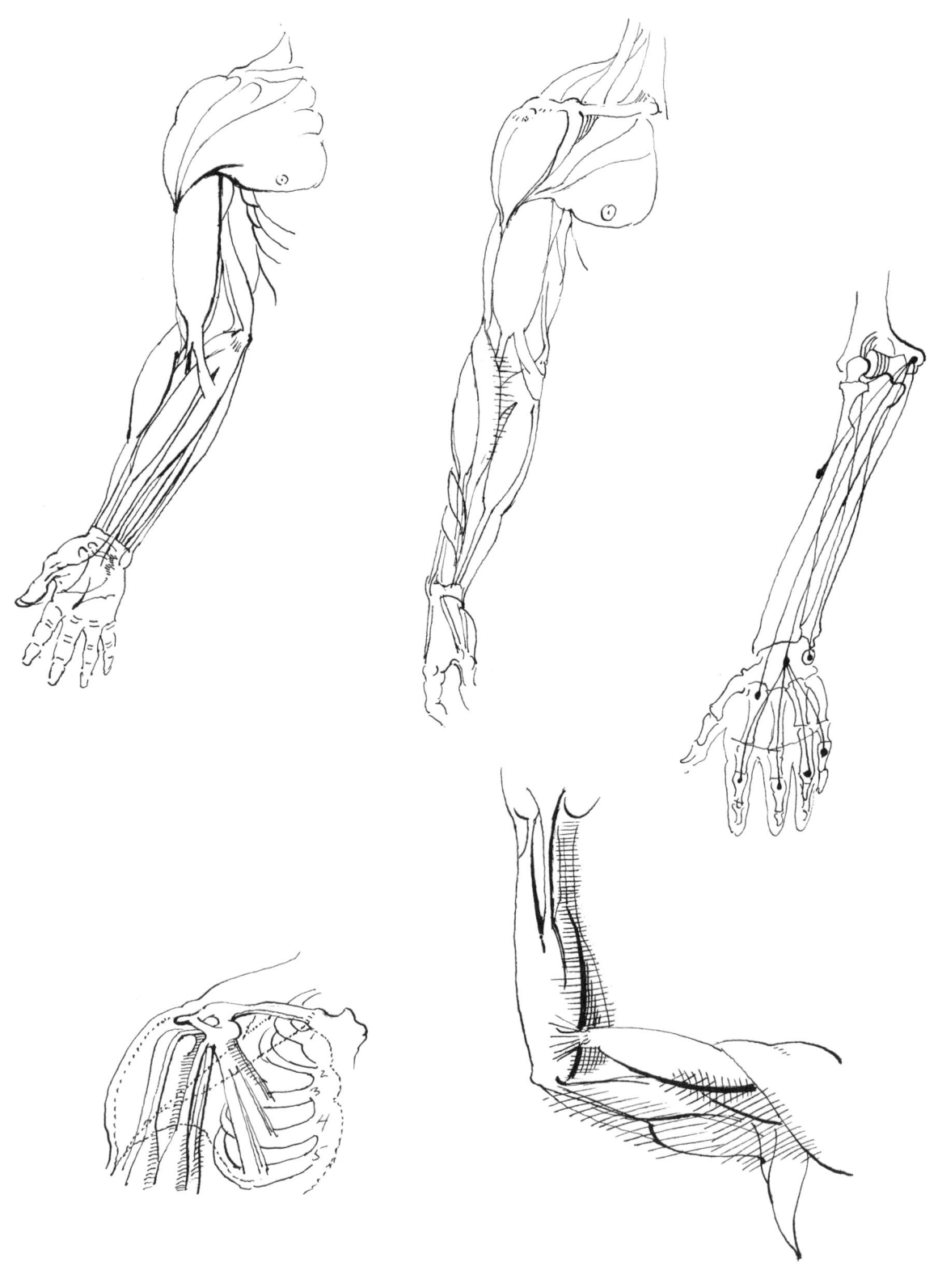

composite derivations
from Richer and Thomson
next 4 pages

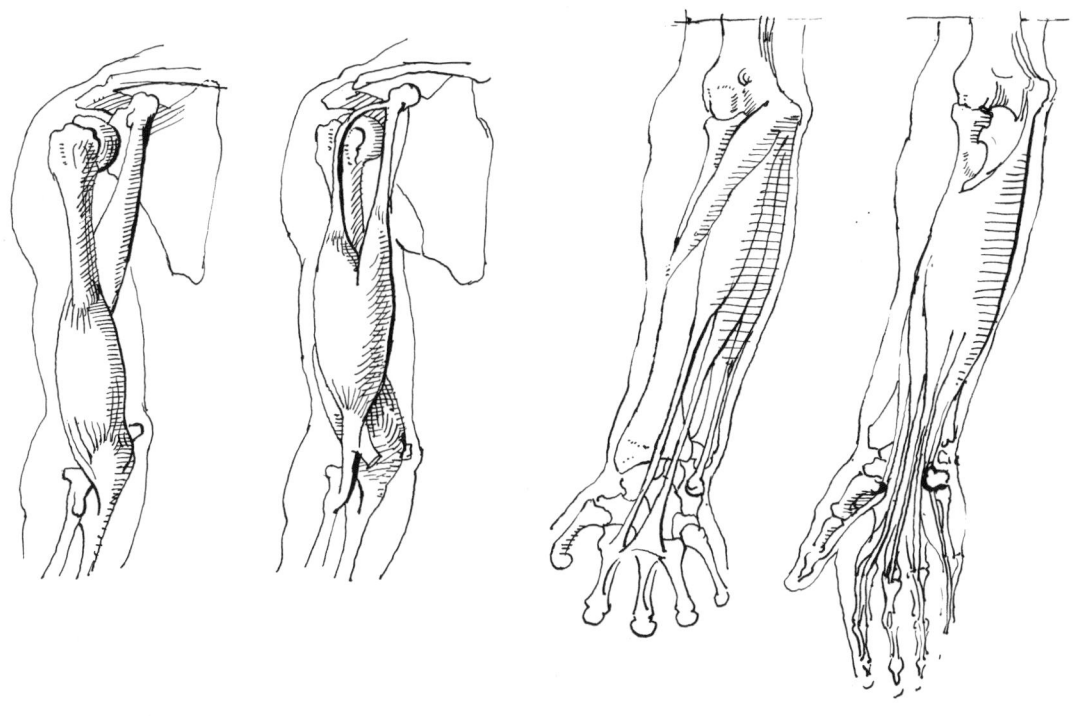

pronation and supination

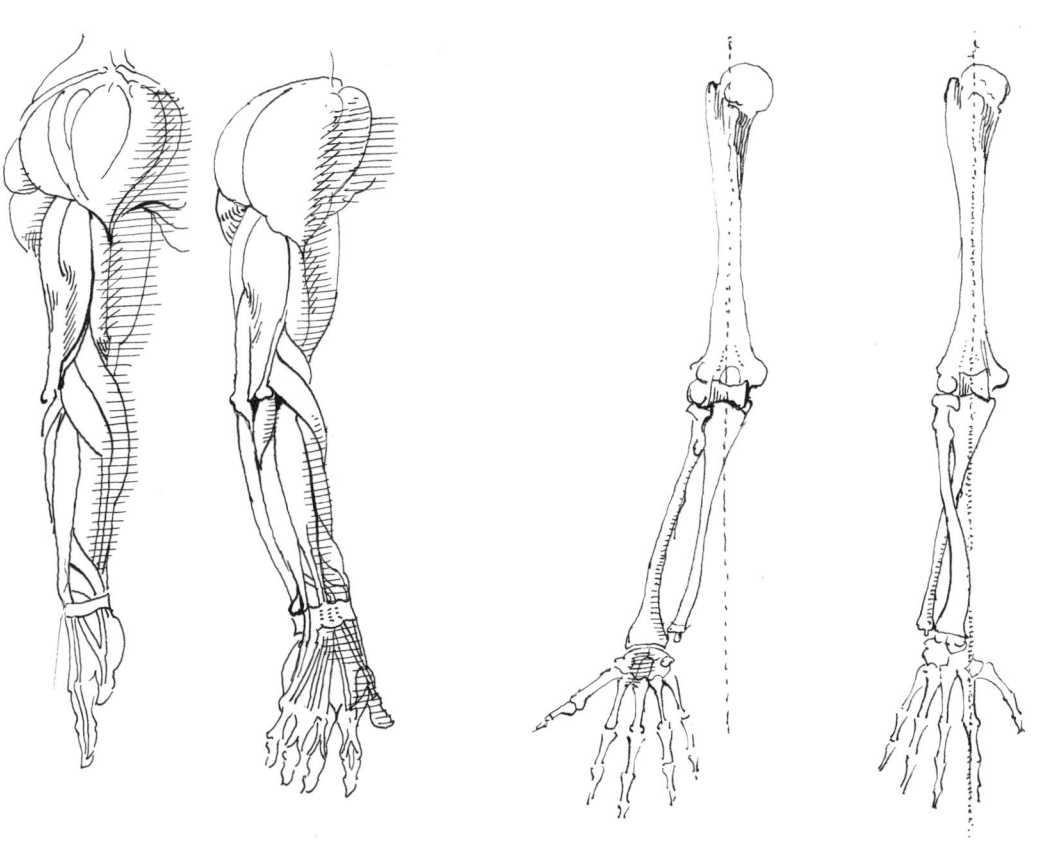

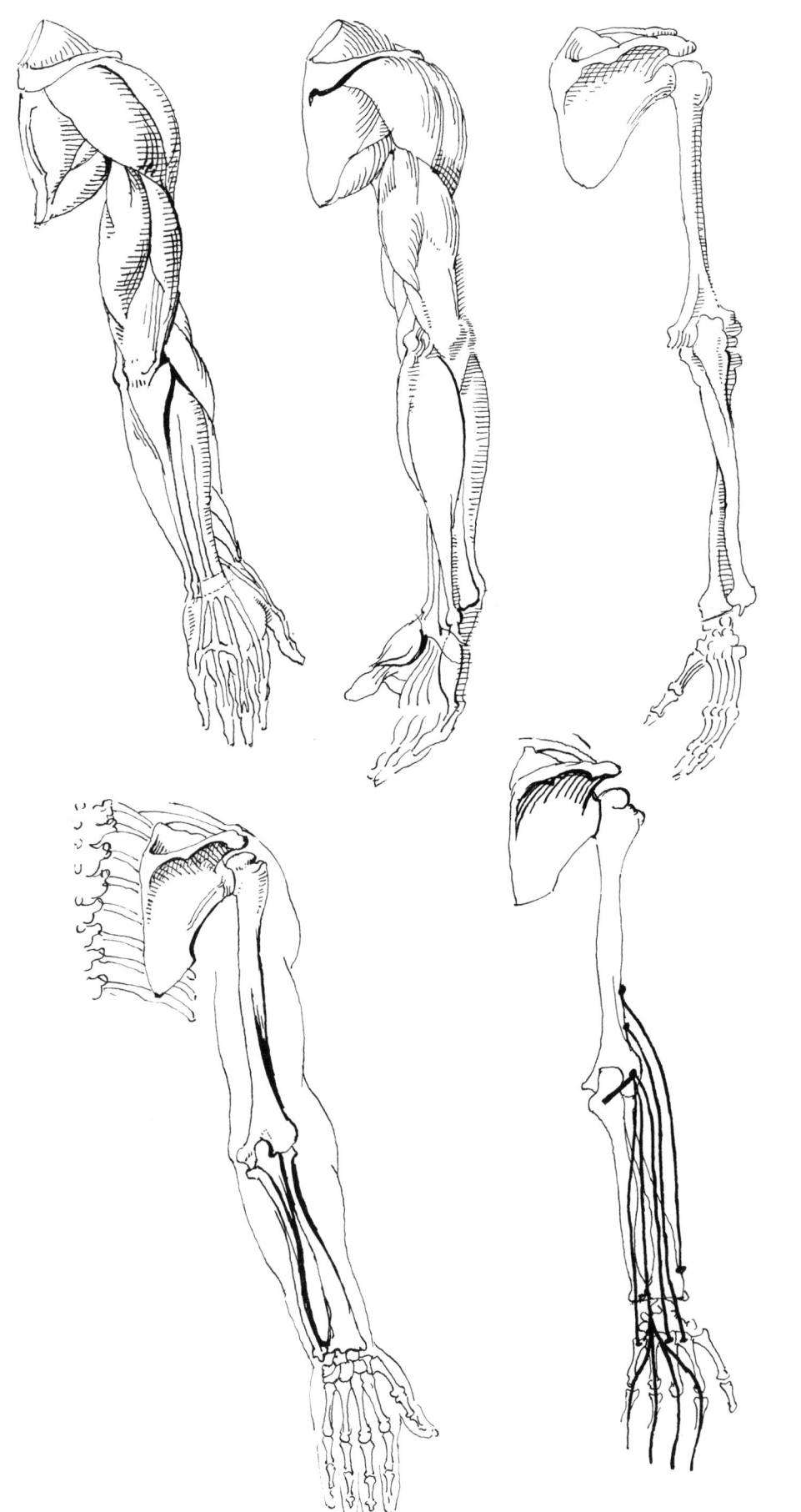

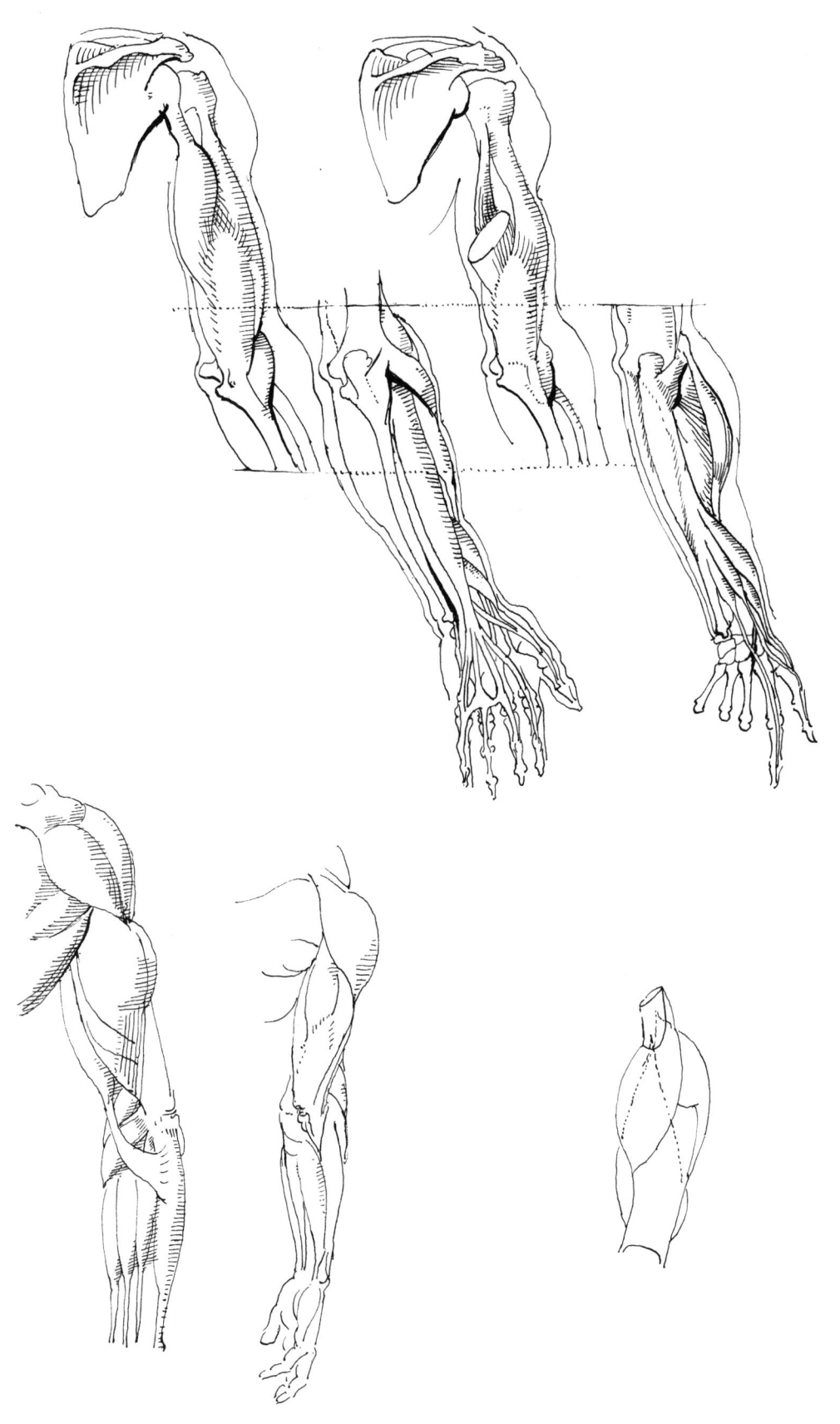

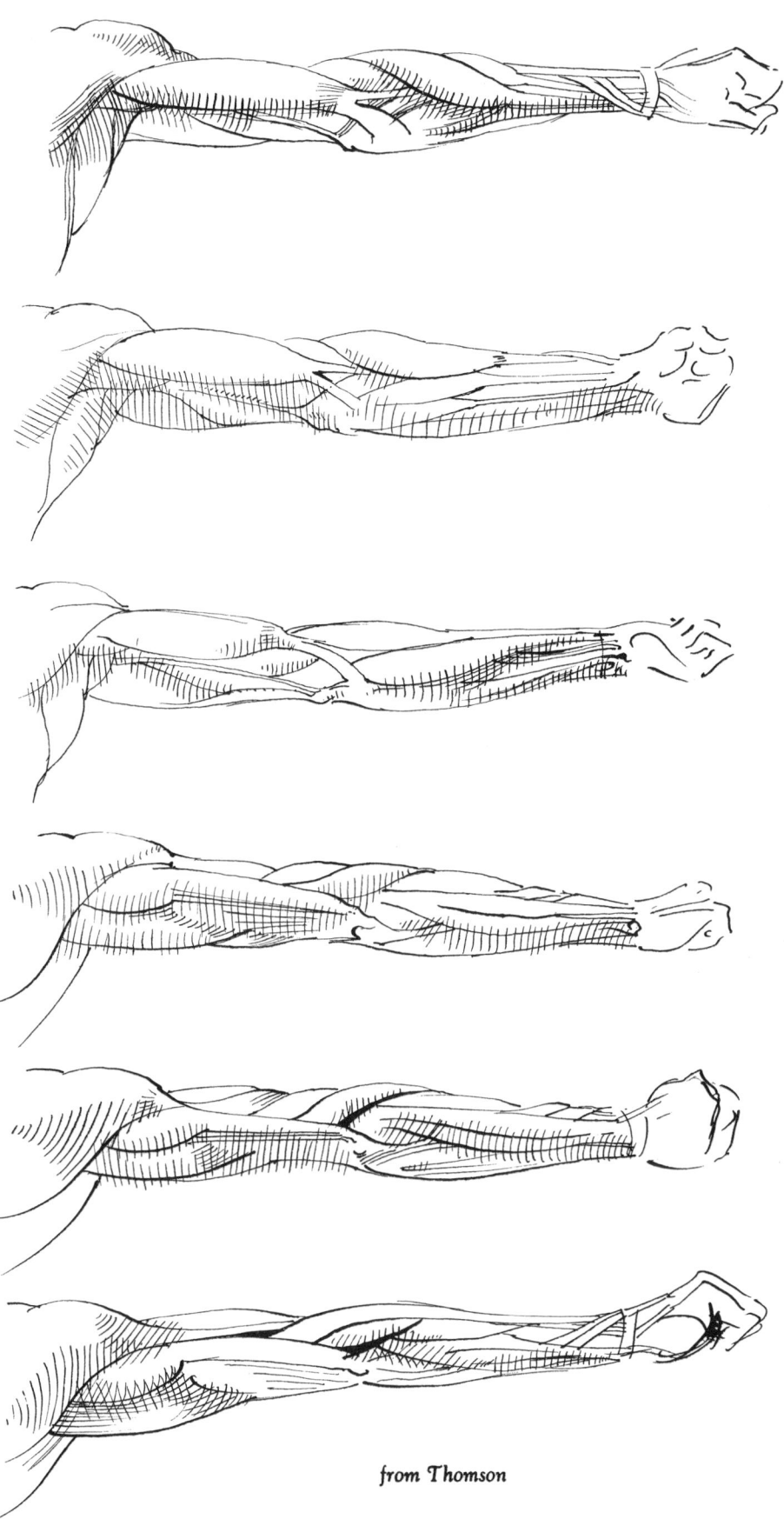

from Thomson

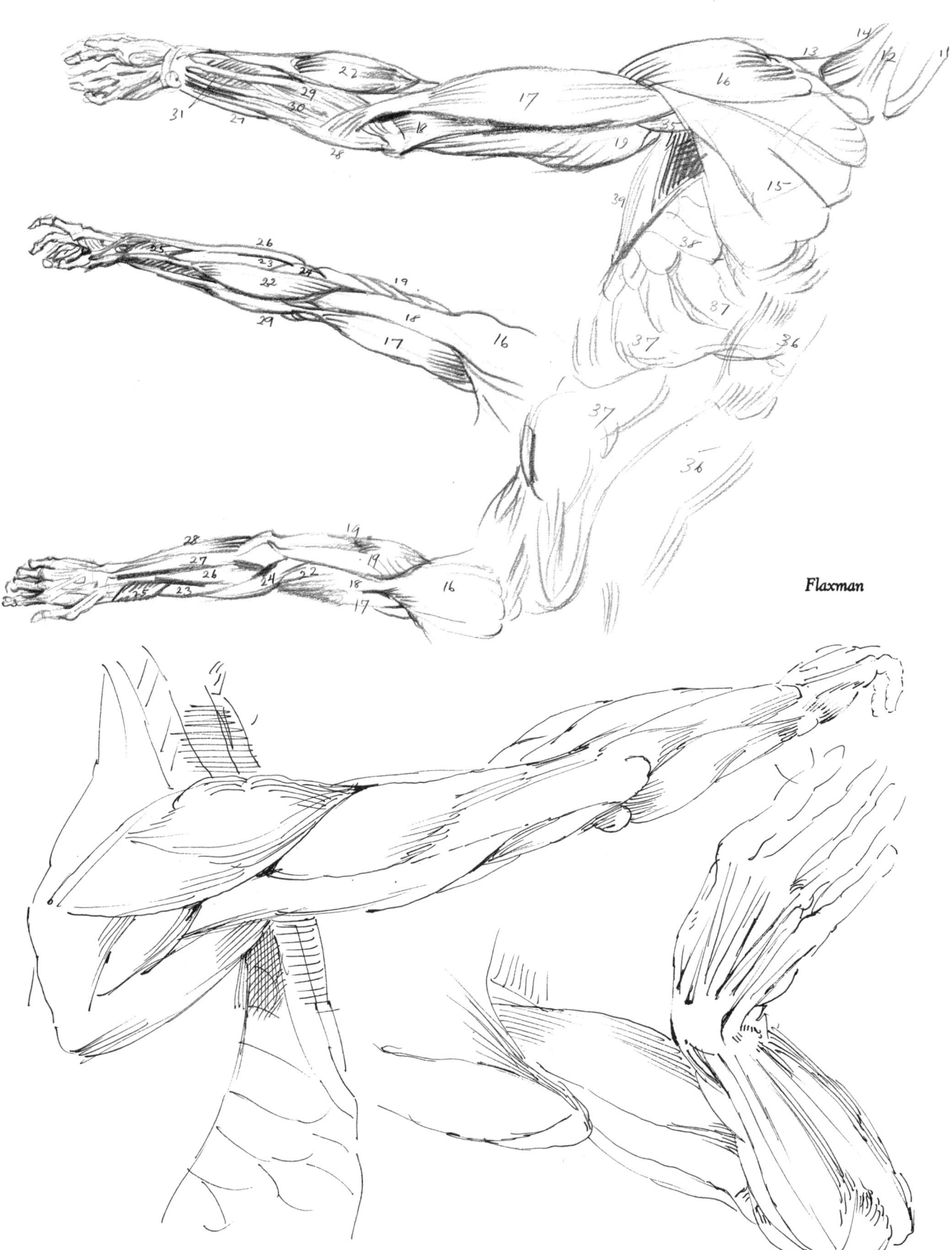

Flaxman

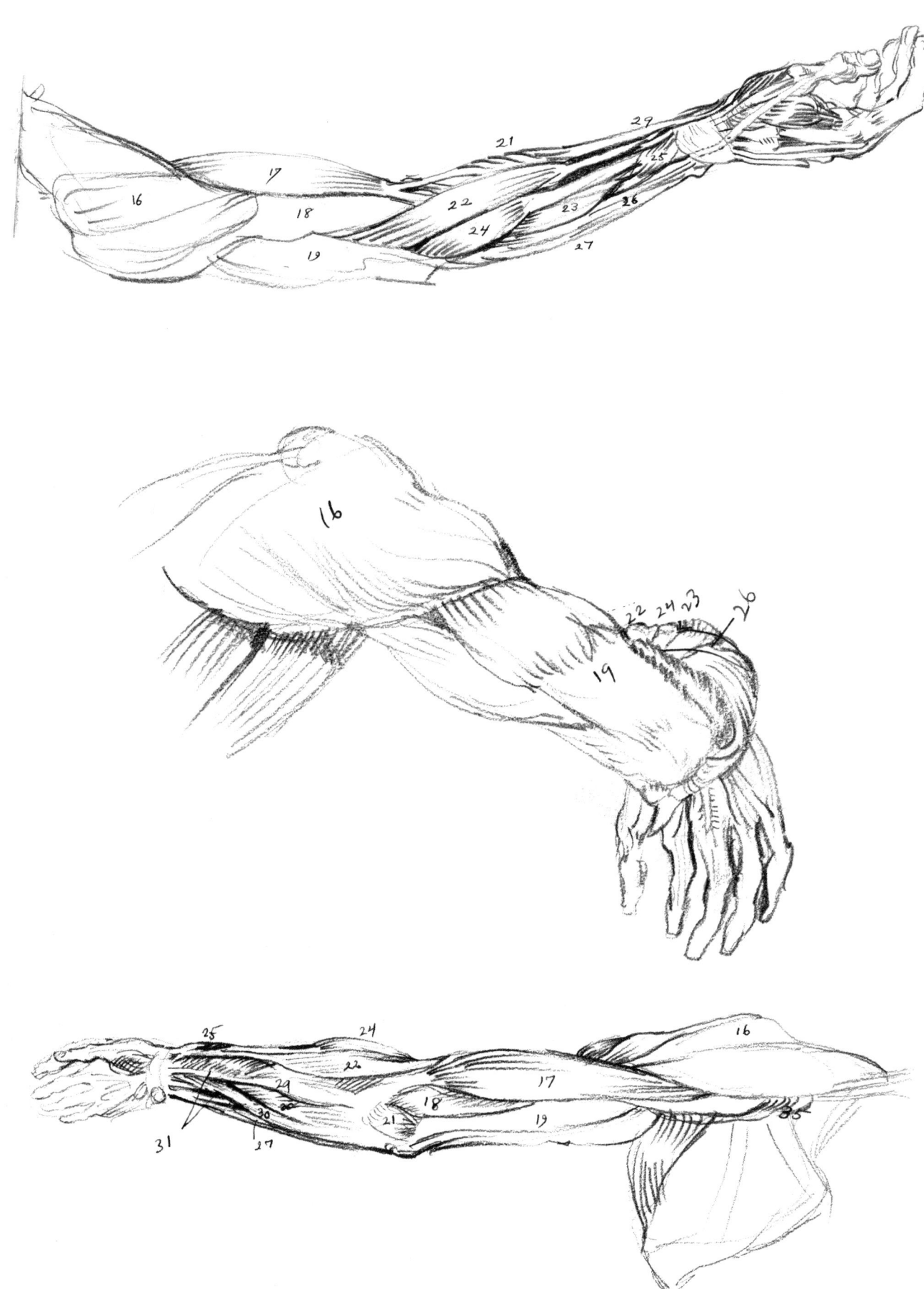

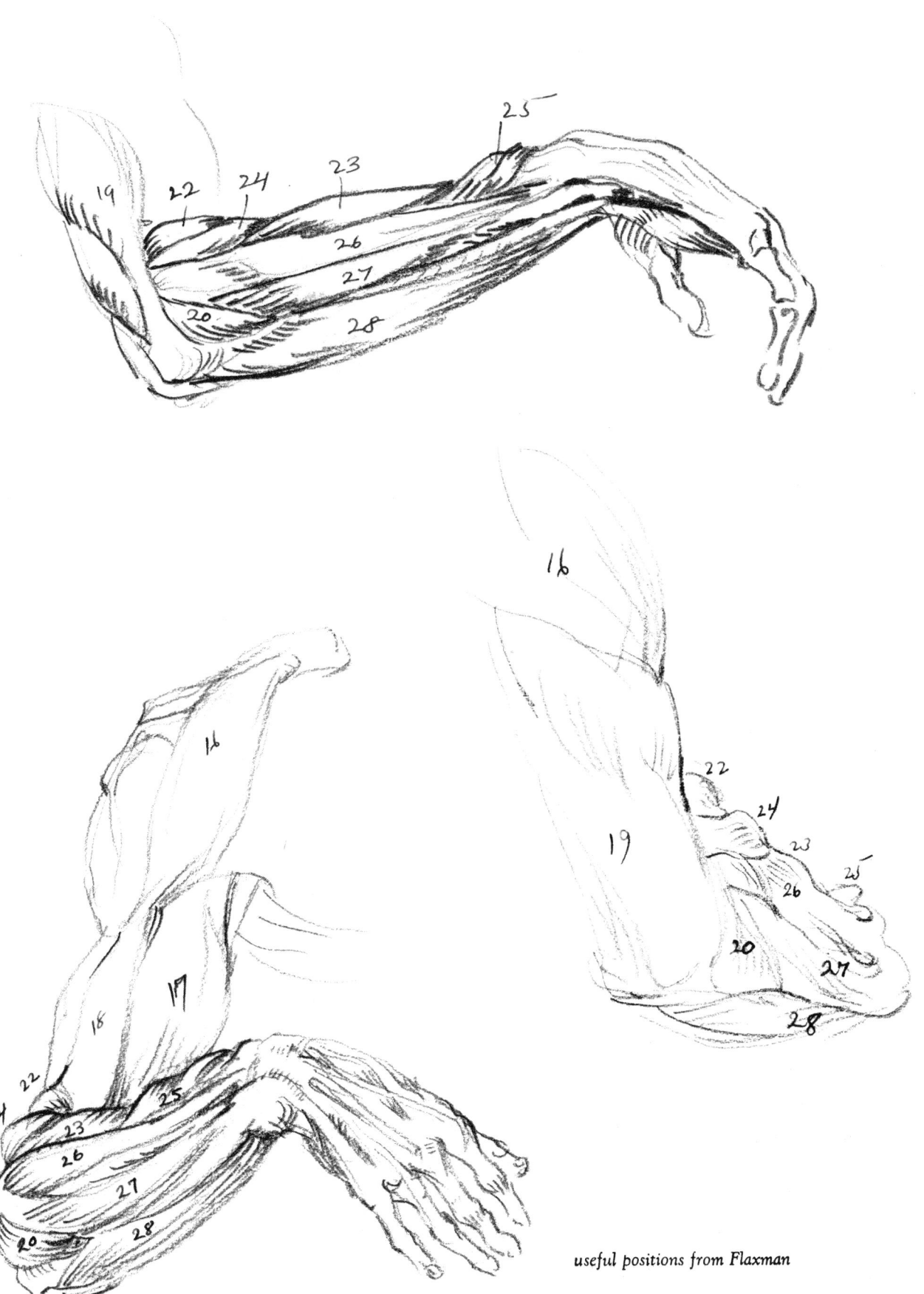

useful positions from Flaxman

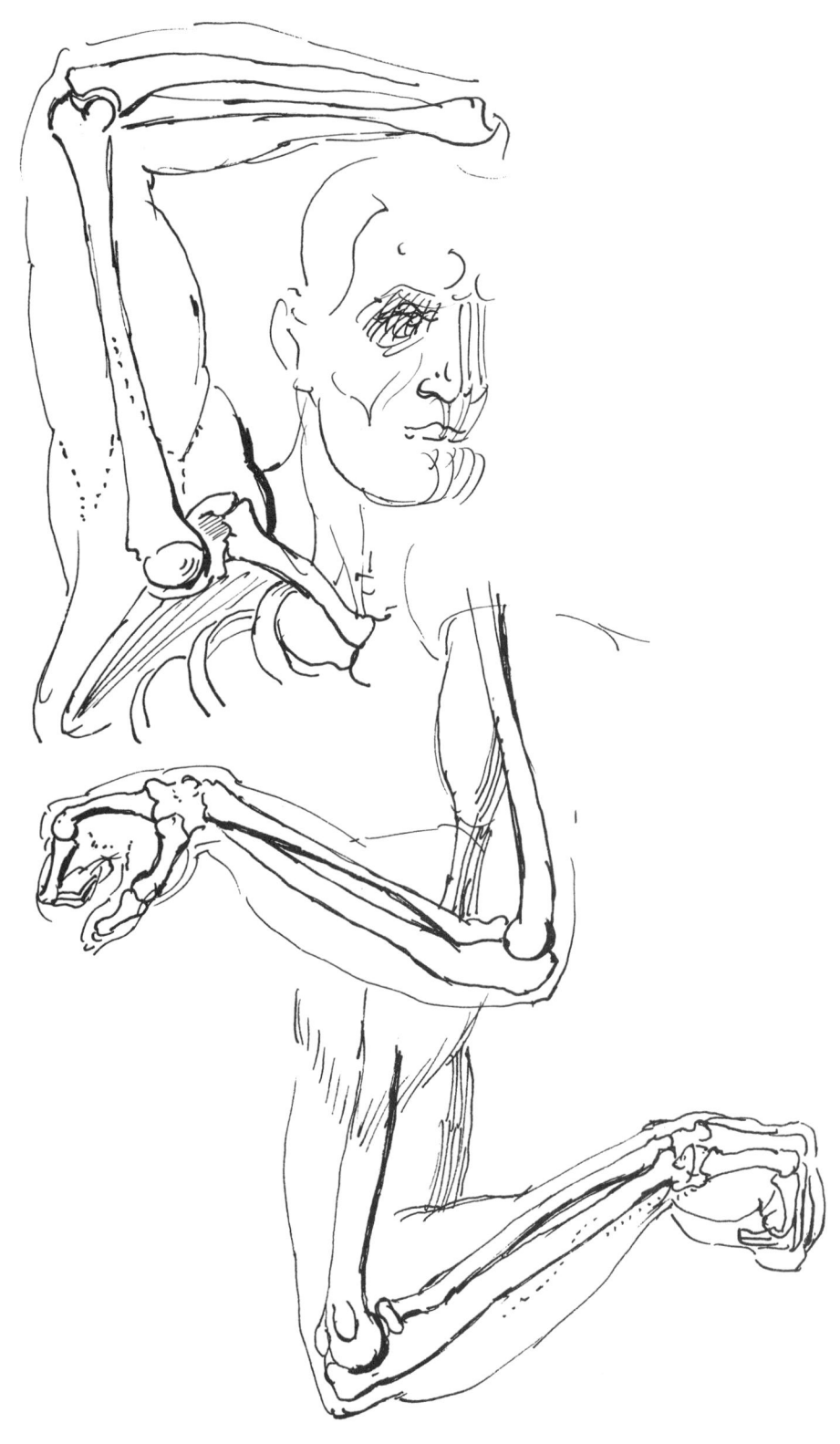

after Fau

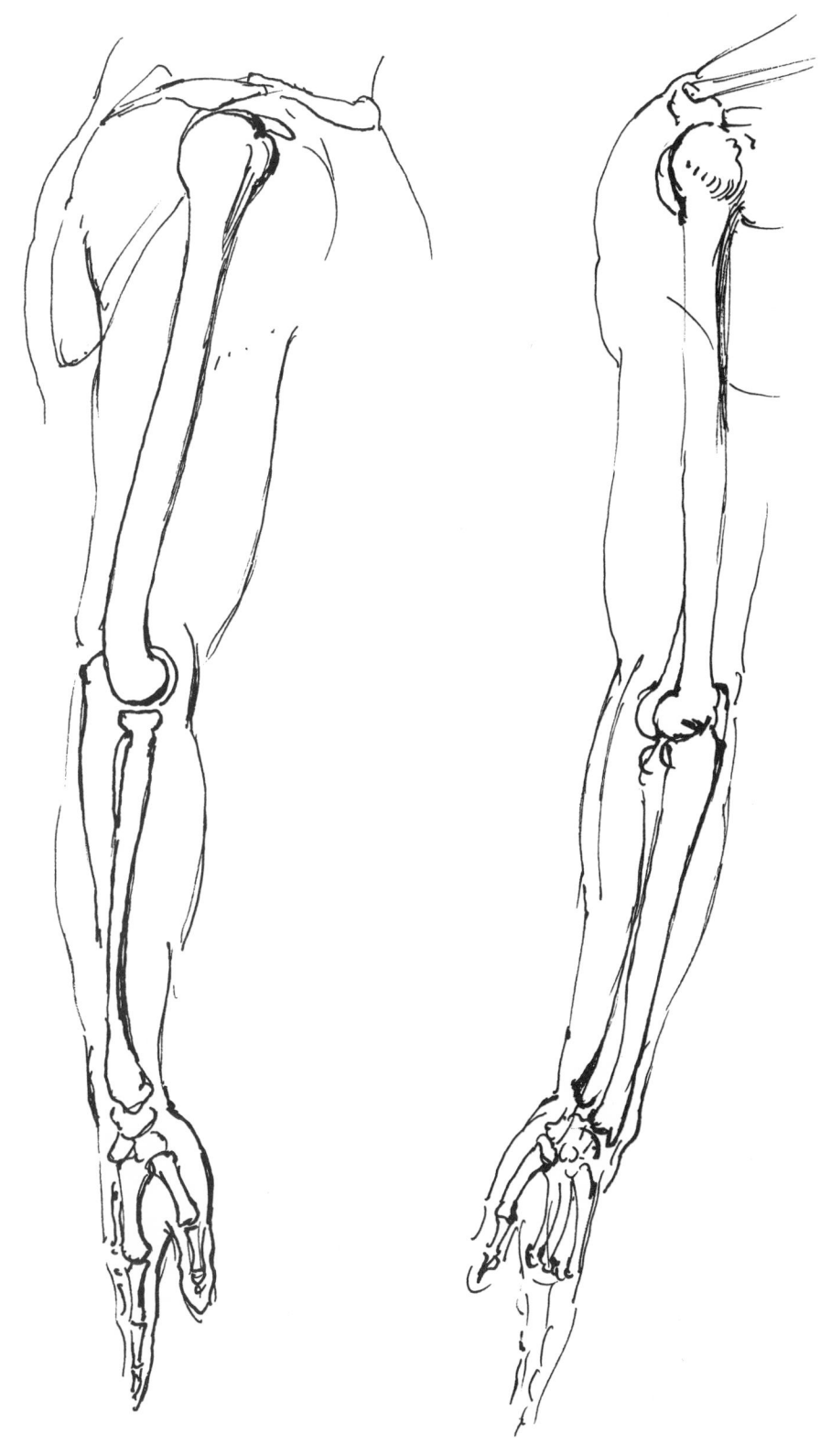

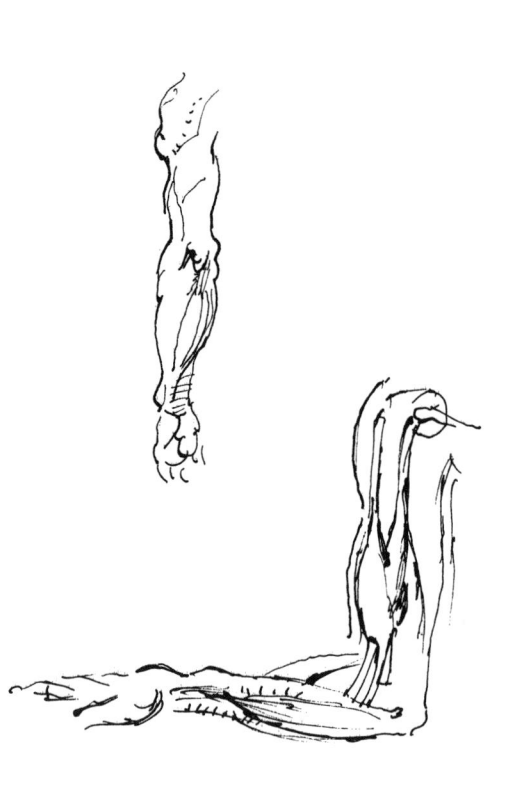

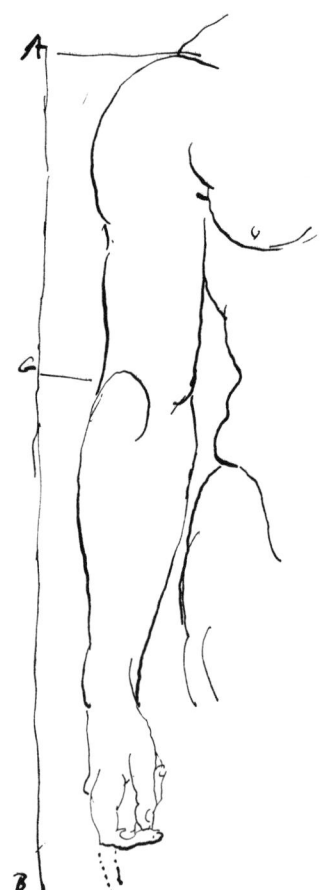

Dürer

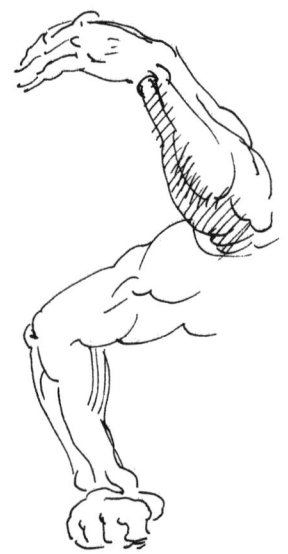

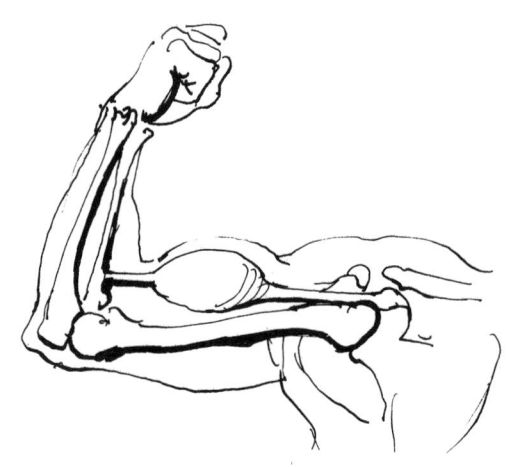

Michelangelo

biceps

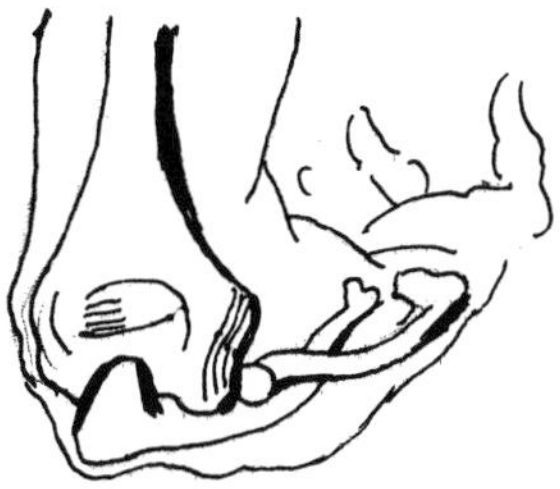

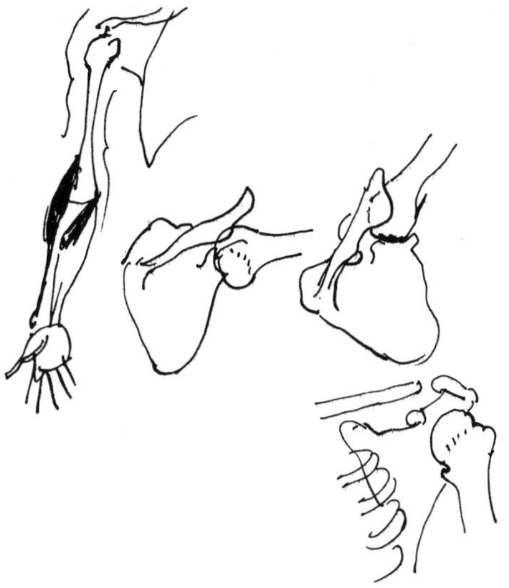

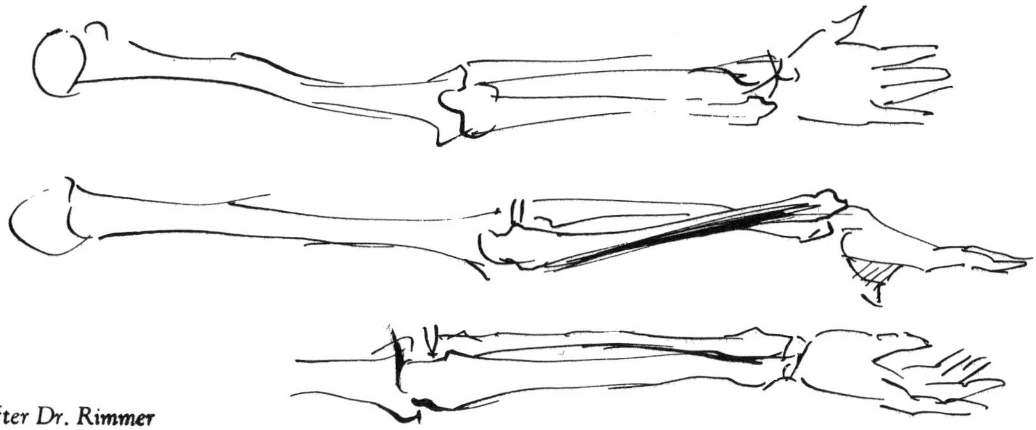

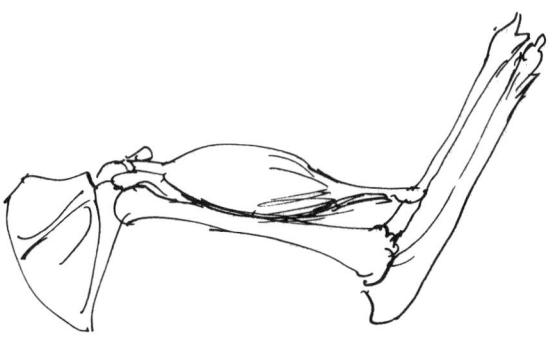

after Dr. Rimmer

biceps

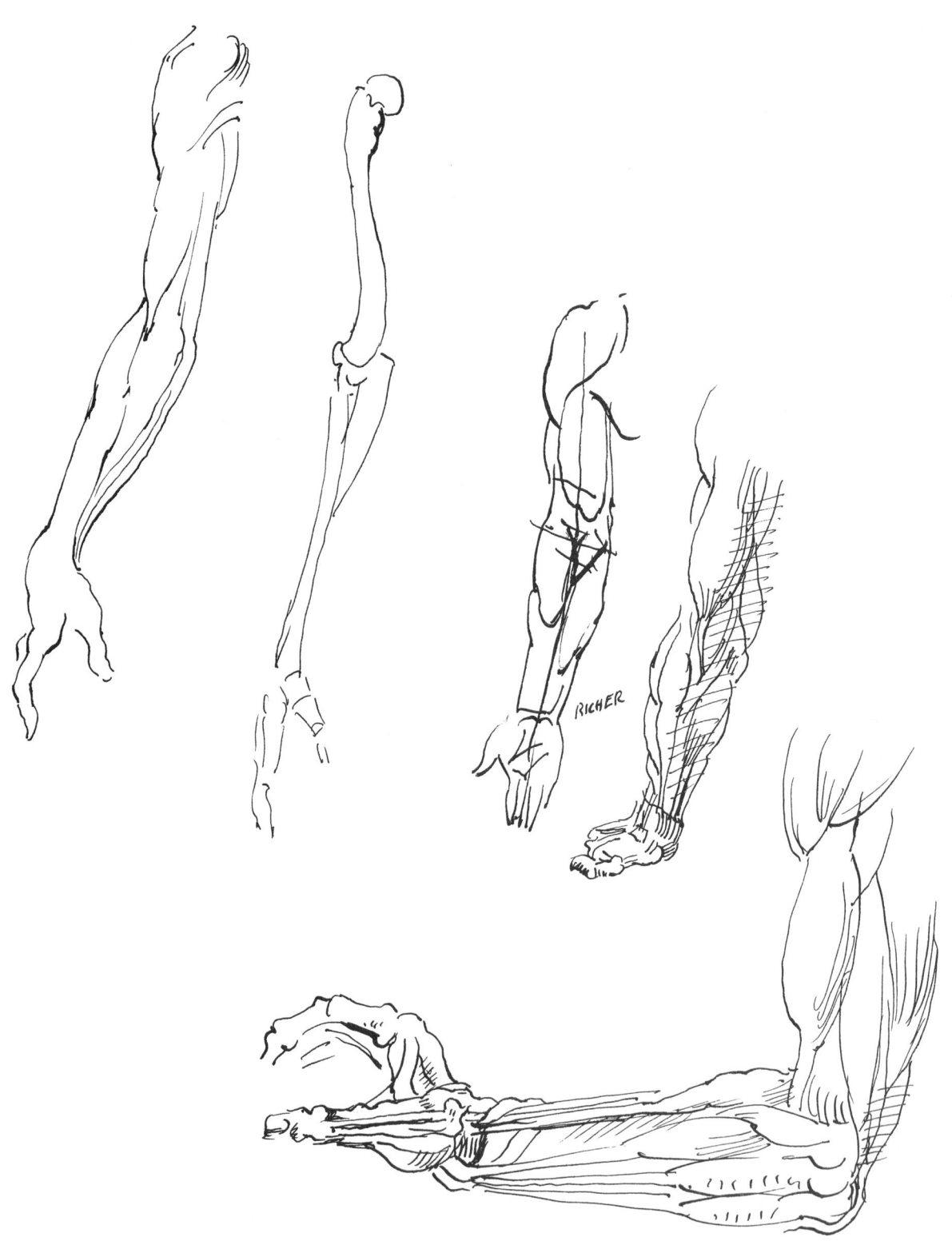

from unpublished
Italian originals in
Cooper Union Museum.

RICHER

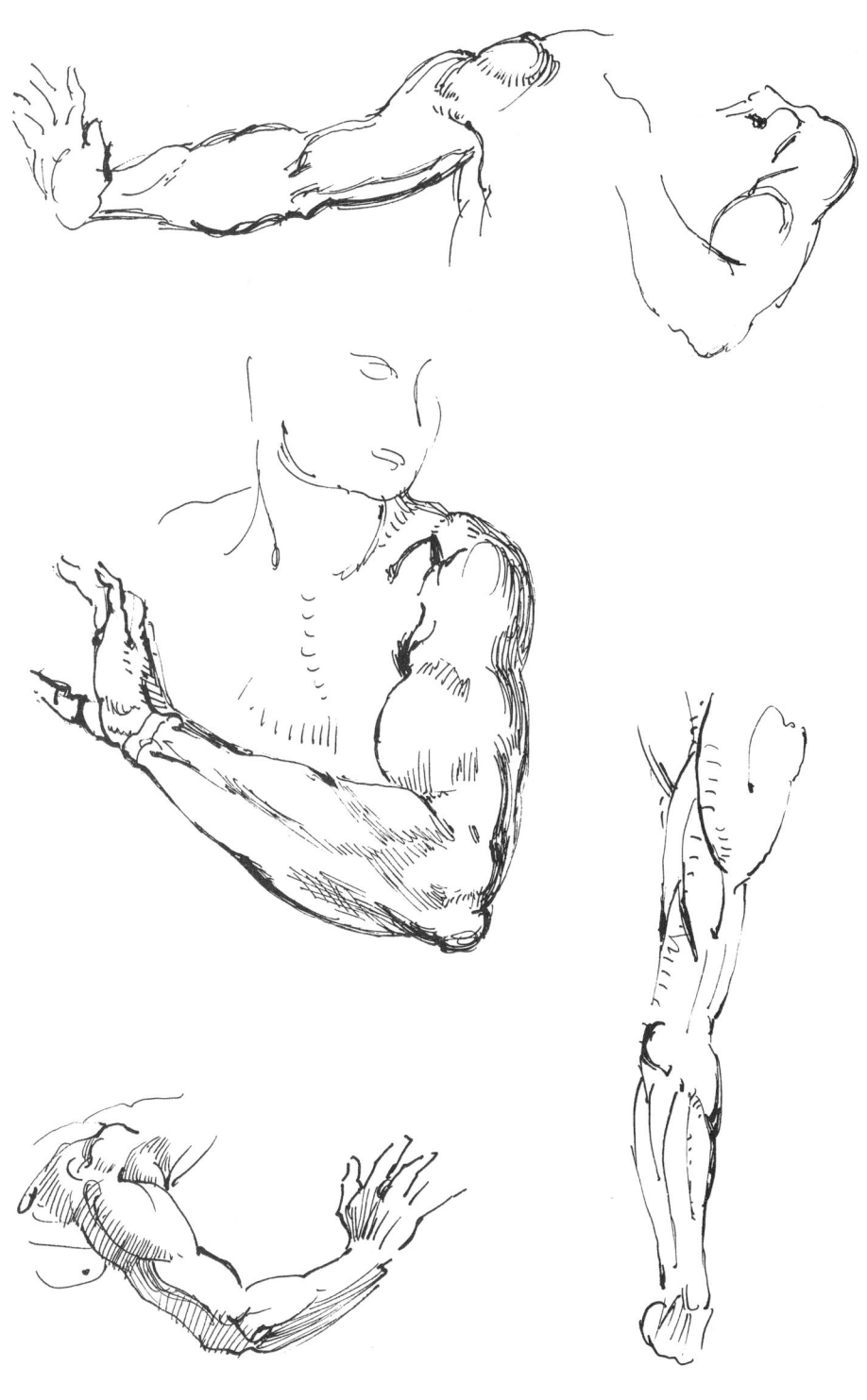

Michelangelo

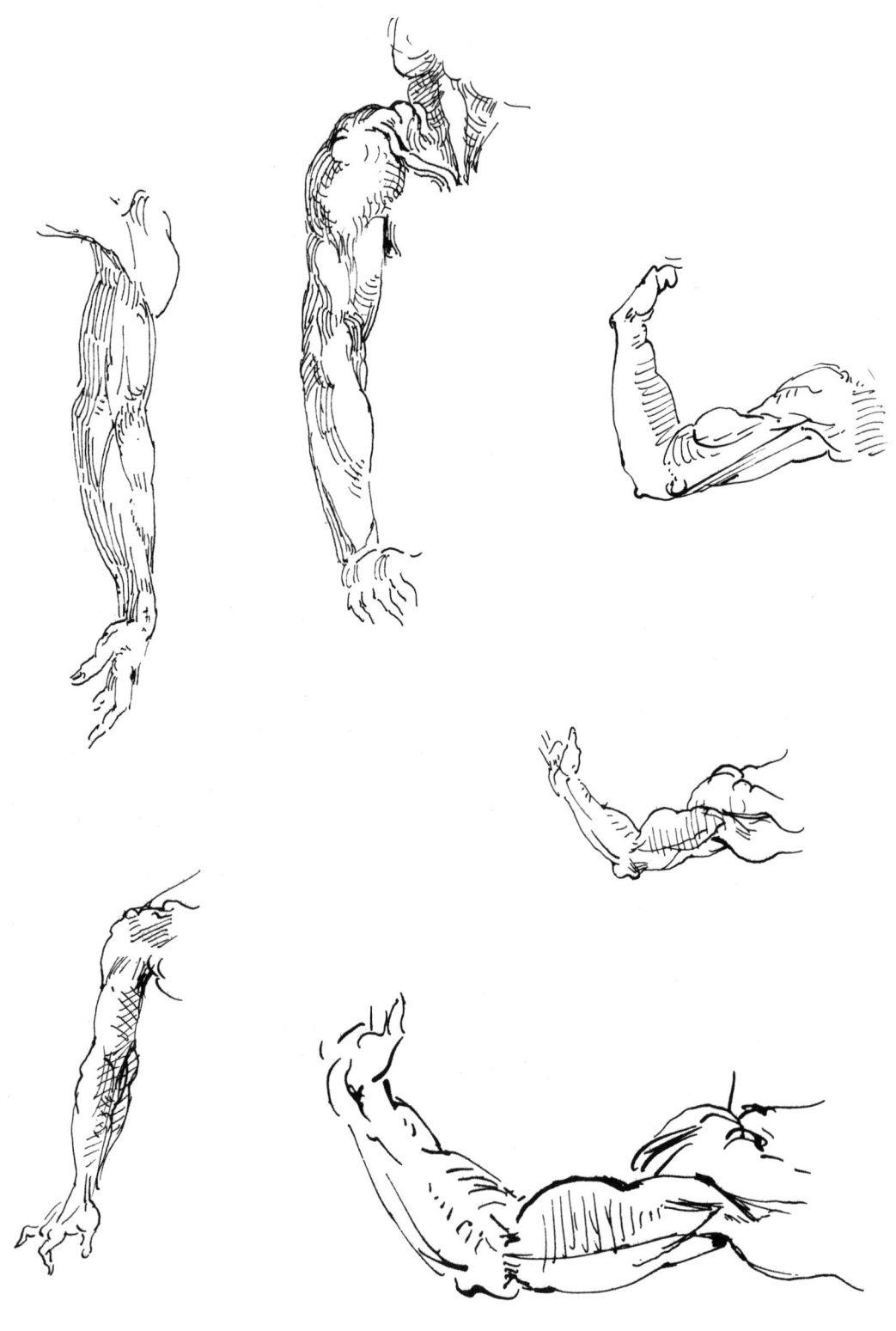

Michelangelo

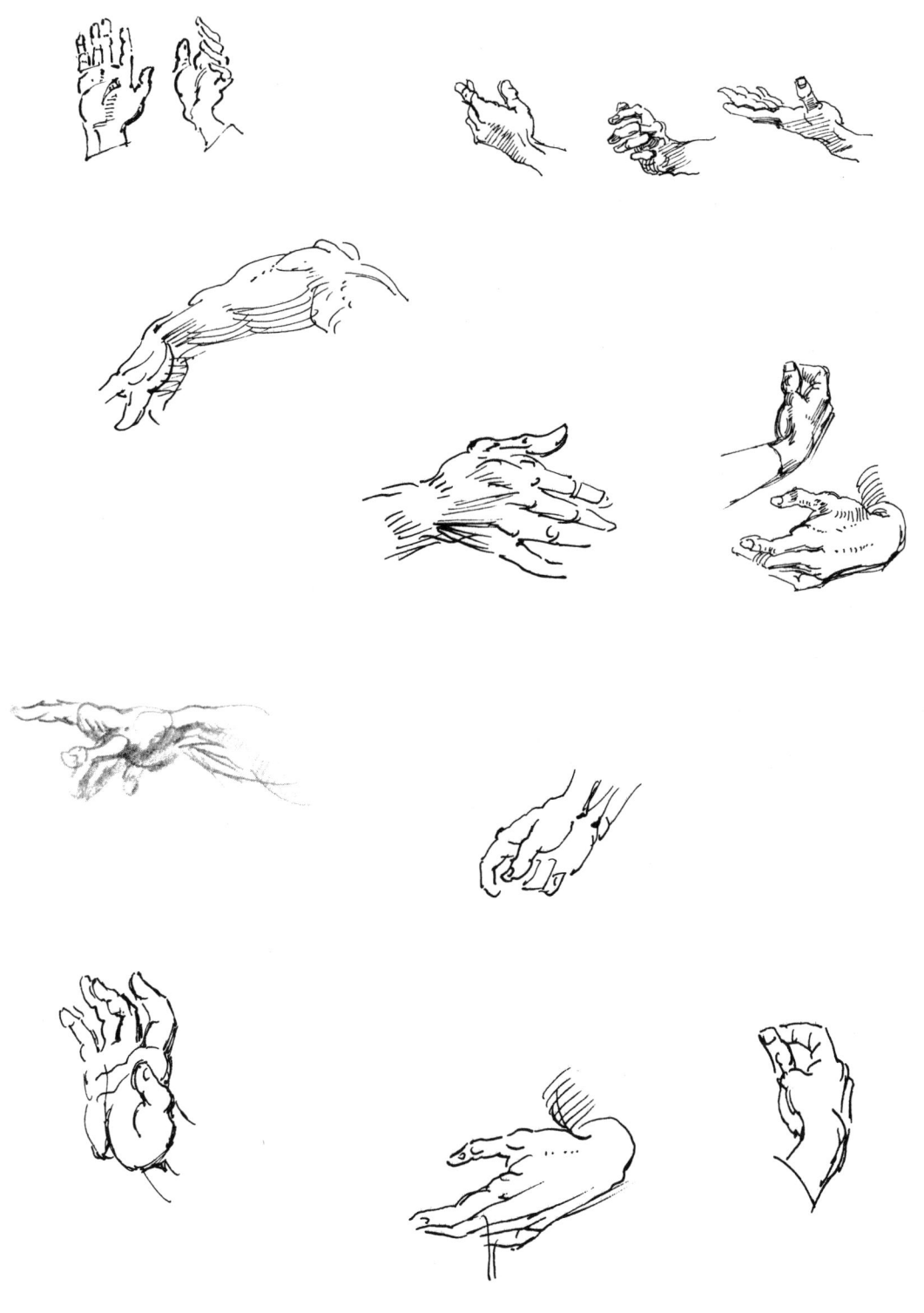

da Vinci, Michelangelo

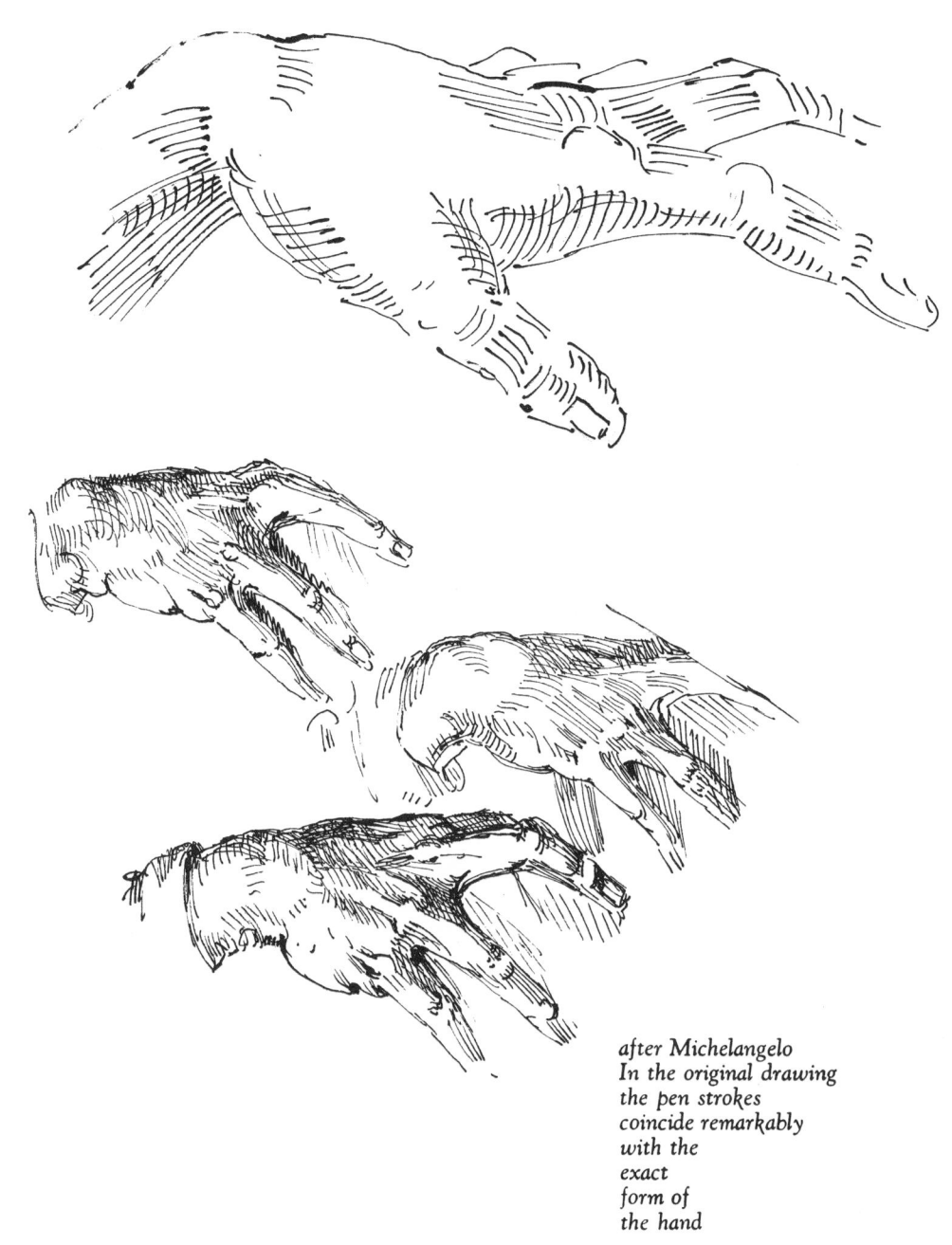

after Michelangelo
In the original drawing
the pen strokes
coincide remarkably
with the
exact
form of
the hand

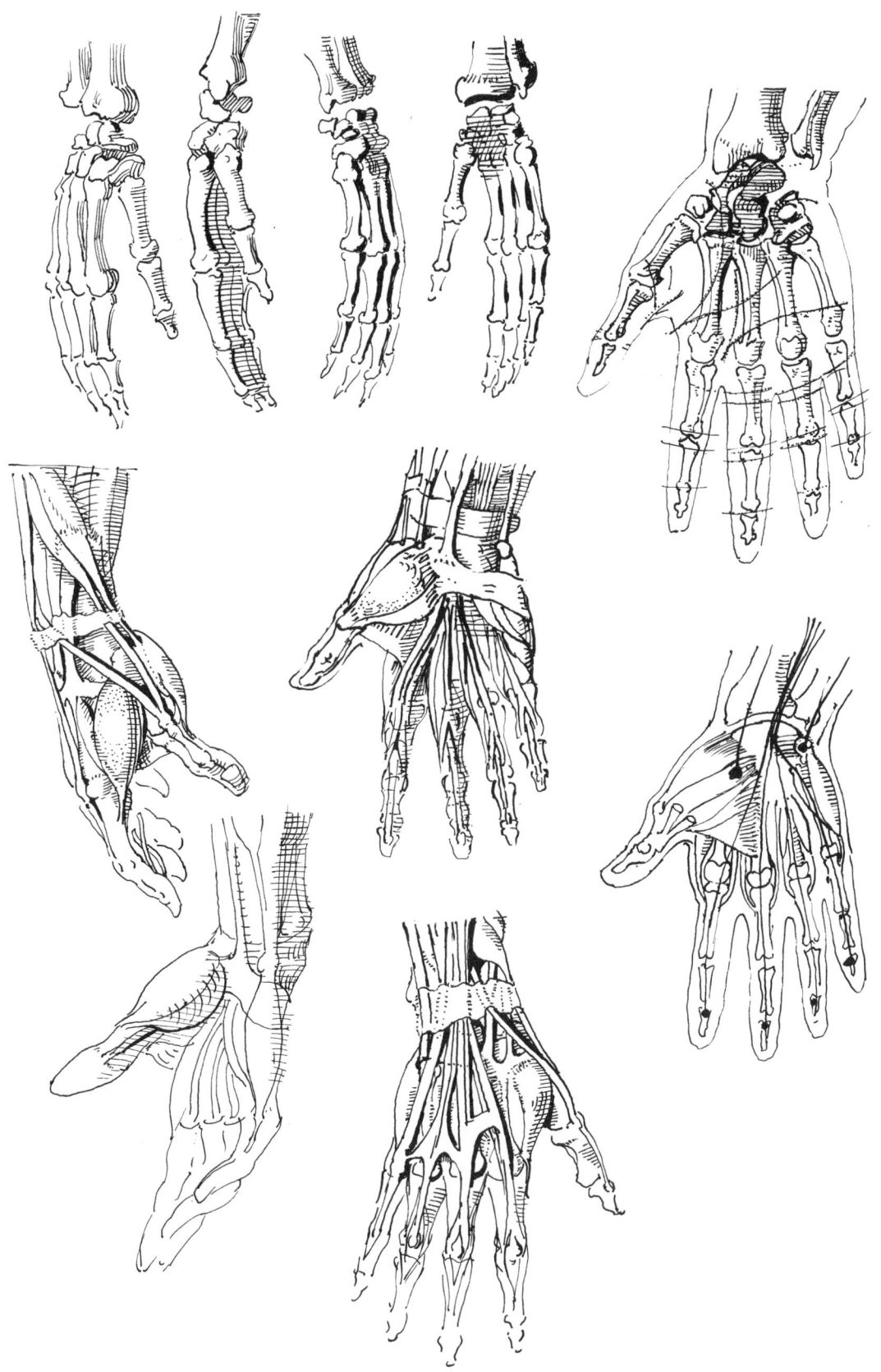

composite of Richer, Schiders and Thomson

Legs-Feet

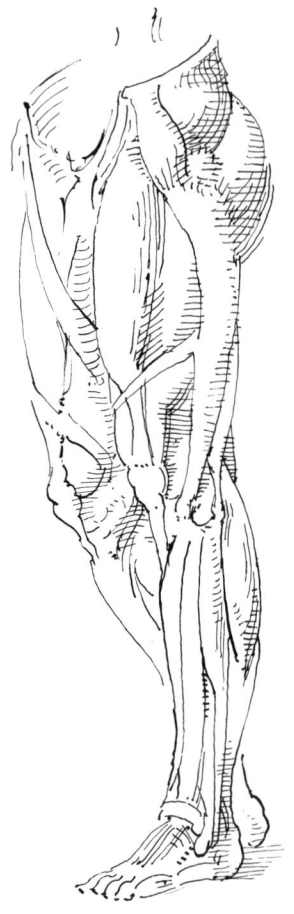
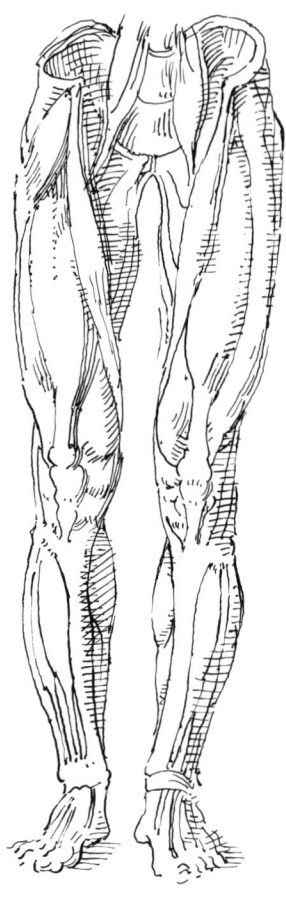
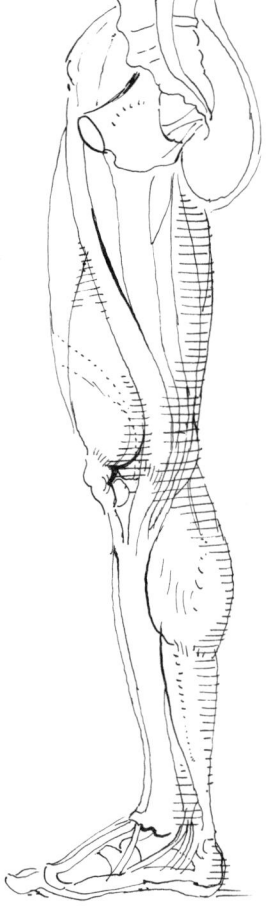

adaptations
from Thomson and Richer
traced fom photographs
(next 6 pages)

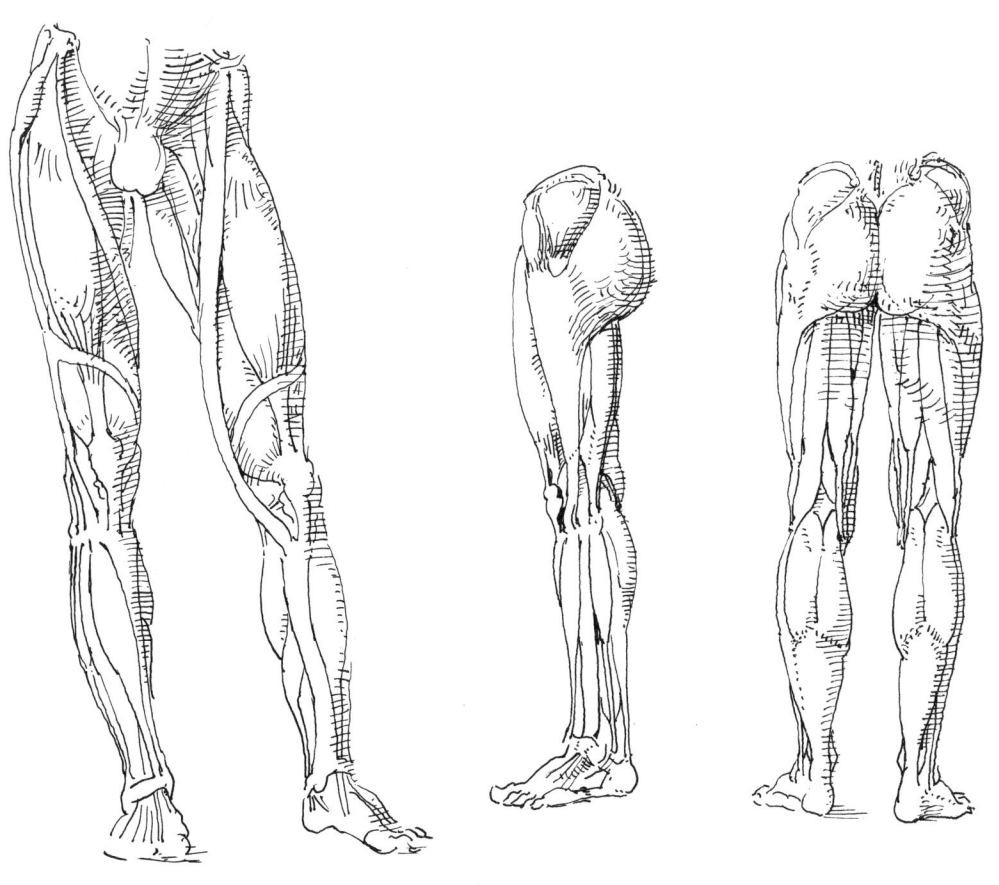

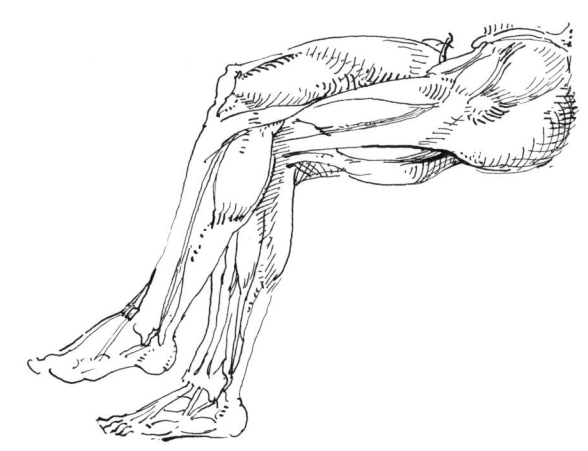

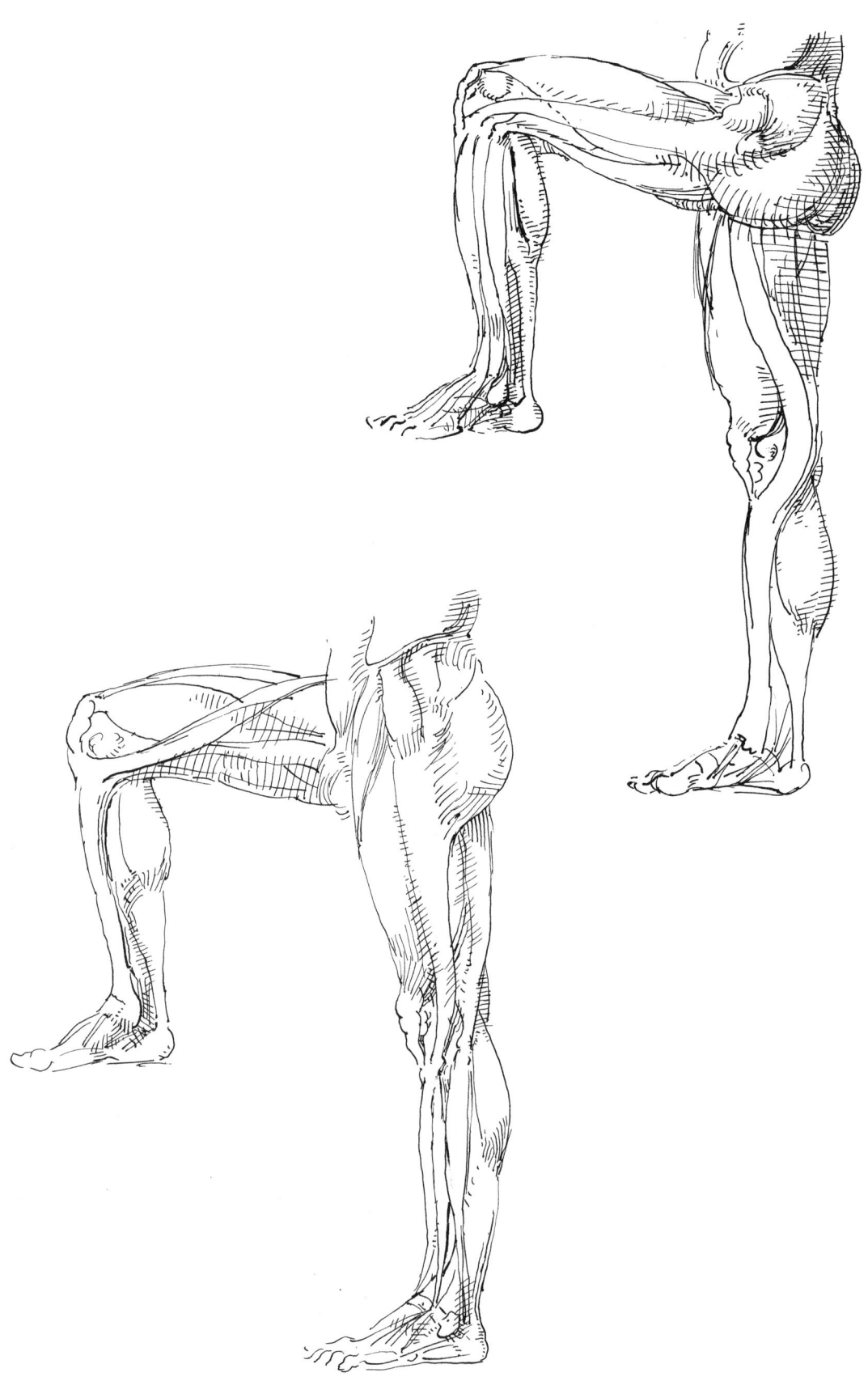

154

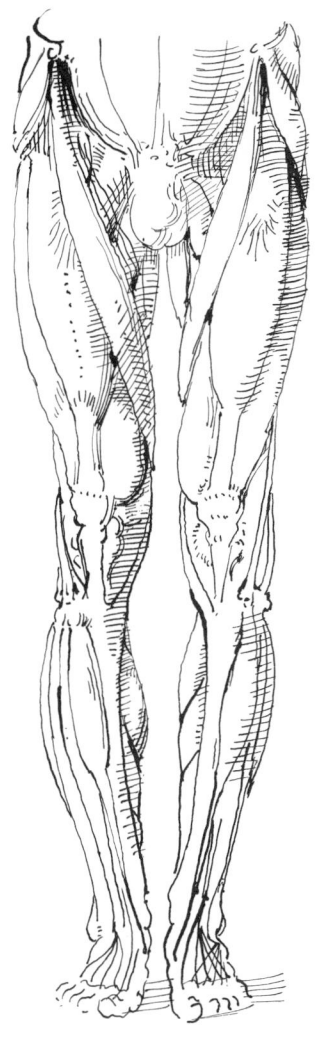

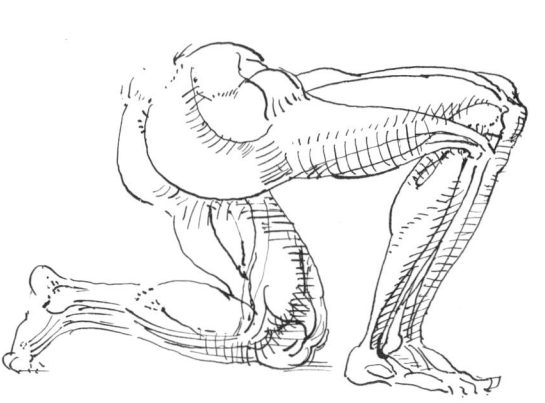

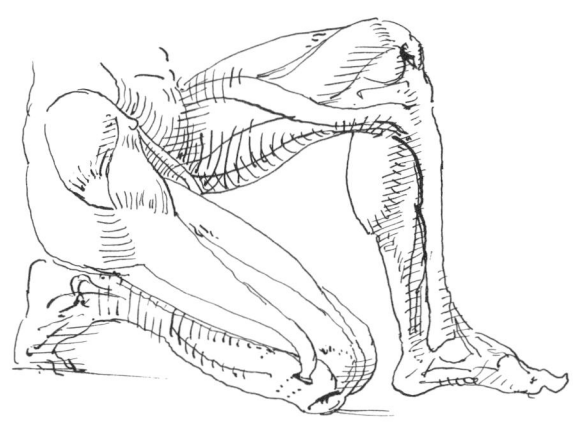

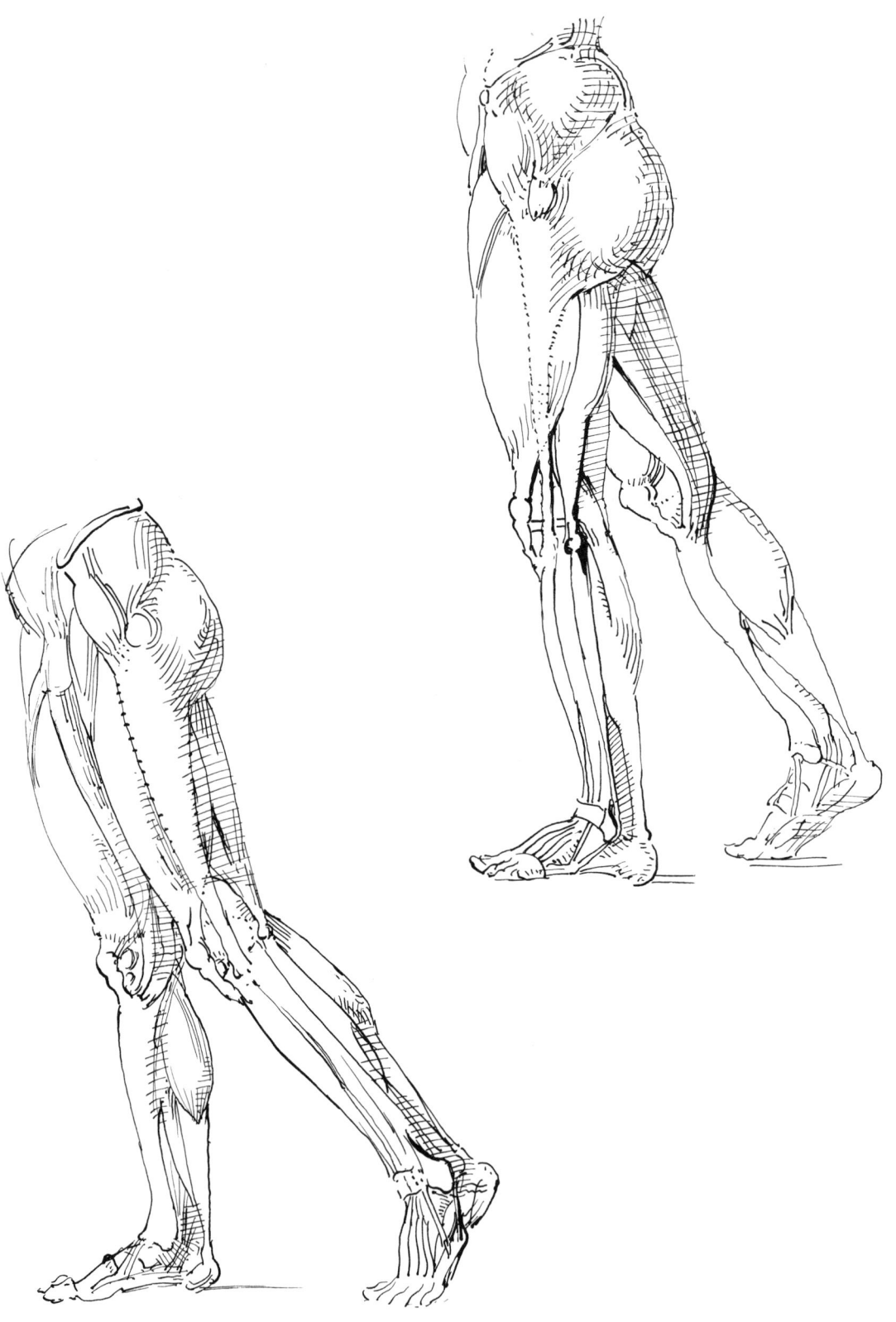

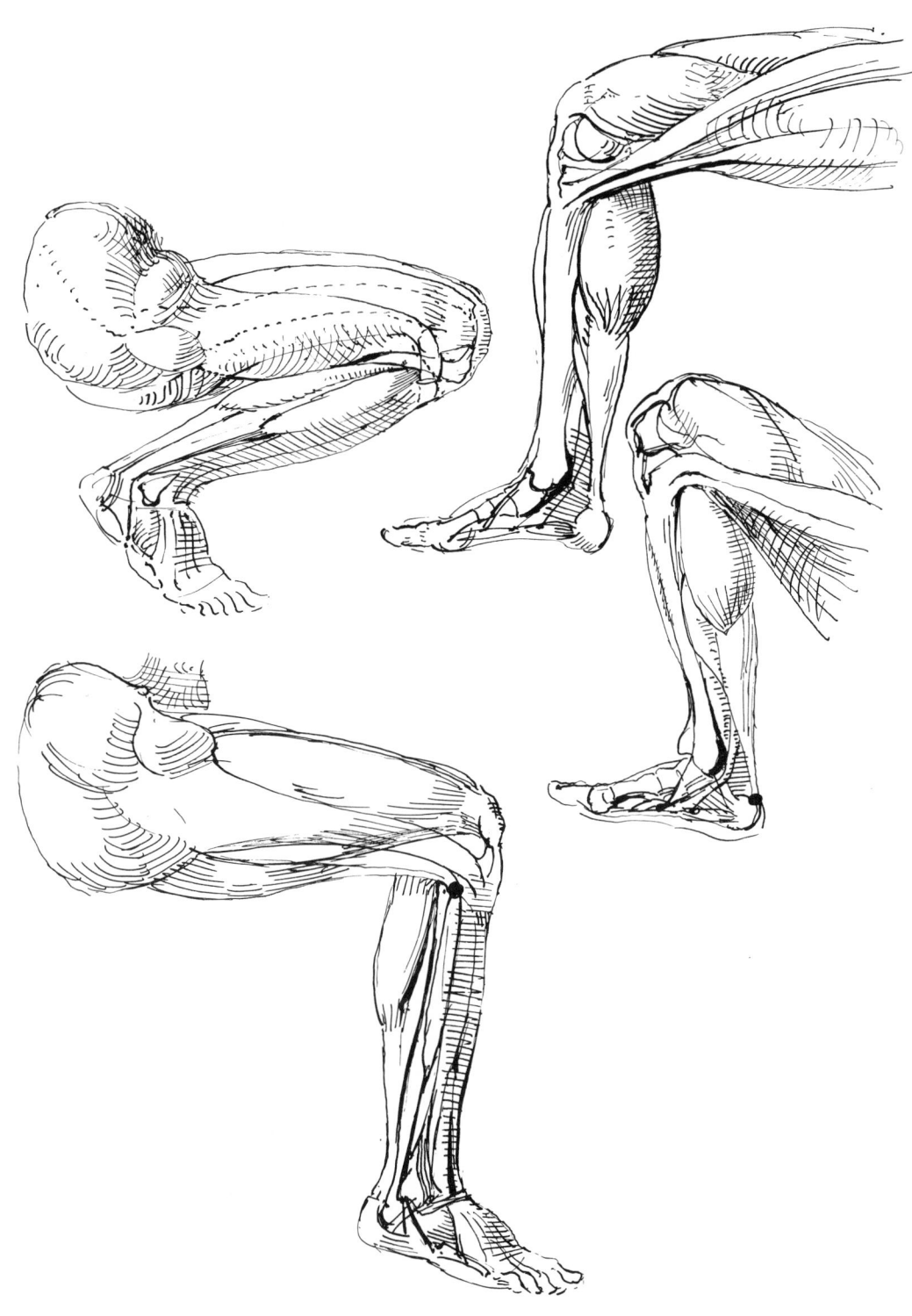

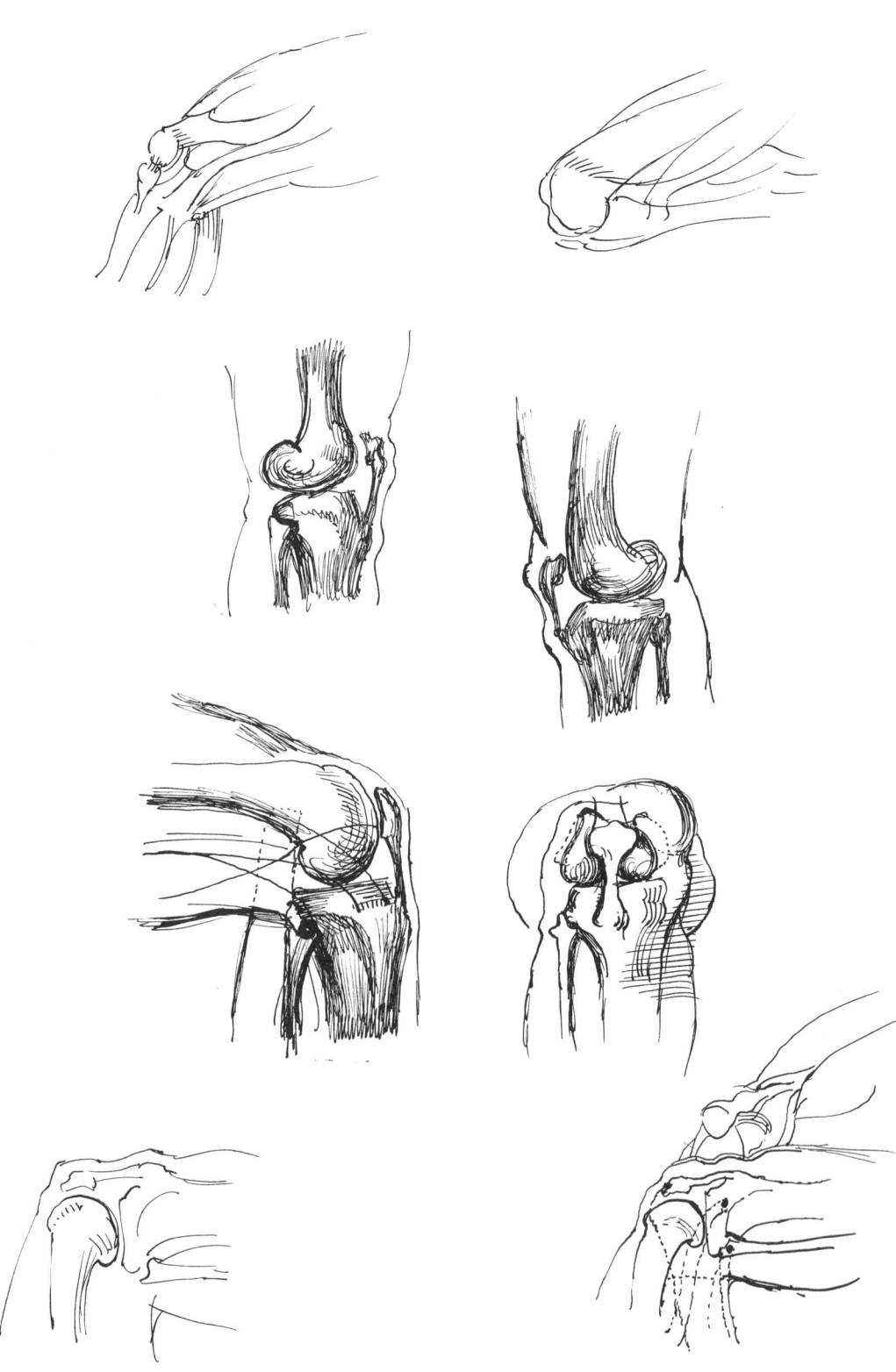

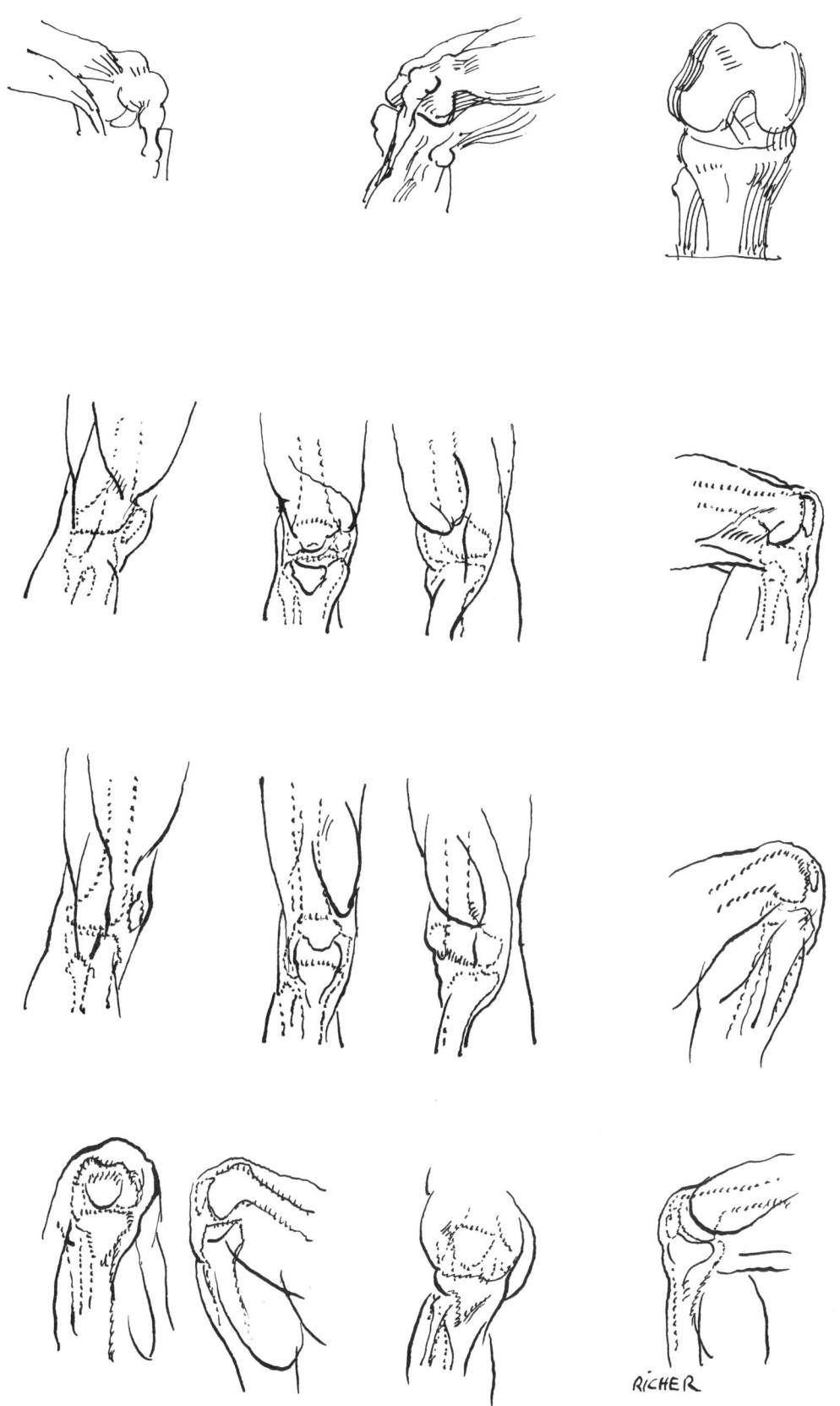

RICHER

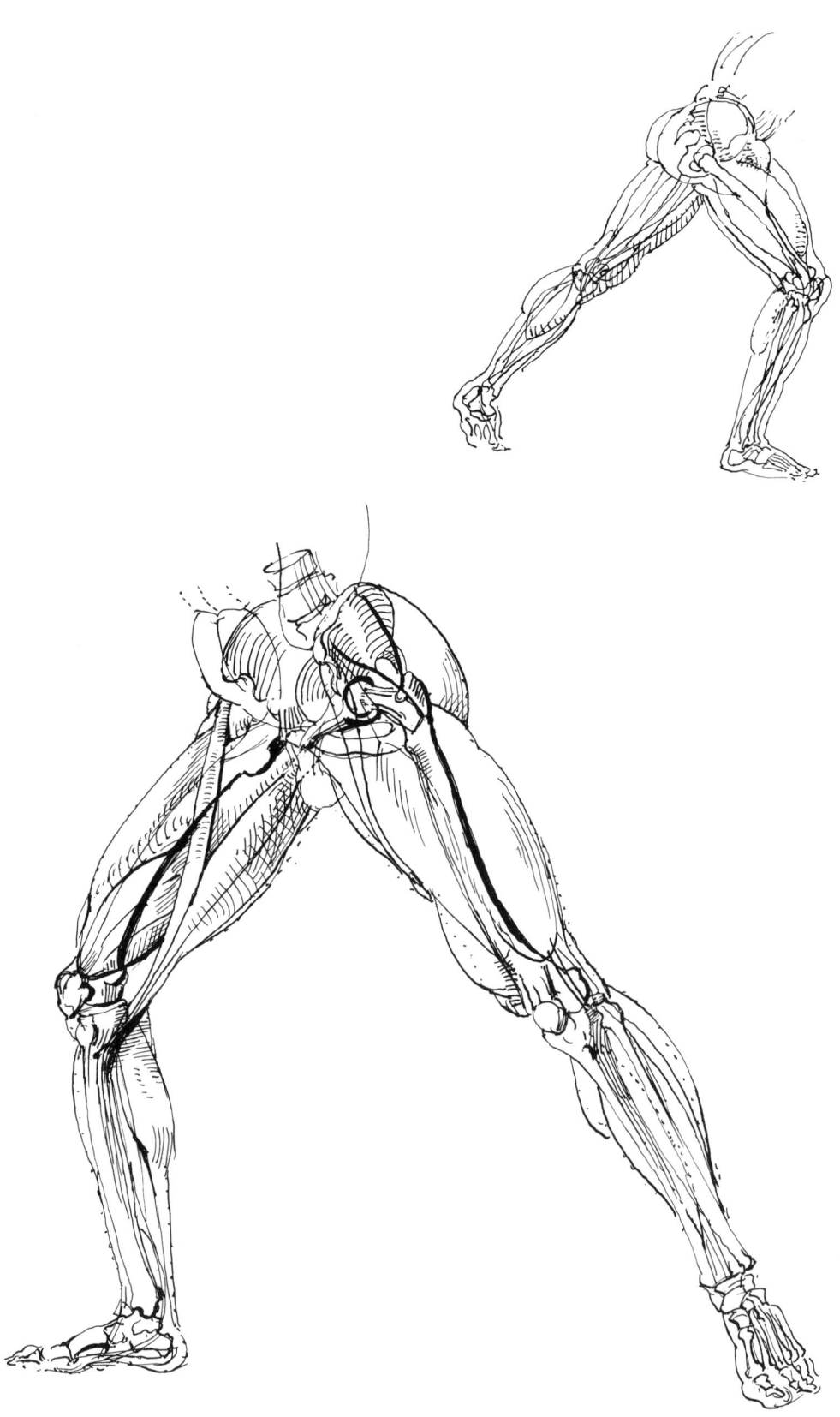

adapted from (du Val) Agasias gladiator

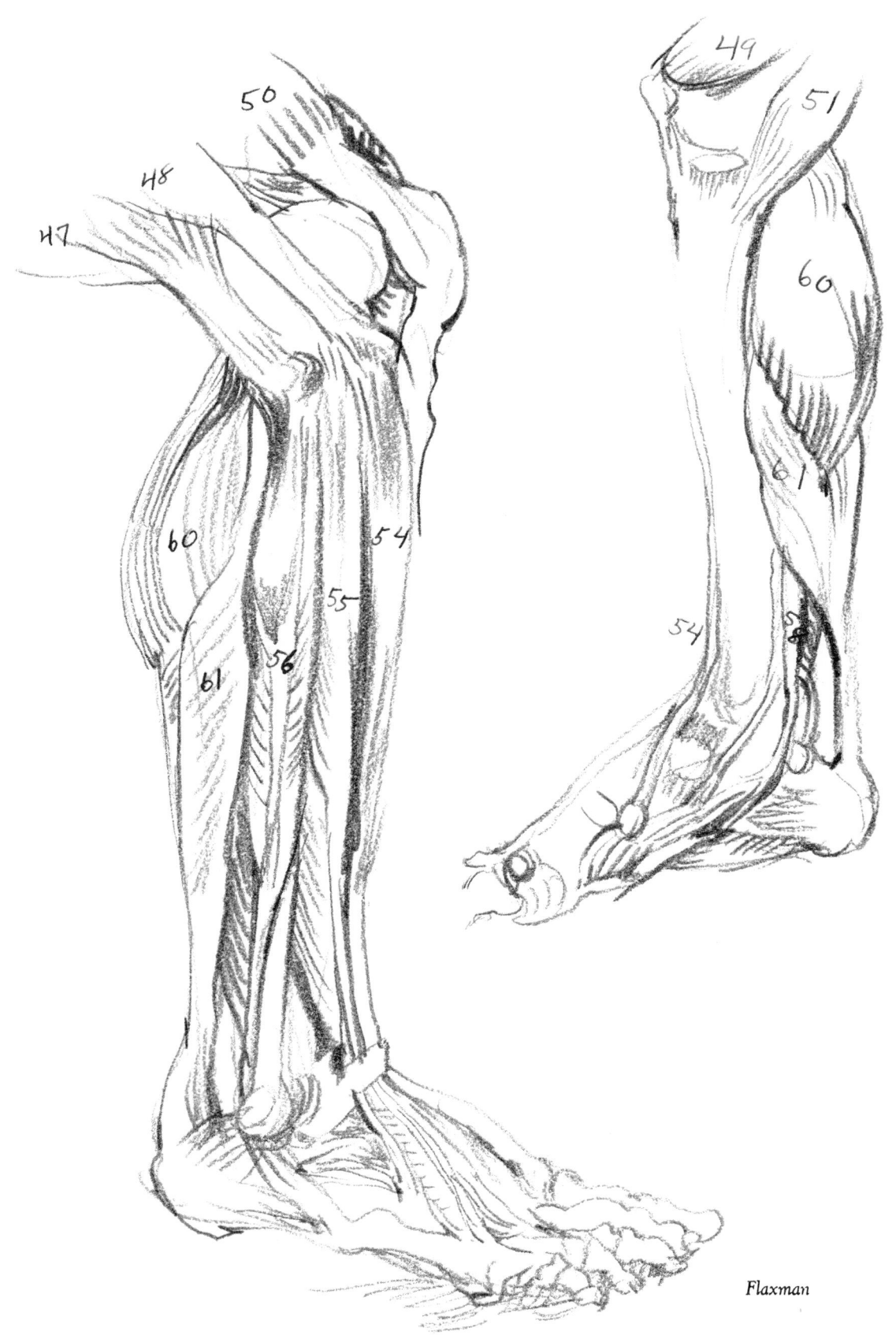

Flaxman

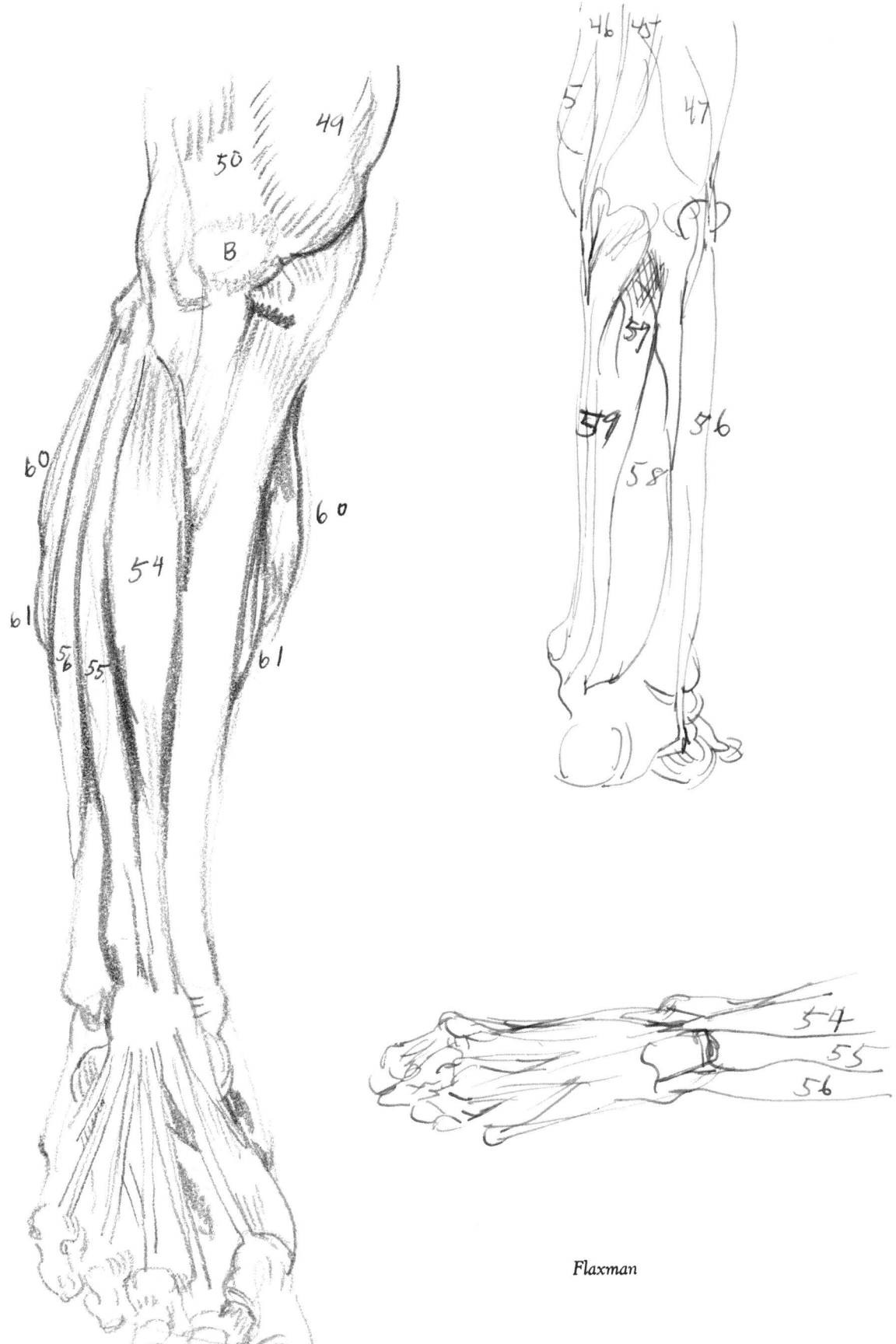

Flaxman

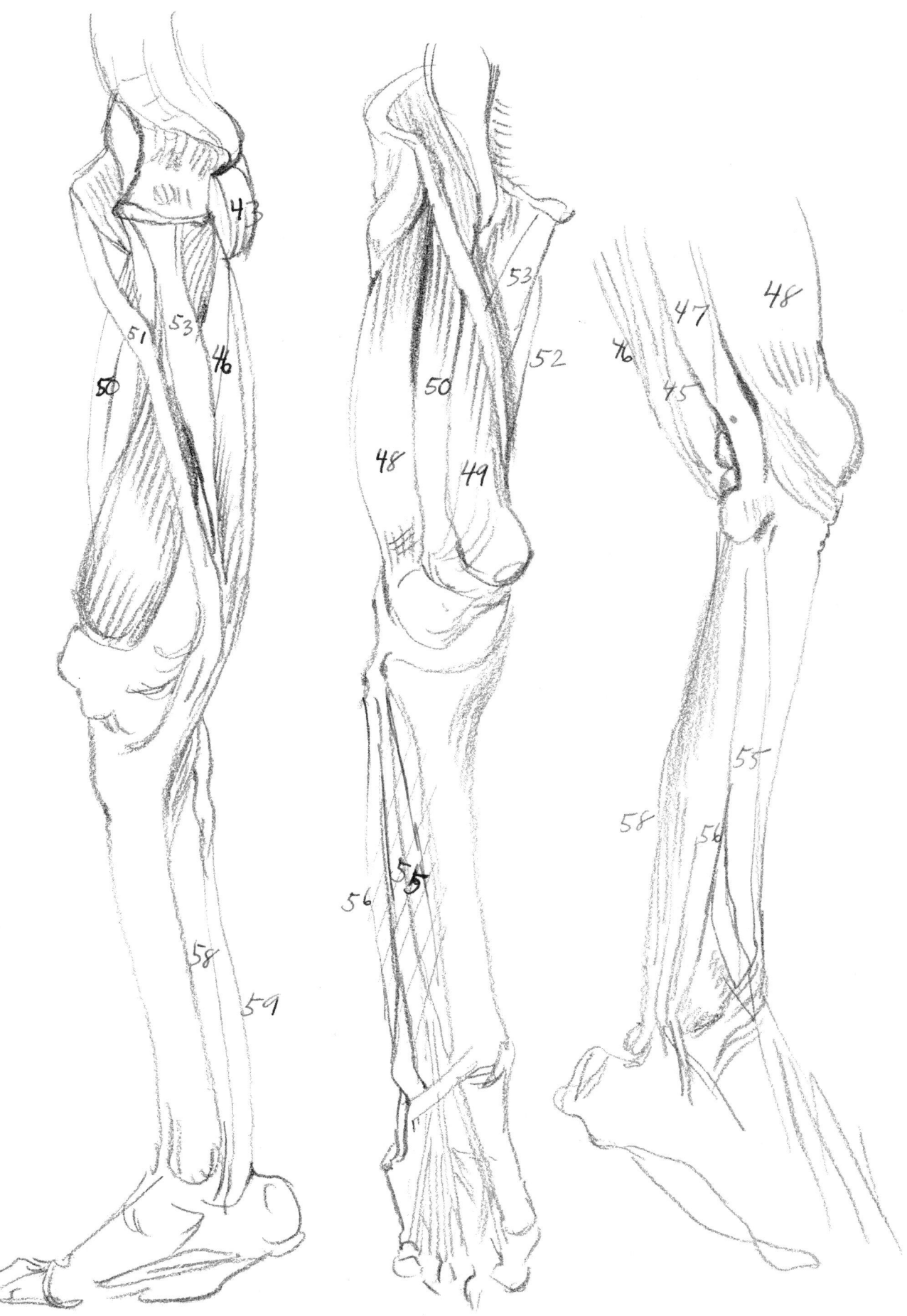

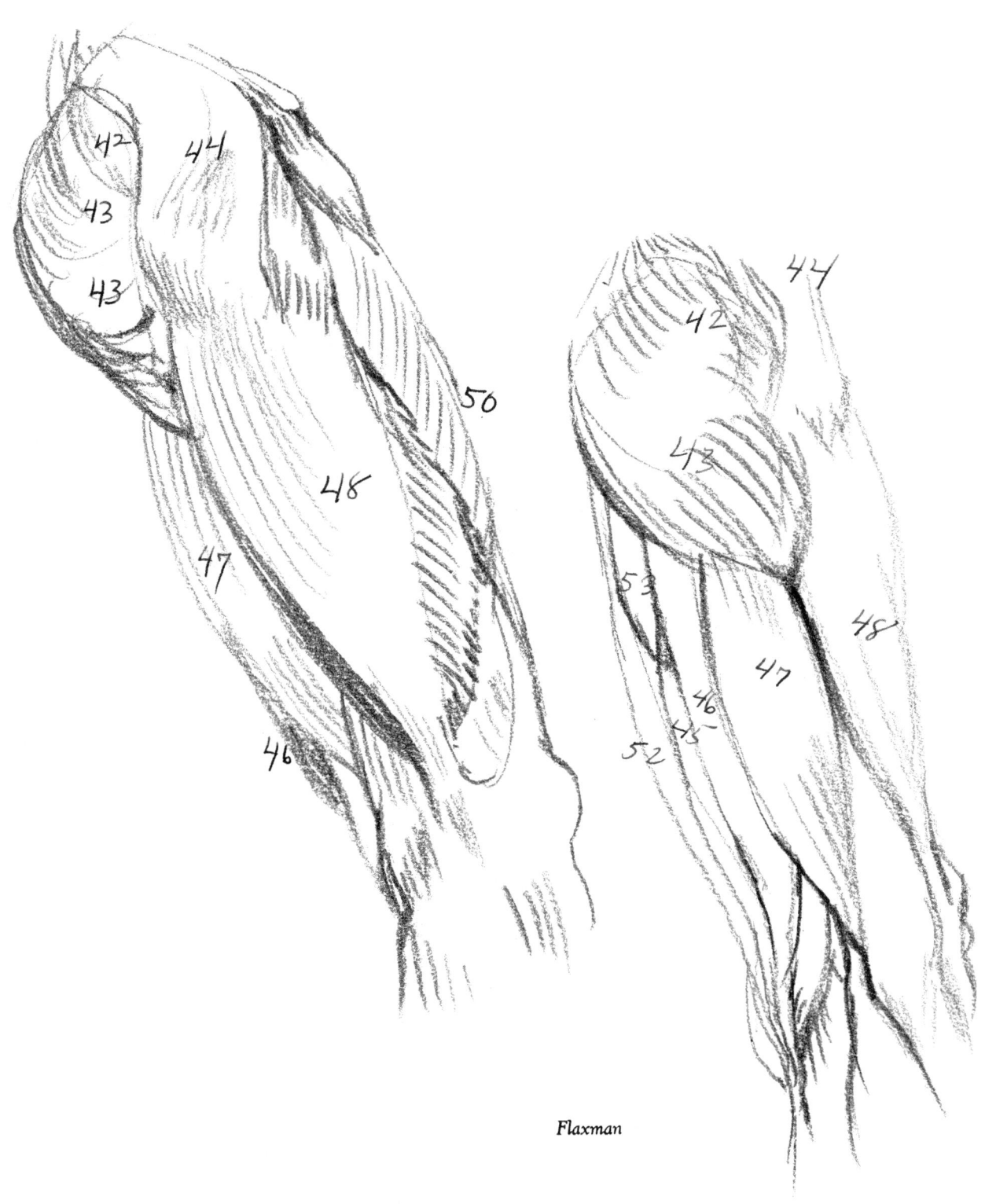

Flaxman

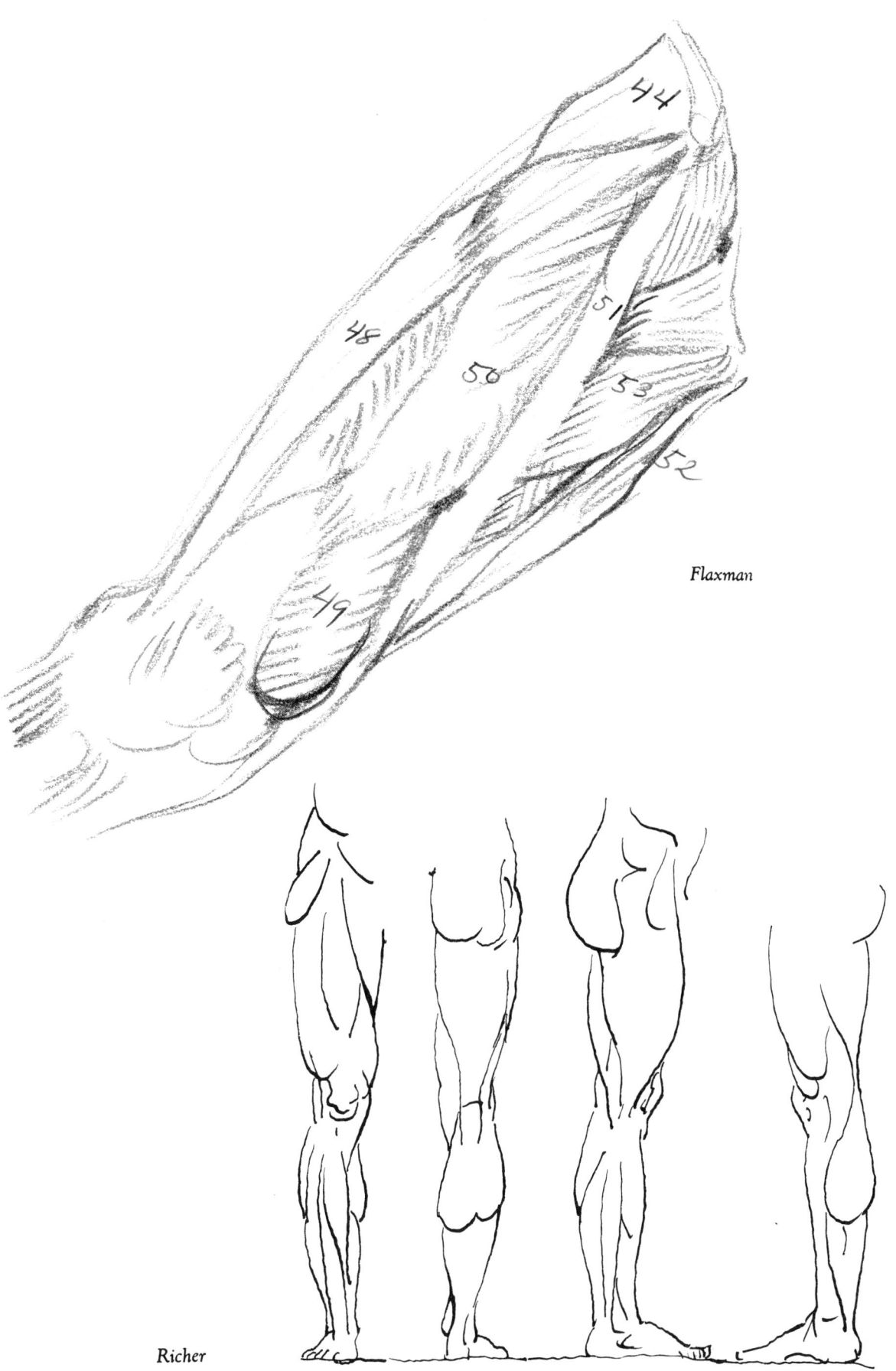

Flaxman

48

50

44

51

53

52

49

Richer

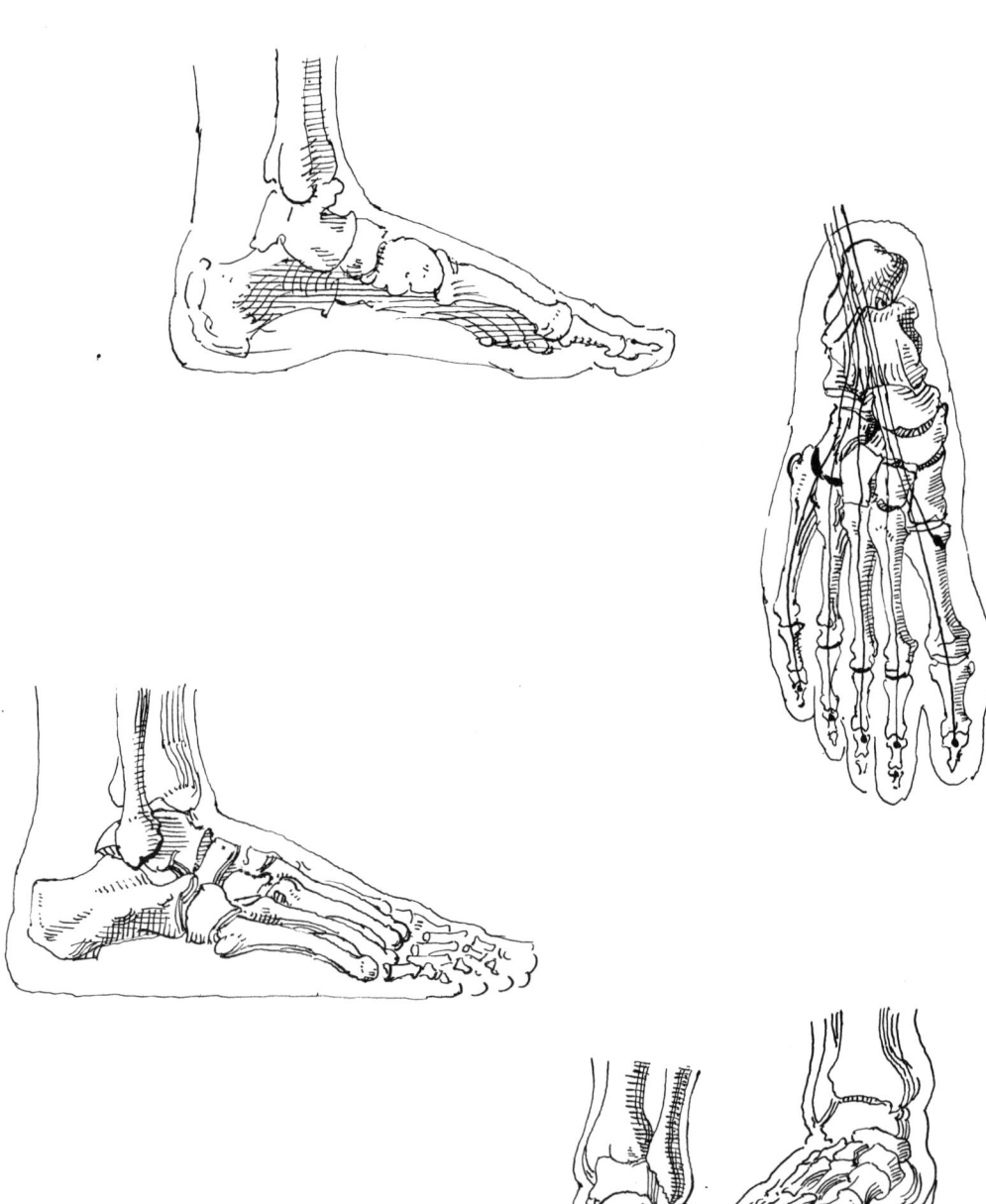

adapted from Sabotta and Thomson and Richer

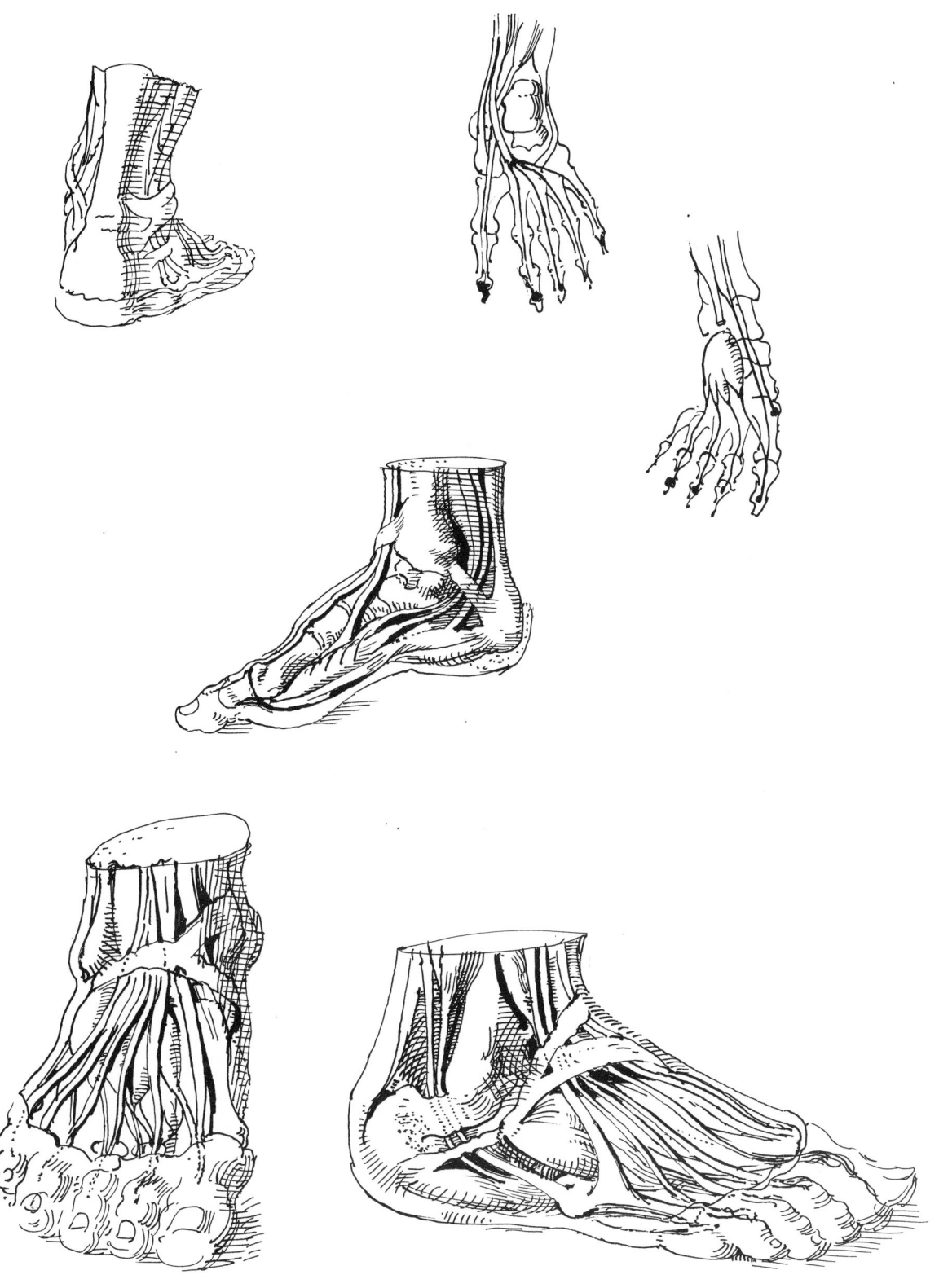

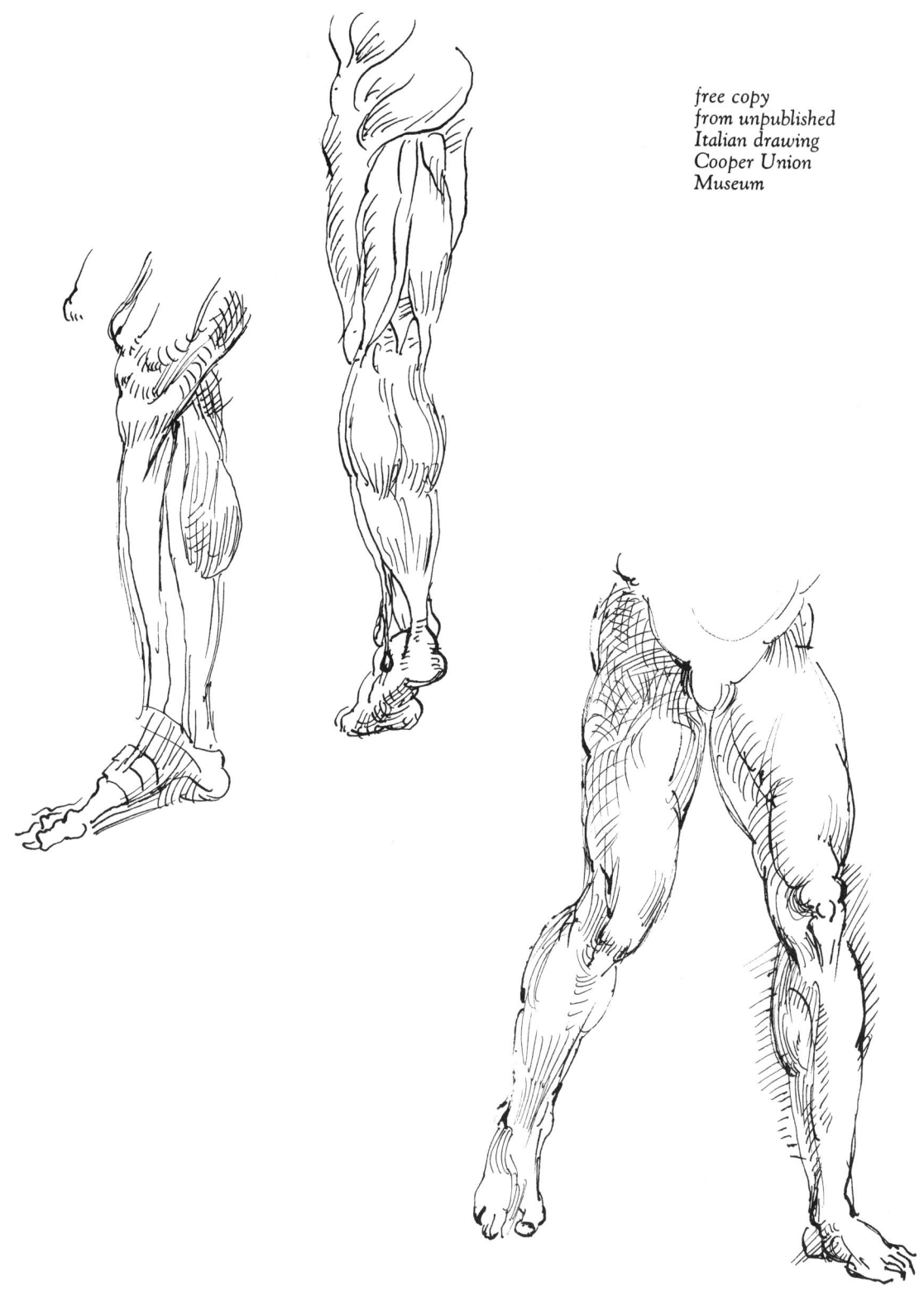

free copy
from unpublished
Italian drawing
Cooper Union
Museum

Raphael

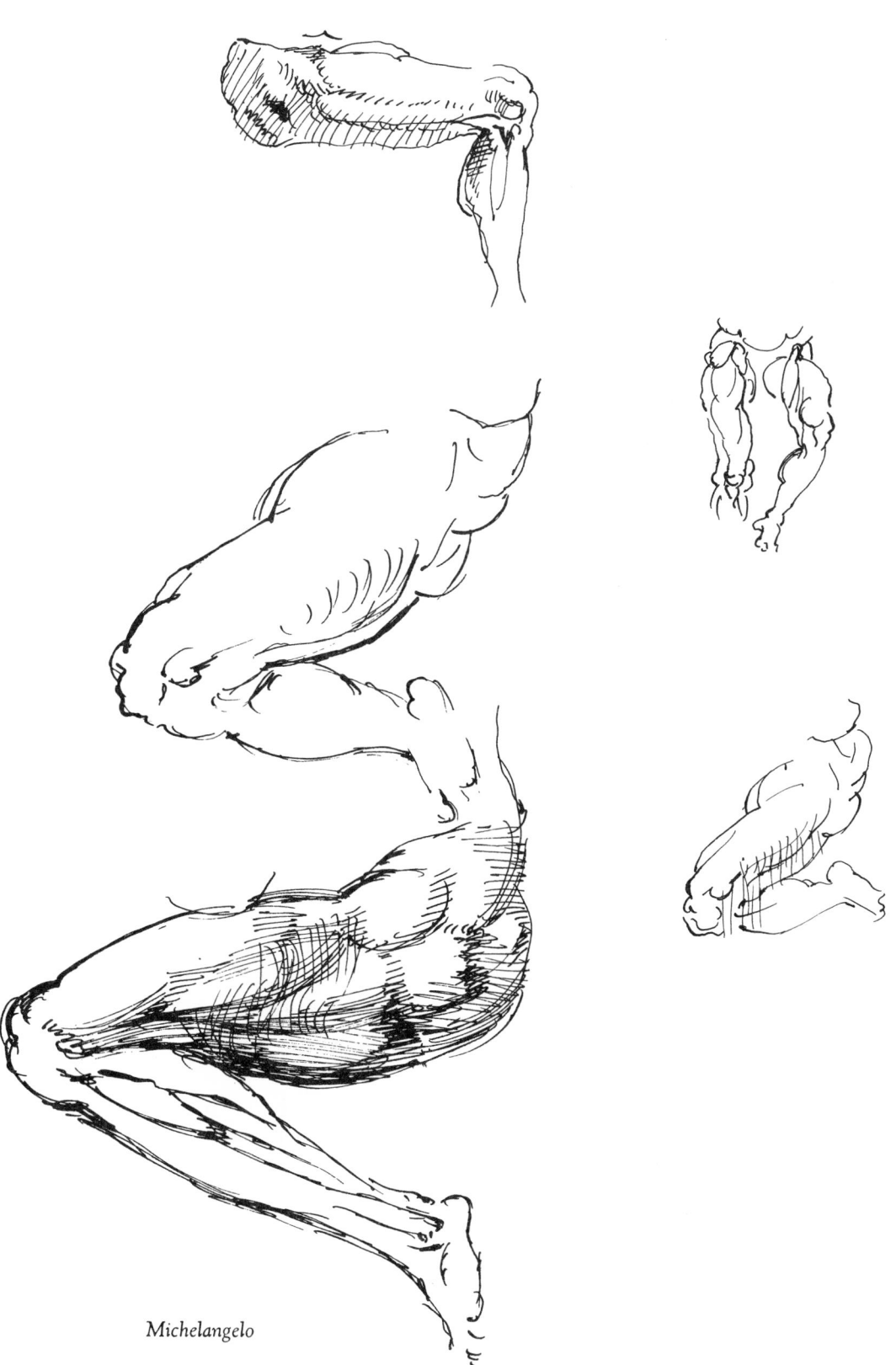

Michelangelo

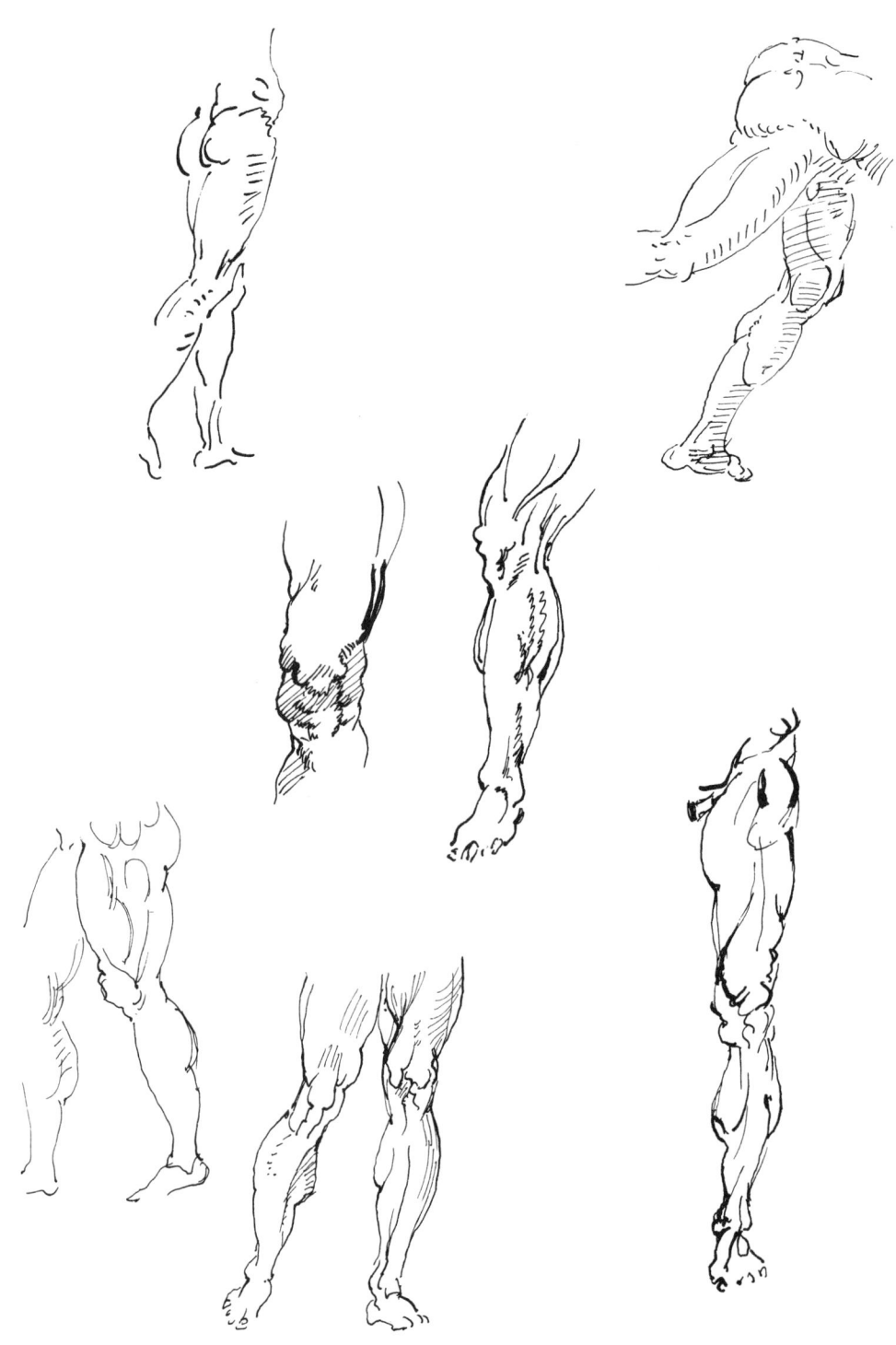

Raphael and Michelangelo

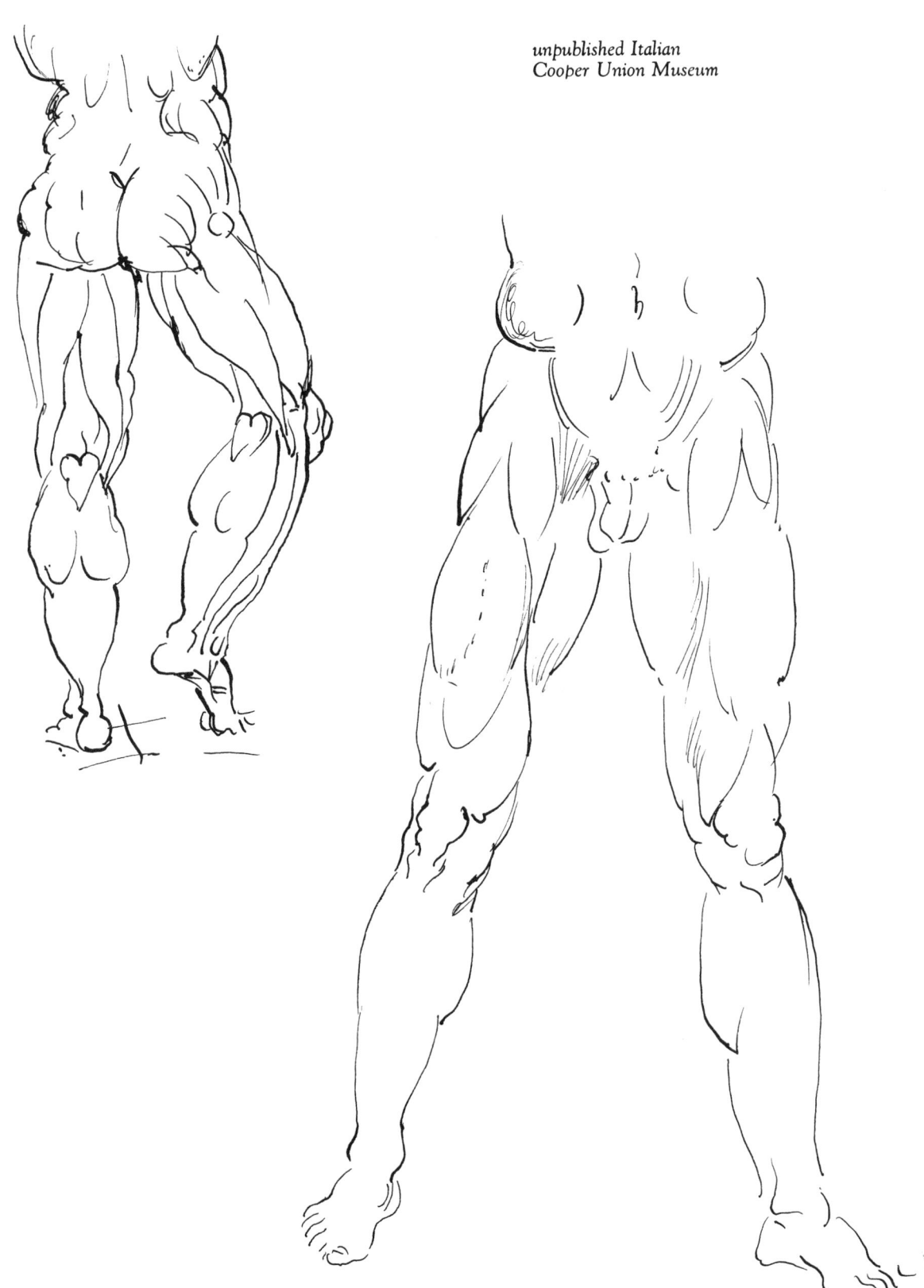

unpublished Italian
Cooper Union Museum

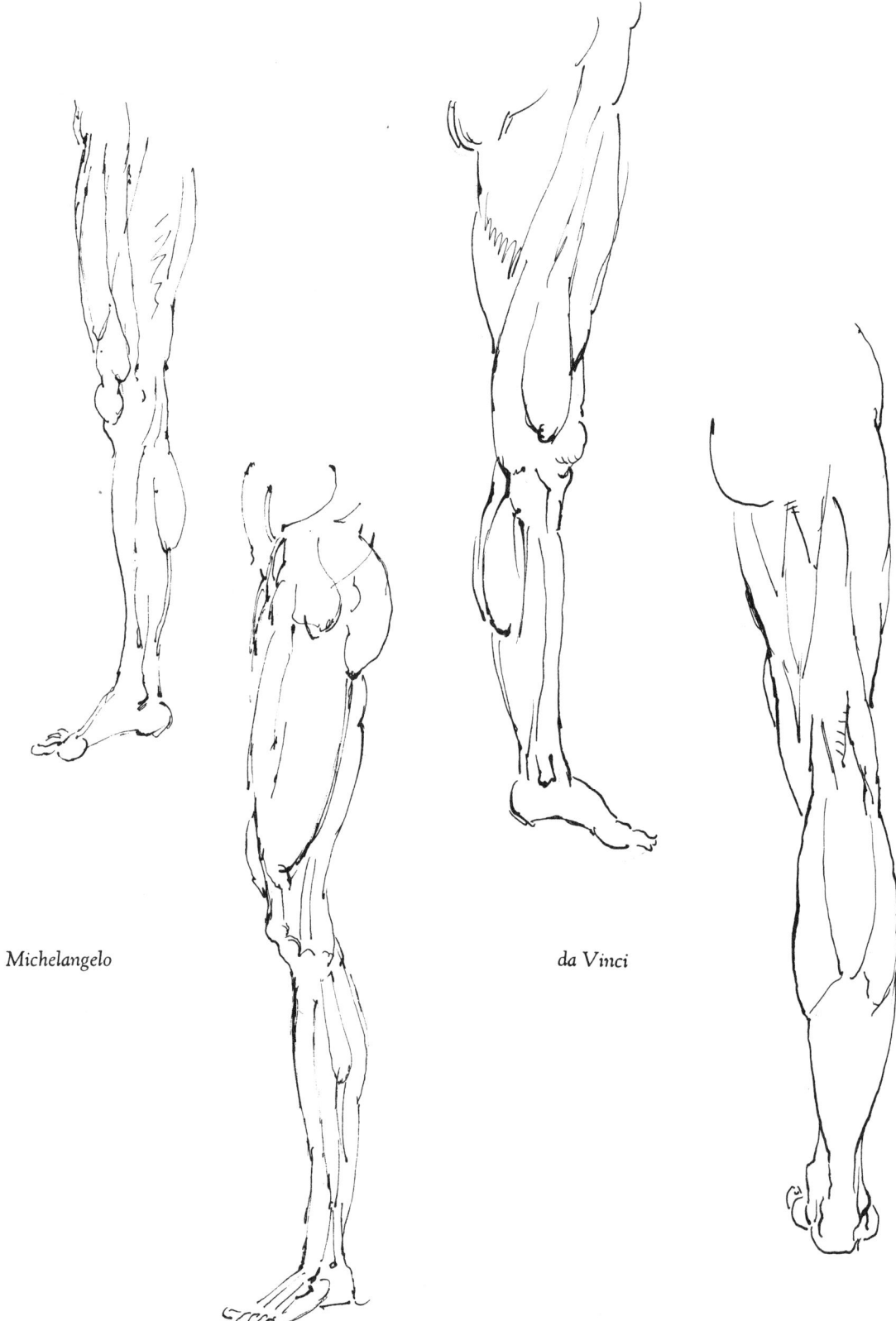

Michelangelo

da Vinci

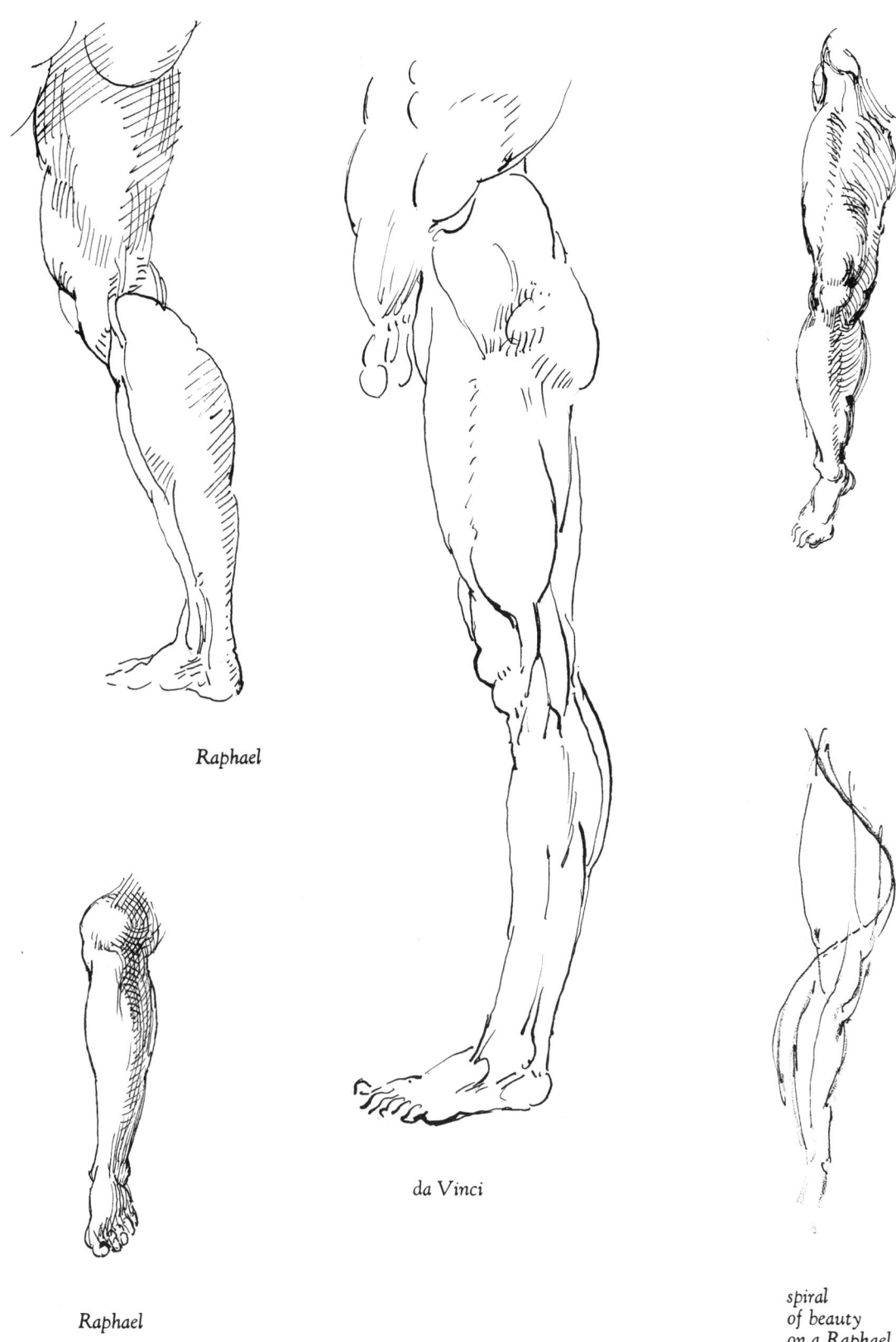

Raphael

Raphael

da Vinci

spiral
of beauty
on a Raphael

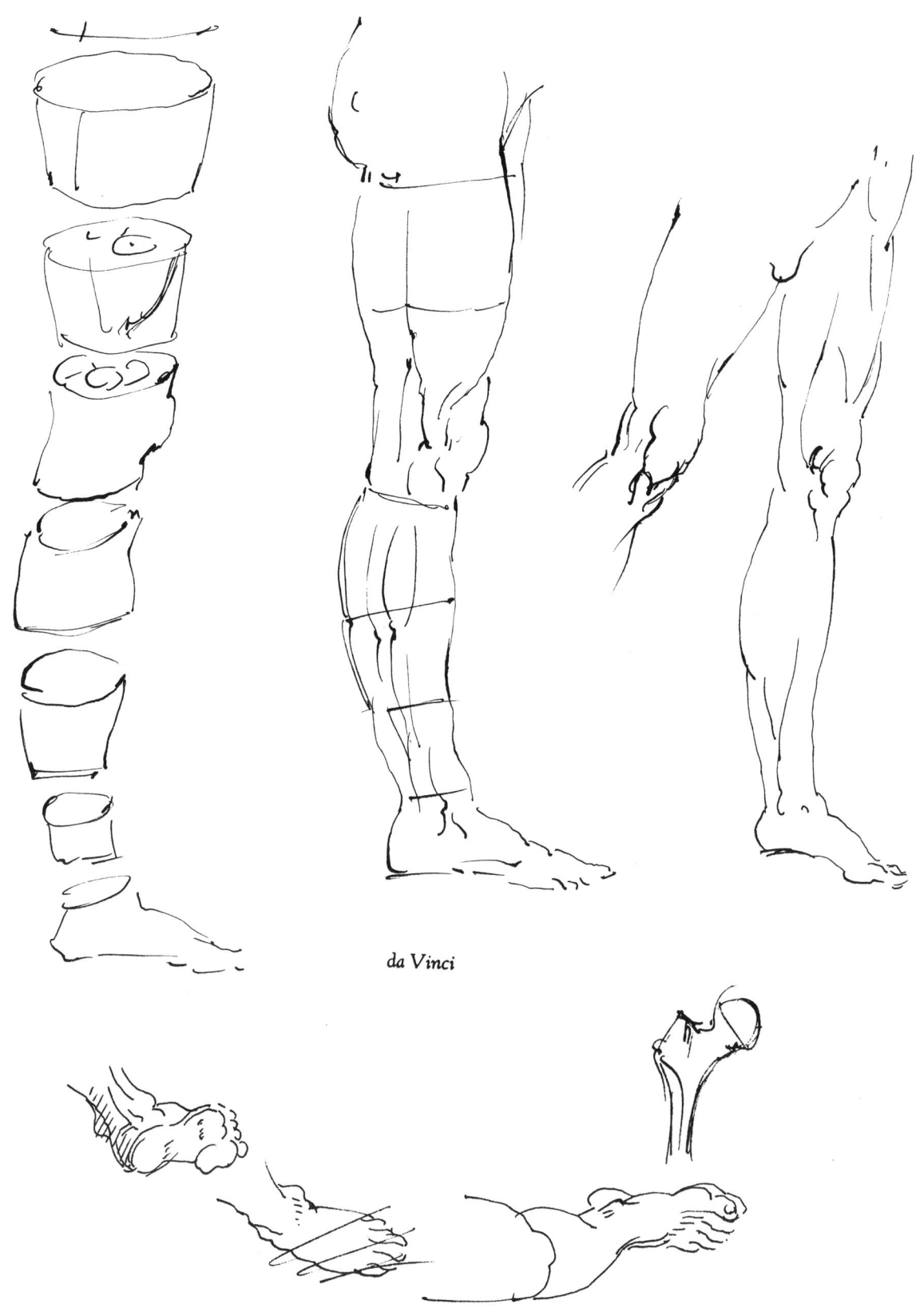

da Vinci

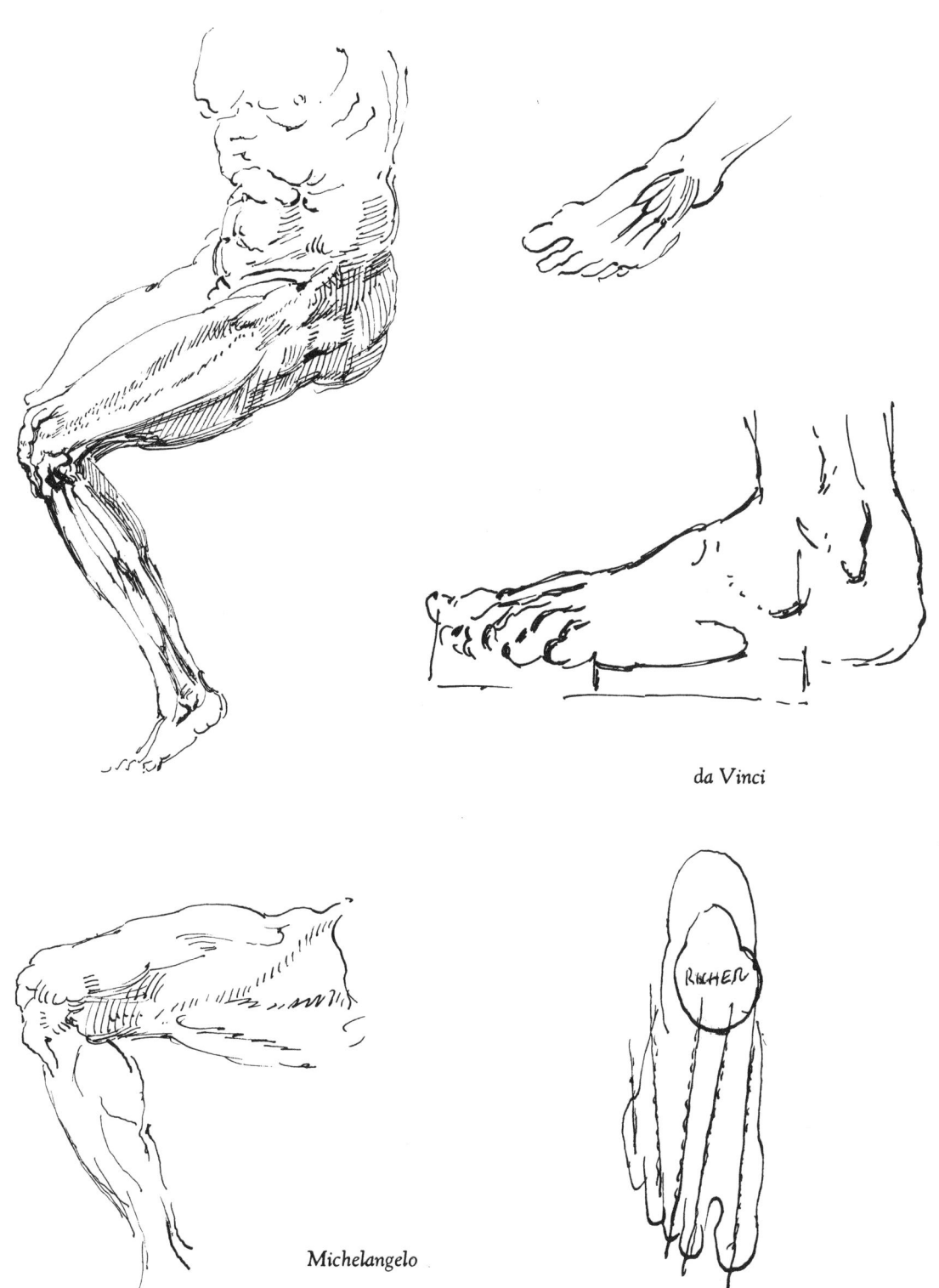

da Vinci

Michelangelo

RICHER

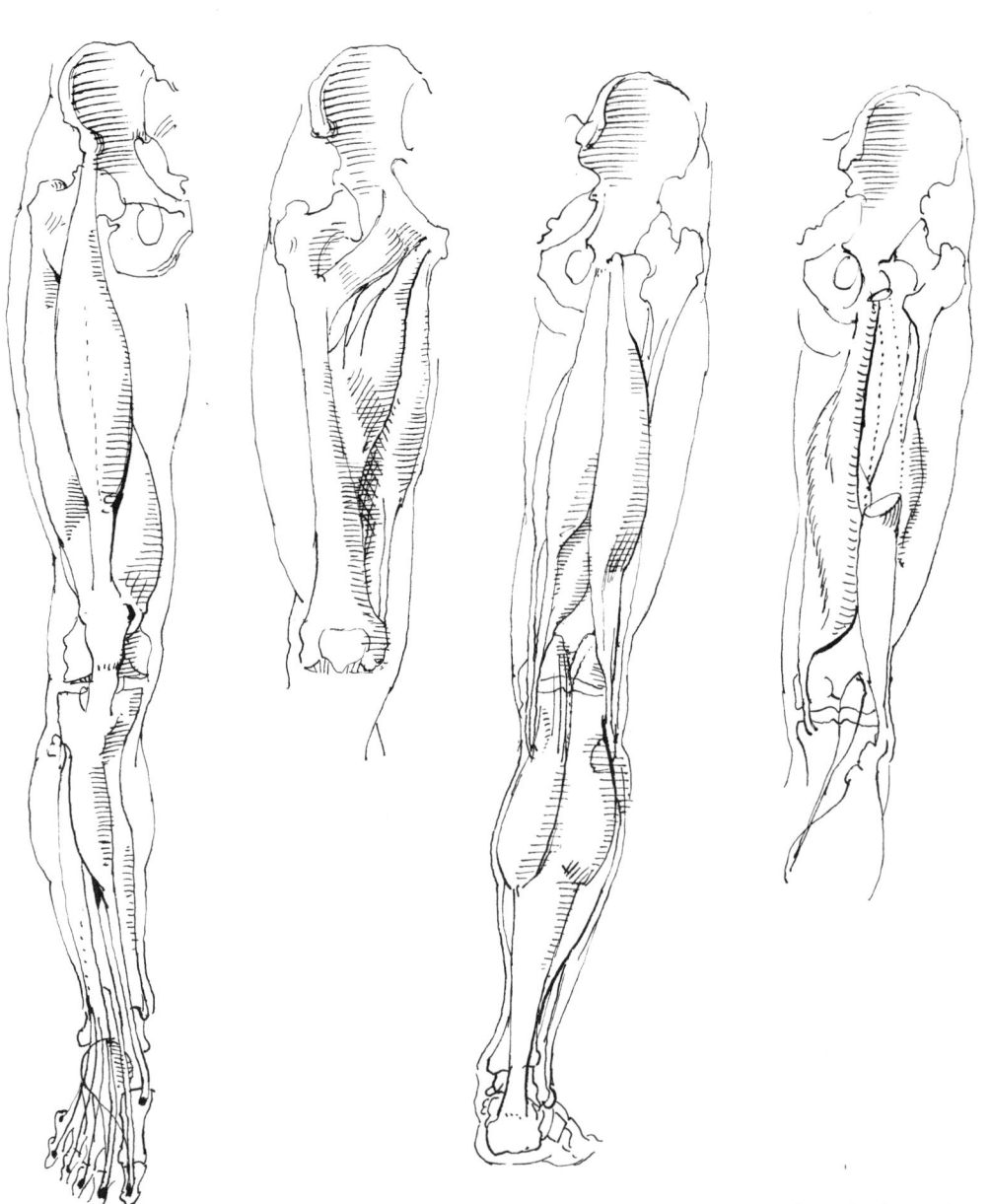

from Richer and Thomson

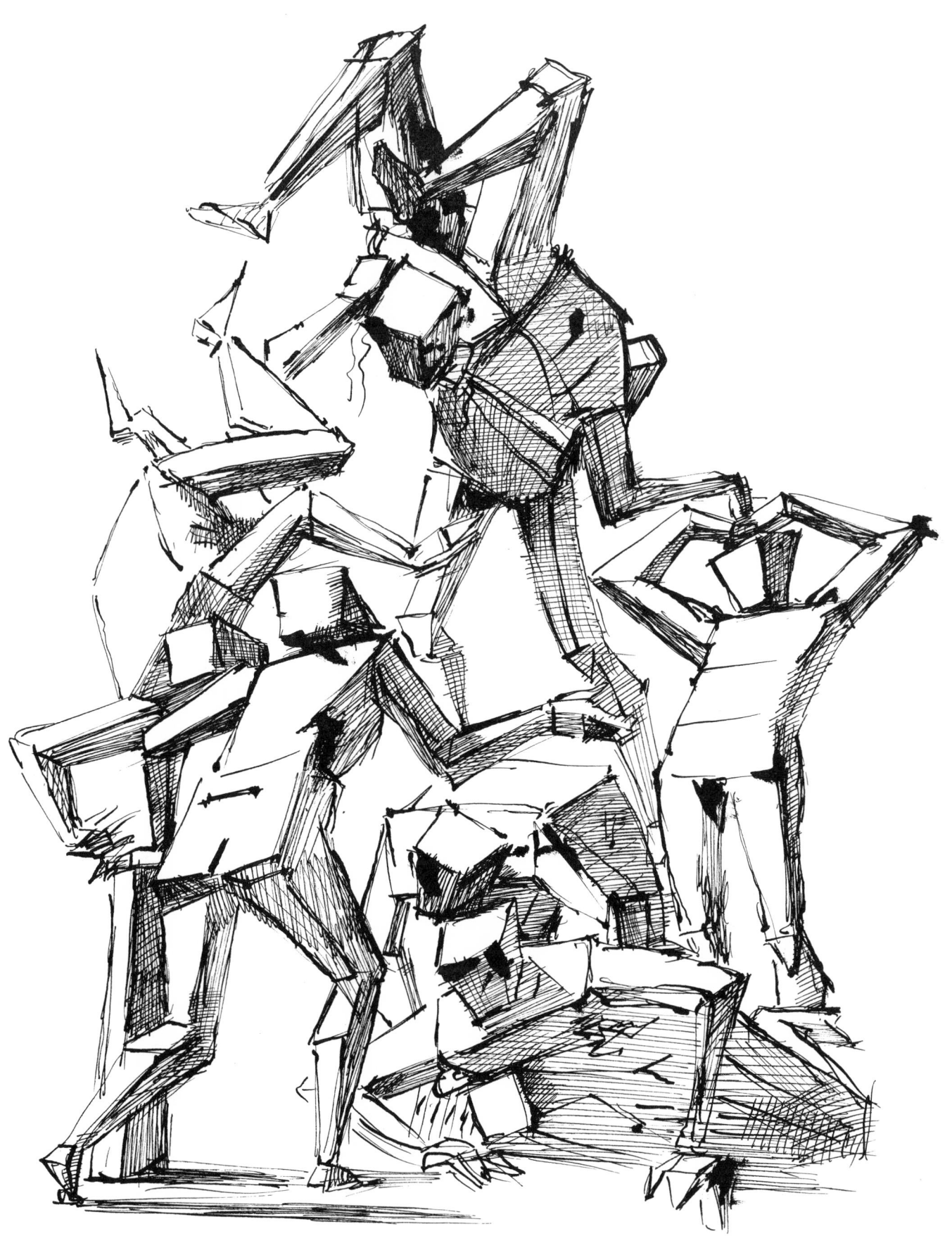

schematic composition Luca Cambiasi 1527-85

Proportions

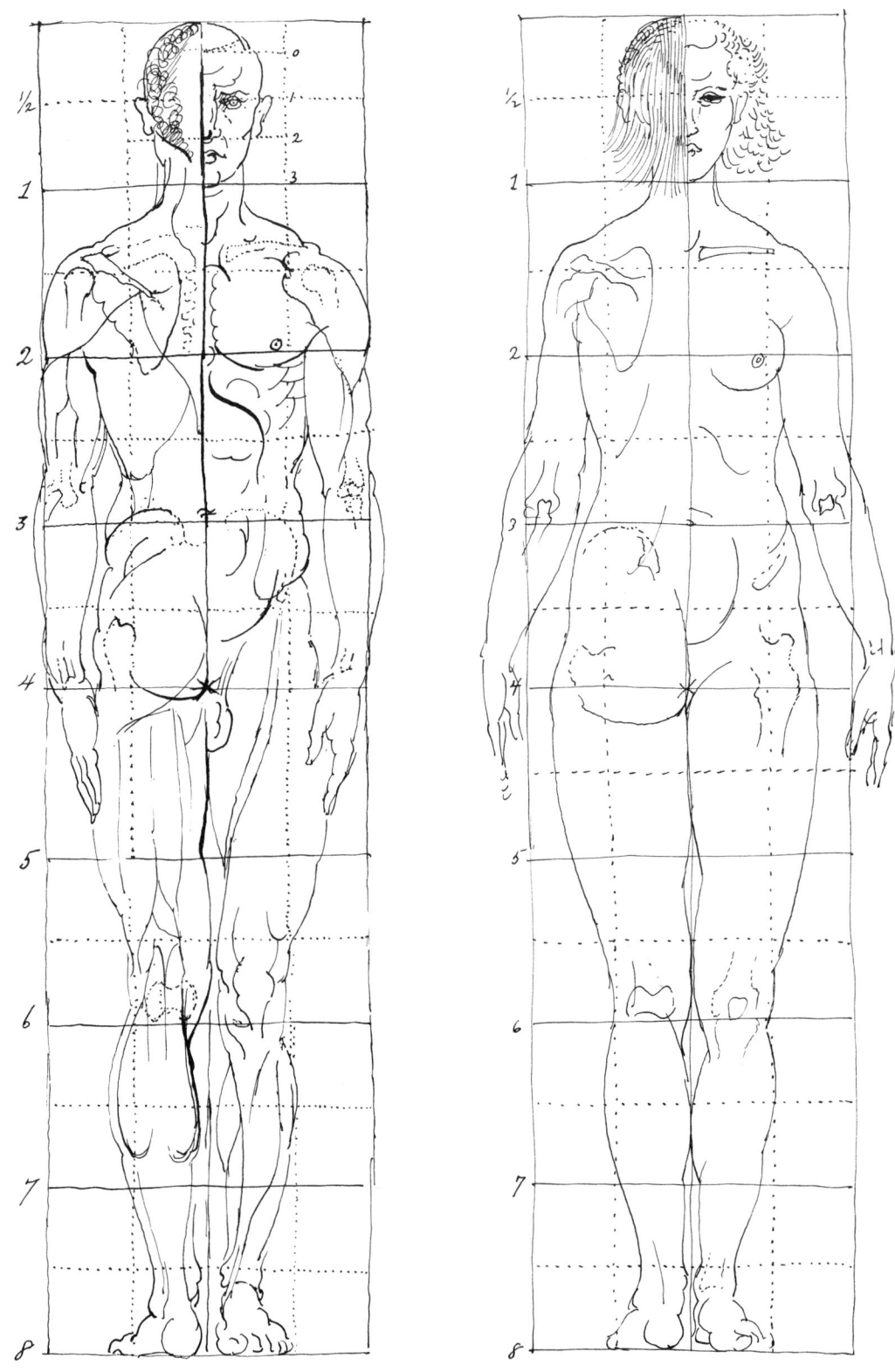

Eight headed proportion—male and female, front
and back, amended from Richer's 7½ head design.

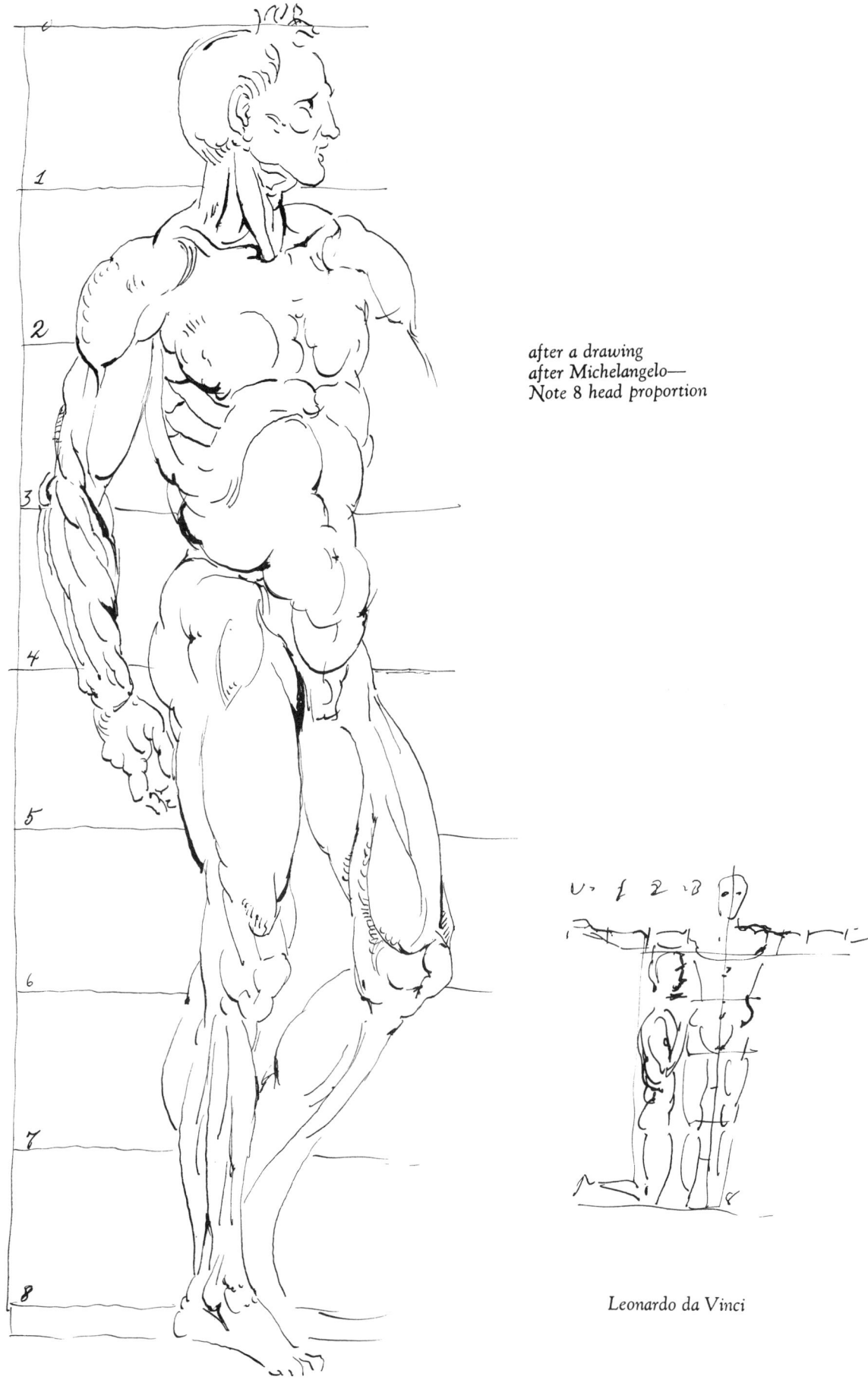

after a drawing
after Michelangelo—
Note 8 head proportion

Leonardo da Vinci

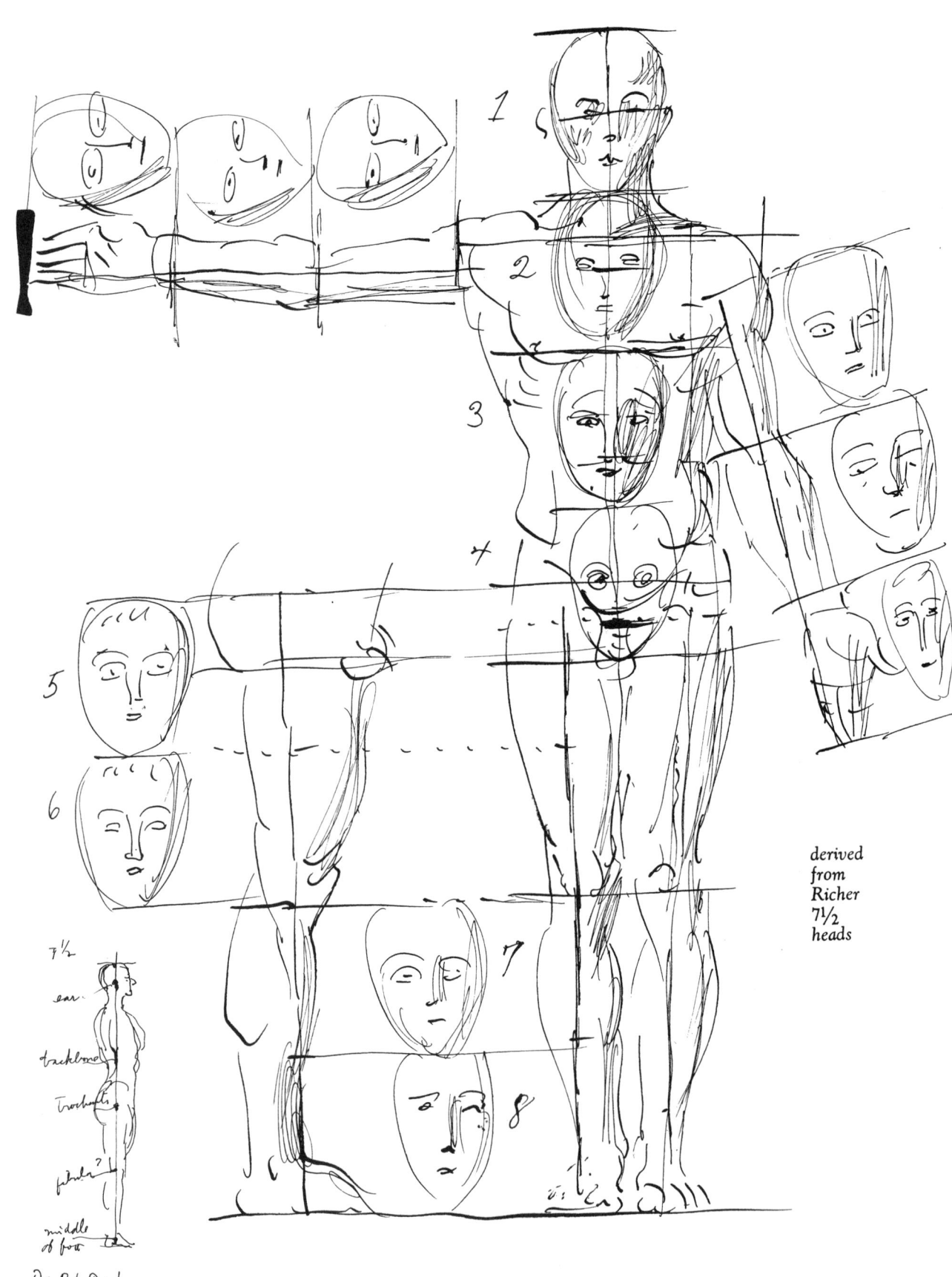

1

2

3

4

5

6

7

8

derived
from
Richer
7½
heads

7½

ear.

backbone

Trochanter

fibula?

middle
of foot

Dr R L Dickinson

Center of gravity according to Dr. R. L. Dickinson's measure-
ment for current American type which is 7½ heads high.

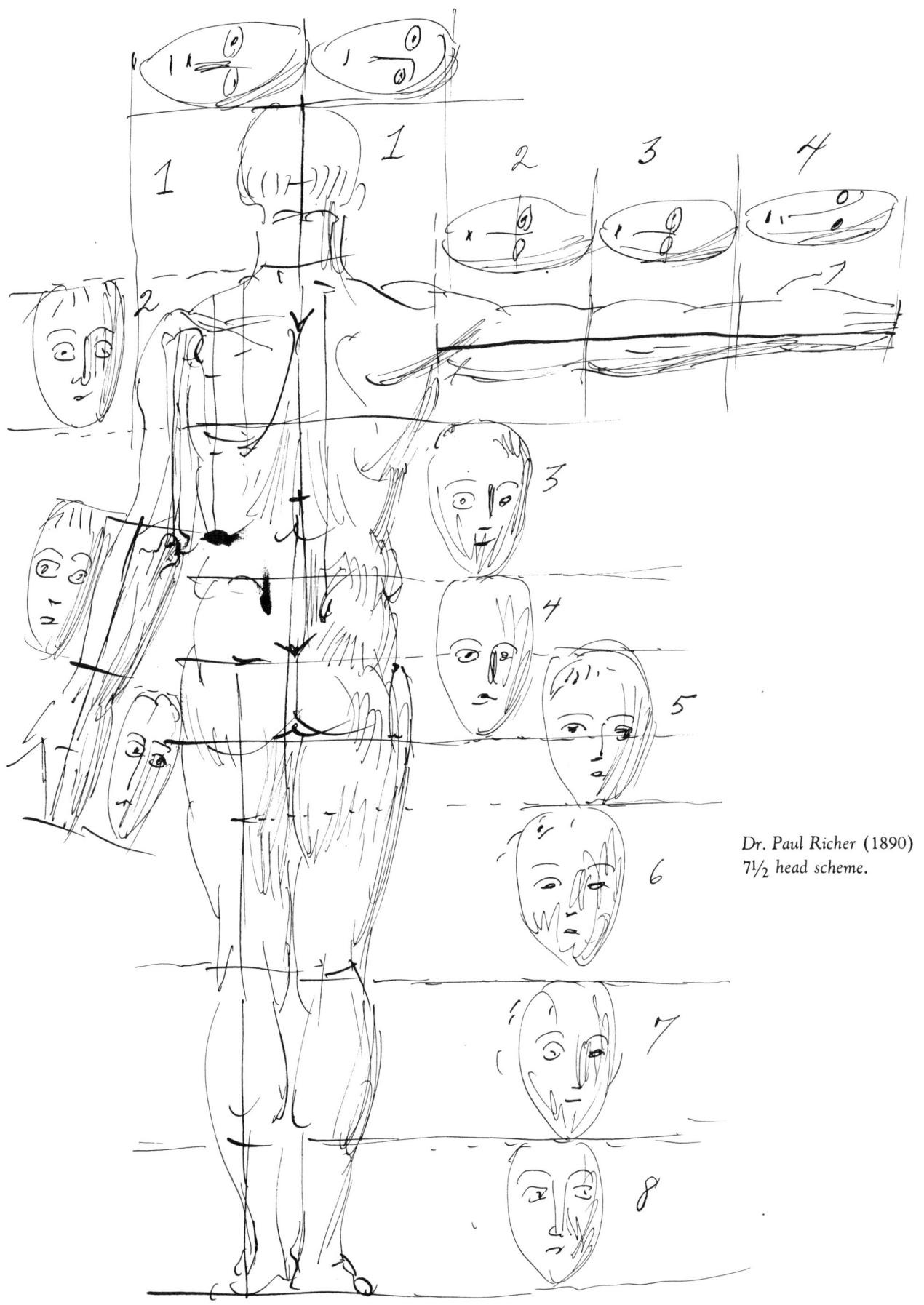

Dr. Paul Richer (1890)
7½ head scheme.

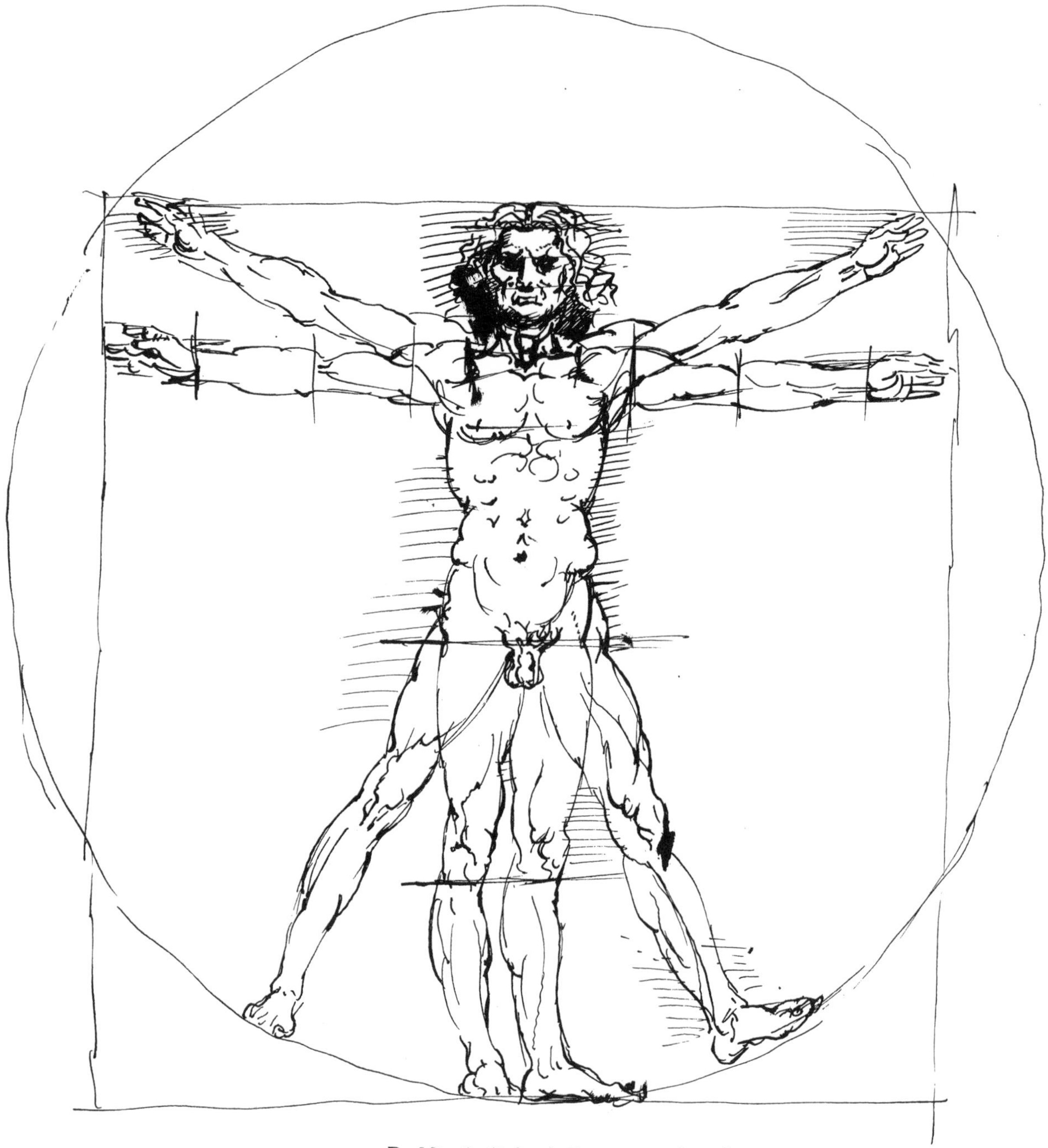

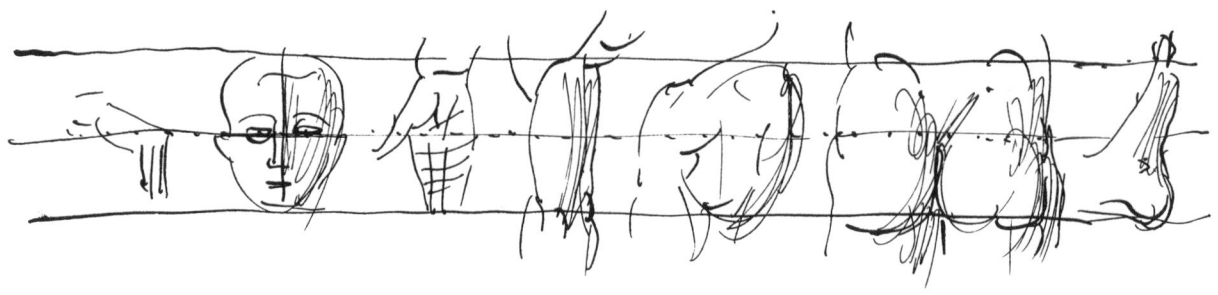

Da Vinci's (8 headed) square and circle

from Richer—a useful table for head and 1/2 head proportion.

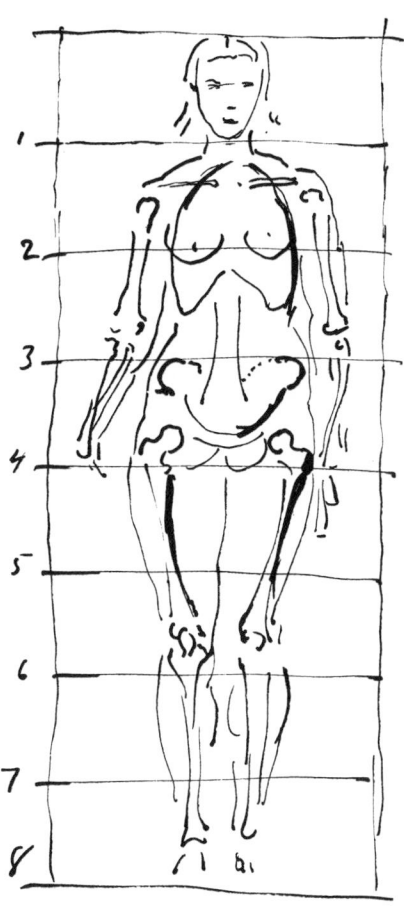

a basic sketch (8 heads)
Persons over 6 feet high are 8 headed

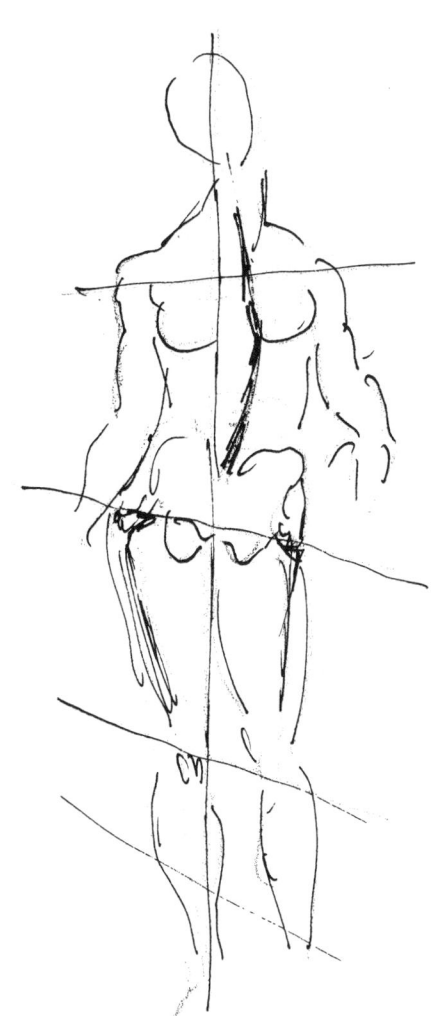

Ingres

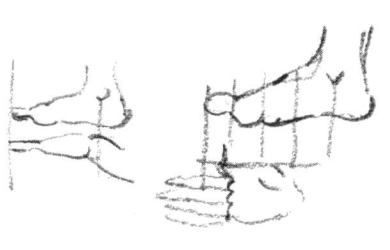

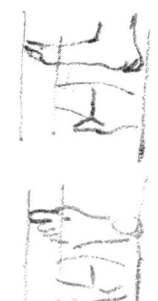

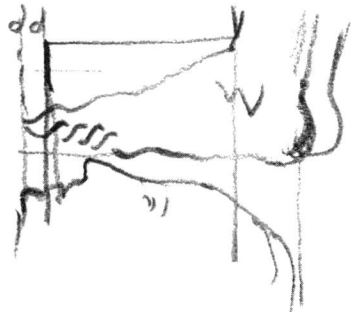

free copies of da Vinci

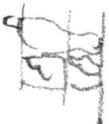

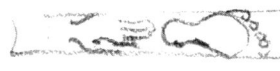

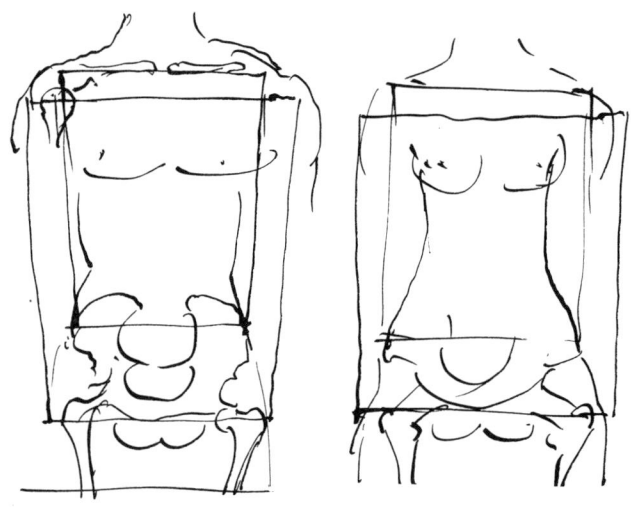

from Richer

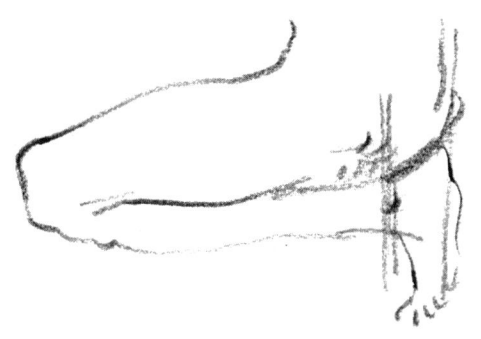

da Vinci

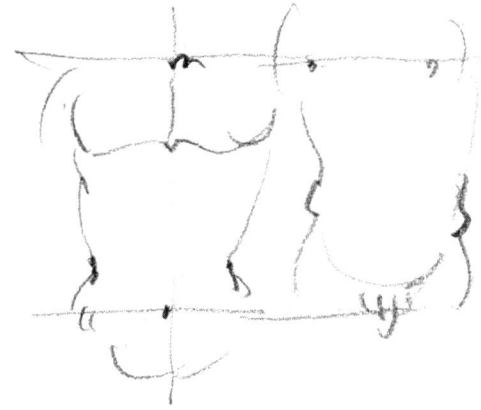

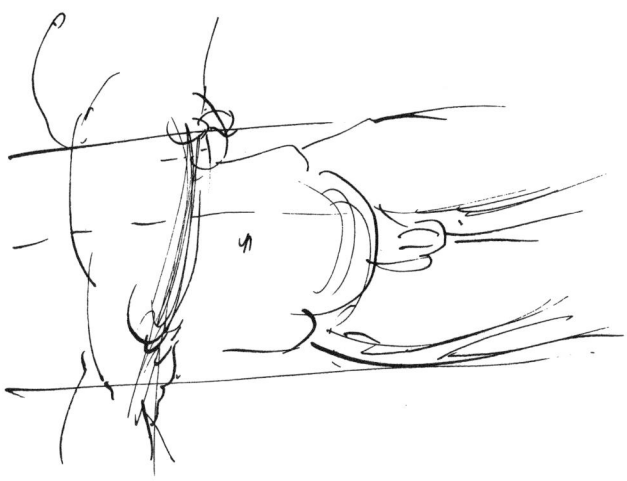

Richer

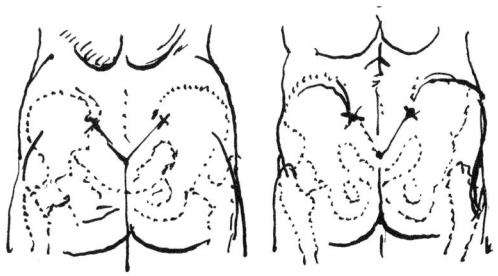

*Richer's
position of
the pelvis
and hip joint*

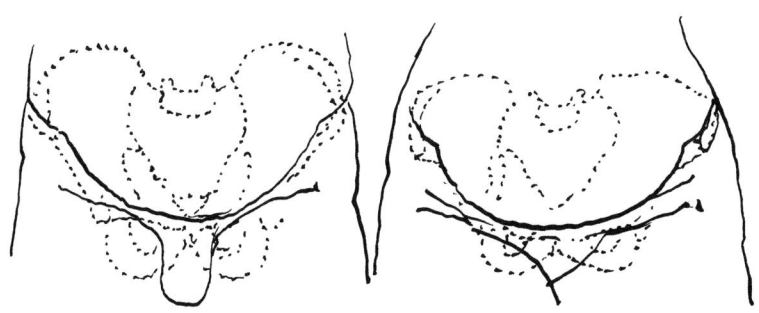

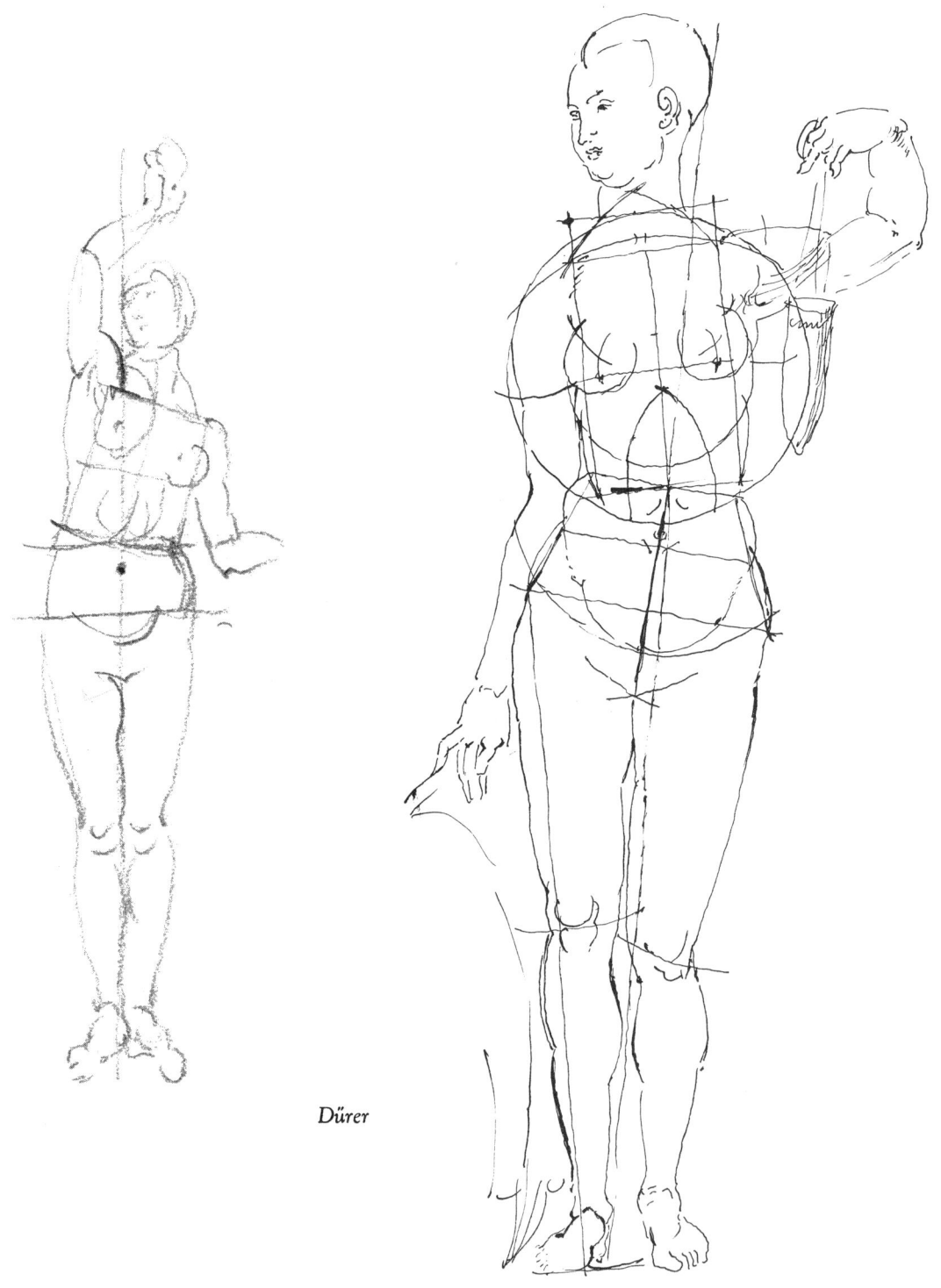

Dürer

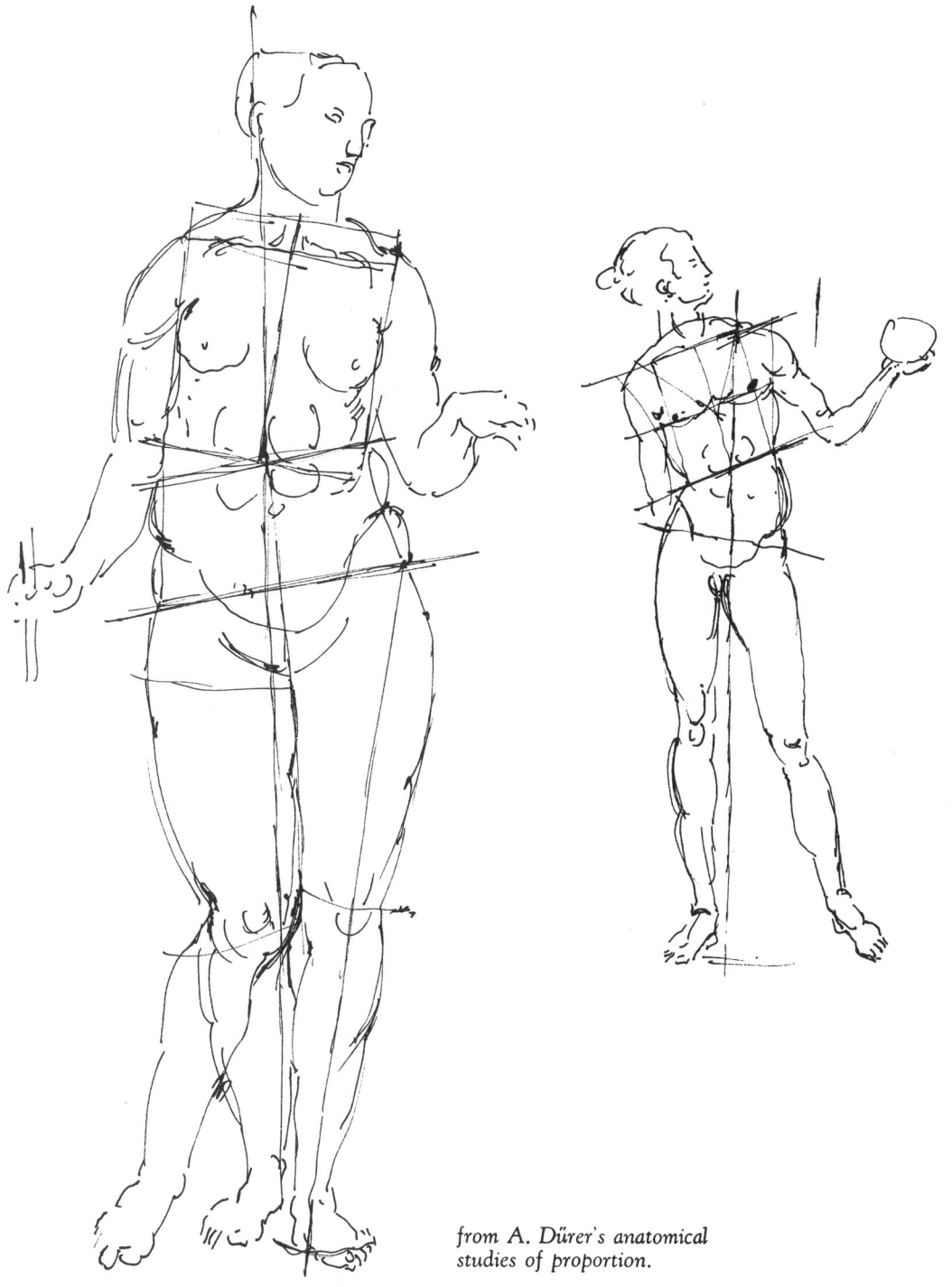

from A. Dürer's anatomical studies of proportion.

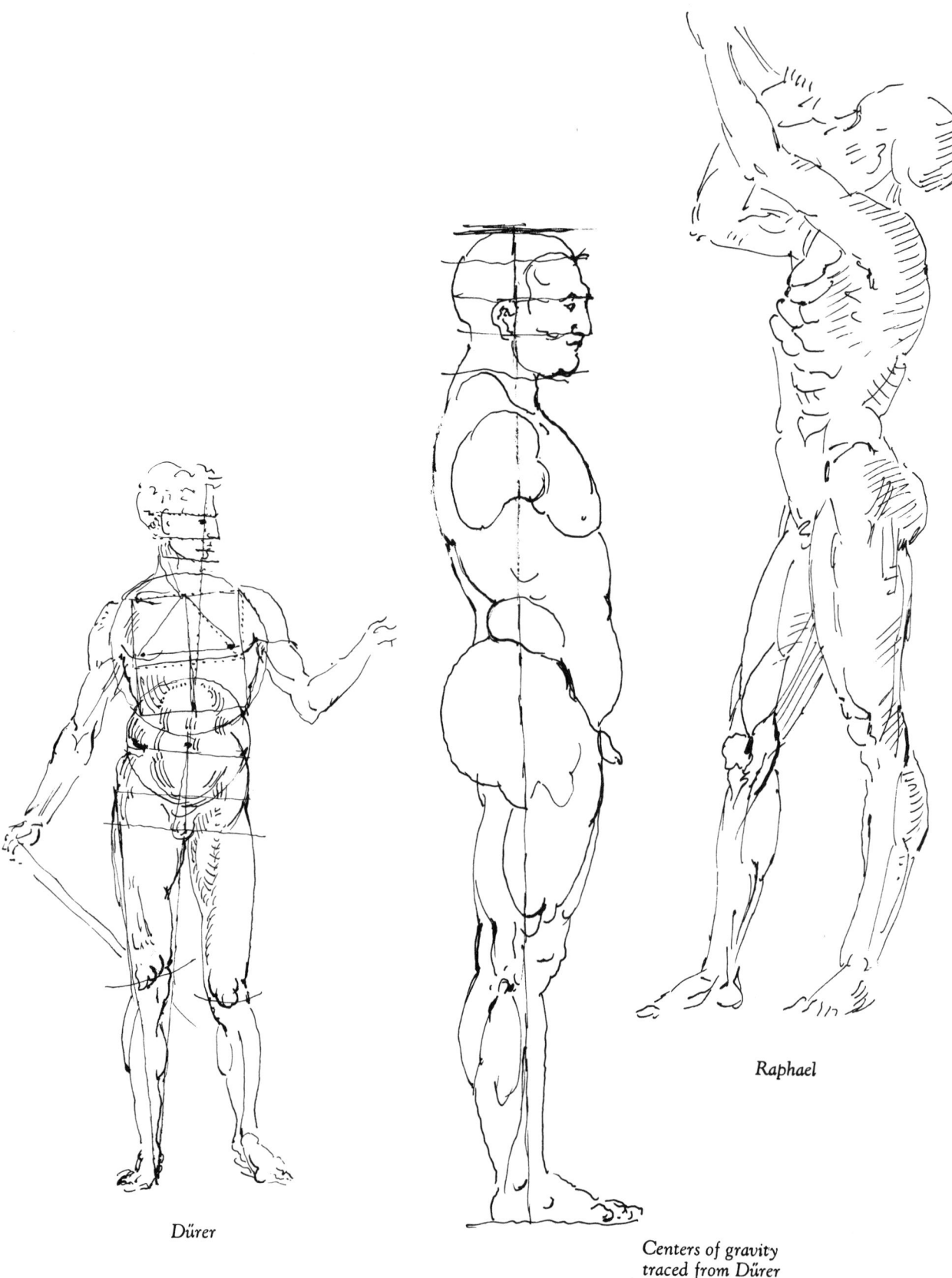

Dürer

Raphael

Centers of gravity
traced from Dürer

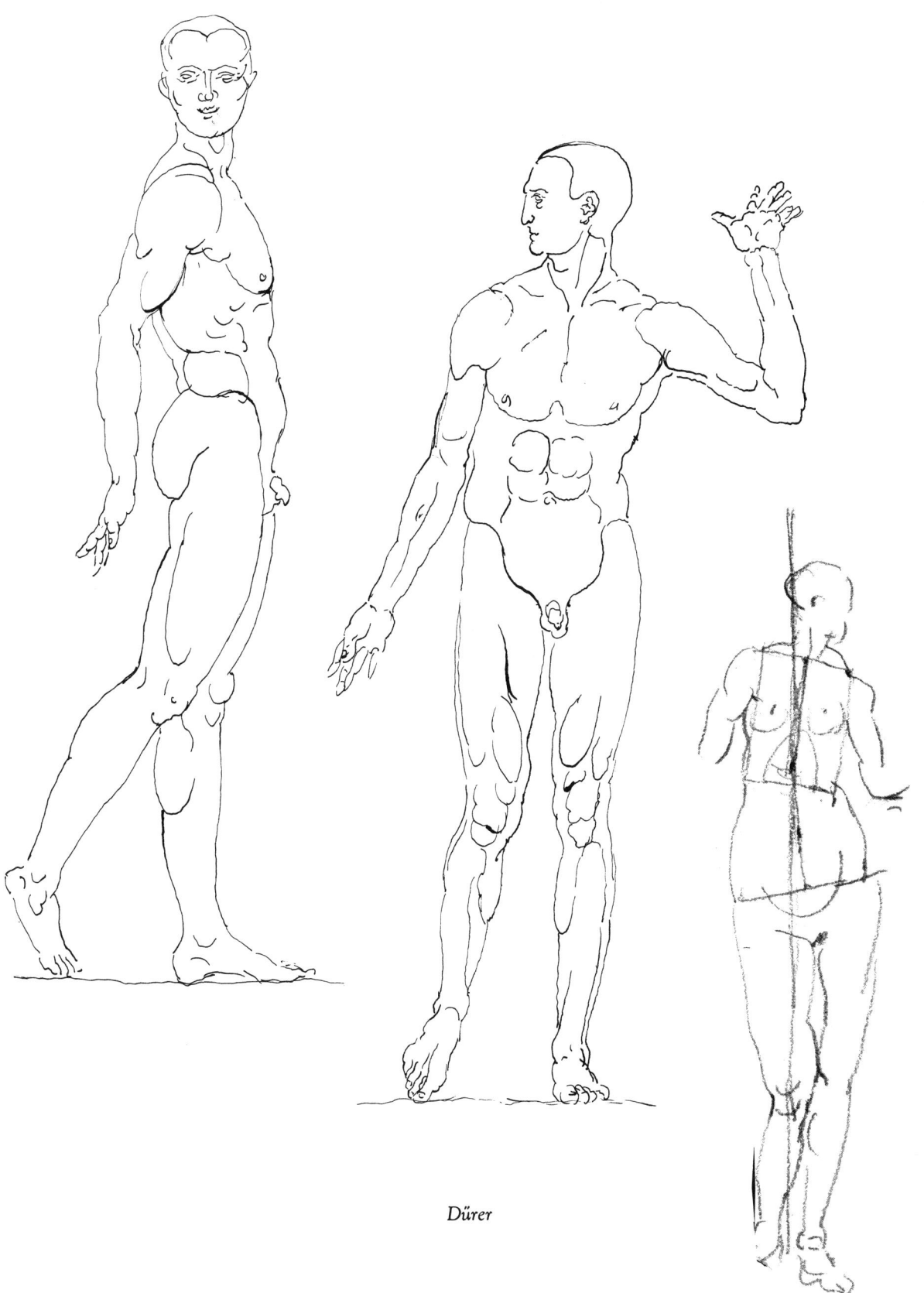

Dürer

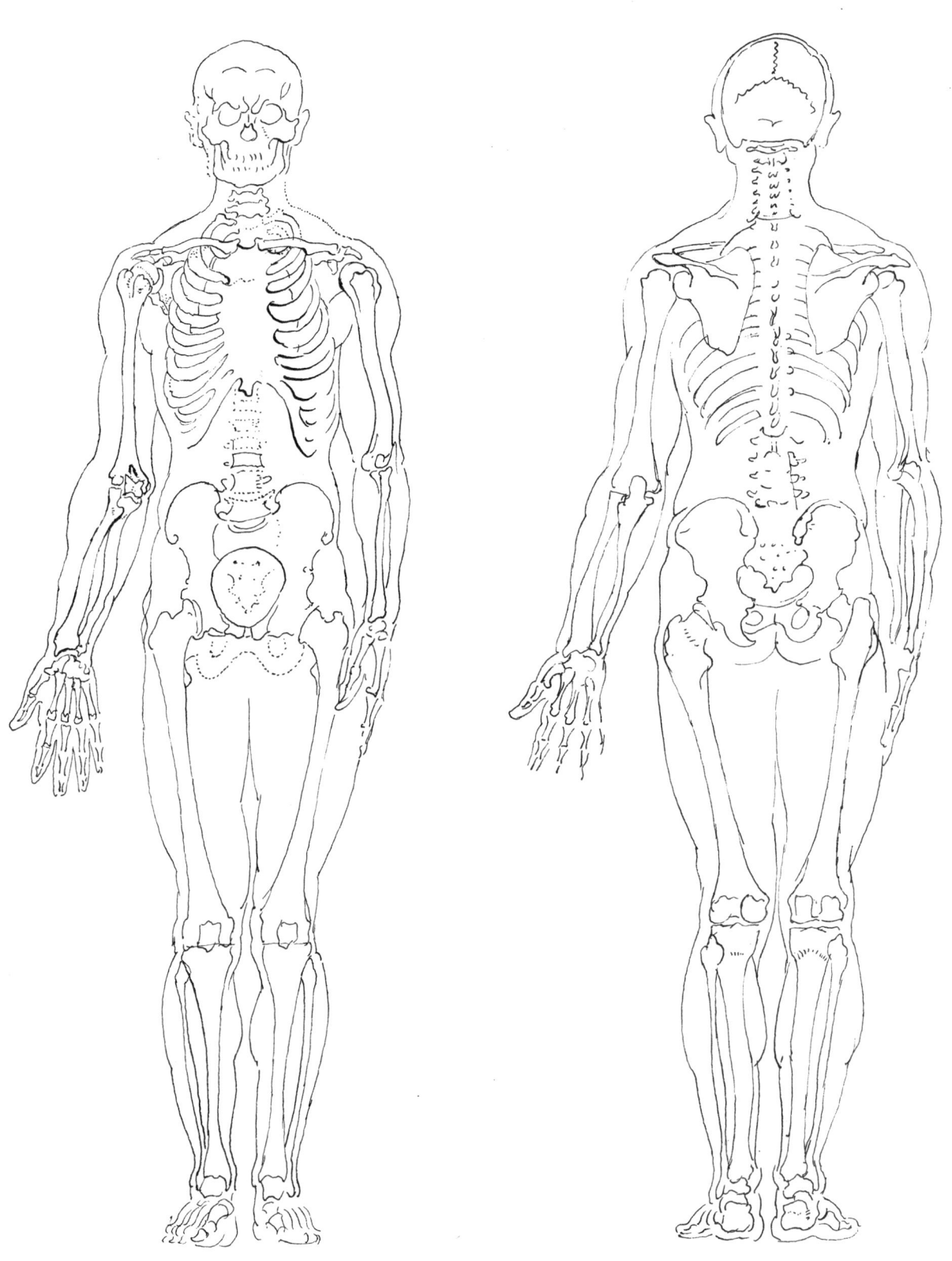

diagram showing position of bones. Note the crossing of the bones in forearm.

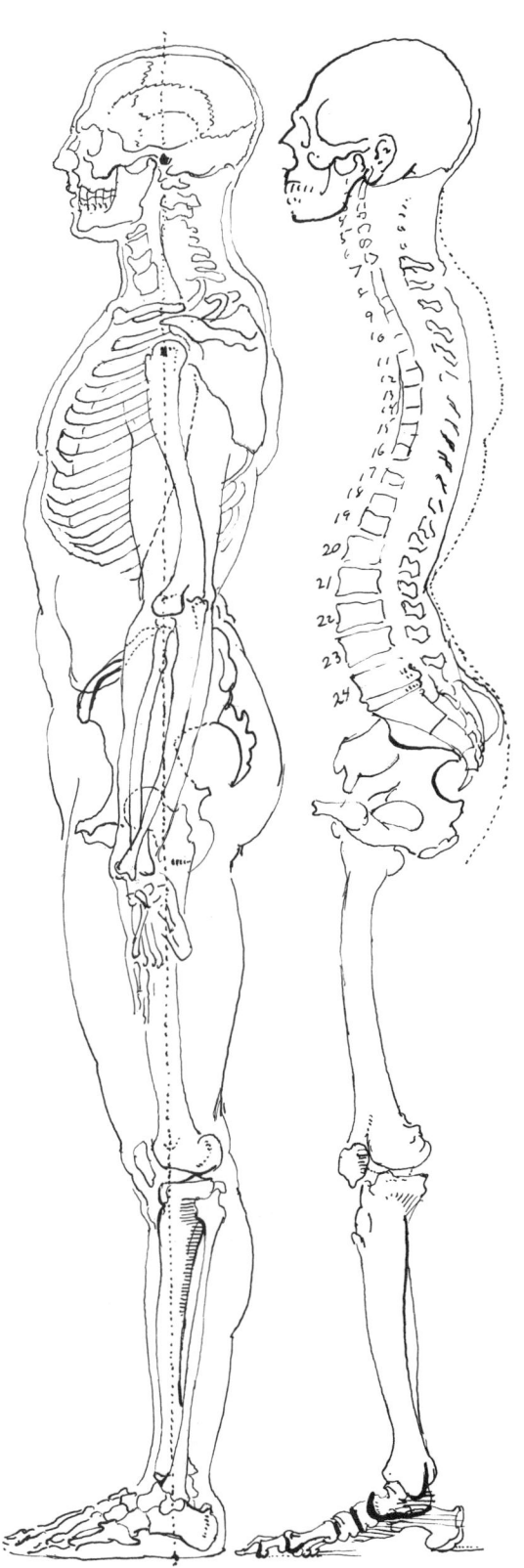

*the same
from
the side
(derived from
many authors)*

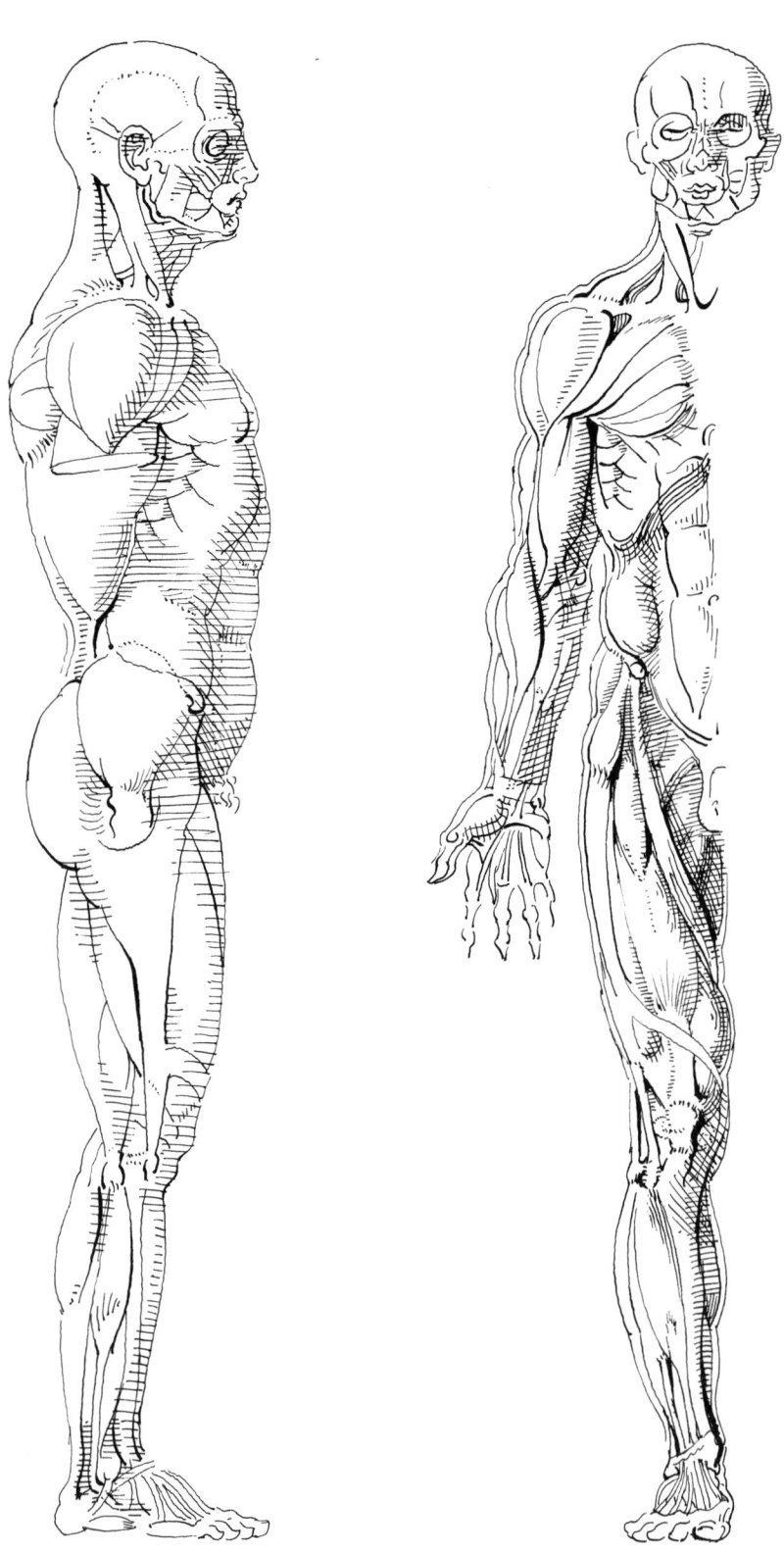

*Muscles of
the whole side*

front and back

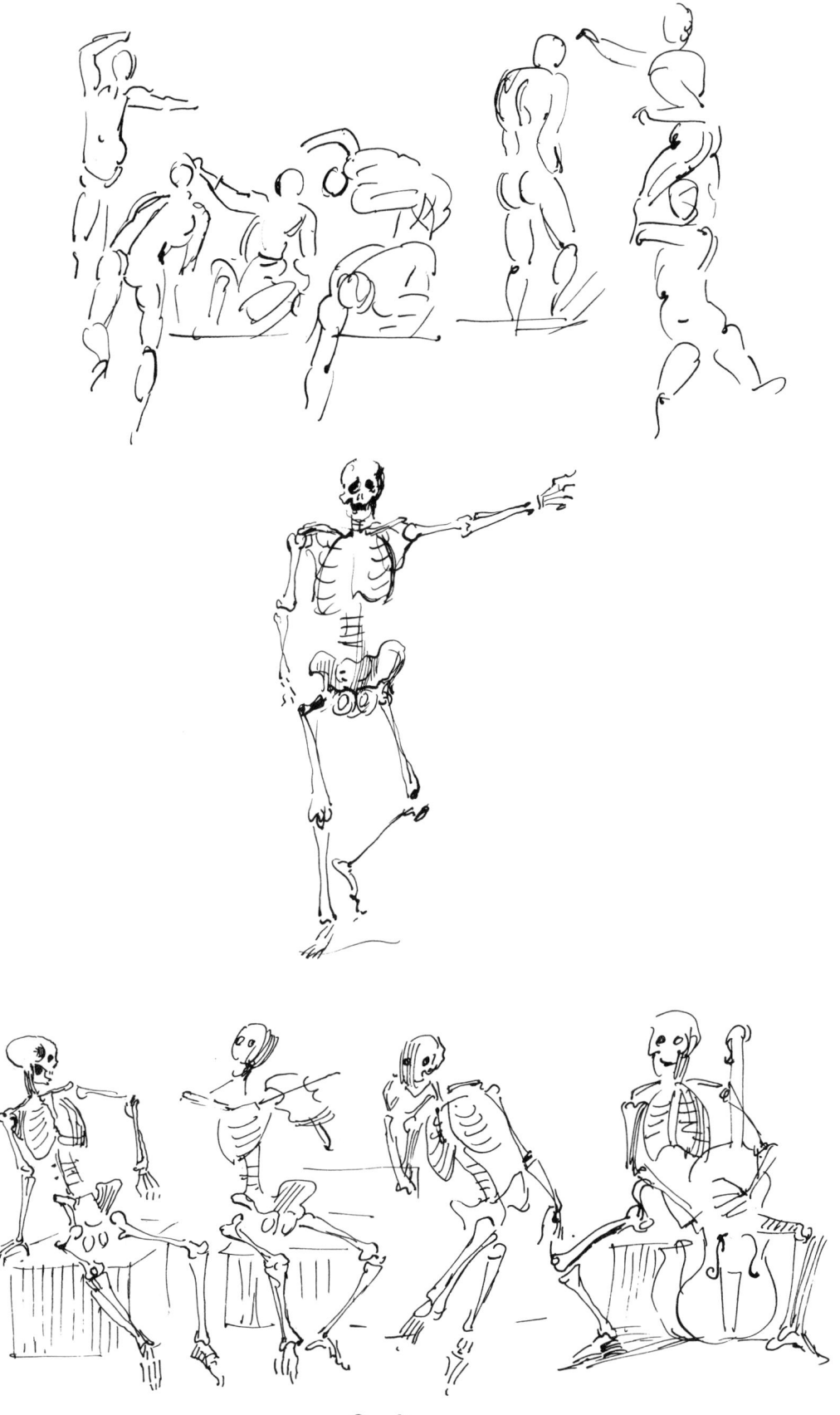

Gamelin

Figure Sketches

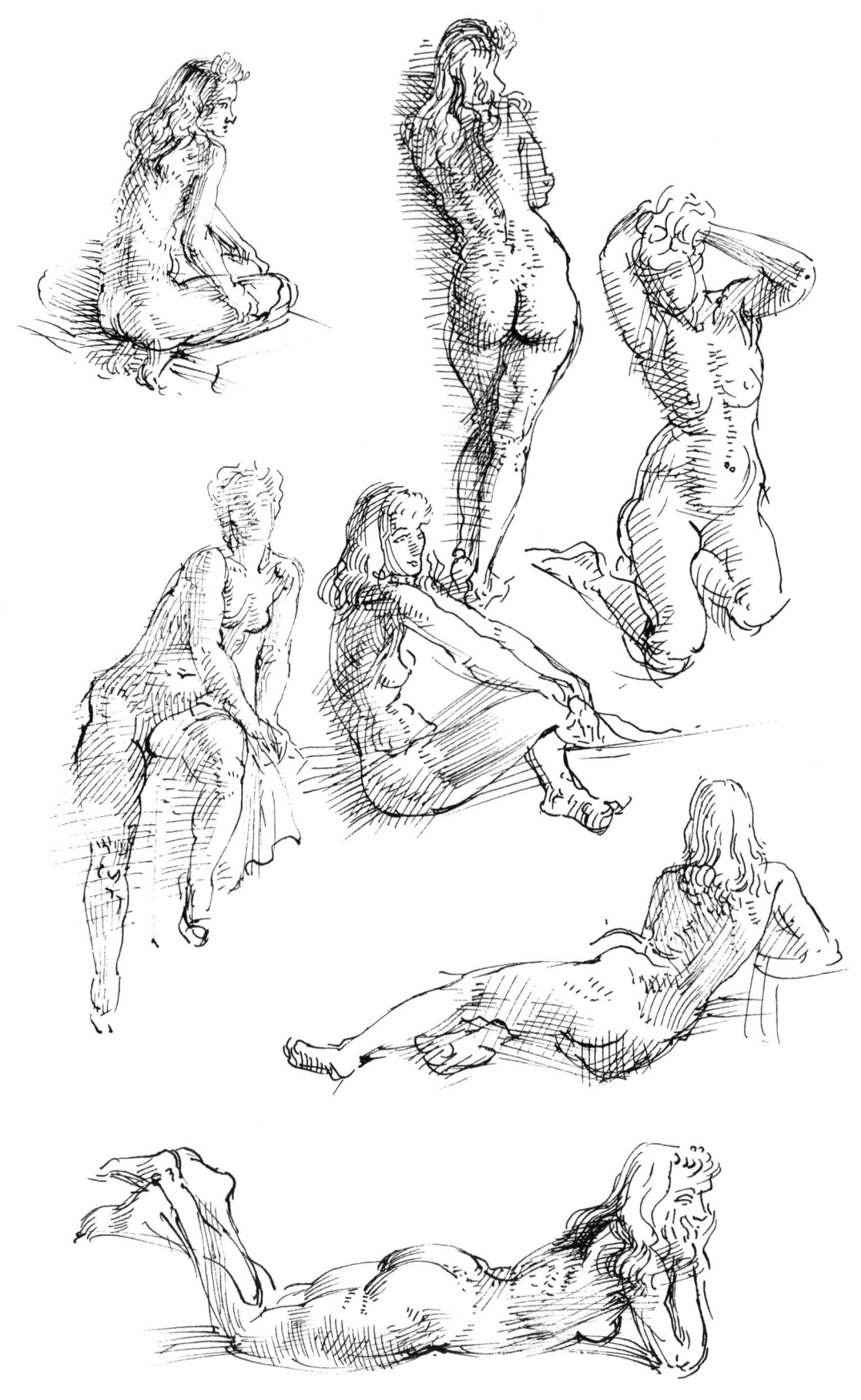

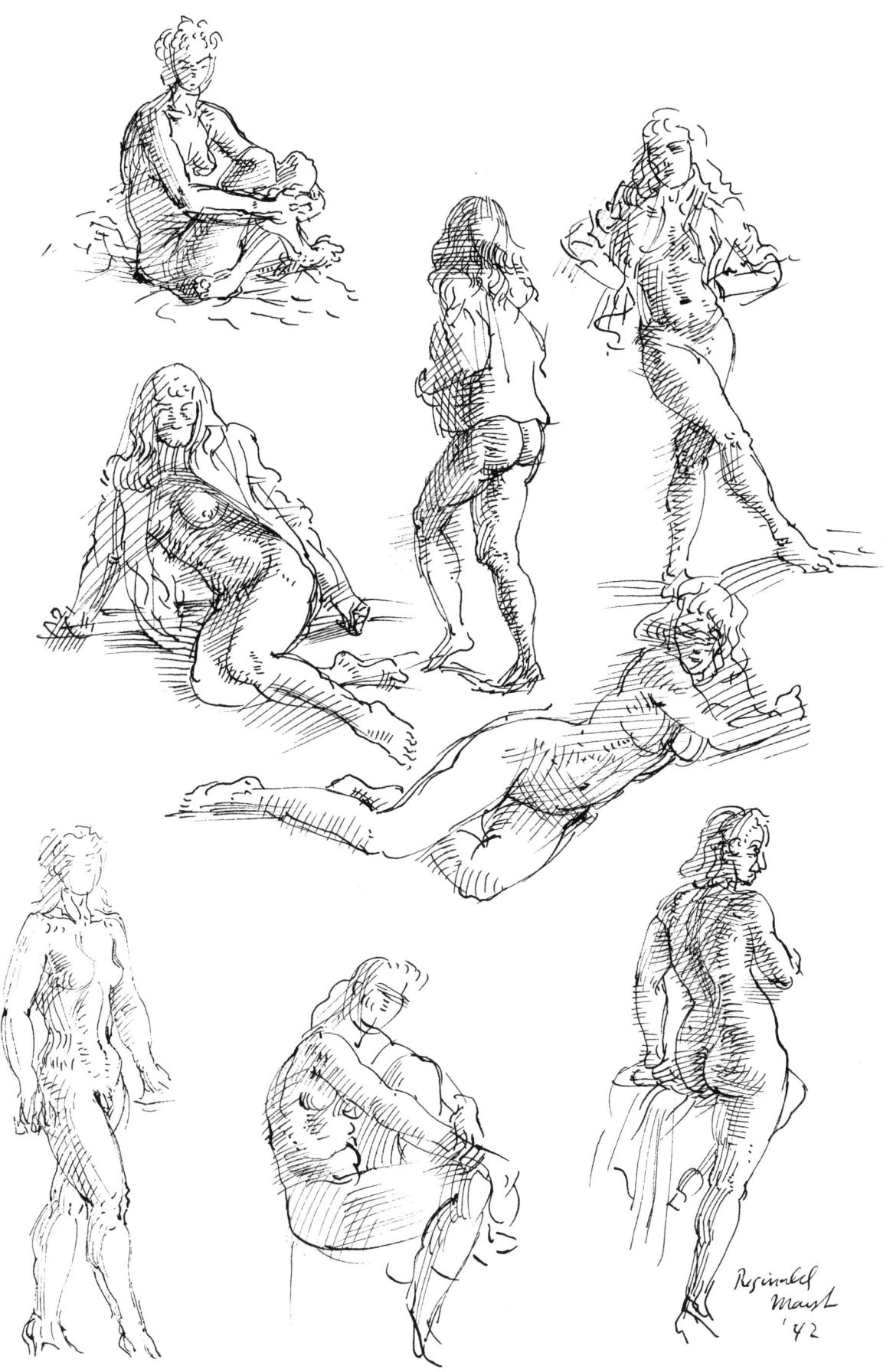

Reginald
Marsh
'42

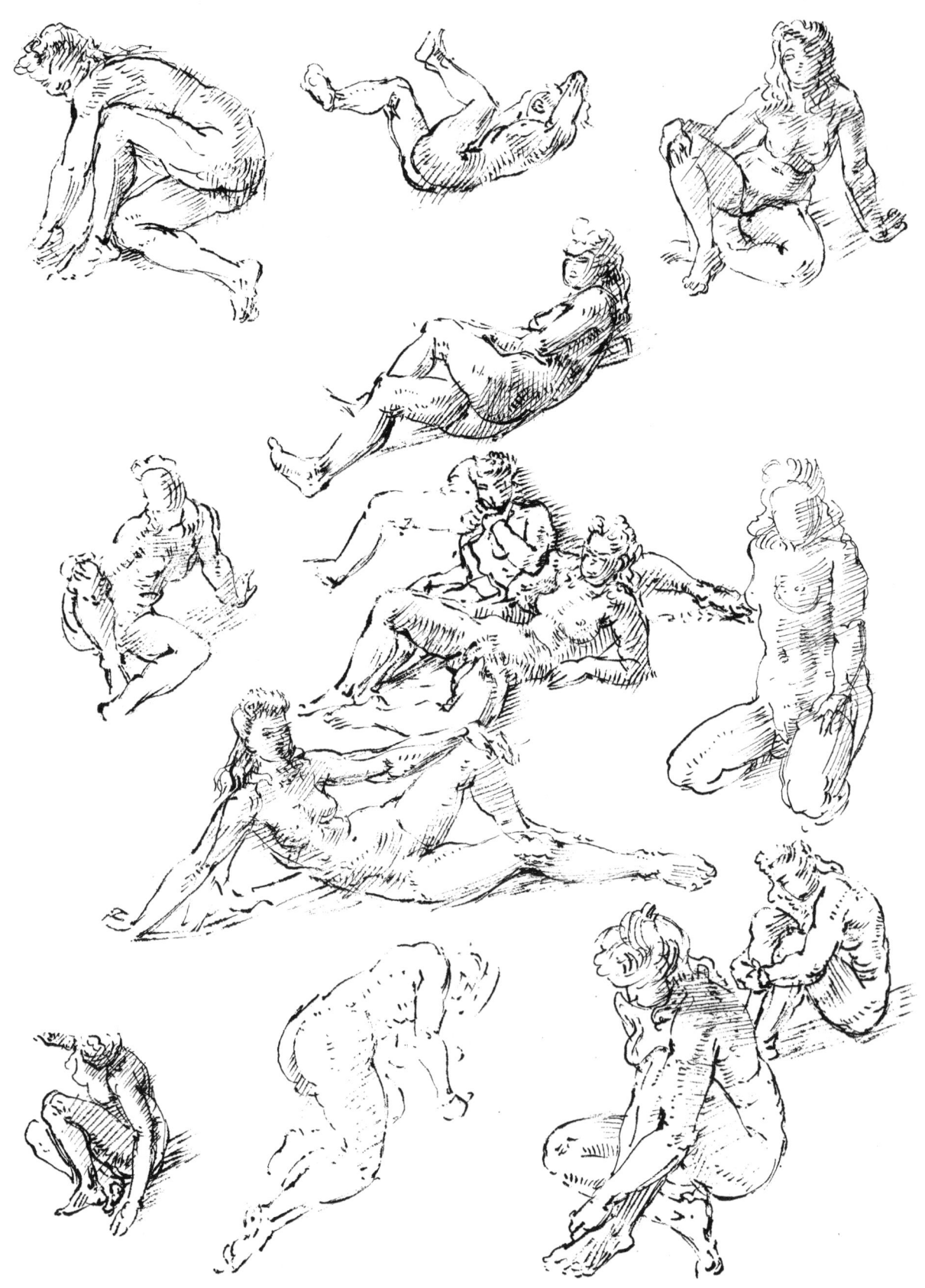

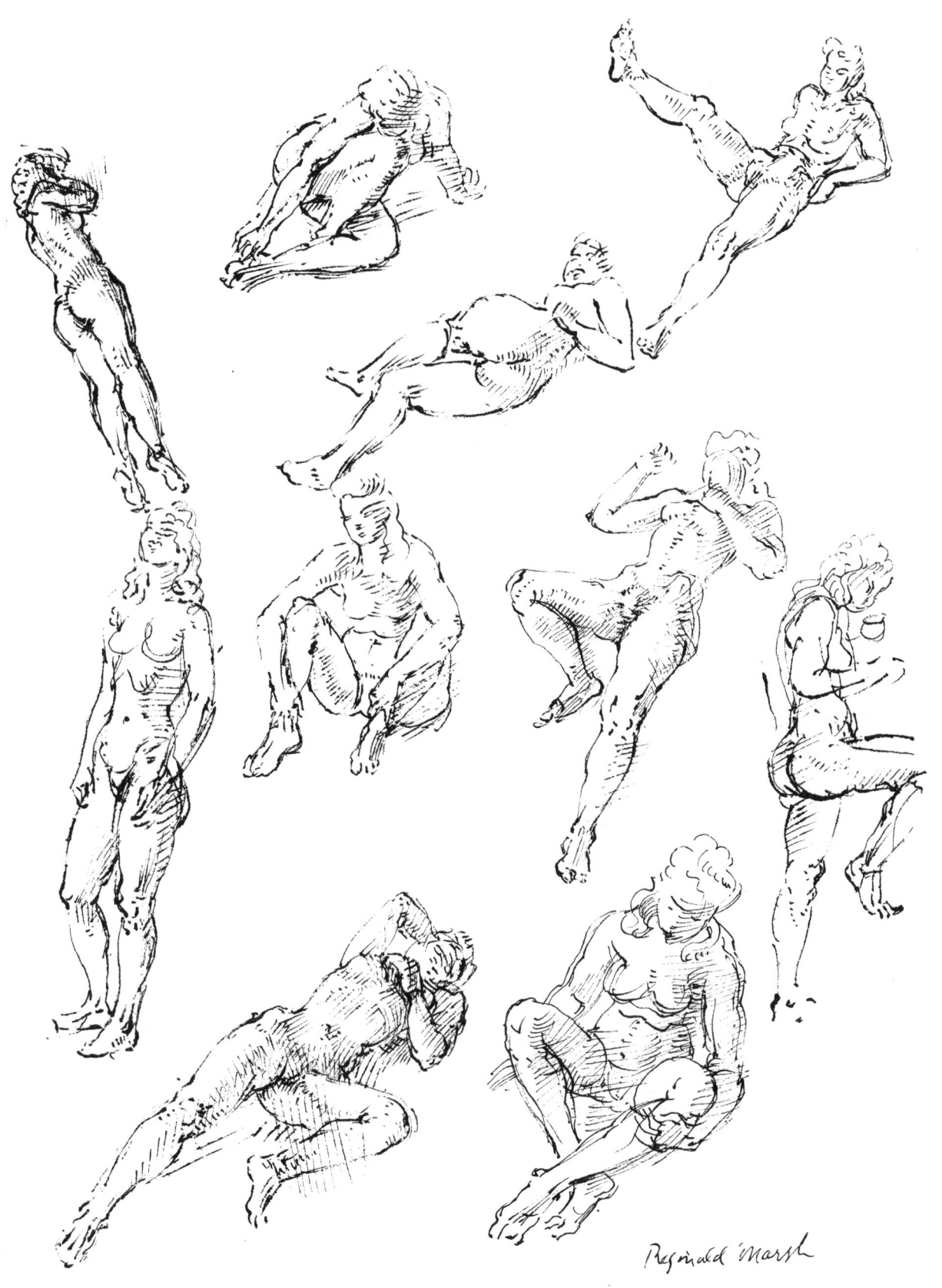

Reginald Marsh

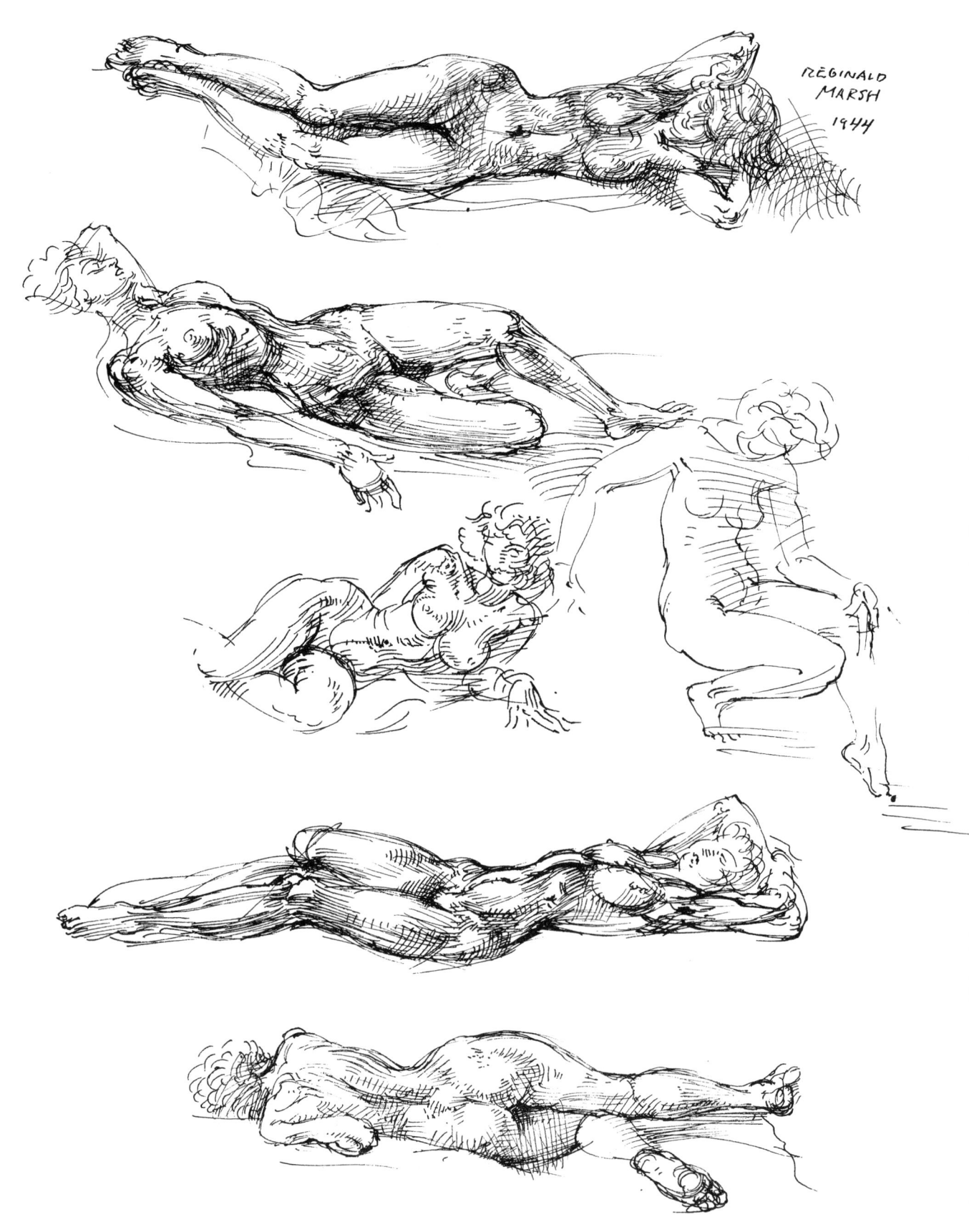

REGINALD
MARSH
1944

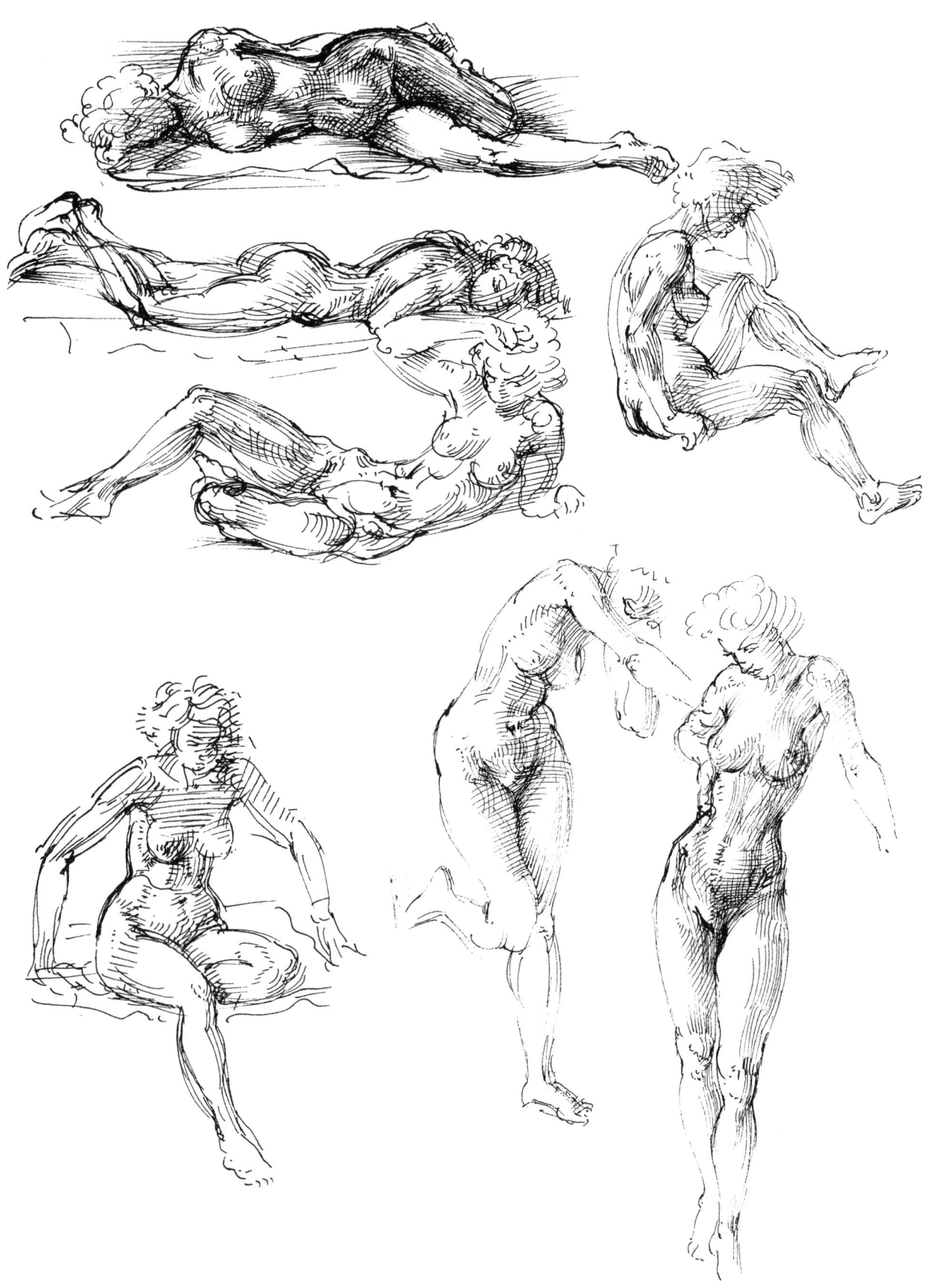

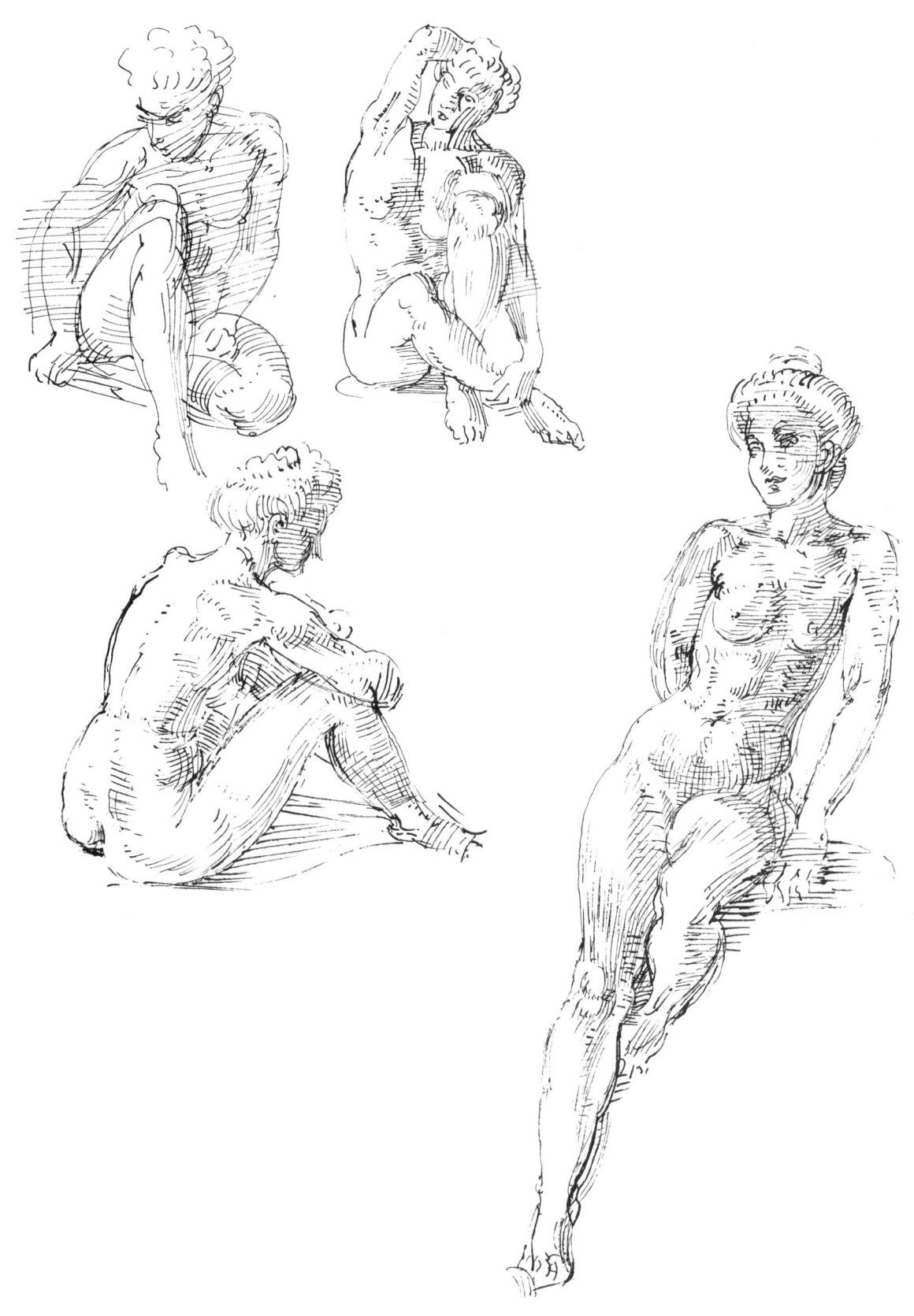

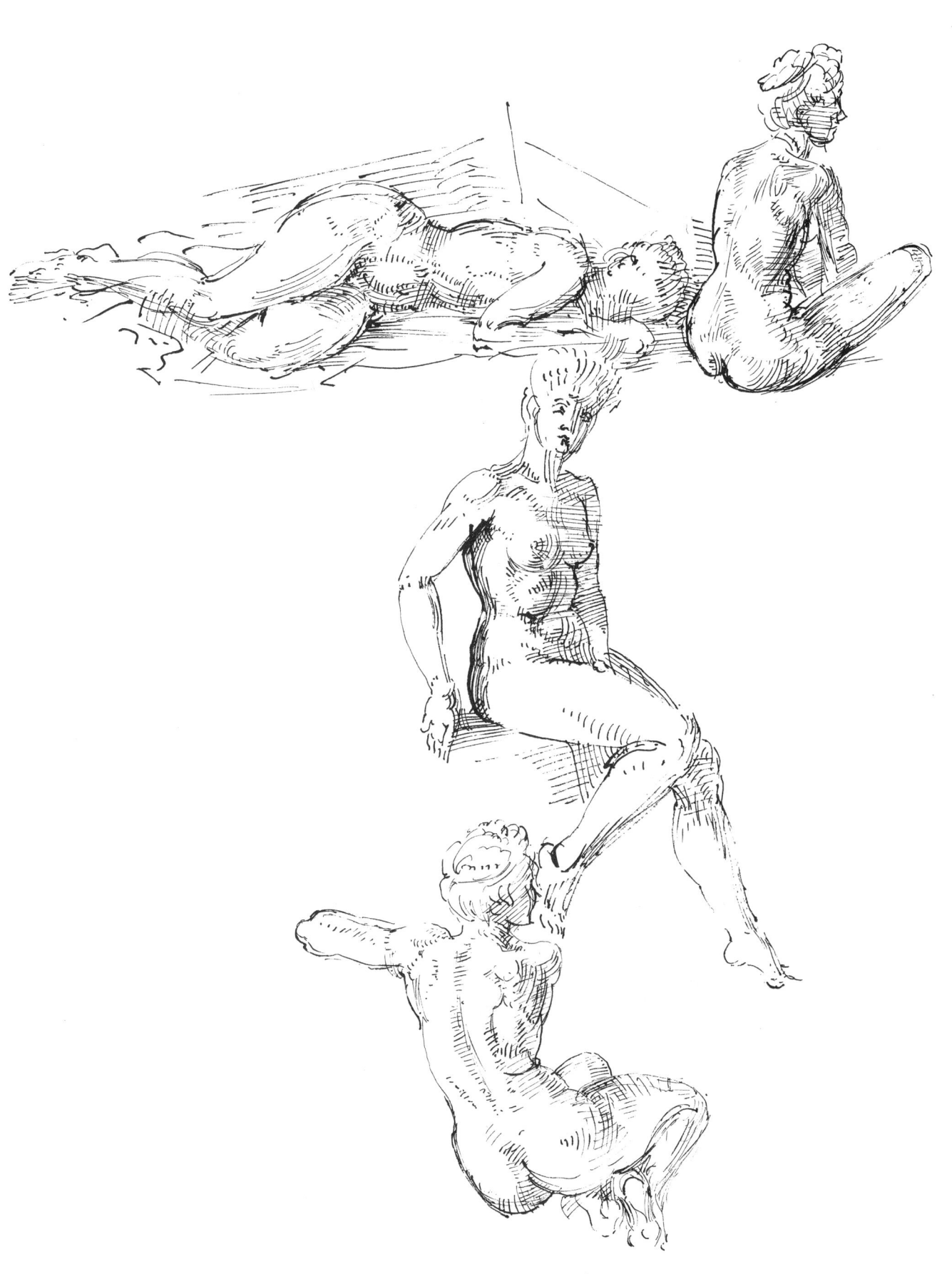

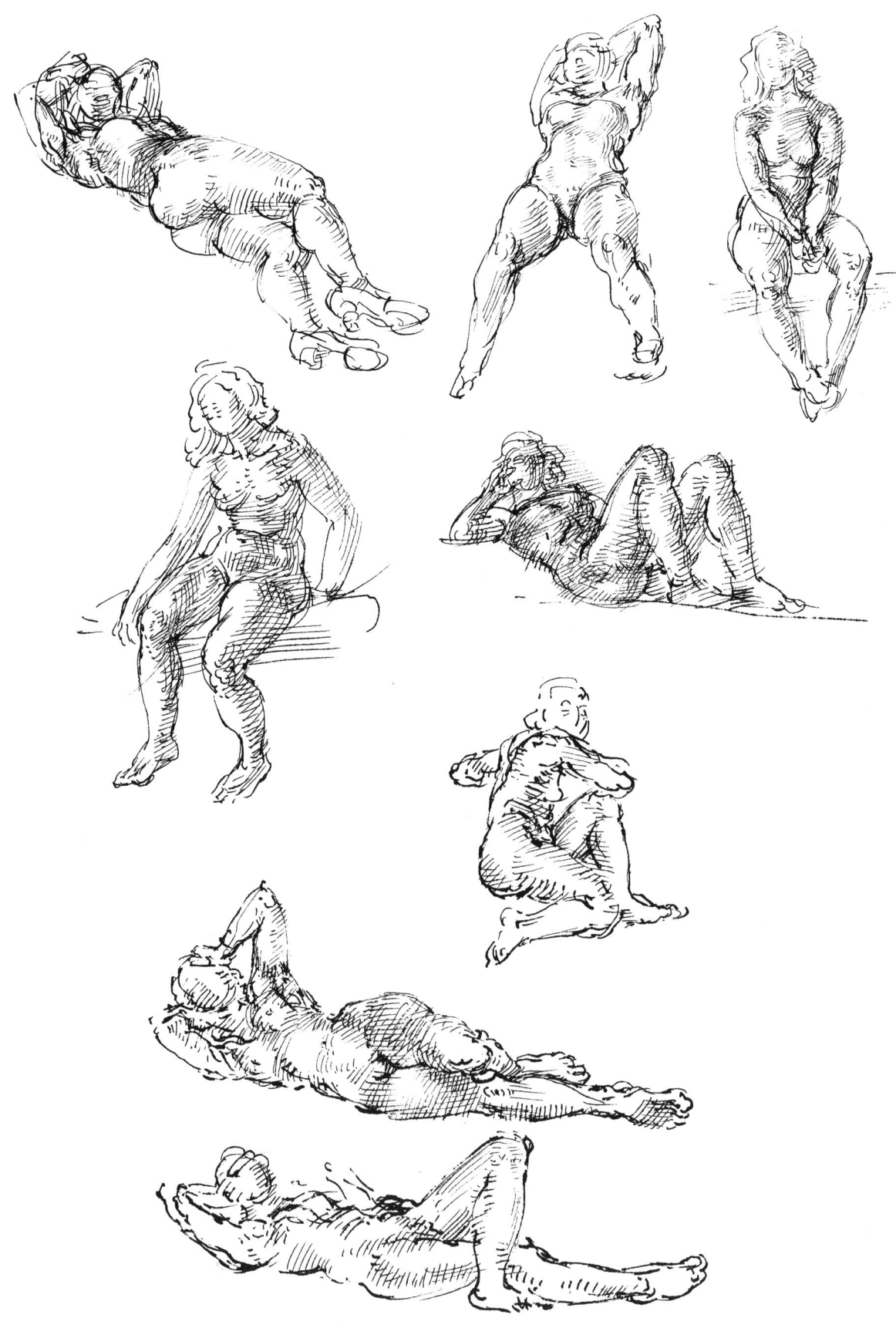

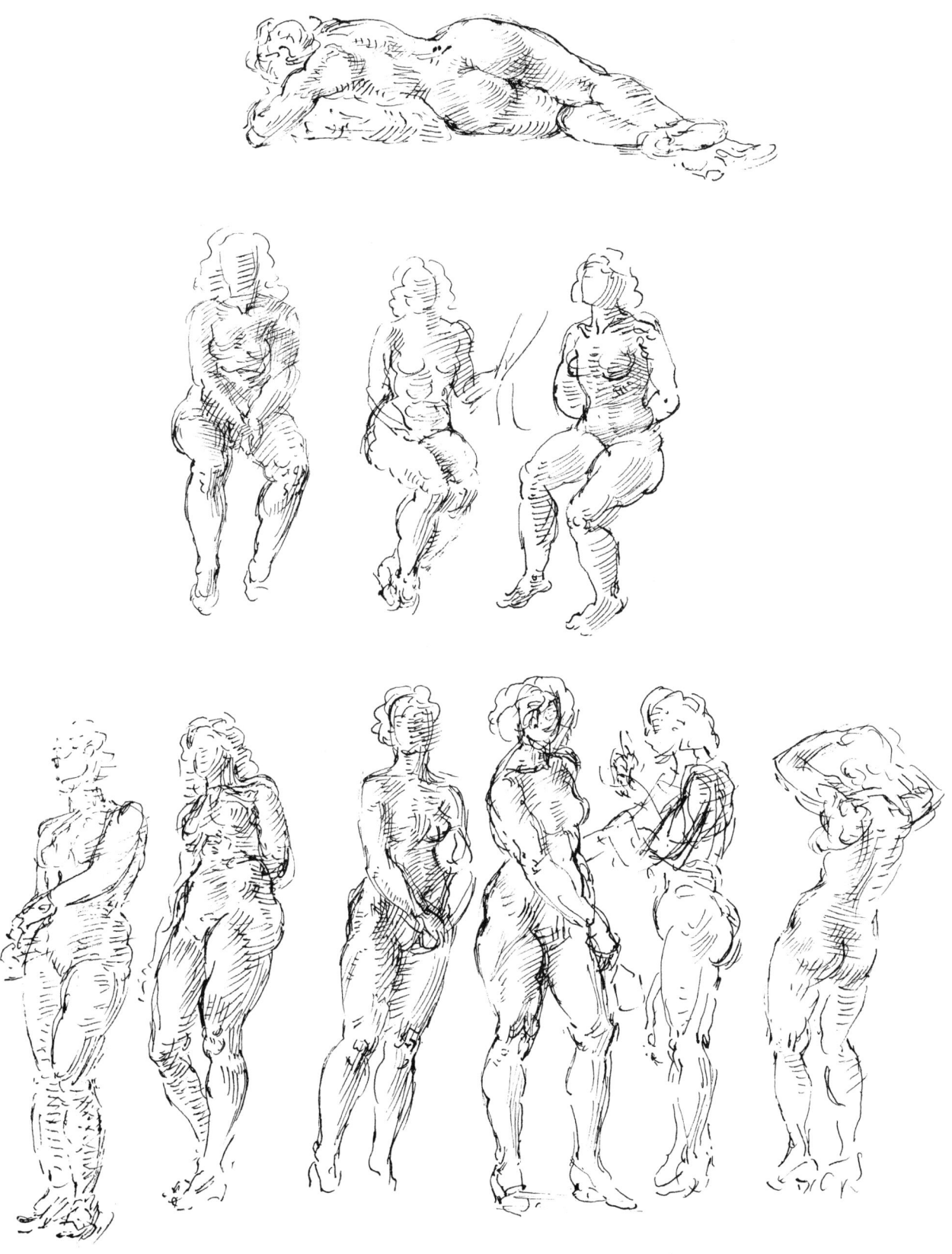

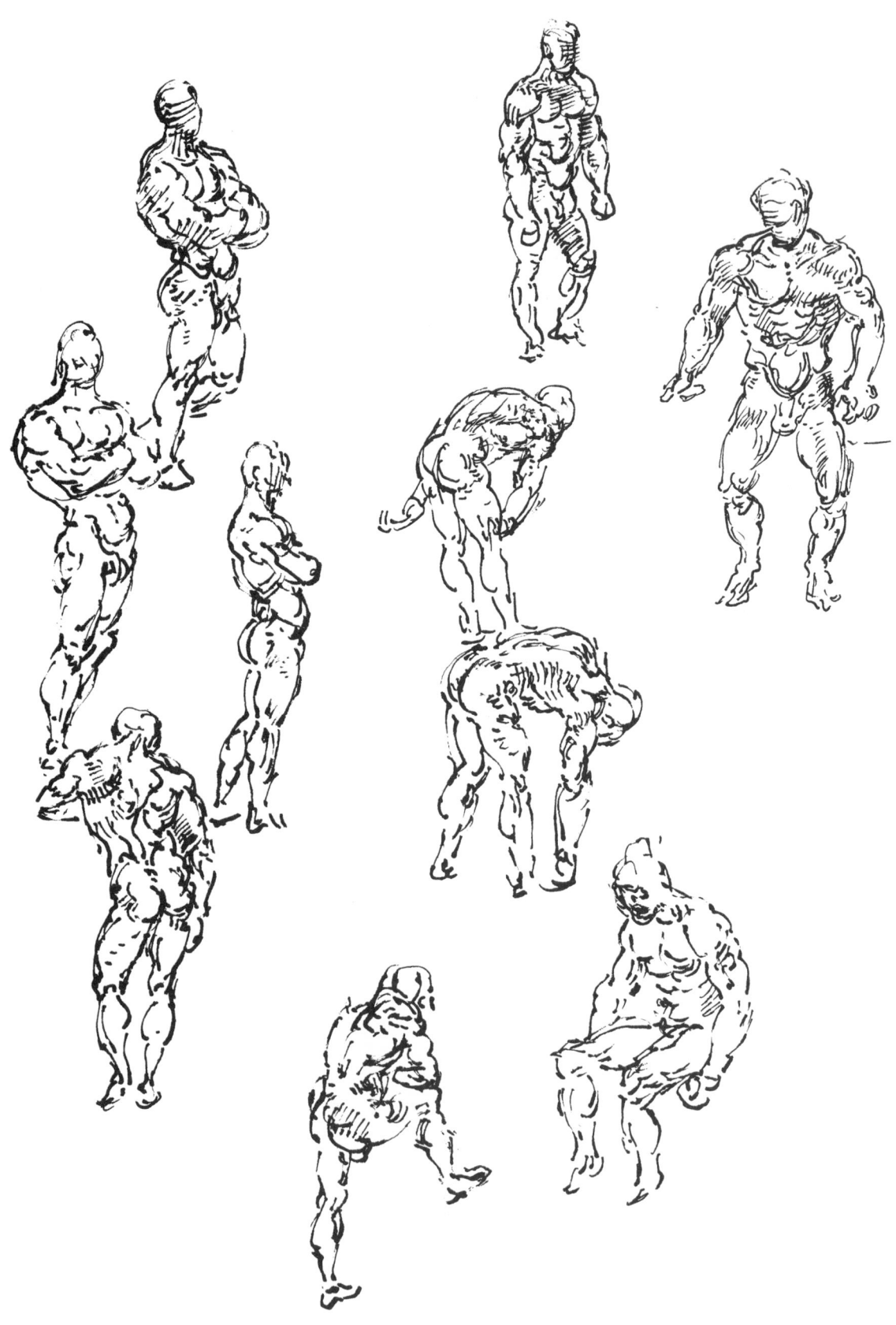

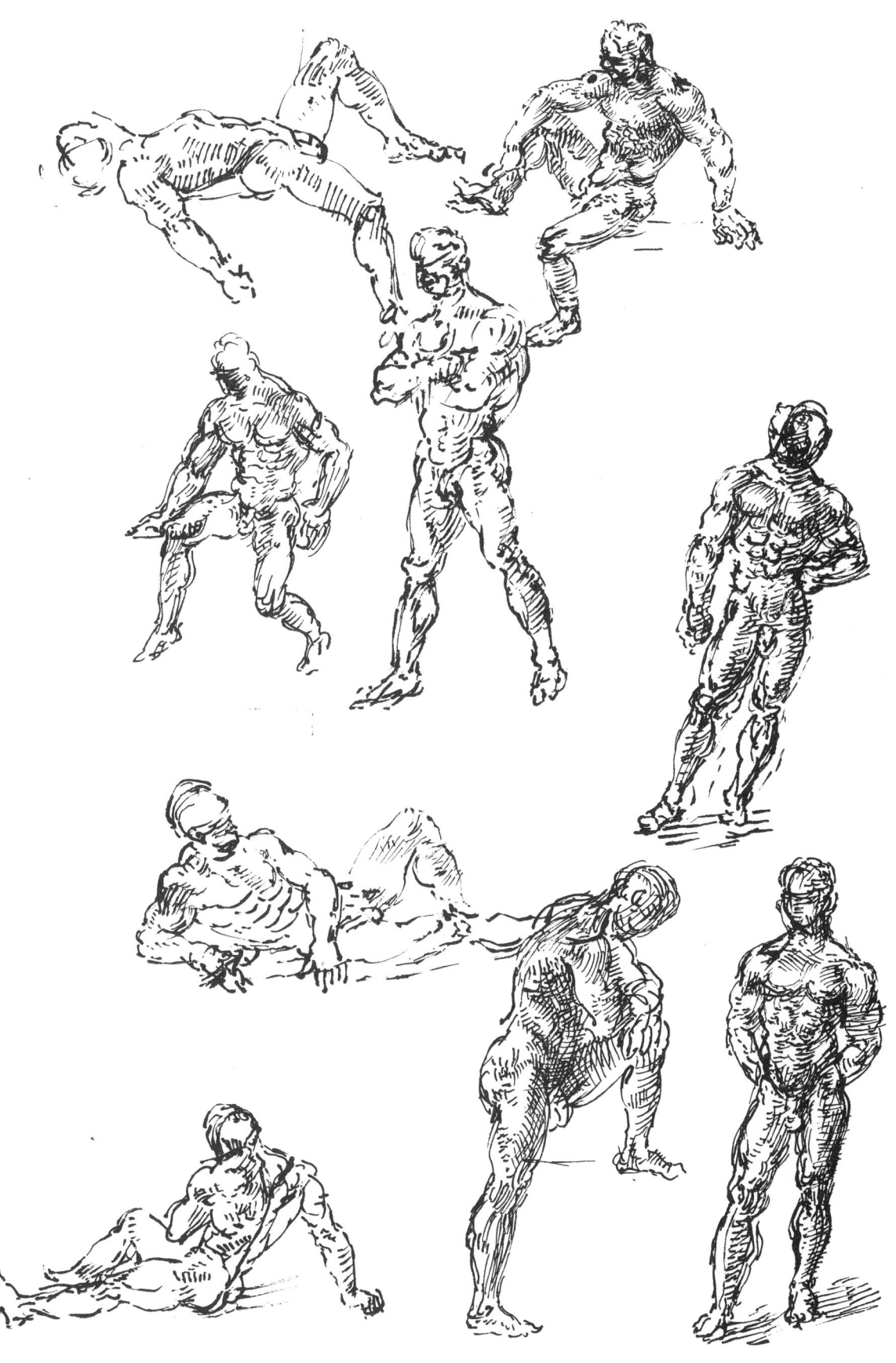

209